MUSIC, *The Glory* AND COSMIC WAR

RESTORING TRUE WORSHIP SERIES: VOLUME 1

MUSIC, *The Glory* AND COSMIC WAR

RUTH WEBB

Music, the Glory and Cosmic War
by Ruth Webb
Copyright © 2025 Ruth Webb

Published by Heart of the Psalmist Inc
P.O. Box 133, Eaglehawk, Vic, 3556
www.tabernacleofdavid.org.au

Design and layout: Tom Carroll
Editor: Susan Pierotti
ISBN: 978-0-9587437-5-4

Scripture emphasis throughout have been added by the author.
Unless otherwise noted, all Scripture quotations are from the New King James Version **(NKJV)** Copyright © 1982 by Thomas Nelson, Inc. Used by permission. All rights reserved.

Scripture quotations marked **TPT are from The Passion Translation®**. Copyright © 2017, 2018 by BroadStreet Publishing®Group, LLC. Used by permission. All rights reserved. ThePassionTranslation.com.

Scripture quotations marked **GW (or NOG)** are taken from *GOD'S WORD* or *Names of God Bible* (GOD'S WORD)®. Copyright ©1995 God's Word to the Nations. Used by permission of Baker Publishing Group.

Scripture quotations marked **CJB are taken from the Complete Jewish Bible.** Copyright © 1998 by David H. Stern. Published by Jewish New Testament Publications, Inc. www.messianicjewish.net/jntp. Distributed by Messianic Jewish Resources Int'l. All rights reserved. Used by permission.

Scripture quotations marked **TLV are from Tree of Life Translation of the Bible.** Copyright © 2015 by the Messianic Jewish Family Bible Society. Used by permission of the Tree of Life Bible Society.

Scripture quotations marked **NLT are taken from the Holy Bible, New Living Translation,** copyright ©1996, 2004, 2015 by Tyndale House Foundation. Used by permission of Tyndale House Publishers, Carol Stream, Illinois 60188. All rights reserved.

All rights reserved. No part of this publication may be reproduced, stored in, or introduced into a retrieval system, or transmitted, in any form, or by any means (electronic, mechanical, photocopying, recording, Internet or otherwise) without the prior written permission of the author.

DEDICATION

To the Chief Musician – my good Shepherd.

To my beloved Laurence – devout, devoted, steadfast, resolute.

I love how we get to harmonise in life, with our family, and in worship to the Lord. The Lord sees all you do. So grateful for your love, support, and allowing me to be me in following this challenging call.

ACKNOWLEDGMENTS

It takes a village to raise a child and also to complete a project like this. I am grateful to the Lord for sending each of you to journey with us, and I am so appreciative of each of you who have walked alongside me in life and ministry.

You are all precious gems whom I love and cherish.

- My precious family: children, grandchildren, and extended family
- Valued and often unseen armour bearers who have encouraged, interceded, and been faithful friends and family
- Faithful T.O.D. worshippers, intercessors, and partners
- Alignments with ARC Global, and The Global Watch
- Each friend who has taken the time to review the manuscript and write endorsements and the foreword
- Each friend who has proofread the manuscript, encouraged the project, listened, prodded with questions, partaken in discussions—including the creative headings.
- Typing pool who enabled the project to start.
- Susan (editor) and Tom (design and layout)

T-H-A-N-K-Y-O-U

ENDORSEMENTS

In Music, the Glory and the Cosmic War, Ruth Webb shares the deep revelations she has received in her life-long search for understanding of throne room worship, the glory of God and the end time spiritual battle. I have known Ruth for over 25 years and in that time have witnessed her passion to offer God the purist worship that delights His heart.

Her experience as a gifted worship leader, watchman, teacher, broadcaster and General in the prayer movement has enabled her to bring true revelation but also warnings about false worship and the danger of demonic influence in our music. She reveals forthcoming shifts and that the worship we enjoy in times of peace will not be sufficient in times of war. She stresses the importance of prophetic worship that releases a sound that surrounds the throne of God and writes of how we then sing from the same song sheet as the angels.

Ruth expresses openly how much of the revelation she has received was forged in the fires of affliction. The fruit is within the pages of this book. I highly commend it.

Jenny Hagger AM
Founder and former Director of the Australian House of Prayer For All Nations and Mission World Aid.
Member of Global Watch Advisory Council representing Oceania.

∼

As the cosmic war intensifies and the world echoes with wars and rumours of war, Ruth Webb articulates a needed shift in how we understand the role of worship in these accelerating times. She captures this shift: "Sounds of war are very different from wedding bells. Earth may prepare for war, but heaven is preparing for a wedding." These words speak directly into the reality of the times. As the end-time narrative unfolds, a new sound of worship is emerging—one that transforms lives and shifts spiritual atmospheres. In a season of acceleration, we cannot remain unchanged. This book extends an open invitation to discover the vital shifts in worship that enable us to break through the cosmic resistance to advance God's Kingdom. A must read for all who desire to see the battle turned at the gate, and His Kingdom to prosper in the days ahead.

Dr. Susan Rowe
Founder, The Global Watch
www.theglobalwatch.com

～

The Lord is sharpening and instructing us all, as a generation of older and younger, in turning our hearts toward one another as fathers and mothers, and sons and daughters, to know and hear Him much better through each uniquely anointed instrument we are.

In 'Music, the Glory and the Cosmic War,' Ruth Webb with the piercing precision of her seasoned words, cuts to the heart of our worship in saying, "The sound needed for this new era is not defined by age, style, or trend but by anointing."

Just as lighting strikes its mark and thunder is heard, Ruth in a God-fearing tone is emphatic that, "No worship team can sing and worship for you. No one else can sing on your behalf. Only you can sing the praises to Him, that need to come from you!"

This book is a saltshaker and heart-sifter, calling forth the holiness of worship in spirit and in truth, where God Almighty and Jesus our Lord are exalted above all in this epic Cosmic War.

Colin Brown
National Board Member of Aglow International Australia
Author: Born for Battle, Dose of Iron, Outside the Camp

∼

Ruth Webb's latest book "Music, The Glory and Cosmic War", reminds us of the centrality of worship in the lives of believers, in both our relationship with the Lord, and of its major role in spiritual warfare. The need for utmost integrity, and the awareness of pitfalls make this book a 'must read' for all those who lead worship, and for any who are part of the heavenly task of bringing others before God's throne. We would do well to take heed of all the wisdom that is laid out for us in this book.

Ruth Fazal
Internationally renowned violinist, worship leader, composer.
www.ruthfazal.com

∼

Music, the Glory and the Cosmic War, by Ruth Webb, is a book packed with powerful, dynamic, teaching. This is not a dainty drink; it is a fire hydrant of prophetic revelation that comes with a depth of insight from Ruth's many years of pursuing the Lord and standing against the works of the kingdom of darkness in her region.

I am eternally grateful to Ruth for stewarding the call God has placed on her life. Through her teaching, we too can enter this end-time, strategic call from heaven to, "Let His glory ring out, filling the globe with our worship, aligned with His sceptre and throne of authority."

Karen Wilson
Oceania War Room—The Global Watch

Over 45 years in ministry, I have been privileged to speak about and lead worship in numerous churches and denominations in South Africa. My long-time concern has been the state of worship found in most churches. I would highly recommend every pastor, church leader, and believer, whether involved in worship ministry or not, read the series "Restoring True Worship". Ruth Webb's passion and extensive research is evident in every page, and it is my prayer that as you read, the Holy Spirit would reveal the true meaning of worshipping Him in Spirit and Truth (John 4:23) and for godly worship to be restored to the churches.

Charmaine Rayment
South Africa

FOREWORD

Ruth Webb's newly revised book "Music, the Glory, & the Cosmic War" carries a much-needed message for the global body of Messiah as the "birth pangs" of the end-time spiritual battles are intensifying throughout the earth.

This important book is packed with extraordinarily profound insights on the role of music and worship as a spiritual weapon to advance and manifest the kingdom of God in Israel and the nations.

As a worship leader on Mount Carmel, Israel, where Elijah confronted the prophets of Baal and repaired the altar of the Lord that was torn down, I deeply resonate with Ruth's message calling the body of Messiah to a deeper, uncompromised, sacrificial worship "in spirit and in truth."

May this book bring greater understanding to enable us all to fulfill our high calling as a royal priesthood, as we prepare the way for the return of the King of Glory, Yeshua.

Karen Davis
Co-Founder/Worship Director
Kehilat HaCarmel
Mt. Carmel, Israel
karendavisworship.com

Born in the U.S. in a Jewish family, Karen had a life-changing encounter with Yeshua (Jesus) in New York City where she was developing her musical talents. Karen and her late husband David Davis immigrated to Israel in 1989 and established Beit Nitzachon (House of Victory) rehabilitation center and Kehilat HaCarmel (Carmel Congregation) in 1991.

CONTENT

Dedication II
Acknowledgments III
Endorsements IV
Foreword VIII

PART ONE

SINGING CANARIES, BEATING WAR DRUMS: Lessons From the Worship Trenches

PART ONE: PROPHETIC SNAPSHOT 2

1. **Mum's Canaries to Global Coalmines** 5
   Israel: The Canary to Civilisation 5
   Music: The Canary to the Church 6
   Window to the Soul 6
   Mum's Canaries, Amazing Songbird and Coalmines 7
   Why Israel? Spine of the Bible 9
   7 October 2023: Alarm to the Nations 11
   Music Peels Back the Veil 12
   Paradigm Shift Needed: What is Our Worship Model? 13
   Come All Ye Faithful: Shift Atmospheres 15
   Health Check – To Sing or Not to Sing? 15

2. **Ctl-Shift-30: Rebooting Three Decades** 17
   Dinosaur Computer to AI 17
   Thirty 18
   Watchman Struggle: 'But I'm a Woman!' 19
   Metamorphoses in Motion 20
   Thirty-Year Storm 22
   Mt Sinai to Mt Zion: Hear His Voice! 23
   New Era: Worship Needs an Upgrade! 25
   Increased Urgency 27

3. **Beating War Drums** 29
   War to Establish Era of Glory 29

CONTENT

King of Glory, Man of War	30
Marching Bands and Beating War Drums	32
Watchmen Play Shofars and Sing!	34
Air Supremacy: Stop the Land War	35
Dragons, Drums, Firecrackers and Missiles	36
War for His Throne, Name, Glory – and *Your* Voice	37
Worship Drums or War Drums?	40
War Drums or Wedding Bells?	41
Setting the Record Straight: Father's Heartbeat	42
New Breed of Psalmists and Intercessors	43

4. Agitated b4 Divine Download 44

Agitated @ University	44
Survival Mode: Music or Food?	45
Green Bible	46
Four Takeaways	47
Uprooting Performance and Entertainment	48

5. Don't Touch the Ark! My Steep Learning Curve 51

Rebuke from the Lord: 'No Flesh in My Presence!'	51
Don't Touch the Glory	52
Presumption on My Part	52
Heavenly Music, Heartbreak and Spiritual Abuse	53
Course Correction	54
Seat Belts On: Eight Turbulent Episodes	54
Recovery, L plates, and Greater Joy	59
Pray for Israel: Prophetic Worship	59
Learning Spiritual Warfare: Pray Bendigo	60
Lead a Ministry – Me? Nobody Will Come!	61
Rejoice! Lessons from the Fire	62

6. Don't Shoot – I'm Just the Piano Player! 64

Covid Lockdowns and 2 Chronicles 20	64
Don't Shoot – I'm Just the Piano Player!	65
Hidden Layers of 2 Chronicles 20: A Fresh Perspective	66
En Gedi: Waterfall and Hideout	67
From the River to the Sea	68
The Lord says, 'I've Got It!'	69
Singing While Eyeballing the Enemy	71

CONTENT

    What Song? 72
    Army in position? Cover the Frontline Troops! 73
    Advance, Ready, Set, Worship! 75

7. Merging Worship and Music **76**
    Our Worship Filters? 76
    Pause and Pray 77
    Worship Defined 77
    Merger: Strumming Heart Strings 78
    Heaven's Model: Bow and Sing! 79
    Liturgy to Loudspeakers: Changed Genres 82

8. Music, Marx and Recycling the Gods **89**
    Return of the 'gods' 89
    Music to Kill By 90
    Return of the Gods and Restoring True Worship 90
    Music and the Sexual Revolution 92
    Lost Ground After Revival 94
    Events in Israel Mirrored in the Church: + and - 96
    Marxism Vs. Revival: Losing a Generation Matters! 98
    Where to Now? War Over Tabernacle of David 100
    Questions to Ponder 101

Endnotes – Part 1 .... **103**

PART TWO

MUSIC AND COSMIC WARFARE
God Created – Lucifer Stole

PART TWO: PROPHETIC SNAPSHOT **106**

9. Music at Creation **107**
    In the Beginning … 107
    Creator Made Sound 108
    God is a Singer! 109
    Sound, Movement: Shift to the New 109

    Let There Be Light! 111
    Light, Sound and Creative Miracles 112
    Made in His Image, We Create! 115
    Music in the Garden of Eden 117

10. Sounds of Eternity 119
    Music for the Glory of God 119
    Glory Sounds of Eternity 119
    Creation Responds: Stars and Icebergs Sing! 122
    Resonance 125
    Groaning Earth 126

11. Music and the Glory 128
    The Glory, The Ark and Sound 128
    Pentecost: Sound of Heaven 130
    Worship in the Book of Revelation 133
    Sounds of Heaven on Earth 134
    Corporate Anointing 135

12. Frequencies of the Glory 138
    Frequencies of His Glory 138
    Frequency of His Voice 139
    Songs Tuned to the Glory 141
    Sympathetic Sound 142
    Deaf Student Heard the Trumpet 143
    Echo and Resonate 144
    Anna Mendez in Australia: Sound to Shatter Glass 145
    How Do We Resonate with Frequencies of His Glory? 147
    Anointed Sound Changes Things! 147

13. Heaven's First Worship Leader – Mutiny! 151
    Perfect Beauty and Skill 151
    Confusing Bible Translations About Lucifer 154
    Lucifer's Ministry: Musician or High Priest? 155
    Dualism: Greek or Hebrew thinking?
    Worship and Intercession 157
    Lucifer's Five-Point Manifesto: 'I Will', Not 'I Do' 158
    Tragic End 163
    Restoring All Things 164

14. Why Lucifer Had to Go — 166
- Wanted Top Job of Supreme Ruler — 166
- God is Holy — 168
- Failed Coup, Bitter Usurper — 169
- Jesus and Satan Spar Over Worship — 170
- Worship Music Corrupted and Hijacked — 171
- Music and Worship Stolen for the 'gods': Marx and Cultural Revolution — 173
- Ludicrous Hyper-grace — 175

15. Battle For Worship — 177
- Root of all Battles: Lucifer's Eviction — 177
- Light Vs Darkness — 178
- Revenge, Jealousy, Anger, Hatred — 179
- Your Voice: Vacancy in Heaven's Worship Department — 180
- Your Voice: DNA and Identity — 181
- Overcoming Sabotage — 182
- Four Lies That Deceive and Undermine Worship — 184

16. Why Music: Divine Mystique or Neutral? — 186
- What is Music? Please Explain! — 186
- Mystical, Unique Gift of Creation — 187
- Chaos to Order: His Glory, Voice and Music — 188
- Has the Church Lost Music's Mystique? — 189
- Music's Purpose and Power: Awaken Souls and Shift Atmospheres — 190
- Dr Jordan Peterson: Music the Highest Form of Art — 192
- Historical Views on Music — 194
- Modernism and Postmodernism — 195
- Heart Vs Postmodern Straitjacket — 196
- 1980s Church Mantra: Music is Neutral — 197
- 'Houston, We Have a Problem' – What, With the Creator? — 198
- Conflict of Christians Advocating Music is Neutral — 199

17. Songs Without Words: Prophesy on Your Instrument! — 201
- Criteria for Evaluating Worship Music: Lyrics or Music? — 201
- Music Breaks Open Dark Sayings — 202
- Prophesy Without Words – How? — 203
- Exploring Realms of Spirit and Sound — 204
- Music to Release Prophets — 205

CONTENT

- Schools of the Prophets Included Psalmists 206
- Prophetic Atmospheres Transform 207
- Songs of Deliverance 207
- Can Anointed Music Help Society? 209
- Sociological Effects of Music: Education, Politics and Culture 209
- Physiological 211
- Neuroscience Reveals Music's Effect on Brain 213
- Psychological 214
- Response to God's Mercy: Holy Living and Worship 216

18. When Entertainment Supplants His Glory 217
- Father's Sorrow: Lightweight Worship 217
- Kabod: Weight of Glory 218
- Stages or Altars? 219
- Raise Up Altars of True Worship Above Strongholds 222
- Night Club or Holy of Holies? 222
- Mimicking the Real: Doodads and Fairy Floss 224

Endnotes – Part 2 227

PART THREE

GOLD FOR WORSHIPPING THE KING
Crafted Into a Calf

PART THREE: PROPHETIC SNAPSHOT 232

19. Are You Paying Attention? 233
- Sinai to Zion: Listen to His voice 233
- Nine-fold Multiplication 234
- Watching the Golden Calf from Heaven's Grandstand 235
- Massacre at Supernova 237
- Blessings or Curses? 238

20. Betrothal to Betrayal 240
- Jilted at the Altar 240
- Wedding Chuppah (Canopy) 241

CONTENT

    Jewish Wedding: Ketubah 241
    Wedding Ring Traded for an Idol 243
    Idolatry is Adultery: Bride Has Another Lover! 245
    Pentecost: Has the Church Rejected the Bridal Gift? 247
    Idols Render Us Unfit for Worship! 248

21. Excuses, Excuses: This Calf Came Out by Itself! 251
    Where is Moses? 251
    Need a God We Can See? 252
    Impatient Waiting for God? 253
    Why Did Aaron Comply? 254
    This 'God' Delivered from Egypt? 255
    Aaron Built an Altar 256
    Mixture and Syncretism 257
    Mixture, Counterfeits and Confusion 258
    Yes … No … Make Up Your Mind! 260
    21st-Century Syncretism 261
    Generational Consequences 262

22. What is the Worst Sin? It is Poisonous! 264
    No Other Gods 264
    Spiritual Dehydration While Active in Worship Team 265
    Idolatry: Hidden Root of Spiritual Abuse 267
    Trading Jesus for Another God 268
    Oops, There Are Demons! 270
    Slippery Slope 272
    Don't Point the Finger at Israel! 272
    Idolatry Our Default 273
    Assessment of Idolatry: Good and Bad Kings 275
    Prophets Concerned with True Worship 276

23. Supernova Sukkot 279
    Global Supernova Festivals 279
    Confusion: Music or Gunfire? 280
    Mystical Music Genre: 'Supernova Psytrance' 281
    Supernova, Hindu Shiva and the Pantheon of 'gods' 282
    Supernova Sukkot, Feast of Tabernacles 283
    Dancing with Torah or Golden Calf? 284
    'And Israel Rose Up to Play': Revelry 284

Singing and the Noise of War 286
Destruction 289
Powerful Promises to Israel 290

24. Gold For Royalty and Worship, Not Idols 292
Gold Represents Royalty: Worship the King of Glory 292
Wealth of Abraham and King David: Fund Building the Temple 293
Gold and Dragons: Bendigo 295
Contention for Glory: Gold and Dragons 297
Gold, Greed and Mayhem 298
Building Our House Before His: Haggai 299
Buy Gold From the Lord! 302
2023 Word to Watchman at Mt Carmel 303

25. The Ark or Golden Calf? 305
Two Icons 305
Purpose of the Ark 305
The Ark Opened After Seventh Trumpet 308
Base of Sinai: Revelry 309
Contrasting Dances 310
A Picture of Worship: Holy of Holies or Outer Court? 310
Last Days House of God: Top of the Mountain 312
Climbing the Mountain of Suffering Love 313
Habitation For the Glory 314

26. Cute and Cuddly Lamb or Cow? 316
Passover Lamb 316
Getting Egypt Out of Israel 318
Bull Vs Calf Worship 318
Cute and Cuddly 320
Don't Dismiss Cute Sins 321
Nip Them in the Bud 322

27. Our Sacred Cows 324
Unknowingly Crossing a Line 324
Our Opinions 326
Adapting Values of the World 328
Greed, Covetousness and People on Pedestals 330
Wealth: Things Made from Gold or Silver 331

Work of Our Hands: What We Own, What We Do ... 332
Dealing With Sacred Cows ... 333
Restoring Worship: Synergy of Anointing ... 333

28. Intercession: Battle at the Gates ... 336

Moses Pleaded With God ... 336
Stand in the Gap ... 337
Who is on the Lord's Side? ... 338
Taking the Sword to Your Relatives – Seriously? ... 340
Turn Back the Battle at the Gates ... 340
Repair Broken Altars: Judgement to Redemption ... 343
Uprooting Demonic Altars, Raising God's Altar ... 344
Restoring the Altar of True Worship ... 346
Summary: Consecrate Altars of True Worship ... 346

Endnotes – Part 3 ... 349

PART FOUR

WORSHIP MUSIC TUNED TO THE GLORY
Activate Angels, Dissipate Darkness

PART FOUR: PROPHETIC SNAPSHOT ... 354

29. End-Time Battle of the Bands ... 359

Clash of Kingdoms, Contention for the Airwaves ... 359
Music and Cosmic Battle to Dethrone God ... 360
Tormenting Sounds ... 361
Grammy Award for 'Unholy' Vs Asbury Revival ... 362
Demonic Music Festivals: False Deities ... 363
Demonic Alliances, Counterfeit Marriage ... 366
Worship the Lamb or the Beast? ... 366
Worship of the Lamb Vs Babylon ... 367
Seduced: Bowing to Satan ... 369
How Music Shapes Society ... 370
Trojan Horse to Worship ... 371
Worship Clashes Intensify in End-Times ... 373

30. Sound of the Blood Needed for His Glory — 375

- The Blood and the Glory — 376
- The Voice of the Blood Speaks! — 377
- Reconciliation Dream: 'Oh the Blood' Our National Anthem! — 379
- The Cross is the Power of God — 381
- Overcoming End-Time Dragon Accusation: Communion — 383
- Heaven's Worship Honours the Lamb — 385
- Bush Praise and Battle Hymns: Songs to Make Demons Run — 386
- Testimony of the Blood — 387
- Applying the Blood Apostolically — 388

31. Exquisite Governing Sound: Wait for Weighty Glory — 391

- Vietnam War, Charismatic Era: My Resistance Broken — 391
- Exquisite Sound Beyond Description — 392
- Return Singing in Tongues to the Church – Urgent Priority! — 393
- Tongues Defeat Babel - Babylon — 394
- Governing Sound — 395
- Sounds From Heaven: Singing in Tongues — 396
- Heavenly Language and Tongues of Fire — 398
- Five Truths About Tongues — 399
- Minimising Singing in Tongues — 402
- Wait For the Weight of Glory — 403
- Your Voice, Corporate Tongues: Powerful Weapon — 405

32. Psalm 149: Nuclear Warhead — 406

- Beyond the Natural: Breaking the Sound Barrier — 407
- Judgement Shockwaves: His Voice and Our Instruments of Praise — 408
- Psalm 149: Spiritual Nuclear Warhead — 409
- Seven Components — 409
- Binding Kings with Chains — 414
- Judging Demonic Kings, Enforced by Worshipping Warriors — 415
- Double-Sided Scroll with Written Judgements — 416
- 'One Sound' Amplifies God's Original Sound — 419
- Ark in Temple: 'One Sound' — 420

33. The Harp: End-Time Instrument — 422

- Harp Resurgence — 422
- Gentle Strength — 423
- Pharaoh: Exodus 15 — 424

Anti-Christ: Revelation 15 424
Tracking the Harp Resurgence 425
Four Reasons for End-Time Harps 426

34. Glory Sounds From Church Confront World Powers 434

Oh, To Be Like the Early Church 434
Paul and Silas Sing 435
Ephesus: Witchcraft and Idol Worship 436
Nullifying the Prince of the Airwaves 438
Battle of Britain: Spiritual Air Supremacy 440
Exalt Jesus, Not Demons 442
Ephesian's New Lifestyle: Sing to the Lord 443
The Glory Terrifies Demonic Kings 446

35. Ark Defeats Dagon: But Yahweh's Glory is *No* Lucky Charm! 447

Ark Vs. Dagon: Showdown in Worship War 447
Dagon's Real Identity: Sea Dragon 448
Clash of Cloud Riders: Yahweh Supreme King 449
Return of the Gods: Dagon, Merman, Mermaid and Mitre Hat 451
Dagon, Dragon: Mystery Babylon and End-Time Victories 451
Dagon Bowed Once, Twice! Rat Plague and Haemorrhoids! 453
Dagon Must Bow Before Yahweh 454
Why the Ark Was Captured 455
Broken Covenant in a Time of War 455
Sound of the Ark Shook the Ground 456
The Ark is *Not* a Lucky Charm 457
Return of the Ark and Stolen Land 458
Gaza: Giants, Judah, ANZACs and Hamas 459
ANZACs at Gaza 460
Gaza and Hamas 461
Worship and the Inheritance of Judah 461
Word From the Lord 462
The Glory and His Sword 464

36. Silencing Babylon: Praise Eruption 465

Relief From Babylon 465
Final Battle Over Worship 466
Anti-Christ Demands Worship – Destroyed by the Breath of God 467

Last Mercy Call to the Earth ... 468
Judgement on Ancient and Mystery Babylon ... 469
Sounds of Nebuchadnezzar and the Beast Imposing Worship ... 469
Lucifer and the Sound of Babylon ... 471
Babylon Will Be Judged ... 472
Babylon's Final Judgement – Silence! ... 474
Tale of Two Women, Two Cities and Two Rivers ... 475
Hallelujah Chorus: All Creation Sings! ... 476
Hallelujahs, The Wedding and the White Horse ... 478
Intergenerational 'One Sound' and the Glory ... 478

Endnotes – Part 4 ... 481

Other Resources by Ruth Webb ... 486
About the Author ... 488

PART ONE

SINGING CANARIES, BEATING WAR DRUMS: Lessons From the Worship Trenches

Then Moses and the children of Israel sang ... 'I will sing to the LORD, For He has triumphed gloriously! ... The LORD is my strength and song ... He is my God, and I will praise Him ... The LORD is a man of war; The LORD is His name.' (Exodus 15:1–3)

Sing to YAHWEH a brand-new song! Sing his praise until it echoes from the ends of the earth! (Isaiah 42:10 TPT)

The LORD shall go forth like a mighty man; He shall stir up His zeal like a man of war ... He shall prevail against His enemies. (Isaiah 42:13 NKJV)

Blessed be the LORD my Rock, Who trains my hands for war, And my fingers for battle ... (Psalm 144:1)

... he appointed those who should sing to the LORD ... as they went out before the army and were saying: 'Praise the LORD, For His mercy endures forever.' (2 Chronicles 20:21)

PART ONE: PROPHETIC SNAPSHOT

As Israel is the canary in the coalmine to civilisation, so music is the canary to the Church. When altars of worship are replaced by stages of entertainment, not only do congregations stop singing, but sexual and financial scandals soon follow. The canary's beautiful song is a metaphoric warning but is also an invitation to stand with Israel and for *every* believer's voice to rise in praise.

War drums are beating across the earth. Behind plots of political manoeuvrings and media manipulations lies a deeper conflict – the cosmic war. The spiritual war of kingdoms clashing is Satan and his cohorts striving to block the return of Jesus to Jerusalem to reign on David's throne.

How do we stand against such darkness? The Lord has been training worshipping warriors in hidden trenches – His spiritual air force, those who will gain air supremacy through sound, song, decrees and intercession.

My story may mirror yours – a journey of learning throne room worship, not merely church worship.

The sound needed for this new era is not defined by age, style or trend but by anointing. What was developed in times of peace will not sustain us in times of war. A paradigm shift is needed.

The Church must now release the sound that resonates with the armies of heaven 'for such a time as this' (Esther 4:14).

Vision of the Rent Veil

In worship, I saw the torn veil, as when Jesus died. Multitudes stood before it celebrating – singing, dancing, laughing and shouting with joy. Though rejoicing, most had not gone beyond the veil. Only a handful had gone in. They were kneeling before the Lord, weeping and lost in awe and adoration. There was a clear demarcation between the two groups.

Upset and troubled, I asked, 'Lord, why do Your people not enter right in, when the blood of Jesus opened the way?'

The Holy Spirit replied, 'The veil was torn the moment Jesus died. The way into the Holy of Holies is through the cross, but many of My people will not fully embrace My cross or take up theirs.'

Then I entered in and knelt. The Lord stood in His royal robes; a holy hush filled the atmosphere. As I worshipped Him, His sceptre was extended towards me – a moment of receiving access, favour, a commissioning, like a divine investiture of authority. Those who had entered before me had also had the sceptre extended.

In this hour of cosmic conflict touching the earth, there is a sound only released from within the Holy of Holies – and this is where our journey into restoring true worship begins.

CHAPTER ONE

Mum's Canaries to Global Coalmines

Israel: The Canary to Civilisation

'ISRAEL IS THE CANARY in the coalmine' is a statement repeated often since the Hamas massacre on 7 October 2023.

The late Australian Prime Minister Bob Hawke said, 'If the bell tolls for Israel, the bell tolls for all of mankind.'

Sad irony for Australia – it is some of Bob Hawke's colleagues who have been ringing the bell!

Israeli Prime Minister Benjamin Netanyahu echoed Hawke's sentiments stating:

> *We are in a battle of civilisation against barbarism. I've been through wars. I've seen horrible things. I've never seen things this horrible. This is a battle of our common civilization.*[1]

The targeting of Israel for persecution and extermination warns us about the possible collapse of Western civilisation. Jews get vilified and blamed when nations are in trouble and want a scapegoat. Among the many blood libels are the following claims: 'Jews run the world', 'they own all the money', 'they killed Jesus'. As King David wrote:

CHAPTER ONE

> *From our very beginning we have been persecuted by the nations. And from our very beginning we have faced never-ending discrimination. Nevertheless, our enemies have not defeated us. We're still here! (Psalm 129:1–2 TPT)*

Music: The Canary to the Church

If Israel is the canary in a coalmine to civilisation, is there a canary in the coalmine for the church? Yes!

This may surprise you – it is when music and worship merge.

The first command spoken through Moses, and reiterated by Jesus, is to worship *only* God. Worship is key to intimate relationship and blessing.

Fulfilling this condition comes with blessings and protection, but it is also vulnerable to sabotage and contamination. Even a little contamination in the fuel of an airliner can end in disaster. An early warning system saves lives from gross darkness.

Window to the Soul

Music and the arts are often called 'windows to the soul'. As such, they reveal the condition of the human heart.

About 2000 BC, the Chinese Emperor Shang said that if he wanted to check on any province, he would simply listen to their music because 'coarse and sensual sounds reflect a sick society.'[2] In premodern China, students were required to read a set of classics, one of which was the *Classic of Poetry*. A preface written to this book said music could provide insight to a society. If the music of a province was orgiastic, he knew that province was in moral decay and needed help.[3]

People understood the principle that music can reflect, corrupt or enhance the heart and soul of a society. Depraved and Dionysiac music reveal a society in decline. For believers, music reveals the heart of worship of either individuals or a group like a local church.

What is the condition of the heart of the Church? Would we be comfortable allowing King Jesus to inspect His provinces on earth? I wonder what His assessment would be? Do we have the courage to invite the Lord to give our worship a spiritual health check?

Mum's Canaries, Amazing Songbird and Coalmines

My mother and grandmother kept canaries. These cute little yellow birds filled Mum's large walk-in aviary. I fondly remember their continuous sweet singing as they flitted around, bringing us immense joy. We kids had to make sure none escaped as we fed them!

The beautiful singing capability of canaries is because of their high metabolism; they inhale *and* exhale oxygen! All this oxygen is why they sing so beautifully. Unlike humans – we breath in oxygen and breathe out carbon dioxide.

After a deadly mine explosion from toxic gases in the UK in 1896, scientists realised canaries would be a perfect early warning system. Their high dependence on oxygen means they are sensitive to carbon monoxide. When canaries stopped chirping or died, it alerted the miners and allowed them to evacuate. Engineers developed special cages so the birds could recover with oxygen.[4] Electronic devices replaced canaries in 1986, but canaries in mines remains a powerful analogy. But the canary analogy goes beyond being an early warning signal.

The ability of canaries to breathe in and exhale oxygen is the reason for their beautiful singing. What a pertinent picture of receiving the breath of God, *Ruach Ha Kodesh* (Hebrew for 'Holy Spirit'). *Ruach* means spirit, breath or wind.

What if we, like the canary, would breathe the breath of Holy Spirit in *and* out? We too would sing beautifully day and night. It reminds me of circular breathing, a difficult technique some wind and brass players have mastered to play long notes by breathing in and out simultaneously!

Songs of praise depend upon us breathing the Holy Spirit in and out. I call it the cycle of praise. He breathes His life into us. We return our breath in songs of praise.

> *You're the reason for my praise;* **it comes from you and goes to you.** *(Psalm 22:25 TPT)*

Canaries are songbirds, created by God in such a unique way to especially sing. We too have been created to sing His praises. Every person is created with a voice, and regardless of being a believer or not, we have the capability to sing. It's not just the 'Christian' thing to do; it is what we were created to do. Singing His praises is our response to our Creator.

Like the canary, toxic air stops the ability to sing. What toxicity stops us? The sound of praise depends on us breathing the breath of God – in *and* out.

Some years ago, we were conducting a workshop to sing scriptures. It was a small group. I was getting each person to sing. Some in the group sang in worship teams; some did not. We soon discovered that all the participants had been breathing toxic lies. They all believed their voice sounded awful. It turned out everyone had been told by a parent, teacher or some important other that their voice was terrible and they should not sing. We spent the entire workshop praying for the participants to break curses against their voices.

The devil has done a good job to shut down the singing voices of God's people by his lies. Singing praises to the Lord is not dependant on a voice to win a singing competition! If we stop breathing in the breath of the Holy Spirit, spiritual toxic gases will soon kill the Church and even poison society.

Ask Holy Spirit what lies you believe and what their source is. Forgive, repent and renounce every lie about your voice. The Lord created you with the unique tone which is your voice. Appreciate what He has given you. Believe His truth. He created you to sing! No worship team can sing and worship for you. No one else can sing on your behalf. Only you can sing the praises to Him that need to come from you.

Prophesy to your breath. The new song of the Lord *will* be released through the mouth of every believer of each generation. The song from every mouth will break evil strongholds!

> *My praises will break the powers of wickedness … (Psalm 75:10 TPT)*

Your songs of praise are needed to help fill the bowls in heaven and is a daily love gift to Him.

> *And my praises will fill the heavens forever, fulfilling my vow to make every day a love-gift to you! (Psalm 61:8 TPT)*

Your songs of praise are more valuable than other sacrifices.

> *For I know, YAHWEH, that my praises mean more to you than all my gifts and sacrifices. (Psalm 69:31 TPT)*

Why Israel? Spine of the Bible

The atrocities of 7 October were a global wake-up call. Sadly, it has also awakened latent anti-Semitism. Sympathy for Israel lasted barely twenty-four hours after the Hamas massacre. The speed and ferocity of anti-Israel rhetoric have been gut-wrenching to watch – Islamists and Marxists uniting in protest against the Jews, and governments pressurising Israel more than terrorist organisations. Worse, even some Christians are now siding against Israel.[5]

After completing a journey around Australia in 1993 to release *Restoring True Worship* (1st edition), I sought the Lord about the future. His direction to start a prayer group for Israel shocked me. I was expecting something about worship. Israel was not on my radar, though clearly on His.

I had to learn on the job. I knew little about anti-Semitism, had never heard of replacement theology and had no clue why standing with Israel mattered! It took another decade of learning – about Israel, spiritual mapping and warfare – before being released to start our current ministry, Tabernacle of David. I discovered that carrying the Father's heart for Israel is essential for prophetic worship.

Israel is the plumbline for all things prophetic, the spine of the Bible. If we fail to grasp God's call and covenant with Israel, we misinterpret scripture, the kingdom, the Church's role, end-time revivals and prophecy itself. They all get skewed.

> *No worship team can sing and worship for you. Only you can sing the praises to Him that need to come from you.*

Replacement theology claims that because Israel rejected Jesus, therefore God rejected Israel and replaced her with the Church. All the promises for Israel now belong to the Church. This is both erroneous and dangerous. It has weakened the Church, like a struggling plant with shallow roots and was the reason for centuries of Jewish persecution, the pogroms and the Holocaust.[6]

During a recent worship watch, one of our intercessors was burdened over the rise of anti-Semitism in Sydney and Melbourne. As we worshipped, the Lord revealed a key: the Church must repent of replacement theology!

7 October 2023: Alarm to the Nations

Following the Hamas massacre, journalist Douglas Murray entered Gaza and Lebanon with Israeli Defense Force troops. He interviewed soldiers, civilians and government leaders on both sides of the conflict. He recorded his insights in his book *On Democracies and Death Cults: Israel, Hamas and the Future of the West* (2025).

Murray observed that in war zones, love and hate coexist. 'When you see war up close, you cannot help but think about what matters most.'[7] He said he kept coming back to the Bible:

> *I call heaven and earth as witnesses today against you, that I have set before you life and death, blessing and cursing; therefore* **choose life**, *that both you and your descendants may live ...* (Deuteronomy 30:19)

Murray concluded that Israel embodies the values of life and covenant – the heart of Judeo-Christian civilisation, which is to love life rather than death. Israel fights, not to glorify war, but to protect life and the inheritance given by God.

If Israel, with all her flaws is the canary to civilisation, why is it so hated? Because God chose her as His nation, a light to the nations. He entrusted her with the covenants, the Torah, the prophetic promises and the Messiah[8] Himself. Jesus will return to rule from the throne of David.[9]

The opposition to Israel ultimately seeks to stop the return of Jesus the Messiah. Quoting from Psalm 118:26, Jesus declared:

CHAPTER ONE

> *... for I say to you, you shall see Me no more till you say, "Blessed is He who comes in the name of the LORD!" (Matthew 23:39)*

How then can true believers in Jesus despise His own brothers and sisters? Israel is not perfect – but neither are we.

Israel is more than a prophetic clock; she is the apple of God's eyes through whom He views all nations. Nations will be judged as sheep or goats by how they treat the Jewish brethren of Jesus and by whether they divide His land through a 'two state solution'.

Israel has already drunk the Lord's cup of trembling. That cup is now empty, passed to those who have afflicted her.[10]

> *Behold! I am about to make Jerusalem an intoxicating cup filled with the wine of my wrath. Any nation around her who dares to drink from it will stagger and fall ... In that day, when* **all the nations join forces against her, I will make Jerusalem like a heavy stone**. *All who lift it will severely injure themselves. (Zechariah 12:2–3 TPT)*

What does all this have to do with music and worship in the Church? Everything!

Music Peels Back the Veil

From music history, and the earlier example given of the Chinese Emperor, I learned that music reflects and shapes society. However, it was my personal experience thirty-five years ago that caused me to see just how influential it is. It felt like the Lord peeled open a can of worms.

I had been part of the worship team of our local church where many described the worship as heavenly. Suddenly, the music flipped. I was disturbed and sought the Lord for answers. It was like He anointed my eyes to see. (More specific detail in Chapter 5, 'Don't Touch the Ark'.) It felt like the Lord used the change in the music to lift a lid, tear a veil or open a window for me to gaze through. For me, it was a warning like the canary that stopped singing in the coalmine.

Did the music cause the problems? It contributed. It was certainly a window to the soul, the early warning, like miners watching a dying canary. The Holy Spirit was waving His red flag: 'Something is wrong. Stop, wake up, adjust, run. The environment is toxic.'

Like a barometer measuring atmospheric pressure, music and worship can reveal the health of a local and even global church. As a window to the soul, music allows us to see things previously hidden. If songs of praise are affected, heed the alarm. If we ignore the warnings, music can add to the toxicity. Music's unique power can exacerbate and compound problems. If we ignore the warnings of 'silent canaries', then prepare for the Lord's own shofar blast! At Mt Sinai, the Lord Himself blew the shofar, and it got louder and louder and louder! All Israel trembled.

Paradigm Shift Needed: What is Our Worship Model?

A pastor once asked me to help develop the worship in his local congregation. As we talked, he said he wanted it developed on the model of what he saw was a successful worshipping church in Australia. As I talked with him, I suggested that though this might have been appealing, the better model to consider was the worship of heaven.

Worship leaders and psalmists are called to release the sound of heaven into the earth, not the sound of earth into heaven! We are called to use music to build His altar of true worship, not stages for entertainment. We must upgrade our thinking about the role of music and worship. Though we may think worship practices have advanced well in recent decades, we now need another major paradigm shift.

The warning to the Church is to properly align with Israel and cease using music for entertainment. Otherwise, we are in grave danger. Judgement begins at the house of God.[11]

In Psalms 106 and 107, David remembered Israel's history. They worshipped God and received blessings, then Israel was seduced by the surrounding culture. They turned to worship other gods, which the Bible identifies as demons, and indulged in all their immoral practices accompanied by distinct sounds and songs. They ended up in wars, conflicts and even captivity. In their pain, they cried out to God. His enduring mercy restored them. Restored to the true worship of God, and His ways of living, they rediscovered *shalom* and blessings.

> **Worship leaders and psalmists are called to release the sound of heaven into the earth, not the sound of earth into heaven!**

The Western Church has been like Israel as described in these Psalms. We have worshipped God and He has blessed us. Then, for various reasons, we embraced the culture of other gods, much of it demonic, even brought some of it into the Church, and now compromise has captured us. We worship either God or something else.

Like the book of Amos, restoring true worship is not just a warning of the dangers of our worship being infiltrated by ungodly culture. There is also a promise of restoration. He desires to bring His people into the freedom, liberty and power of worship as He had intended. The cry to restore worship to the Lord's original intent has shifted from a cry to a roar.

Come All Ye Faithful: Shift Atmospheres

In a dream, I heard multitudes of God's people singing the carol 'O Come all Ye Faithful'. A few people had begun singing at a major shopping centre in a Muslim-majority area. But as they sang, more and more believers joined them, resulting in a major shift occurring in the atmosphere.

I believe the Lord is calling His faithful ones to step out and sing. Maybe it's not a shopping centre, but anywhere there is hostility in the Spirit. Biblically, music has a vital role in creating a worship environment that transforms atmospheres. When music and worship align correctly with the throne of God, they function as a powerful weapon in tandem with the hosts of heaven. This is critical in a time when the cosmic war of the ages is spilling onto the earth.

When earthly psalmists release the sounds of heaven, the sound breaks major strongholds. As divisions of angelic armies hear these sounds, it is the trumpet call in the Spirit for them to spring into action. Heaven and earth engage together in songs of deliverance. When we understand the Lord's intention for music and worship, one gets to see why there is such a war over it.

Health Check – To Sing or Not to Sing?

Canaries stop singing in a coalmine when toxic gases choke out oxygen. Likewise, when God's people stop singing, it warns of fleshly toxins stifling the environment.

Paul encourages us that when we 'yield freely and fully to the dynamic life and power of the Holy Spirit, [we] will abandon the cravings of [our] self-life' (Galatians 5:16 TPT). He warns that our flesh wars against and offends the Holy Spirit.

Many churches have shifted to performance-driven worship with loud bands or complex tunes drowning out

CHAPTER ONE

congregations. Participation wanes; even singing in the Spirit fades. Regarding the canary warning to the Church about worship practices, first God's people stop singing, then they die.

While writing this chapter, I had a dream of an international prophet calling to renounce compromise. She said we had reached a strong, pertinent crossroad and we must choose between the Holy Spirit and our flesh. As we sat and waited on the Lord, suddenly I saw an external flash of light, which simultaneously went right into my spirit. Behind me, others were also being touched as a fresh wave of the Holy Spirit moved among us.

We are possibly in the greatest crisis of civilisation in history. The enemy fears a singing Church empowered by worship that is aligned with heaven's throne. He has sought to dilute and pollute our worship, sabotaging our greatest weaponry. Remember the works of the flesh include sexual immorality, idolatry, witchcraft, contention and revelries. Witchcraft can operate through soulish prayers and music and seek to control people through manipulation and intimidation. We face a crossroads: will we breathe the Spirit's oxygen or the world's poison?

Conduct a health check: are all God's people singing? Can we hear the voices? Has the band drowned the voices out, or are people not singing because they are convinced their voices sound terrible? We need to reclaim Spirit-led worship to silence Babylon's sound, rather than the Church's sound being silenced by Babylon. A new sound for the new era is being raised up. It is the sound of a tribe who praise and follow the roaring Lion of Judah. Will you add your voice to that sound? You must choose.

In the next chapter, I share how God called me thirty years ago as a watchman to sound this alarm.

CHAPTER TWO

Ctl-Shift-30: Rebooting Three Decades

Dinosaur Computer to AI

THE FIRST EDITION OF *Restoring True Worship* was published in late 1993. Thirty years later:

- *the world has changed.*
- *technology has changed.*
- *language has changed.*
- *the season has changed.*
- I have changed.

But the message has not. If anything, it has become *more* critical. The last three decades have exposed us all to drastic changes in the world.

Three decades of change are demonstrated by the technology and especially the equipment used for the first edition.

Thirty years ago, I had a dinosaur computer – a museum piece! It had no hard drive at all and a total of 1 MB of RAM! Files were stored on floppy discs. It was one of the earliest desktop computers, and ours had won the computer of the year! I did not start writing with a monitor but hooked up to an old television set that was two feet thick!

Thirty years on, technology changes hourly. AI can now assist with research, fact-checking and editing suggestions, all within seconds.

Thirty

Throughout the Bible, the number 30 signifies a right time, or maturity, to minister or reign. Joseph became second-in-command in Egypt at age thirty. At age thirty, David became king. Jesus began public ministry around age thirty.[12]

Thirty years ago, in response to the Lord's call to be an Ezekiel 33 watchman, I released the first edition of this book, *Restoring True Worship*.

Though the first edition was something I had lived, I told little of my story in it, partly because we were still living it. But in this rewrite, I share our personal story because the valuable lessons learned in the trenches and deeper healing along the journey provide necessary insights for the battles faced today. Perhaps this is now a right timing for the Body of Christ to be ready, even desperate, to receive a deeper and more mature message. The message which had begun as a personal and regional issue has now shifted to one of global significance.

Thirty-plus years ago, I was part of a worship team where many described the worship as heavenly. I thought a vision the Holy Spirit had deposited in my heart some fifty years ago was coming to birth. But while on maternity leave from my role as music director, the music shifted from heavenly to earthly and, sadly, demonic fingerprints were also clear. My world fell apart, as did the lives of many others. After seeking the Lord, His revelations, though shocking, became the material of this book and the direction of our ministry.

Watchman Struggle: 'But I'm a Woman!'

I was reluctant to write, and to rewrite, this book. My hesitations were a combination of the amount of work, warfare and resources needed, as well as dealing with reactions. Music and worship can be a very touchy subject – even a sacred cow! (In the original edition, I had a chapter titled 'Music, the Department of War or Peace?')

Thirty years ago, my first excuse to the Lord was 'But I'm a woman, therefore no one will listen to me'. The old attitude toward women in any sort of leadership was a genuine concern, with good reasons. My second fear was that though I had a music degree, I did not have theological training. The Holy Spirit had forbidden me from going to Bible College.

The Lord dealt with my reluctance and fears by reminding me of the stern warning in Ezekiel 33. For prophets and watchmen who do *not* sound the alarm when an enemy is threatening, the consequence is on their heads. But if they sound the alarm and people ignore the warning, then the responsibility no longer rests on the watchman.

For the rewrite, I needed a confirmation, and received two! Because of the technology changes shared earlier, I did not have the original three hundred and fifty pages in a usable digital format. This was a critical starting point. The Lord's answer was a typing pool, and the amazing team finished the task in one month! I still needed to know, did the Lord really need me to do this? Was a fresh and expanded version really needed?

Just as the typing pool recovered the original manuscript and we were about to go to Israel, I had an unforgettable dream about the golden calf. The first edition had one chapter called 'The Golden Calf'. Six months after the dream and our visit to Israel, 7 October occurred where Hamas attacked so many precious Israelis at the Supernova dance party. (The connections are in Part Three.)

Three times in thirty years, the Lord had spoken to me about the golden calf incident. The Lord burned its importance into my spirit. When God speaks once, we must listen. When He repeats and repeats, we must stop and pay attention – what is the Spirit of God saying? He had my attention; I had my confirmation.

At Mt Sinai, the golden calf incident marked Israel's covenant with God amid His powerful Presence. Roll the years and pages over to the book of Acts, and Pentecost birthed the Church with a similar divine encounter. Both were pivotal moments showcasing God's power, yet both faced fierce resistance.

At Sinai and Pentecost, people made choices. Sounds and music accompanied both – some holy, some profane. The messages of Mt Sinai and the golden calf are so profound that neither Israel nor the Church can afford to ignore them, especially in the strategic time we are in.

Not only did I get my confirmation, but the original singular chapter grew to multiple chapters in Part Three of this edition.

Metamorphoses in Motion

The world has changed

The world has changed drastically over the last thirty years, impacting us socially, economically, politically – and spiritually:

- the rise of terrorism – 9/11, 7 October
- major realignments in the Middle East since the Arab Spring of 2010[13]

- unseen viruses, closed borders and churches during the Covid pandemic
- anti-Semitism not seen since the Holocaust from October 2023 onwards
- persecution of Christians at its highest since the early Church
- global elites wanting a world government and religion to 'save' the planet
- fact checkers, misinformation and fake news to silence critics
- increase in wars (even on the verge of nuclear), record-breaking volcanoes and earthquakes

All as Jesus warned for the end-time, that such events would be signs of birth pangs.[14]

Language and morals have changed

Language often changes over time. Words take on new meanings. New words are created to suit new narratives. Without giving in to political correctness or declining morality in a changed world, we have sought to update some language. We have also taken the opportunity to include recent incidences and experiences.

I have changed: mother to grandma

Thirty years ago, I was mother to two young children. Today, I love being grandma to three young children.

Life changes us! In our thirty-year journey, we discovered warfare we didn't know existed. From rejections, accusations, loss of income, strained friendships and ministry doors slammed shut, the rugged wilderness taught us to really lean into Him. But, oh, the joys and depths of revelation, provisions and new friendships and open doors! So much spiritual and personal growth accompanied this journey.

One volume to multiple

The first edition was akin to a textbook with some three hundred and fifty pages. *Restoring True Worship* was originally an overview of the Biblical call and function of music to minister to the Lord in worship. This new edition calls us higher from the defensive to the frontline of the battle for civilisation. It is now divided into a series of four volumes.

Thirty-Year Storm

The original publication was controversial. It was either loved or hated, and sometimes me with it!

On the negative side, it seemed to hit a raw nerve – or some sacred cows! Folks reacted with varying degrees of anger. Sadly, this also included some spiritual leaders.

On the positive side, we had hundreds of messages from people who were encouraged. The consistent messages were like this one: *'Music trends in church disturbed me, but I thought it was just me. If I expressed any concerns, they dismissed me and claimed it was my problem. You have put into words exactly what I have been feeling. Because I don't understand music like you do, I thought I was wrong. I have been so grieved. Thank you.'*

Was there any change? The answer would have to be, yes, but slower and less than I would have liked!

It brought assurance and courage to many intercessors who had previously doubted their own discernment.

Some churches took our newsletters and published them for their whole congregations.

The late Joan Morton of Aglow Australia took the now out-of-print *New Season, New Song* (a smaller version of first edition) and distributed to all the presidents across Australia.

Some church leaders came to our meetings (or us to theirs) and they adopted some things into their churches.

Some leaders who had been critical of the first edition of the book, apologised for previous hostilities. Mostly apologies came, not so much from reading the book, but from observing the changes God did in me, and in the extraordinary worship times that developed in our ministry.

Mt Sinai to Mt Zion: Hear His Voice!

Mt Sinai shook at the Presence of the Lord.[15] In Hebrews 12:18–29, the Lord says, 'but *now*.' This is a *now* word for His Church. He is bringing us to His holy mountain, Mt Zion. At Mt Zion, there is the gathering of innumerable angels and the blood of Jesus on the mercy seat is a voice speaking on our behalf.

If Mt Sinai was scary for Israel, Mt. Zion causes the fear of the Lord to fall on us all as the shakings intensify. He says to us, '*See that you do **not** refuse Him who speaks*' (Hebrews 12:25). His voice should not be trifled with!

The first edition of this book came about because I heard what I can only describe as the audible voice of God. I have only heard it booming like that twice in my life. It shook me and solidified a message I would not give except for hearing Him speak. When His glorious and powerful voice thunders, the only way to respond to is to worship – and obey!

> *Give unto the LORD the glory due to His name; Worship the LORD in the beauty of holiness. The voice of the LORD is powerful; The voice of the LORD is full of majesty. And in His temple everyone says, 'Glory!' (Psalm 29:4, 9)*

His voice causes everything to shake.

> *Once and for all I will not only shake the systems of the world, but also the **unseen powers in the heavenly realm**! (Hebrews 12:26 TPT)*

Everything is being shaken, even our understanding of worship and music especially as it pertains to unseen powers. We hold too many mindsets and paradigms that are not Biblical and need adjusting. He is calling us higher, and to Mt Zion.

What should be our response to His voice shaking everything?

> *Since we are receiving our rights to an unshakable kingdom we should be **extremely thankful and offer God the purest worship** that delights his heart as we lay down our lives in absolute surrender, filled with awe. For our God is a holy, devouring fire!(Hebrews 12:28-29 TPT)*

Our response to His voice is to be filled with gratitude and offer the purist worship. After He shakes off all our stuff, a pure sound of worship emerges out of us that aligns with His kingdom. Hence, we must leave Mt Sinai, including the golden calf debacles, and come up to Zion.[16]

> *... magnificent mountain, you are the mighty kingdom of God ... For Zion is the mountain where God has chosen to live forever. (Psalm 68:15-16 TPT)*

From Zion, the Lord leads a triumphal procession against His enemies, with God's people singing praises. There is a pure and powerful sound of glory. When heaven and earth align in this sound, it shifts things in the spirit realm and on the earth.

New Era: Worship Needs an Upgrade!

Our friend Bruce Lindley said in his book *A Whole New Era*, 'Sometimes in history there is accelerated change.'[17]

As the new millennium ticked over, an acceleration occurred on 9/11. Other key moments, as listed in the previous section, provide a snapshot of the speed at which momentous changes have occurred.

When the Arab Spring occurred, it looked like a real spring season with all its turbulent shifting winds. But the continuing shifts seemed to indicate a hot summer of harvest, reaping what we have sown – both good and bad.

But these decades do not just reflect seasons, but a new era, or epoch. Life continues to change dramatically and drastically. It is a totally new day for nations, for Israel and for the Church. We are in a critical time in history, a tipping point.

Worship in a time of peace is different from in a time of war.

In his book, Bruce Lindley speaks of a new sound for the new era.[18] In *Restoring True Worship* (this volume and series), I am seeking to articulate that sound, how to identify it, facilitate it and encourage its creation.

In my lifetime, there have been significant shifts taking place in worship and music – even a revolution. I have been privileged to not only observe but also participate. Yet these changes developed during a time of relative peace. Worship in a time of peace is different from in a time of war.

Churchill was a wartime prime minister. He did not suit peacetime. Donald Trump is a wartime president. Where we have had worship developed during peace, we must upgrade our thinking and worship to be appropriate for a time of war.

We need bridal worshipping warriors. They carry a different heart posture and a distinct sound. They are not what the natural mind thinks, and these differences are essential if worship in a time of war is of the Holy Spirit, not flesh.

In the next chapter, we discuss the sounds of a 'season of war'. (And no, not contradictory.) But shifting from peace to war requires a different sound.

Psalm 50 speaks of the glory coming out of Zion, and with it a sound.

> *Out of Zion, the perfection of beauty, God will shine forth. (Psalm 50:2 NKJV)*

> *With the rumble of thunder he approaches; he will not be silent, for he comes with an ear-splitting sound! All around him are furious flames of fire, and preceding him is the dazzling blaze of his glory. (Psalm 50:3 TPT)*

The psalm is saying, 'Remember the sights and sounds of Sinai'. But there is a greater blazing glory and ear-splitting sound coming from Zion. His sound does not need us to turn up the amplifiers and speakers. It is His sound, coming out of His Glory. The glory, sometimes described as light, has frequencies that relate to sound, because light and sound are connected but operate at different speeds and frequencies. If we want to welcome His Glory, we must expect it is accompanied by a sound.

Daily, events are shifting us to align more and more with God's prophetic timeline. Is the worship we have loved and been blessed by sufficient for this day? Psalm 40:4 speaks of a *'new song for a new day'*.

And what of our foundations, not just of the Church, but of our mindsets about worship? In this time of the Lord shaking everything, it is vital our foundations are solid.

Turkey in 2023 had severe earthquakes which caused badly constructed buildings to collapse. The higher a building is to be, the deeper the foundations need to go. The Church, and the sounds coming from the Church, need to be on solid foundations, especially in this time of severe testing and shaking.

Jesus called His Church *Ekklesia*, which is a legislative and governing assembly. This includes legislating through His sounds. As cosmic war rages, for us to legislate the Lord's will and sound in our music and worship, we need an urgent upgrade: first, to secure our foundations, to go deep, remove any sand and get onto His rock; second, to be equipped to hear and reproduce the sounds of heaven on earth for this strategic time in history.

Increased Urgency

Thirty years on, the message of *Restoring True Worship* is not redundant but more insistent. We are in a critical time of history, a season of war, spiritual and natural. Some say World War III has already started. Israel, the West and the Church face existential threats. You cannot compromise with those who want to kill you! Rather, we need to arise, confront and overthrow every enemy.

The cry from watchmen, and the prayer movement worldwide, is reaching a climax not heard in thirty years. Despite the growth of prophetic worship in this time frame, the Lord keeps calling us higher. The worship we enjoyed in a time of peace will not be sufficient in a time of war. We must shift our sound.

For some, it may be little tweaks. For others, it will require far greater changes. Regardless, we must all press into God's Word for His answers: we must heed His voice, His warnings, and discover His vision for worship, not ours.

It is crucial we allow Him to shift our understanding, be freed from a lack of knowledge that destroys us and come higher, to hear the sounds coming out of heaven. Amid the greatest of shakings, there is a pure worship that delights the heart of God!

This is a fresh, loud trumpet call for a new and glorious sound of praise, perhaps even a new worship revolution! This is a fresh call to 'offer God the purest worship that delights his heart'.[19] Come with me as we discover fresh and renewed revelations, needed for this time in history.

CHAPTER THREE

Beating War Drums

War to Establish Era of Glory

KINGDOMS ARE CLASHING IN the spirit realm and manifesting on the earth! Each week, war drums beat louder and faster with increasing ferocity and intensity. Their pounding throbs are greater than since World War II.

When kingdoms clash, there is a war for the throne, for who will rule. Each kingdom has its own signature tune, its own distinct sound. What if those sounds and tunes are also weapons of war? What if those sounds are used to contend for the throne? In the spirit realm, the cosmic war is led by Satan trying to block the King of Glory, whereas true worshippers of Jesus welcome Him.

Psalm 24 concludes by asking, 'Who is this King of glory?' The answer explains the current war: 'The LORD strong and mighty, The LORD mighty in battle' (Psalm 24:8). The King of glory comes amid war. The Passion Translation frames the answer this way:

> *He is YAHWEH,* **armed and ready for battle,** *the Mighty One, the invincible* **commander of heaven's hosts!** *Yes, he is the King of Glory. (Psalm 24:10 TPT)*

CHAPTER THREE

As we welcome the King of Glory, demonic kingdoms resist Him. The manifestation on earth is a natural and spiritual intensity that most of us have not known before.

Many of us baby boomers have lived in the peace gained by two world wars and the sacrifices of the previous generation. Many of us have fathers, brothers or uncles who served in the military, and their stories and attitudes made us privy to a wartime mindset.

Though the period of war we are in is different to what our forefathers experienced, there is a vital question to ask: will our worship and prayer, developed during peacetime, sustain us and be effective in a time of historical warfare? Do we understand the urgency of the time? Do we understand what we are up against? Are our weapons primed and ready?

Demonic powers love war and death. It is the devil's domain. They desperately want a nuclear World War III to abort the Lord's harvest plans. Sadly, warmongers agitate for conflicts because they benefit with increased wealth and power, regardless of cost to nations and families.

The sound of heaven rises above this frenzied sound of bloodlust. The heartbeat of the Father is a different rhythm to the manic war drums of the dragon. Anointed glory sounds surround the throne of Adonai. These sounds of light and glory resist, penetrate and destroy darkness. In a time of trouble, we need deep worship in His Presence to sustain us. We need the rhythm of heaven, the reassuring sound of Father's heartbeat.

King of Glory, Man of War

> *The LORD is a man of war; The LORD is His name. (Exodus 15:3)*

God Himself is a warrior. As already described, the King of Glory is armed and ready for battle (Psalm 24:10).

'Lord of hosts' is one of the most used names of God in the Bible – over two hundred and fifty references, with sixty in Isaiah and forty-six in Zechariah. Many prophetic words are spoken in the name of the Lord of hosts. He is the commander-in-chief of the armies of heaven. 'Host' refers to an army, which can be angels, even all of creation, as when the sun stood still for Joshua to win the battle or hailstones took out enemies. When He speaks as the 'Lord of hosts', He is speaking with the authority and backing of all of heavens armies.

Psalm 29 says His voice is powerful and majestic, across oceans, splintering strong trees, symbolic of strong men. His voice is an ear splitting sound that can shift the mountains of Lebanon and Hermon (Psalm 29:6).

> *When the nations are in uproar with their tottering kingdoms, God simply raises his voice, and the earth begins to disintegrate before him ... (Psalm 46:6 TPT)*

Invoking the memories of Psalm 29, Isaiah 30:30 says, 'The LORD will cause His glorious (majestic) voice to be heard'.

The Lion of the Tribe of Judah emits a formidable sound, powerful and terrifying, or gentle and comforting, a sound a frightened lion cub would long to hear. Yet the same voice terrifies demonic kings and shakes powerful men and nations. The voice of the Lord shakes and shatters everything, including the systems of the world and demonic structures.

Even His breath can vaporise His enemies.

> *And then the lawless one will be revealed, whom the Lord will consume with the breath of His mouth and destroy with the brightness of His coming. (2 Thessalonians 2:8)*

There is a song of praise from the ends of the earth which stirs up the zeal of the Lord, the Man of war. He responds with a battle cry of a mighty warrior.

> *Sing to the LORD a new song, And His praise from the ends of the earth ... The LORD shall go forth like a mighty man; He shall stir up His zeal like a **man of war**. He shall cry out, yes, **shout aloud**; He shall **prevail against His enemies**. (Isaiah 42:10, 13)*

As we hear the war drums of men, it is a signal for us to increase His praises. Our praises rouse Him to arise as the man of war to deal with His enemies.

> *He makes wars cease to the end of the earth; He breaks the bow and cuts the spear in two; He burns the chariot in the fire. The **LORD of hosts is with us;** The God of Jacob is our refuge. Selah. (Psalm 46:9, 11)*

Marching Bands and Beating War Drums

For centuries, marching bands accompanied soldiers to war. They marched with military precision as rolling snare drums and pounding bass drums kept the rhythmic beat. Trumpets and drums transmitted signals across battlefields.

Scripture shows many similar uses of music. Specific instruments and sounds call out for God's help in times of trouble, to prophesy and to engage angel armies. Do we hear the spiritual drums calling His army to march to the rhythm of heaven? For disciplined precision, we must be in step with His timing. Quick march!

Silver trumpets and shofars

Numbers 10 specifies two silver trumpets. They are to be blown at the start of each month and in a time of war.

> *When you go to war in your land ... then you shall sound an alarm with the trumpets, and ... you will be saved from your enemies. (Numbers 10:9)*

The silver trumpets sound an alarm, a fanfare, a war cry. The Lord reassures Israel and us – if these are blown in a time of war, He will rescue from the enemy.

IDF Chief Rabbi Shalom Gore blew a shofar at the Western Wall as Jerusalem reunified on 7 June 1967. It was a sound of victory.

At Jericho, seven priests blew seven shofars in front of the Ark as Israel marched around the city. On the seventh day, they marched seven times. When the shofars sounded, the people shouted and the walls came down.

> *... As soon as they heard the blast of the shofars, they raised a massive shout of jubilee like a thunderclap, and all at once the thick walls of Jericho collapsed! (Joshua 6:20 TPT)*

Some have tried to work out the science of frequencies to see if it was the sound of the shofars, shouting or marching that caused the fortified walls of Jericho to collapse. Undoubtedly, obedience activated the Lord's hand. No doubt embedded in the Lord's instructions was a phenomenon of sound. Research shows low frequencies destroy things, even human organs! We do know that when marching soldiers cross delicate structures like wooden bridges, they are commanded to march out of step since sympathetic resonance can, indeed, cause bridges to collapse. (See more information in Chapter 12, 'Frequencies of the Glory.')

In the book of Revelation, there are seven angels with trumpets. When sounded, calamities are released on the earth.

> *... seven angels bringing the last seven plagues, for with them the wrath of God is finished. (Revelation 15:1 TPT)*

The first trumpet is linked with incense from worship and intercession (harps and bowls).[20] These trumpets complete the Lord's judgements on His enemies. God Himself sounds the final trumpet (shofar). This last trumpet signifies the overcoming of the final enemy, death itself. God resurrects us with 'incorruptible' bodies.[21] His voice repeatedly sounds like a shofar in the book of Revelation.[22]

Watchmen Play Shofars and *Sing!*

The watchmen on the walls of a city are the gatekeepers, prophets and intercessors watching over cities and nations. Watchmen are instructed to warn of danger or imminent war by sounding shofars (trumpets). Some watchmen may protest about needing to blow trumpets and especially to sing, but it is part of the job description!

> *... When ... a watchman ... sees the sword coming upon the land,* **if he blows the trumpet (shofar) and warns the people** *... (Ezekiel 33:2-3)*

> *Your watchmen shall lift up their voices,* **With their voices they shall sing together.** *(Isaiah 52:8)*

Blowing shofars is not just a metaphor for sounding the alarm; the shofar also represents the voice of God Himself.

But don't forget the bit about singing, often left out when this verse is quoted. When God answers our prayers, watchmen celebrate and break into singing. They *sing together*!

They are in agreement for Zion. There is a musical sound connected to the armies of heaven, and in the watchman's call. Watchman do not just speak together – they sing! They shout in triumph and sing for joy. Such songs are as much a part of defeating the enemy as are the warnings.

Watchmen engage in all these aspects of sound: warning, warring and victory.

Air Supremacy: Stop the Land War

In World War II, the Allies knew they had to have air supremacy to defeat Nazi Germany. So too in the spiritual realm, victory in heavenly places must precede success in earthly wars. In World War II, extraordinary victories and miracles came through prayer and praise. (Specific stories are told in Chapter 34, 'Glory Sounds of Church Confront World Powers'.)

Scripture reminds us that natural weapons do not win spiritual wars. But in the heat of battle, it is easy to forget and react instinctively. The Lord has given two recent warning dreams.

One of our intercessors dreamed of the Emu War in Australia, 1932. Emus, our native animal, can run up to fifty kilometres an hour and damage crops. Post-WWI soldier-settlers on Western Australian farmland were being inundated by emus. The Australian government deployed the military with machine guns to cull them. The emus won! Their speed and agility outwitted military might.

In my dream, the Spirit of the Lord warned of China's intent to destroy Australia and Oceania. The war was aerial only, signifying spiritual warfare. Planes using natural or carnal weapons were shot down. Only accurate, succinct spiritual weapons brought victory. Children were vulnerable, dependent on air force victory. Upon awakening, I realised that the spiritual air force's success was necessary to avert a land or natural war with China.

In the natural, the Chinese communist party is threatening Taiwan and Oceania islands – right in my backyard, a picture of the dragon's war drums beating.

These dreams are vital for Oceania churches to grasp. In the natural, we are militarily vulnerable, but also spiritually, as too many churches are asleep or blissfully unaware of the spiritual battle at hand, its nature, size and importance. Hear this watchman alert.

Dragons, Drums, Firecrackers and Missiles

Beating war drums across the earth signals the dragon's aggressive warpath after Israel and the church. Revelation 12 provides insight into the cosmic war as the fiery red dragon pursues the woman who birthed the Messiah – Israel. His intent was to devour the child Jesus at His birth, killing Him. But Jesus' resurrection and ascension defeated the dragon, who now targets Israel, but the Lord protects her. The dragon then pursues her offspring, those with the testimony of Jesus.

Revelation 12 identifies the dragon as the ancient serpent, the devil, Satan – evil personified. Yet the world portrays dragons positively in movies, games, martial arts, children's colouring, and cultural festivals as fun or for good luck.

My city hosts the largest Chinese Imperial dragon in the southern hemisphere (an effigy connected to Chinese culture. More in Chapter 24, 'Gold for Royalty and Worship, not Idols'). During public festivities, the drumming and firecrackers that accompany the dragon are believed to drive away demonic and malevolent spirits. Observing this in our streets has given me a unique perspective on using music and worship in warfare, especially over the footsteps of the dragon.

Do not let the dragon's superficial huffing and puffing deceive you. Believers must not underestimate this vicious war. The dragon's murderous intent employs multiple deadly devices. In the spirit realm, loud demonic drumming agitates for war to knock out God's people.

The dragon's firecrackers against Israel resemble drones, cruise missiles, ballistic missiles and potential nuclear warheads. Deranged calls stir up rage, hate and destruction.

> *… But woe to the earth and the sea, for the devil has come down to you with great fury, because he knows his time is short. (Revelation 12:12 TPT)*

War for His Throne, Name, Glory – and *Your* Voice

The dragon's intimidation is to cause all the earth to bow and worship him. Only the redeemed can avoid worshipping the dragon.

> *So they worshiped the dragon … and they worshiped the beast … **All** who dwell on the earth will worship him, whose names have not been written in the Book of Life of the Lamb … (Revelation 13:4,8)*

But the Lamb always wins. He never loses.

> *They will go to war against the Lamb, but the Lamb **will defeat** them, because he is Lord of lords and King of kings … (Revelation 17:14 CJB)*

Revelation 15:4 states that eventually all nations will bow before the Lord. The key is the blood of the Lamb. Heaven's songs honour Him.

> *And they sang a new song, saying: 'You are worthy to take the scroll, And to open its seals;*

> *For You were slain, And have redeemed us to God by Your blood Out of every tribe and tongue and people and nation.' (Revelation 5:9)*

In contrast to demonic drumming, heaven erupts in beautiful worship songs to the Lamb of God. Victory in this war season demands sounds and songs honouring the blood of the worthy Lamb.

In Revelation, Michael and his angels defeated and ejected the dragon from heaven. This overthrow has major implications for worship (see Part Two). Even amid troubles on earth, there are victorious statements: *'the dragon **did not prevail**', 'they overcame, conquered him completely'.*[23] The book of Revelation contains triumphant language over the dragon.

As war drums beat across the earth, the war for true worship rages in the heavens, on earth – and in the church! We contend with our King for His kingdom.

War for the throne and His holy name

Terrorists insist *'Allah Akbar'* ('Allah is greater'). The Warrior Bride proclaims Yeshua, Messiah, is King of kings and Lord of lords. Interestingly, Islam mostly bans music, but God surrounds His throne with exultant choirs of praise. Perhaps this fact alone tells us much.

War for true worship

In this war season, key questions arise: who and how will we worship? The choice is to worship in the beauty of holiness or with fleshly entertainment, pacification, gratification. What influences our worship – the Holy Spirit, His word or popular trends? Is our worship aligned with His plumbline and throne or with Hollywood and culture, where blaspheming rock stars are treated like gods?

Worship and glory belong to God alone. The ancient serpent, the dragon, demands and steals it. This contention for God's throne, holy name and all nations to worship in Spirit and truth is also a war for Judeo-Christian foundations of civilisation.

War for truth and righteousness

Jesus warned of end-times deception. Truth is always the first casualty in war. Cancel culture drives information wars through fake, twisted or forbidden news.

In Nazi Germany, Goebbels' Ministry of Propaganda and Public Enlightenment conquered the populace by spreading ideology via controlled media and theatre.

Today, Israel faces enemies on all fronts, including public opinion. In an August 2025 700 Club report, Netanyahu noted his historian father realised every genocide against Jews was preceded by lies and blood libels.

Jesus told us His Father only approves worship based on truth![24] Therefore, the war for truth and righteousness impacts the true worship of Almighty God. How can we believe lies about Israel, while worshipping the Holy One of Israel, who is *the* truth?

> *Jesus told us His Father only approves worship based on truth!*

> *How can we believe lies about Israel, while worshipping the Holy One of Israel, who is the truth?*

War for glory sound

A greater glory is coming like a tsunami wave, which is triggered by underwater earthquakes. The sound waves and frequencies of earthquakes are beyond the human ear but heard by animals. The glory also has sound waves and frequencies. These are not detected by the natural ear but in the Spirit.

Sound of praise accompanied the Ark into Jerusalem; similar sounds are needed to accompany this glory wave. Contending for worship akin to heaven comes by resisting counterfeit sounds of earthly 'freedom' at night clubs.

War for your voice

War rages for your voice to resound in praise and be heard in society. Many of God's people are afraid of their voice being heard, thinking their voices sound bad. Yet, your voice is linked to your DNA and identity. Let the Father's love penetrate your heart. Learn how He delights in you and created your voice! The enemy silences your voice because it is beautiful and powerful. Embrace who He has made you, including the sound of your voice. Then lift your voice – even roar – in praises to Him.

Is there a correlation between your voice being heard in society and first being heard in the spirit realm?

Worship Drums or War Drums?

As nations teeter on the brink of World War III spiritually, we hear war raging in the unseen realm and war drums calling to war.

But which call are we hearing? And what drums are we hitting, soulish drums or Holy Spirit warring? Are we releasing worship drums or soulish war drums? There is a difference.

It is too easy to get stirred up emotionally as we hear propaganda and easily cross a line to use carnal weapons. On the one hand, drums can release the sound of God's voice thundering through every demonic stronghold. On the other hand, they can stir up unholy wars, not instigated by God, but by the enemy seeking to bring destruction.

In this season of war, we must discern and be in step with the rhythms of Adonai, the man of war. It is His battle. He is the one who destroys the weapons of man and demons.

War Drums or Wedding Bells?

The sounds of war are very different to wedding bells. Earth may prepare for war, but heaven is preparing for a wedding.

The destructive sounds of war drums activate hate, greed and lust. Wedding bells ring out sounds of love, joy and connection. The Song of Solomon speaks of a new bridal season associated with cooing doves and love songs.

> *The season for singing and pruning the vines has arrived. I hear the cooing of doves in our land, filling the air with songs to awaken you and guide you forth. (Song of Songs 2:12 TPT)*

Singing doves are to awaken love.

> *Can you not discern this new day of destiny … There is change in the air. Arise, my love, my beautiful companion, and run with me to the higher place. For now is the time to arise and come away with me … How beautiful your eyes of worship and lovely your voice in prayer' (Song of Songs 2:13–14 TPT)*

In this time of clashing of kingdoms, coming higher with Him is critical. The sound the Lord wants to release is unique and powerful and comes through His redeemed and spotless bride. It is in the opposite spirit to warmongering.

CHAPTER THREE

Setting the Record Straight: Father's Heartbeat

Some misunderstandings arose after the first edition of *Restoring True Worship,* with some believing I said drums should never be used in worship. That is incorrect.

Those familiar with our ministry know we have an excellent prophetic percussionist–drummer. Anointed drums and percussion inspired by the Holy Spirit can prophesy by capturing the Spirit's rhythm and releasing Father's heartbeat. They enhance the atmosphere while underscoring other musicians and singers. Sometimes, worship is punctuated with no drums, like musical rests; that is different to prohibition! Being led by the Holy Spirit is always key for any instrument.

In the first edition, I highlighted some negative drums uses. I cited three instances revealing the instrument's vulnerability, thus urging sensitivity and careful use:

a. ancient use of drums accompanying child sacrifices in Moloch worship.

b. drums fuelling the sexual revolution, often tied to occult practices.

c. drums inducing demonic trance in some cultures.

I have witnessed some tragic drum misuse in the house of God, so I remain cautious. However, prior to such experiences, I even taught drums and percussion. Drums themselves are not the problem; it is how they are played, and whether the player is truly submitted to the Lord. Drums can empower or destroy worship, making or breaking it.

Any musical instrument can aid God in His battles or resist Him. For negative or unwise use of drums, other instruments or voices, repentance and re-education are better than eradication. But if not possible, absence is a better option than bombardment.

Musical flexibility is essential to flow in the Holy Spirit's river. This applies to all instruments but is especially vital for drums.[25] As a worship leader, I am uncomfortable when dominating drums with incessant beats hinder adjusting tempos and intensity as the Spirit leads.

We need musicians who are called by the Lord to be teachable and who know how to flow with the Holy Spirit, not just skilled players. Wait for the Lord to bring them – and pray for them.

New Breed of Psalmists and Intercessors

He is calling for a new breed of psalmists and intercessors, young and old, to release His victorious sounds in the war for our nations. They will release:

1. a sound of high praise
2. a sound that terrifies demons and releases God's judgement on principalities and powers
3. a pure sound without mixture or a sniff of the world
4. a sound originating in heaven yet heard on earth
5. a sound in sync with the Father's heartbeat
6. an intimate sound

Worshipping warriors, intercessors, *Ekklesia*, this critical time demands alignment with our Master's drumbeat. His sound is urgently needed.

CHAPTER FOUR

Agitated b4 Divine Download

WHEN THERE IS TALK of nuclear World War III, the Middle East as a cauldron ready to explode, struggling economies and vitriolic hatred against Jews and Christians, why is restoring true worship an important consideration? Why is the subject of music a vital consideration?

A good question.

Agitated @ University

I should have been as happy as Larry, as the saying goes. Life was good. There was no logical explanation for my disturbing disquiet as my thoughts exploded with questions. With hindsight, I now know the unease and questions was actually the Holy Spirit stirring me to find some necessary answers and ultimately set the course of my life trajectory. The ensuing download would also download a blueprint for the Church in a time of war – a time like now!

The discomfort in my soul did not make sense. As soon as I was saved at age eleven, the Lord made it clear my call was in music and I needed to prepare to gain the necessary skills. I had just walked through a series of miracles to land a scholarship to study music at The University of Melbourne, and I got to study piano with one of the most sought-after teachers, one of Australia's finest renowned concert pianists. I had a great circle of friends, many Christians. It was the early 1970s, and though the Vietnam War was contentious on university campuses, life was pretty good. I should have been enjoying the moment. Instead, I was overwhelmed with a Jacob-type struggle with the Lord.

I knew I had some years of hard study in front of me but was excited to fulfil the dream. Unexpectedly, I started to feel agitated. Learning skills to perform and entertain was now my world, but I felt uneasy about devoting years of my life to developing skills just to entertain people with pleasant music. It seemed crazy. Music was in my veins. My mother was a piano teacher. At age four, she began giving me lessons because she couldn't keep me off the piano while imitating students as they left. Dad was a lay pastor and Mum was heavily involved with teaching religious education and Bible clubs in schools. The call of the Lord to music was clear. Everything was now in place, so why did these questions hound me?

The Lord's ways are amazing! Every facet of life has His orchestrated fingerprints on it when we surrender to Him. Like a good Hebraic rabbi, He puts questions into our hearts that guide us to His solutions. He did not just give me the answers; He set me on a course to find them.

Survival Mode: Music or Food?

When war, crises or disasters cause a scarcity of basic necessities, is music as vital as food, medicine, shelter and being safe? When circumstances press and survival is paramount, how important is music? Is there an unknown or unidentified value within music that makes it equivalent to those necessities of life?

In a time of war, does music just provide temporary and momentary distraction and relief to lift your spirit while trying to just stay alive? In a time of war, does music give marginal relief or can it help you win the war? Is there a sound that will help you persevere and even press towards victory? Is music just a luxury item that one can live without, or does it have some eternal property that is essential for life?

These were some questions I wrestled with before the Lord. I needed to resolve the matter. I needed answers!

Green Bible

I asked the Lord if there was a value, a purpose for music, that in a time of crisis would be as necessary as food and shelter. Could humans live without it, or was it just to entertain us and make life more pleasant? The Lord's answer came as an instruction.

I was to read the Bible from Genesis to Revelation and highlight every reference to music and discover what He had said. Challenge accepted, and having chosen a green pencil to underline, I soon had a green coloured Bible.

Biblical answers flooded my soul with peace as I read of David playing his harp before King Saul, and later as king, he brought the Ark into Jerusalem accompanied by specific music. At this time in the mid-1970s, I had heard no sermons nor read any books on this matter, except what I was reading in the Bible. It was like these passages of scripture were vivid, alive, in neon lights. The Holy Spirit was illuminating and downloading revelation.

During this time, I also learned about music therapy. Even secular textbooks mentioned the first ever example of music therapy was young David playing his harp to deliver Saul from demons. That was a shock to discover this in the literature and teaching at university! I learned of the relationship between music and the brain – not only fascinating, but scientific research confirming the great Creator had indeed wired us humans for sound.

Now I was getting some deep answers for these questions.

As my progress in piano accelerated, doors in the music world began opening for me to perform. They were not bad – they were amazing! But these were not the doors of the Lord. Within no time, life took challenging twists and turns. My father passed away, and a sporting injury left me unable to complete the extra piano studies I had been granted. The Lord reminded me of His call and pathway. When we commit our way to the Lord, He has ways to remind us and to get us back onto the narrow path!

Four Takeaways

Having turned my Bible green from highlighters, I found four major takeaways about music that have been fundamental to my life and ministry. I will expand on them in the following chapters. They are critical for the time we live in now.

1. *Worship is about God, not me*

Biblical worship is specific and consequential. It is God's priority. He is to be the recipient of all glory and honour. Worship is when we are in awe of our Creator and bow to Him. It encompasses our offerings of thanksgiving and gratitude to Him. It is from us, and to Him. It is for His benefit and pleasure, not ours.

2. *The Ark and glory sound*

The Ark represents the complete Presence and Glory of God. After King David failed to bring the Ark into Jerusalem, he sought the Lord for the correct protocol. One of those changes was to choose specifically appointed musicians singing prophetic songs beside the Ark. Prophetic worship surrounds the Lord in heaven and is meant to do the same on earth. The purpose of this music is not to attract humans but to summon angel armies. It is a sound that surrounds the throne of God. This sound is akin to the red carpet welcome for the King of kings. It is a sound that is like the bodyguards and officials who accompany and surround the King of the universe.

3. Music and demons

It was a profound moment to discover music therapy literature acknowledging David, the shepherd boy, playing his harp for King Saul as the first known episode of healing and deliverance through music. The implication of this is huge. What if the reverse is also true? What if music can welcome demons and activate ill health? Sadly, many New Age and Buddhist influences have now infiltrated through music therapy. I would say largely because the Church has failed to take up the role to disciple nations and because the Church has too often debunked much of the supernatural realm, especially its connection through music and the arts.

4. 2 Chronicles 20 is a pertinent scripture

The Holy Spirit is highlighting this vital scripture to His people. Singing praises to the Lord while facing grave danger, repeated, achieves much more in the spirit realm than we have often realised. (More in Chapter 6, 'Don't Shoot - I'm Just the Piano Player!')

Uprooting Performance and Entertainment

After receiving this download at university, there came a day I will not forget. I was waiting for my piano teacher in his room. I had just completed what would be my last exam and was waiting to receive his feedback. As I stood waiting, the Holy Spirit spoke to me about performance and entertainment.

Being taught by a concert pianist, I was being instructed in how to perform and, by default, entertain. The Lord showed me that while the musical training was necessary to gain skills for His call, there were some aspects that would violate what He had called me to. He asked for my permission for Him to uproot from my spirit the ungodly things deposited in my soul that would contribute to performing and entertainment.

There was clarity in the prayer for Holy Spirit to separate between the skills I needed to serve and worship Him and the harmful unnecessary mindsets of striving for perfection to please and entertain man. There was a prayer of renouncing and fresh dedication of the gift to serve the Lord. All glory to the Lord for the spiritual and natural results of that day! Though my teacher was thrilled with my progress from an average student to a top student, the most important upgrade that day was to be freed from the spirit of performance.

Entertainment is not sustainable when persecution is around. When persecution and trouble are around, entertainment will not win the war!

As harassing cancel culture grows, we need to worship deeply in His Presence. The ever-increasing challenges force us into His throne room. In a time of war and distress, would it not be better to release the sound that welcomes and accompanies the Lord of Heaven's armies?

> *Entertainment is not sustainable when persecution is around. When persecution and trouble are around, entertainment will not win the war!*

CHAPTER FOUR

In the world of worship in the Church, people often view music as a warm-up for what they perceive as the main event, the message. Perhaps music is used to draw a crowd, help folk feel energised, inspired or comfortable? When individuals view music with these motivations, it can lead to a mindset that suggests music is nice, but not essential.

In Australia, we frequently have the extremes of wildfires and floods. What role does music play then? Jesus warned that in the end-times, there would be much deception, wars, famines, pandemics and earthquakes. Is the call to move into a higher realm of worship on earth, as it is in heaven, vital equipping for important end-times tasks? Is it possible that worship of the saints could be needed to release God's angel armies and overcome Satan at Armageddon?

Is there an essential role for music in the end-times or when life is in survival mode?

CHAPTER FIVE

Don't Touch the Ark! My Steep Learning Curve

IMAGINE STANDING IN UZZAH'S shoes as David brought the Ark to Jerusalem.[26] Would you, like me, instinctively reach to steady it? Or would you trust God and keep your hands off? In that moment of pressure, it's a tough call to know what we would do, but know for sure, the Lord would not be impressed if we dared to say, 'But I protected the Ark'.

We all long for the manifestation of His Glory, but could we inadvertently mishandle it? Having a desire for the glory and pursuing it has certainly challenged me!

Rebuke from the Lord: 'No Flesh in My Presence!'

Amid some disagreements in our ministry, the Lord spoke to me forcefully in a dream. His voice thundered through my sleep: 'No flesh shall glory in My Presence. Not your flesh, and not their flesh!' I felt my whole body shake at His word. I woke up with the fear of the Lord throbbing through my whole being.

How often in the Body of Messiah do our disagreements and divisions smear the glory of God and His reputation? It is not about being right – it is about His reputation!

CHAPTER FIVE

Don't Touch the Glory

We cannot mess with the Lord's holy name and get away with it! The Creator of the universe and Redeemer of our souls will not share His Glory with our flesh, our idols or sacred cows.

> *Thus says God the LORD, Who created the heavens and ... the earth ... 'I am the LORD, that is My name; And **My glory** I will **not give** to another, Nor My praise to carved images.' (Isaiah 42:5-9)*

When God's people pretend allegiance to Him but simultaneously bow to other things, it steals His Glory and dishonours His name.

> *Listen carefully ... you who ... claim to worship the God of Israel ... See, **I have purified you in the furnace of adversity ... so my name will not be dishonored.** I will not yield [give] My glory to another. (Isaiah 48:1, 10-11 TPT)*

Honouring His holy name, His Glory and Presence is the same for Israel and for you and me. It is too easy for us to discredit and bring shame to His name. As Christians, we can easily presume we are walking in His ways when we are doing the very opposite.

Presumption on My Part

While grappling with music's role at university, I was especially impacted by King David's appointment of specific skilled musicians to accompany the Ark and minister in the tabernacle and temple.

Naively, I thought a similar assignment today was reasonably straightforward – get your musical skills, love God and be set apart to serve Him, though achieving those things is neither easy nor simple. But I underestimated the real challenge.

It is too easy to do the equivalent of touching the Ark in our day. Honouring God's strict protocols to accompany His Glory is more difficult than we realise. We often overlook how we will face the devil's fierce resistance and our own susceptibility to idolatry. If King David struggled, why would today's Church fare any better?

Heavenly Music, Heartbreak and Spiritual Abuse

In 1978, armed with a music degree, I began teaching secondary school music in Bendigo, Australia, and joined a vibrant church with 'heavenly' worship. The skilled, tight-knit worship team touched many who encountered the Lord. We supported artists like Larry Norman and Chuck Girard on regional tours. As music director, I played piano, wrote songs, trained musicians and led worship seminars for our national denomination. After three years, I left teaching to pursue God's call. Laurence and I married and started our family.

I envisioned bringing God's Glory into the church, like David with the Ark. Perhaps my overconfidence was akin to King David's when he set out for the first time with the Ark. Did I touch the Ark? Not intentionally or knowingly. But somewhere the 'oxen stumbled' and the Lord's name was dishonoured. Did anyone or something die? It felt like it.

The heavenly worship crumbled, my calling stalled and over the next decade, our congregation shattered and scattered. We observed fifty-plus marriages end in divorce, a culture of control over the people (counterfeit leadership) and, later, money issues that led to a pastor being jailed. Many from that season still struggle spiritually.

Detailing the reasons for spiritual abuse would take an entire book. Suffice to say, in our experience, the change in music reflected the deterioration of the soul of the congregation. Despite many great attributes, intimidation and mixed worship left a trail of destruction. Sadly, this tragic tale is not an isolated incident. As I shared the message of *Restoring True Worship* across Australia, I discovered the spirit of control is so widespread, it is the largest obstacle hindering revival.

Course Correction

Desiring the glory is good, but pursuing the glory in a wrong way is dangerous. Following His ways are safe; our ways are not! He will not share His Glory with anyone.

For the sake of His holy name, judgements and shakings begin at the house of God. They are redemptive course corrections.

David learned from his mistake, which enabled him to bring the Ark safely into Jerusalem. I learnt from my mistakes and the Lord opened extraordinary doors in glory realms. If you have had a journey like this, expect a wonderful turnaround as you pursue His healing and direction.

Like David, I misunderstood the glory. Somewhere my heart drifted across a forbidden line and it was kidnapped. Despite being at every meeting and serving the Lord, I had become dry and backslidden. My life was about to be shaken beyond recognition.

Seat Belts On: Eight Turbulent Episodes

If you are in an aircraft when severe turbulence hits, if you are not wearing a seatbelt, it can be frightening, even dangerous. The force of hitting luggage compartments or the roof can cause severe head and spinal injuries or even death. Our season of severe spiritual turbulence lasted more than a decade, with at least eight severe storms. Many days I wondered if I would survive, but God's grace was our seatbelt. Life can seem like that in this new era. We must keep pressing in to hear His voice and learn from Him.

1. Maternity leave

From 1987 to 1988, I took maternity leave from being music director at the church and felt the first niggles in my spirit. At first, I dismissed them and attributed them to pregnancy hormones. Something had changed in our music department and the sound coming out of it. Despite my musical training, I could not pinpoint the problem. After our baby was born, the misgivings grew. This time, I dismissed it as post-natal problems! Eventually, reality hit – it was not hormones but Holy Spirit red flags!

2. Ministry cut short

Changes in the music department soon affected me personally. At thirty-three, the senior pastor abruptly cut my ministry off, claiming my public ministry was finished, and as a good teacher, I should raise the next generation of worshippers – a passion of mine, but not the full story. In David's tabernacle, ministry spanned ages twenty to fifty; my calling was just beginning, not ending! This apostle's word clashed with the Holy Spirit's deep call in me, leaving me in turmoil. Worse, the leader's son, my student, replaced me. Though gifted, music wasn't his calling. I had prepared my whole life for this. It was a bitter pill to swallow.

3. Cracks in the foundations

Now the Lord had my full attention! Personal loss of call and vision after years of dedicated work left me confused and distressed. With a grief-stricken heart, I cried out to the Lord.

He showed me cracks in the foundations of the congregation. It was no longer just the worship department being affected by trouble: marriages and financial issues were surfacing. I quickly discovered the cracks in the foundations were not just in the church – they were in me too.

4. Idols of the heart

The Lord showed me a vision of the pastor on a pedestal and me bowing down to worship him. Discovering an idol in my heart was sickening! I was shocked. Really shocked. Confronted. Humbled. Repentant.

It got worse. He then revealed His gift of music had become an idol too! No wonder my heart was backslidden, and I had felt soooo dry!

It was painful to discover my first love had evaporated and the flame of revival nearly extinguished. It was a shock to discover the same sins that caused Israel grief had happened to me inside a vibrant Pentecostal church. What a warning! Hours morphed into months of repentance, weeping, praying and seeking the Lord. I laid aside the ministry I had trained for and devoted my whole life to. I put it all on His altar. More tears, and more repentance.

5. Spirit of rock

One day, the Lord's audible voice broke in on housework and changed our lives forever. I was making the children's beds with the turbulence momentarily forgotten. Suddenly the Lord's voice was like thunder: 'The spirit of rock has entered the church.' I was shocked. Nor did I really understand what He meant. In time, I came to understand it was both the music and culture of the sexual revolution.

I had been asking Him what had happened to the music department where heavenly music had been replaced by a raucous sound. As the music became more jarring, the control became harsher. Young children and older adults cried from the pain. Sound levels were measured at ninety decibels at the back door.[27] This change was so grievous. I continued pursuing the Lord with questions. Again, He spoke firmly: 'If it is not repented of, it will destroy true worship.'

I had a season of Q&A with the Lord. Some answers fuelled more questions. Graciously, the Holy Spirit poured in download after download. (The spirit of rock is the subject of Volume Two in this series.)

6. Training a worshipper: peeling onions of healing

The Lord revealed deep anger in my heart. I had stopped playing the piano – period. I felt dumped and unwanted, despite obeying His call. Prayer brought understanding but not relief from grief. We might know why we are in pain, but removing the pain is a separate healing journey.

One day, the Lord warned me that my anger was about to descend into dangerous bitterness. I had to make a choice. He urged me to play the piano, give thanks and worship Him alone, with just Him and me. This felt a daunting task. My heart was broken, and I wrongly believed I needed a congregation to accompany in worship. Like many, I'd been told my voice was worthless, cursed by careless words. Healing was needed, as was a change of mindset.

As I chose to worship Him at the piano, I wept and the Lord mended my heart. He also taught me how to follow His lead in worship. He was not after a singer who could win 'The Voice'. He wanted my heart clean and my voice added to His choir of praise. In this season of clashing kingdoms, every worshipper's voice is vital to turn back the battle at the gates.

7. Write a book

His next instruction was to put what He had taught me into a book. The thought of writing, and facing fallout from a controversial subject, left me feeling like jelly. My excuses were: 'I'm not a writer', 'I am a woman', 'I don't have a theology degree.' How could I get out such a message? As I continued to seek Him in worship, I sensed God's strength like steel entering my spiritual spine.

The Holy Spirit ended my debate with two challenges. First, He asked, 'If you had little time left, what would you do?' I replied, 'Write the book.' Without critics to face, I'd be free. He urged, 'Get to it!', exposing my fear of man.

Second, Ezekiel 33:2-7 revealed the watchman's call: sound the alarm and responsibility is fulfilled; fail to warn and the guilt is mine. If my book is wrong, it can be discarded, but disobedience to God's call is on me. If people do not heed the warning, it is on their own heads. The fear of the Lord overcame fear of man.

As a young mum, amid church devastation, learning to write and use technology while grasping this revelation was daunting. We also needed much deliverance and healing. It was a process like peeling onions, with lots of layers. As I worked on each chapter, the Holy Spirit would highlight where I had not overcome in that area. I would stop typing, repent and pray through the issue. Allowing Holy Spirit to expose and uproot issues from our lives is neither fast nor comfortable, but it brings joy and spiritual maturity. The spiritual warfare was intense.

8. Resignation

We remained in the church as long as possible, despite the increase in heartbreak. I wanted to flee, but the Lord insisted I deliver His message to the leadership first. As former music director, He said I had the responsibility and authority to speak. If the watchman does not warn, who will?

Once the material was submitted, and having received outside counsel, the Lord released us to resign quietly, avoiding gossip or influencing others. When our departure was known, we lost all church friends, my music students and my income. Our spiritual and social network vanished. I had been labelled a 'false prophet and heretic'. Weeks later, we discovered fifty others, including a prophet, had also left, silenced by a controlling spirit – none of us had dared talk to each other. But in a way, this was good. Leaving had to be a work of the Holy Spirit, not idle gossip.

We identified with Abraham; we did not know where we were going or what to do. Simply trust the Lord and follow Him. Listen. Obey. Worship.

Recovery, L plates, and Greater Joy

Eight is the number of new beginnings – exactly what the Lord did through our eight shakings! At times, it felt like the end, but it was actually a new start. After releasing *Restoring True Worship* across Australia and New Zealand, people requested a demonstration of the written material. This occurred as the new day dawned and three new doors opened.

King David took only three months to recover after the death of Uzzah. My restoration took much longer, decades in fact. If you are someone who is recovering from spiritual abuse, do not rush. Full recovery is slow, and the Holy Spirit has the exact recovery process for you to heal.

Pray for Israel: Prophetic Worship

Expecting a future in worship ministry, I was surprised when the Holy Spirit led us to start a prayer group for Israel. I knew little about prayer or modern Israel and was unaware of replacement theology or its anti-Semitic roots.

Learning on the job, we explored Hebraic roots, visited Israel and befriended Messianic believers, discovering our 'grafted in' identity.[28]

We discovered our connection to the land through the ANZAC charge at Beersheba. The Feasts of the Lord, like Passover, became a fixture on our calendar. Loving the Jewish people and understanding their pain transformed my heart. I discovered my call as a 'Ruth', who said: *'Your people shall be my people, And your God, my God'* (Ruth 1:16).[29]

The Lord taught us deeply. The correct Biblical order is for alignment with Israel to *precede* prophetic worship. The unity of Jew and Gentile as one new man unlocks His Glory and its sound. The richness of the alignments with His heart, His land and His people is incalculable.

> *The correct Biblical order is for alignment with Israel to precede prophetic worship. The unity of Jew and Gentile as one new man unlocks His Glory and its sound.*

Learning Spiritual Warfare: Pray Bendigo

The Australian Prayer Network identified Bendigo as a key spiritual portal for Australia – the tail of the dragon. At the turn of the twenty-first century, Pray Bendigo united churches for weekly corporate prayer.

In the year 2000, the pastors appointed me, with Lois and then Muriel, to lead the prophetic intercession team. This was a strategic training ground, a baptism of fire and a steep learning curve in spiritual warfare and mapping. Through both prayer journeys, for Israel and Pray Bendigo, I led worship and honed this new skill.

Founded during the 1850s gold rush, Bendigo hosted revival and glory but was also the headquarters of various religions. Australian prophet Adam Thompson described Bendigo as not just a spiritual portal but a spiritual vortex; I call it a hamburger with the lot. Despite indicators of spiritual contention, the Lord has earmarked it for great glory!

My introduction to warfare assignments was the construction of a large Buddhist temple (stupa), replicating a major Tibetan temple, to launch Buddhism in the southern hemisphere. The Lord gave us a prayer strategy which took several months. As we completed the assignment, a rare tornado swept through the city without warning. The trajectory was idol sites, thankfully with minimal damage but confirming the prayer strategy.

As we were concluding this assignment, the Lord gave a clear direction: 'Raise up an altar of true worship above all the idolatrous strongholds'. It was shortly after this we began our current ministry of 'Tabernacle of David' with this mandate.

Lead a Ministry – Me? Nobody Will Come!

After receiving the Lord's mandate, we went to key pastors in the city, seeking confirmation if this vision was from the Lord or not. Though receiving encouraging confirmation, I really struggled. I was sure nobody would come! I would have preferred for the vision to be attached to an existing ministry, not start a new one. How could I lead a ministry? Rebuilding confidence takes time.

In July 2003, we launched the Tabernacle of David Bendigo for worshippers and intercessors to gather in throne room worship. Though not in large numbers, some people travelled several hours to attend, often taking back what they learned to their own churches.

In 2005, the Lord spoke audibly, directing me to host the Gold to Glory worship conference with David Swan in Bendigo Town Hall. Built during the gold rush, its gold-leafed walls, like a holy of holies, were ideal (gargoyles prayed over and covered). The glory fell as churches miraculously united in worship, repenting to the Chinese church for goldfield injustices. People flocked from the streets; the local newspaper verified the reports. David Swan still speaks of the glory that manifested.

As the conference concluded, an apostle, stunned by the event, apologised for criticising my book's first edition, affirmed my call as a worship leader in the holy of holies and recognised me as an apostle of worship. Doors opened to minister across Asia and Israel, aligning with like-hearted worshippers for three-day worship marathons over twenty years.

Rejoice! Lessons from the Fire

Despite the church tragedy, I rejoice. The journey changed me. It made me go deep. It taught me to repent and grow in Him. Without the shaking, I would not have been ready for His Presence – idols must go! Throughout the turbulence, God's goodness was my refuge, a strong tower.

I am grateful for the course correction and lessons by my loving heavenly Father. Forgiveness, healing and deliverance are real and vital. Brokenness before God invites His fullness, like crushed olives yielding anointing oil. The Holy Spirit taught me how to worship and to lead others into His Presence.

A calling is costly to fulfil. It needs repentance, obedience, travail, prayer and worship, not mere intellect or gifting. Only the Lord's fire forges worship's sound for this season's spiritual war. Anointing and authority demand a price – they are not cheap.

After a worship conference, a young musician asked me to pray to give them my anointing. I refused and gave a challenge, asking: 'Will you pay the price for the anointing and authority God has for you?'

CHAPTER SIX

Don't Shoot – I'm Just the Piano Player!

Covid Lockdowns and 2 Chronicles 20

SOME HAVE AFFECTIONATELY RENAMED BC and AC as 'before Covid' and 'after Covid'. In our part of Australia, we had some of the worst lockdowns globally – Melbourne, two hours away, was even worse. The 2020–2022 pandemic tested relationships, faith, churches and ministries. Some pastors fought court cases; others went to jail. The Lord placed great emphasis on 2 Chronicles 20.

When our government tried to prevent us from singing in our services, this became a red line – it was a hill to die on. As lockdowns dragged on, I realised 2 Chronicles 20 would be vital for the entire decade of the 2020s, a season of spiritual and natural war and of great instability.

Did we learn to honour the glory of the Lord during that hazardous time? We certainly learned new and creative ways to worship, especially via Zoom!

In 2 Chronicles 20, multiple armies threatened Israel to throw them out of their inheritance, the Promised Land. This threat has repeated through history, more recently since 7 October 2023. The chant, 'From the river to the sea', heard in our streets and universities is a blatant reminder of the threat of 2 Chronicles 20.

The church also faces multiple fronts of opposition, undermined morals enforced by law-fare.

In 2 Chronicles 20, the Lord gave instructions for victory. They were to appoint a special unit of singers and musicians to praise God at the front line! The worship band were to be in front of the trained and armed soldiers. Yep, 'don't shoot – I'm just the piano player' comes to mind. (I literally had the saying came to mind in a situation in Jerusalem – keep reading!)

Why would the Lord emphasise this scripture in our own time of turmoil? We are in a time of the glory of the Lord. It is a time when He demonstrates His power over His enemies while we sing His praises. Though this passage is well known and discussed frequently, I would like to explore some often overlooked factors.

Don't Shoot – I'm Just the Piano Player!

What was the strategy the prophet gave that would cause Israel to prosper? The part we often refer to is based on v. 21, 'Send the musicians and singers out in front of the army'. Israel would prosper if they heeded this word: release the Lord's song and sound before anyone discharges any weapons!

To the human mind, how crazy! Is this suicidal? Praising the Lord on the front line while eyeballing a murderous enemy is no easy feat! Yet when you have the word of the Lord and you understand the role and realm of music and sound, it is totally sensible.

While I was in East Jerusalem for seventy-two hours of worship, an IDF commander sent some of his soldiers to learn about and interact with Christians who stand with Israel. The pastor asked us to sing over the soldiers!

Many IDF soldiers carry their assault rifles or machine guns as they shop and walk the streets. Going to the keyboard, my biggest challenge was eyeballing a soldier, sitting in the front row with a weapon in hand facing in my direction! I felt safe, as they were friend, not foe. But it was a surreal moment and a little unnerving. As a musician, I am not used to facing loaded military weapons! The song came to mind: 'Don't shoot, I'm just the piano player'.

In that instance, the soldiers were deeply touched as we sang 'Pray for the Peace of Jerusalem'.

These were friendly soldiers, not enemies. I thought about 2 Chronicles 20 and what it would be like to be sent out to sing in front of a physical hostile army with lots of soldiers, all with their weaponry facing me!

Hidden Layers of 2 Chronicles 20: A Fresh Perspective

As believers in the twenty-first century, we have the advantage of reading scripture with hindsight. We know the story from the start to the end. We know the dire circumstances Israel faced, what God told them to do, and most importantly, we know the end of the story. We have the advantage of knowing the outcome. Israel did not.

Facing fear, the threat of annihilation from so many enemies, Israel did not know how it would end. They did not know how God would respond. They did not know when or even if God would answer them. All they knew was that they needed to seek the Lord and then respond in an act of faith.

The Israelites did not know how the Lord would help them that day. We do not know how He will help us either, but we must trust Him. We have to trust the prophets gave an accurate word, and then make sure we are in correct position.

For a few minutes, let us put aside knowing the end results. Let us also overlay the events of 2 Chronicles 20 with some situations we face, like the pandemic and world events pushing and shoving against the Church.

Let us lay aside any presumption we may have that God will answer us in the same way He did for Israel. It is a powerful strategy, but we should enquire of the Lord for ourselves as Israel had to do.

Let us consider current events in the same way Israel had to, not knowing the end result. We do not know how the Lord will answer our intercessory worship and acts of faith.

In this way, let us review how we view or implement the strategy, especially in this time of global instability where the cosmic war is in our faces.

En Gedi: Waterfall and Hideout

The Dead Sea is one of the lowest places on earth; it is also one of the hottest. The waterfall nearby at En Gedi is a beautiful oasis and a welcome relief. It was also David's main hideaway from Saul. As it is likely this is where he wrote 'As the deer pants for water', it makes sense that it was written in this spot.

In a visit to En Gedi, we also found the thorn tree from which the crown of thorns was made and pressed into the head of Jesus. Each thorn is around twenty-five to thirty centimetres long and as sharp as can be. It gave me a new appreciation for the blood of Jesus to deal with mockery sent at our minds.

As the crow flies, En Gedi to Jerusalem is around forty kilometres, but, as the Dead Sea is the lowest point on earth, the hills up to Jerusalem means it is a hundred and fifty kilometres by road. Arab nations used to invade from the south of the Dead Sea and could be almost undetected until not too far from Jerusalem.

King Jehoshaphat received word of multiple enemies, a conglomerate of different tribes, gathering at En Gedi to drive Israel out of the Promised Land. Jehoshaphat was King of Judah, the southern kingdom. He had followed the Lord and had peace until he allied himself with Ahab, king of the northern kingdom. The Lord had warned him about helping the wicked.[30] Our alliances are critical. Are they of God or not? Wrong alliances can bring trouble.

Jehoshaphat soon found out. En Gedi, originally inhabited[31] by Israel's arch enemy, the Amalekites, was now Judah's territory. Israel's consortium of enemies was coming from Syria. They were not coming for a coffee or a peace deal – they wanted possession! And it would take war to resist.

Though afraid, and partly to blame, at least King Jehoshaphat called the nation to fast and seek the Lord. The king himself prayed. National prayer and fasting are vital in overcoming enemies.

From the River to the Sea

Across the globe, intellectuals in universities and activists in our streets chant, 'From the river to the sea'. Sadly, some Christians do not correctly align with scripture on these matters.

What river and what sea? Currently, Israel's eastern border is the Jordan River which flows into the Dead Sea. The Mediterranean Sea is its western border. This chant is exactly the threat seen in 2 Chronicles 20 – to throw Israel out of her land, the land covenanted by the Lord. The slogan being chanted in our streets means to obliterate the Jewish nation. Some of these activists are actually calling to finish what Hitler started! They are calling for a second Holocaust.

Israel has always had to deal with enemies, but since 7 October 2023, it is in an intensified battle for survival. Most of its neighbours are unfriendly, with Iran the major threat.

Iran's many proxies are in the same geographical region where the enemies in 2 Chronicles 20 were based. Sadly, today's threats extend beyond the physical. A psychological war is also being waged through media and Western governments.

We are in an epic clash of kingdoms. Bible morality is a target of intense hatred. Many would love to see Jews and Christians removed from the planet.

The Lord says, 'I've Got It!'

The first word Israel received was very encouraging.

> *Thus says the LORD to you: 'Do not be afraid nor dismayed because of this great multitude, for the battle is not yours, but God's ... You will not need to fight in this battle.' (2 Chronicles 20:15)*

Repeatedly in scripture, the Lord says, 'Do not fear.' In Jesus, we have the great assurance: His perfect love casts out fear. Jesus told John:

> 'Do not be afraid; I am the First and the Last. I am He who lives, and was dead, and behold, I am alive forevermore. Amen. And I have the keys of Hades and of Death.' (Revelation 1:17–18)

Comforted, Jehoshaphat invoked the Lord's promises in 2 Chronicles 7 about praying at the temple in times of trouble. He remembered Israel's history coming out of Egypt, and now these same enemies were at it again.

> *... here they are, rewarding us by coming to **throw us out of Your possession** which You have given us to inherit. (2 Chronicles 20)*

This was not a battle to ignore, or hope would go away. This was a battle for existence and holding onto the promises of God. Too easily in the church, we know Jesus won the victory, and we can fail to realise the enemy wants to dispossess us. Sometimes we must fight to keep our possessions and promises.

As Israel sought the Lord, the Spirit of the Lord came upon one of the prophet psalmists, a Levite of the Asaph order. They received explicit instructions that would shift them beyond their normal mode of operation. For Judah at that time, for Israel and the Church right now, it is a spiritual battle. We cannot fight the venom projected at us in the natural.

How often do we hear the words, 'The battle belongs to the Lord' and think, *Great, now we can sit back and just be spectators*? The battle belonging to the Lord means He is the commander-in-chief. It does not mean we sit back in comfortable armchairs watching the action. No, it means we must wait on our orders from the commander of angel armies. Israel had to overcome natural fear, show up and be in the right position. It meant being where He told them to be.

> *The battle belonging to the Lord means He is the commander-in-chief. It does not mean we sit back in comfortable armchairs watching the action. No, it means we must wait on our orders from the commander of angel armies.*

How often, amid upheaval and conflict, do we forget two key truths found in verse 20?

> *Hear me, O Judah and you inhabitants of Jerusalem:* **Believe in the LORD** *your God, and you shall be established;* **believe His prophets,** *and you shall prosper. (2 Chronicles 20:20)*

When we hear God and believe Him, we will be established. To be established is to be supported with strong pillars, a firm or permanent state, something we can trust. We will prosper when we believe the true prophets of the Lord.

The Israelites did not know how the Lord would establish and prosper them. All they knew was they had to believe in the Lord and the word of the prophet. We do not know how He will prosper or establish us either. We too must believe in the Lord and trust Him. We also have to trust the prophets who have given an accurate word. The Lord has been shaking the prophetic movement in recent years, so that it can be trusted. It is important to have reliable prophetic words.

Singing While Eyeballing the Enemy

Singing in front of friendly armed soldiers was one thing, but quite another to do that before hostile soldiers. To the human mind, it is sheer madness to send a worship team to the front lines and face a hostile army equipped with weapons of war when you simply have a musical instrument. It takes a whole other level of obedient, intense and intentional praise to the Lord while facing arrows, guns, tanks and missiles. It takes a special kind of courage and faith to be eyeballing a vicious enemy with nothing more than just your musical instruments and a word from God!

Yet in the spirit realm, that is what is being asked of worship teams. Paul warns the spiritual battle is with major principalities and powers. These are global and regional powers, like Daniel discovered with the prince of Persia. They are not just your local militia – this is the cosmic war with principalities.

In spiritual warfare, the enemy aims intimidatory threats at our soul – our emotions and minds. What will happen? Will we get shot? Will we survive? 'Will it really work?', 'Your sound is terrible', 'You have the wrong song'. How many casualties do we see in music worship teams?

Too often, Christians casually speak of this as a brilliant strategy. But I wonder, those who say this, have they been in a worship team in hostile territory? For our brethren in many countries, this is their reality. We have had a taste of it a few times in China, and in East Jerusalem when militant Islamists were attacking the church. But for the persecuted churches, it is a daily occurrence.

I get concerned when I hear believers gleefully speaking of this strategy but continue with a life of ease. Do we understand the anointing required for such confrontation? Do we understand the spiritual battle we face? Do we grasp what sort of songs are needed? Do we understand what is being asked of the worship team? Singing praises while facing threats, taunts and real weapons is a total test of one's faith.

What Song?

The King appointed musicians to sing praises to 'the beauty of holiness'. But they were on a battlefield, not in the holy temple. They faced an evil enemy, cursing threats and spewing hatred. Their song and heart posture had to be in total contrast, in the opposite spirit to their enemy.

What song did they sing? A simple song about the goodness and mercy of God.

> *Praise the Lord, For His mercy endures forever.*
> *(2 Chronicles 20:21)*

Their ears had to be deafened to the enemy spewing intimidatory threats and curses. With hearts racing, the musicians had to declare that God is good. Was it a nervous sound or a strident rebuttal to the enemy?

They were not singing *at* the enemy to say how wicked they were. No, they focused on the Lord, exalted Him and declared His mercy. They were declaring, in the hearing of their enemy, the mercy of God. Even when in earshot of the enemy, it is vital to declare who God is. We do not have to remind the devil that he is defeated. Just declare who God is and that His mercy is eternal.

The Hebrew word for mercy is *chesed*. Because it is such a powerful word encompassing who God is, people have written entire books about it. Essentially, it means the goodness, the kindness, the faithfulness of God. The writer to Hebrews speaks of God's throne as a throne of grace where we can obtain mercy.

> ... *receive mercy's kiss and discover the grace we urgently need to strengthen us in our time of weakness.* (Hebrews 4:16 TPT)

Israel's history is filled with the mercy of God. The birth, death and resurrection of Jesus is all the mercy of God towards us all. His mercy is eternal!

Army in position? Cover the Frontline Troops!

Do we ever consider the level of engagement needed by the whole army, or do we just want to send the musicians out and let them risk their lives, while the rest cheer from the sidelines?

The musicians had to be in correct position, but so did the whole army. Although Judah went first, it is important to remember the army followed close behind them. The army must also show up and be in position. Worship leaders, musicians and singers need their backs covered by prayer. How many worship leaders and musicians fall, get taken out or fail to arise to potential because they are not protected by other watchman and intercessors?

Today's armies call their crack frontline troops commando units, Navy SEALs or Green Berets. They are specially trained elite units. Yet when they go on a mission, they are not alone; they have vital back-up, including intelligence, air support for strikes and specialised transport vehicles. They have all the necessary support.

How many worship leaders and musicians have been trained for such battles? How many possess the equipment needed – and I don't just mean musical instruments? How many support units do we have for such battles? It is fine to love the strategy but are we prepared to provide adequate cover for our worship teams?

I once spoke with the support person of a well known worship leader and asked about the prayer support for this person. I was stared at as if to ask what I was talking about; they had no clue what I meant. Knowing the sort of warfare I have experienced, I could only imagine what this worship leader went through. I was rightly concerned. Sadly, that worship leader soon had a moral failure.

Musicians and singers need their backs covered. The war for worship is real. This is the arena Lucifer operated in and knows too well. All of Israel had to show up, not just the musicians. The task must not be left to the worship team alone. The whole army of God must be actively engaged. Is the army of God equipped and manned properly? Do we provide the intel that the musicians and singers need? Do they have the practical and spiritual support needed?

> **Musicians and singers need their backs covered. The war for worship is real. This is the arena Lucifer operated in and knows too well.**

The rest of the army must also release their own sound and faith in God's mercy. The worship team cannot worship for you. Every soldier in the Lord's army must worship for themselves. Musicians and singers are facilitators. Don't leave all the heavy lifting to them alone.

The whole army must enact faith in the Lord of hosts and not leave it all to the Davids, like when he went before Goliath.

> ***Position yourselves, stand still*** *and see the salvation of the LORD ... Do not fear or be dismayed ... for the LORD is with you. (2 Chronicles 20: 17)*

When *all* of Israel was obediently in position, God acted!

Advance, Ready, Set, Worship!

> *Now when they began to sing and to praise, the Lord set ambushes against the [enemy], who had come against Judah; and they were defeated. (2 Chronicles 20:22)*

Once Israel was in position and obediently singing, God acted. But the Lord didn't wait until they had been in worship for some hours. He showed up when they *began* to sing. It is said fifty per cent of any task is getting started. Overcoming fears, getting into position and getting started are all vital parts of the process. Advance, ready, set, worship.

God showed up and the enemy fought each other. Israel moved in to collect the spoils, which took three days to do. On the fourth day, they blessed the Lord and went back to Jerusalem with joy. The fear of God fell on all the surrounding countries while Israel had peace. What a divine turnaround.

Honouring Him in our day of trouble is key to aligning with heaven for victory. We must hear His voice, obey and then build altars to worship Him.

CHAPTER SEVEN

Merging Worship and Music

WHEN YOU HEAR THE word 'worship', what do you think of? Your favourite worship leader, your favourite song, an act of service, or do you prefer defining the word 'worship'?

Recent decades in the Western Church, worship music has become an industry. The growth and changes in worship music, even in my lifetime, have been vast, resulting in many genres of worship music developing. Many now believe that worship and music are synonymous.

Scripture often aligns music and worship together. But not all worship includes music, and not all music is worship to the Lord. Our propensity towards entertainment and professionalism have muddied the waters as we have tried to amalgamate the holy with the profane.

Discussing worship can be quite contentious. Personal musical tastes and genre preferences are generally strong, affecting choices of worship music and affect many arguments!

Our Worship Filters?

We all have filters. Our worldview of life (Biblical or secular), our upbringing, our theological stance and preferred musical genres, these all influence our choices as well as our capacity to assess things – even how you interpret what you are reading here.

Some people object to the words 'worship' and 'music' being in the same sentence. They hold the strong view that worship is primarily an act of bowing before the Lord or an act of service. Yet throughout scripture, there are many musical responses in worship. So, which is correct? Can worship and music be in the same sentence?

Pause and Pray

With all our different prejudices, ideas and tastes in music, it can be quite easy to mishear what the Spirit of God is saying, even through this material. Would you be brave enough to pause before going further? Yes, even stopping now, in the middle of reading this chapter?

Be still for a moment and invite the Holy Spirit to speak to you. Are there any prejudices and filters that would hinder you from hearing what the Holy Spirit wants to say to you? Give Him permission to clean your spiritual windscreen, so you can see more clearly. *Selah.*

Worship Defined

Technically, it is right to suggest that music is not worship. Two words are used in scripture for worship. Both the Hebrew *shachah*[32] and Greek *proskuneo*[33] mean to bow down, do reverence to, adore, to be prostrate – especially in a reflex homage to royalty or God.

Most scriptural examples of these words are when people are bowing or raising their hands. Worship is not passive. It is a response to the awe and majesty of a most holy God. Encounters with Him, or receiving fresh revelation of Him, demands a response from us.

> *I will worship you, YAHWEH, with extended hands as my whole heart erupts with praise! (Psalm 9:1 TPT)*

Worship is a response to our Creator and Redeemer. Our responses will come from our whole being; heart, arms, hands, legs, feet, mouth etc.

Merger: Strumming Heart Strings

Though worship and music are not the same, they do overlap with an important merging point, expressed best by the psalmist:

> *Melodies of praise will fill the air as every **musical instrument, joined with every heart, overflows** with **worship**. (Psalm 92:3 TPT)*

Music and worship merge as songs and hearts *join* in response to encountering Almighty God. Worship and music are like a marriage; love is given by God, our hearts respond in a song of praise. God created music as a powerful gift through which we can respond to Him. Though responses can be non-musical, music uniquely facilitates a *corporate* response from God's people. Being able to worship Him *together* is unique, unifying and powerful.

> *Music and worship merge as songs and hearts join in response to encountering Almighty God.*

Our hearts are like harp strings. As we respond to Him in awe, the harp strings of our heart release songs of praise. Worship responses and music go together.

> *My loving God, the **harp in my heart will praise you**. Your faithful heart toward us will be the theme of my song. Melodies and music will rise to you, the Holy One of Israel. (Psalm 71:22 TPT)*

Our heart containing a harp may sound poetic, but I want to suggest it is more. In watching an ABC documentary on music and the brain, the narrator said each electrical neuron of the human brain responds to each note of the piano![34] The difference between piano strings and harp strings is that harp strings are vertical compared to the encased horizontal strings of the piano.

And perhaps the Chief Musician woos us by playing the strings of the harp in our heart!

Psalm 100 speaks of entry into the Lord's presence as coming through gates of thanksgiving and courts of praise. Continue through the courts of the temple and you come into the holy place of His Presence. The inference is thanksgiving and praises are the entrance or gateway to worship or bow in His Presence. King David speaks of songs of worship.

> *Your wonderful words will become my **song of worship**, for everything you've commanded is perfect and true. (Psalm 119:172 TPT)*

David puts the Word of God into songs of worship. Some translations use the word 'say' instead of 'sing'. The Hebrew word used is *anah* and means to heed, to pay attention to, to respond, to answer, to bear witness to. Specifically, it is to sing, announce or sing together.

Heaven's Model: Bow and Sing!

The highest example and model for worship is in heaven, and there are multiple examples of worship merging with music.

In Revelation 4, the four creatures around the throne worship day and night with singing.

> They **worshiped** without ceasing, day and night, **singing**, 'Holy, holy, holy is the Lord God, the Almighty! (Revelation 4:8 TPT)

The four creatures were responding to the holiness of God. They were joined by twenty-four elders who bowed, surrendered their crowns and sang.

> ... **worshiped** the one who lives forever and ever. And they surrendered their crowns before the throne, **singing**: 'You are worthy, our Lord and God, to receive glory, honor, and power, for you created all things ...' (Revelation 4:9–11 TPT)

In this instance, they bowed, worshipped and sang in response to the Creator. We have the benefit of pictures from NASA[35] showing extraordinary images of the stars that cause us to want to join heaven's song, 'You are Worthy'.

Continue to Revelation 5 and the merging of music and worship increases. An elder announced, 'Jesus, the Passover Lamb, is the only one able to open the seals on the scroll.' As the Lamb, the Lion of Judah takes the scroll, twenty-four elders, harp in one hand and prayer bowl in the other, bow, worship and sing.

> ... they fell facedown at the feet of the Lamb and **worshiped** him. And they were **all singing** this **new song of** praise to the Lamb ... (Revelation 5:8 TPT)

What did they sing?

> You are worthy to take the scroll, And to open its seals; For You were slain, And have redeemed us to

> *God by Your blood Out of every tribe and tongue and people and nation ... (Revelation 5:9)*

But it didn't stop there. The worship and the song grew. Choirs of innumerable angels joined the songs of worship. With an amazing crescendo, all in heaven **and on earth** worshipped the Lamb and sang!

> *... the voices of myriads of angels in circles around the throne, as well as the voices of the living creatures and the elders – myriads and myriads! And as I watched, all of them were **singing** with thunderous voices ... Then **every living being** joined the angelic choir ... **in heaven and on earth** ... were **worshiping with one voice** ... (Revelation 5:11-13 TPT)*

What were all these choirs singing?

> *Worthy is the Lamb who was slain ... Blessing and honor and glory and power Be to Him who sits on the throne, And to the Lamb, forever and ever! (Revelation 5:12-13)*

The corporate song in heaven grew from four (creatures) to twenty-four (elders) to millions (angels) then to all of creation. Only God knows the exact number. Worship began as a response to the holiness of God and the extraordinary and victorious sacrifice of Jesus the Passover Lamb.

This is a powerful pattern for us: to merge worship (bow in awe), singing, music and prayer. The worship of heaven is not stagnant; their reason for worship shifted. First, it was honouring the Creator, then the Redeemer, then the King on the throne.

Nor is worship in heaven a private expression. Everyone in heaven is engaged to offer songs of worship. And those on earth sing from the same song sheet as the angels! It is not an individual offering. It is a unified corporate expression. Heaven and earth sing the same song.

Go to Revelation 7 and another spectacle occurs. An uncountable crowd is in heaven from earth. Speculation is that they are victorious ones from the tribulation *'from every nation, tribe, people group, and language'* (Revelation 7:9).

They stand around the throne of God, singing their testimony: 'Salvation belongs to our God'. The response of heaven is amazing. The four creatures, twenty-four elders and all the angels of heaven respond in worship, amazed at the overcoming power of salvation.

> ... *and they **all fell on their faces before the throne and worshiped God, singing**: 'Amen! Praise and glory, wisdom and thanksgiving, honor, power, and might belong to our God forever and ever! Amen!' (Revelation 7:1--12 TPT)*

The most powerful expression of worship is corporate bowing of hearts while singing His praises. Composers should write, worship teams should facilitate, spiritual leaders should require inspirational songs that *all* can sing in response to the holy One, Creator, Redeemer, who sits on the throne.

Heaven's worship as a model for us on earth is crucial for the end-time battles.

Liturgy to Loudspeakers: Changed Genres

Singing revivals have recurred throughout history. Luther's reformation and Wesley's, Salvation Army and Welsh

> *The most powerful expression of worship is corporate bowing of hearts while singing His praises.*

revivals, to mention a few, were all marked by *all* the people singing. The Lord's Presence is full of joy; it is an atmosphere that inspires singing.

The rapid growth in worship music has aligned with the moves of God, and the re-establishment of the nation of Israel. Both frequently coincide. We will quickly overview this large topic. And remember, real life does not fit into neat definitions. Often different genres merge with variations and permutations.

> **Heaven's worship as a model for us on earth is crucial for the end-time battles.**

- *Church worship*

Music tailored for a specific denominational setting, with a set time limit and an assortment of things to fit into the schedule: preaching, Bible reading, announcements, offering, communion. Singing is often considered a warm-up for the important sermon, aiming to inspire faith, convey theological truths, and create an atmosphere of reverence and connection. This will vary according to locality, personnel and denominational or theological perspectives. Hence the categories of Traditional and Pentecostal, but many overlap.

- *Traditional/evangelical*

Three hymns (and some contemporary songs) interspersed with Bible reading, sermon, offering and maybe communion.

- *Pentecostal*

A block of three fast songs followed by one slow song, and perhaps thirty seconds of singing in tongues. The service will follow with preaching, announcements, offering, communion and a last song.

- *Jesus Revolution, charismatic*

The movie *Jesus Revolution* highlighted the shift in the 1970s as guitars, drums and whole bands gradually joined the chorus of praise. The charismatic era overlapped the period of the Jesus Revolution, with some differences. A key factor in the charismatic revival was 'Scripture in Song' developed in New Zealand. Straight scripture was set to simple tunes, providing a great way to learn the word. The charismatic era was also instrumental in the release of singing in tongues.

- *Soak*

Worship music, whether by a live band or recorded, creates an atmosphere to connect with the Lord. Gentle soft melodies and minimal lyrics characterise it. Ambient sounds encourage listeners to 'soak' in God's presence without distraction – suitable for prayer, meditation and reflection. Sometimes scriptures are read. Instrumental music is featured, incorporating elements like strings, special effects, and piano. It is more personal than corporate. It is about surrendering to Him, fostering intimacy and being replenished in Him. Some healing ministries use this to assist people to focus their hearts to receive from the Lord.

- *Evangelism*

A deliberate choice to make the worship music appeal to, or draw in, those outside of the church. Some have stated pipe organs and choirs will not reach the general populace; therefore, we need to plug into a sound system and contemporary culture.[36] It contrasted with Billy Graham crusade choirs and traditional singing and won millions to Jesus.

Before we were married, we were part of an Aussie bush band attached to our evangelism team. It was not worship per se but deliberate outreach. We dressed in colonial gear and sang folk songs with gospel lyrics while the evangelism team gave out tracks and spoke with people listening. Many have done similarly with different cultural music or rock bands and so forth.

- *Contemporary worship music: technology and transformation*

Hillsong, Planet Shakers, Bethel, Vineyard and Elevation Worship exemplify Contemporary Worship Music (CWM), a distinct genre recognised in the music industry. CWM integrates advanced technologies – loudspeakers, dynamic lighting, lasers and fog machines – to become polished productions tailored for busy audiences seeking spiritual connection. In the late 1980s, Geoff Bullock, a key figure at Hillsong, visited our church to share their philosophy: creating worship music that resonates with modern culture to attract new congregations. Years later, on a podcast, Bullock reflected on this approach, expressing regret over excesses that led to personal grief and soul-searching.

- *Warfare worship*

Thanksgiving, praise, proclamation and worship intentionally inviting God's presence is considered a powerful weapon in the spiritual battle with principalities and powers. It is based on Biblical examples like Jehoshaphat's singers routing enemies (2 Chronicles 20) or Paul and Silas's praises shaking prison foundations (Acts 16). This worship declares God's sovereignty, combats personal sin and fosters spiritual victory by shifting focus from fear to the Lord's sovereign power. It is not merely preparatory but the battle itself, as worship aligned with heaven creates an atmosphere to dispel darkness. Angelic activity is divine intervention, causing demonic influences to flee.

- *Prophetic worship*

Prophetic worship is spontaneous and Spirit-led. Music, song, dance and other arts are guided by divine inspiration, often conveying God's heart, messages or revelations to the congregation. Rooted in Biblical examples like the psalms or King David's worship, it blends structured songs with impromptu creative expressions, such as new lyrics or melodies. Once common in charismatic and Pentecostal settings, it fosters intimacy with God, spiritual breakthroughs and sometimes spiritual warfare, aiming to align worshippers with God's will.

- *Davidic/throne room worship*

Worship inspired by King David in the spirit of the tabernacle of David. It emphasises passionate and Spirit-led praise as described in the Bible when David was before the Ark. It involves heartfelt adoration, singing, dancing and playing instruments to honour and exalt the Lord, often in a spontaneous and joyful manner. There is a priority of intimacy with God. This worship is a journey from reverence to exuberance. It includes prophetic elements, intercession and a focus on God's presence as seen in the tabernacle of David, where continuous worship was offered 24/7. Modern expressions may incorporate contemporary music, creative arts with banners and shofars.

> *In this challenging time of end-time clashes of kingdoms and cosmic warfare, is our current understanding and practice of worship able to sustain the turbulence and warfare?*

- *Prayer houses*

This is a combination of worship and prayer, frequently referred to as being in the spirit of the tabernacle of David. The terms 'harp' and 'bowl' are frequently used.

- *Reflection: Music, Bridge to Divine*

Worship begins with hearts bowed to God. When worship merges with music, bowed hearts spill over into songs of praise. We express praise through arms, hands, legs, feet and voices. Worship teams are meant to facilitate corporate worship, uniting congregations to honour God together in one sound.

In this challenging time of end-time clashes of kingdoms and cosmic warfare, is our current understanding and practice of worship able to sustain the turbulence and warfare? Does your worship need to be upgraded?

Let's go back to our filters and consider a few questions.

- What model of worship do you use as a template? Does it need a makeover so you can step up?
- Are you in the right tribe or place for worship according to your call?
- Have you invited the Holy Spirit to help with cleansing and adjusting some filters?

Perhaps you prefer to tuck away this information for a rainy day, a day when the battle is in your face and you need worship reformed.

If the corporate worship you are involved with focuses more on receiving blessings than giving to God, it may need a health check. Do we attend worship to receive or to give a sacrifice or praise? Would you join a Christian gathering solely to *give* sacrifices of praise? Do you get fully engaged and participate in worship? Do you sing?

We are entering an era where worship and music must unite to create a powerful, victorious sound. Warfare today requires our worship on earth to unite with heaven. Through Spirit-led worship, we align our hearts so we can hear the sounds of heaven and bring them to earth as David did with his psalms and harp (1 Chronicles 16:4–6). As we allow the Holy Spirit to work within us, our songs will harmonise with heaven.

This convergence is not just musical; it is transformative of hearts and mind. It echoes the biblical call for heaven and earth to rejoice together.[37] By internalising these truths, we shift from passive recipients to active conduits to foster deeper participations and spiritual victory.

Getting us all on the same page to define how music and worship merge and some historical developments is advantageous before plunging into the realms of the return of pagan gods and how they use music. As we consider the use of music in pagan worship, we become more aware of the battle for worship – even through worship.

CHAPTER EIGHT

Music, Marx and Recycling the Gods

IN 2022, JONATHAN CAHN released his brilliant book, *Return of the Gods*. While reading it, I was astounded to discover some of the exact quotes I had used thirty years ago in *Restoring True Worship* (1st edition). While Cahn's book is not about music per se, he gave a few specific examples.

Return of the 'gods'

Cahn suggests that everything we are experiencing now, and what we see unfolding in the nations today, goes back to the gods of the ancient world. He provides a brilliant spiritual overview and distinctly identifies and enunciates the worship of the pagan dark trinity of Baal, Ishtar and Moloch. He presents clear examples of the gods' return, covering the when, how and why. These have returned with a vengeance, especially in Western civilisation. He draws profound historic and spiritual parallels from the past to today, showing clearly when and how the same ancient pagan gods have returned.

Cahn argues the ministry of Jesus and the Gospel drove out the gods from society. However, where the West was once blessed by being founded on Biblical morality and laws, as society has increasingly rejected Christianity, pagan gods have returned with a vengeance. The words of Jesus have been activated. In Matthew 12:43–45 Jesus warned if a house or *generation* were cleansed of unclean spirits, but not filled with God, seven more spirits would return. The latter state would be worse than the first.

Music to Kill By

In his chapter, 'Children of the Altars', Cahn used a heading: 'Music to kill by', and quotes hymns and music used to accompany the sacrificing of children to Moloch. He quotes ancient poems describing the music used to drown out the cries of babies being sacrificed to Moloch. In *Restoring True Worship* (1st edition), I quoted those *exact* same poems and descriptions of the music used to accompany the heinous heartbreaking practice of child and human sacrifice. Cahn quoted from Plutarch who had said, *'the music was especially strategic'*.

Large slabs of *Restoring True Worship* (1st edition) could fit under Cahn's heading 'Music to Kill By'. I had used the same quotes because the Lord showed me the music of the gods had infiltrated the 1980s church! I referred to music that accompanied ancient pagan worship and how it has now facilitated the re-entry of the gods into society.

Return of the Gods and *Restoring True Worship*

Though expressed with much less clarity and punch as Cahn, the two messages harmoniously align. For those interested in the subjects, and for those involved in worship ministry and in the arts, it would be valuable to read both books side by side.

Volume Two will address this controversial topic in depth. For now, I need to lay a solid biblical foundation for the intense battle over worship, including the music. Music's role and power in the supernatural realms are critical in this end-time battle, waged by both the Lord and imposter gods. (Later chapters, like 'End-time Battle of the Bands', explore this further.) Ignoring this battle has serious consequences.

Spiritual warfare, cosmic war, often operate through the music of culture. It is the nefarious force behind the events we witness in our culture, most often brought to earth through music and the arts. Without understanding music's role in these battles, readers may dismiss much of this material and Volume Two, *Spirit of Rock* as mere opinion. Many believers fail to discern the supernatural battle for worship, viewing music as amoral or neutral. Two reasons explain this.

First, as the late Michael Heiser noted, recent Church history too often lacks awareness of supernatural realms, unlike the early Church. It is hard to fathom, as a belief in God being supernatural is foundational to Christianity! Without this foundational principle, misunderstanding and misinterpretation of scripture occur. Principalities and powers seek to overthrow our Creator, who is King of the universe: with Israel, the Church and music as key battlegrounds.

Second, people love music and hold strong opinions, especially in the church, but few grasp how it works in the supernatural realms or how the gods use it. Many are unaware of how big a role music plays in their own lives. In a school assignment, I challenged my year 8 students to fast from music for twenty-four hours. Most found it impossible, citing its presence in shopping centres, TVs, gyms and more. Those who partially succeeded struggled, realising their dependence on it – they couldn't live without music!

Understanding the role of music in the spiritual battles is vital to empowering us to discover and boldly release the Lord's powerful sound.

CHAPTER EIGHT

Music and the Sexual Revolution

Cahn speaks of the sexual revolution of the 1960s and the gods that re-entered the West through this movement. This was the major thrust of *Restoring True Worship* (1st edition). The Holy Spirit had spoken to me, like an audible voice, about the god behind the music of the sexual revolution. It was one way the gods had punctured the defences of the Church.

Cahn quotes ancient writings of Mesopotamia and summarises: 'Ishtar parades involved harps and drums, music and rhythm … the parades were known for something else – the **bending of gender**.'[38]

Holy One

One specific reference of Cahn's totally shocked me. He spoke of Ishtar being referred to as 'the holy one'. And he quotes from an ancient hymn to Ishtar called 'Holy One'. Like 'gay pride' marches today which are accompanied with music and bands, it was sung with instruments at the ancient parades of Mesopotamia and the Middle East – for bending gender!

> *The hymn sang; 'The people of Sumer parade before you; They play the sweet ala-drums before you.*[39]

Why was this a shock? Two reasons.

1. Isaiah repeatedly calls God 'the Holy One of Israel'. The title reveals the Lord's majesty and purity. He is the one true God whose throne is over Israel.

> *I am the LORD, your Holy One, The Creator of Israel, your King.* (Isaiah 43:15)

For Ishtar to claim the holy name of God is so blasphemous it leaves one speechless!

2. In 2009, I released a worship album called 'Holy One'. My song, 'Holy One' is the key song.[40] The song is based on Revelation 5 where Jesus, the Lamb of God, is found to be the only one worthy to open the scrolls. When we first started singing the song, the prophet intercessor working alongside me kept seeing snakes in the spirit and became engaged in a torrid spiritual battle. Meanwhile, the rest of us were blessed as we sang praises exalting Jesus! It always puzzled me why there was such resistance when we were exalting Jesus. Now I know.

Cahn reveals these ancient parades equate with gay pride parades today. At the time of writing my song, I was totally unaware of the ancient song, and its use for Ishtar parades. No wonder my song 'Holy One' had stirred up spiritual war! Since discovering this information, we have used my song deliberately and powerfully in warfare, especially in Pride Month.

No wonder there is a spiritual war over my song and any time we sing and decreed the Holy One of Israel; King David exhorted us to sing to the Holy One of Israel. The enemy always activates counterfeits to undermine and mock the Lord's purity and strength.

> *My loving God, the harp in my heart will praise you. Your faithful heart toward us will be the theme of my song.* **Melodies and music will rise to you, the Holy One of Israel.** *(Psalm 71:22 TPT)*

This is a potent and authoritative song in the spirit realm, releasing a sound proclaiming the holiness of the one and only

God, who has placed His powerful, pure name upon Israel. Come, Church, sing more songs about the Holy One of Israel!

Lost Ground After Revival

In the 1960s through to the 1970s, the Spirit of God moved powerfully. As the movie *Jesus Revolution* showed, revival broke out among many hippies. Then a move of the Holy Spirit spread through traditional churches, known as the charismatic movement. I witnessed both of these at university, in my family and in the church where I grew up. Repentance and worship were key factors in both revivals. My own resistance to the Holy Spirit broke down as I witnessed the beautiful and unique sound of singing in the Spirit, and the miracles released through praise. (See Chapter 31, 'Exquisite Governing Sounds: Wait for Weighty Glory?')

> *Within a decade of the Jesus Revolution and the charismatic renewal, the enemy used his deception to infiltrate and subvert beautiful music.*

Within a decade of the Jesus Revolution and the charismatic renewal, the enemy used his deception to infiltrate and subvert beautiful music.[41]

In an advertisement for a conference to be held at Morningstar in the latter part of 2024, Dutch Sheets lamented what happened after earlier revivals. He asked some provoking questions. 'How do you experience one of the greatest outpourings of the Holy Spirit in church history, and yet the long-term fruit is you have lost ground, even lost an entire generation?'

Dutch stated that the move of God during the 1960s and '70s had been one of the greatest revivals in history. Some suggest fifty million were saved in those outpourings, yet it is suggested that among those young people, today there are only about two per cent who have a Biblical worldview. He asks, 'What happened?' People got saved, but the church did not disciple nations.[42]

> *People got saved, but the church did not disciple nations.*

Instead, unbelievers were the ones discipling nations in universities, schools, legislature and media. Many hours every day, society was being saturated with Marxist doctrines and worldview. Meanwhile, the church occupied just a couple of hours a week. Even then, not all were teaching morality or filtering world events through the Bible.

In May 2022, a disturbing survey from researcher and pollster George Barna of the Cultural Research Center at Arizona Christian University found that just thirty-seven per cent of US-based pastors hold a 'biblical worldview';[43] this means sixty-three per cent hold a *non-Biblical* view of the world! In a similar survey, Barna questioned Christian parents and found a similar result. Speaking about the survey results, George Barna said, 'This is another strong piece of evidence that the culture is influencing the American church more than Christian churches are influencing the culture.'

The Bible should be our filter on the news, history, all choices of lifestyle, marriage, sexual behaviours, how to bring up children, run a business, choose a church and who and how you worship. If only thirty-seven per cent of pastors and parents allow the Bible to influence their worldview and choices, what are most 'Christians' in the Western Church believing and being taught?

If this is the true state of the Church, no wonder the world is in such a mess. But there is more!

Events in Israel Mirrored in the Church: + and −

What happens in Israel in the natural is often mirrored in the Church spiritually, both positively and negatively.

When the modern state of Israel was born in 1948, a great healing revival swept the churches with ministries like Oral Roberts'. In 1967, the Six Day War reunited Jerusalem. In the Church, the Jesus Revolution broke out among the hippies, as referred to above. Many who were saved were young Jewish people, and some of these are leaders in Messianic ministries today. In 1973 when the Yom Kippur War caught Israel off guard, Israel took back the Golan Heights. The Church took back 'high ground' as the charismatic renewal broke out everywhere and released gifts of the Holy Spirit back into the church.

On the flip side, there are losses to consider. After the greatest miraculous victory in the Six Day War in June 1967, Israel took back control of Jerusalem. They even hoisted their flag above the mosque on the Temple Mount and reunified Jerusalem. But within hours, international pressure caused Israel to relinquish control of the Temple Mount back to the Jordanians, and keep the 'status quo'. The consequences of that episode continue to play out in today's conflicts.

Former paratrooper Rabbi Yisrael Ariel was one of those young men privileged and amazed to be part of liberating Jerusalem. But as he reflected upon the heartbreak of not being able to keep the Temple Mount, he realised Messiah had not yet come and they were not ready to rebuild the temple. In 1987, The Temple Institute was founded to prepare for rebuilding the third temple. It has prepared temple furniture, ritual objects, priestly garments and musical instruments, and trained priests and musicians.[44]

The example of the 1967 war is profound for the church. Much ground was won but also lost. Many were saved in the Jesus Revolution and yet the Church has largely been unable to resist the onslaught of Marxism and secularism throughout Western civilisation.

How did the greatest revival lead to losing our culture? Did we focus solely on preaching the gospel for salvation, neglecting Jesus' command to disciple nations? Discipleship requires discipline and teaching. Leaders like Lance Wallnau have emphasised discipling nations through the seven mountains of influence: family, religion, government, business, education, arts and entertainment, and media.[45] Christians must bring the gospel of the kingdom into these areas to counter Marxism's infiltration.

A key often overlooked is the one I explore in *Restoring True Worship* (1st edition). The 1960s–1970s spiritual outpouring was powerful, but by the 1980s, the church embraced the music and culture of the sexual revolution. This invited demonic influence, weakening the church, much like a fractured ship sinking under ferocious seas.

As The Temple Institute prepares for the Messiah, is the Church readying for Jesus' return through its music and worship, returning to biblical morality and discipling nations? Are we preparing a sound to engage with the hosts and choirs of heaven that will together defeat the system and gods of Babylon?

The end-time Church needs a paradigm shift regarding worship – not some minor tweaks at the edges but a profound reformation! The end-time Church has the privilege and call. We cannot resist the devil by using the devil's sound or his music! We are meant to release the sound of heaven onto earth, not the sound of earth, let alone hell, into heaven!

Consider these probing questions:

- Has the Church's music influenced society, or has society's music influenced the Church?
- Did the Church adopt the music and values of culture lead to compromise, or was music just a symptom of deeper issues?
- Do we compromise worship by embracing worldly values that gratify the flesh?
- Do third-person lyrics undermine worship where we should sing directly to God? After all, it is Him we worship!
- Has the Church embraced music with non-Biblical or evil roots, thus making it complicit in spiritual harm?
- Does our music glorify God or slide into idolatry?
- Has music, introduced as worship, eroded true worship and brought consequences?
- Are we reaping the consequences of not discipling nations, allowing ideologies like Marxism to infiltrate unopposed?

We cannot resist the devil by using the devil's sound or his music!

Marxism Vs. Revival: Losing a Generation Matters!

Western culture has increasingly rejected Christianity, embracing Marxism, which undermines Judeo-Christian society, leading to lawlessness and violence as spiritual and natural boundaries are breached.

Born in Prussia in 1818, Karl Marx, a baptised Catholic of Jewish descent, declared himself an atheist. Exactly what happened remains unclear. Somewhere, disappointment occurred; he became angry at God, and the demonic realm influenced him. Marx blamed religion for society's problems, wanting to elevate the status of man and remove the Creator, reminiscent of Psalm 2! He called religion the 'opium of the people', and with his friend Friedrich Engels, wrote the *Communist Manifesto* (1848), advocating revolution.

Marx reduced human issues to class and money, urging the working class (proletariat) to overthrow the capitalist (bourgeoisie) for a classless, stateless society with collective ownership, echoed today in phrases like 'you will own nothing and be happy'. Cultural Marxism applies these ideas to transform societal norms, targeting family, religion and traditional culture.

Since 9/11 and 7 October 2023, fears of Islamic terrorism have grown, but street protests reveal an alliance between cultural Marxists and radical Islamists, united in hostility towards Jews, Christians and the God of the Bible.

Australian journalist and author Greg Sheridan, in a June 2024 Sky TV interview, highlighted the growing threat to Christianity in Western nations. He noted a secular trend of tolerating Christianity only temporarily, but laws increasingly imposing restrictions and punitive penalties. Sheridan cited the Australian Law Reform Commission's hostility to Christianity and asked the question: 'Why has culture turned against Christianity?'[46]

In the 1970s, theologian David Noebel's book *Marxist Minstrels* warned the Church, citing FBI testimonies to Congress of record companies' roles in the sexual revolution by using pop groups to capture young hearts and minds. Today, Marxism targets toddlers via Disney and libraries, with books, songs and characters celebrating demonic entities or read to them by those confused about gender.

While the Church is often busy planning next Sunday's potluck, Marxism and Islamists wanting a caliphate have got a forty-year-plus game plan to disciple nations and dominate culture. Marxism has purposefully sought to ridicule and undermine Judeo-Christian society while dominating culture through demonic, occult-driven strategies, targeting education, media and entertainment, especially music. They recognise the power of music to pervert and penetrate culture. Marxists treat music like a superpower, while the Church shrugs it off as 'just vibes' or 'neutral'.

By dismissing Marxism's threat and compromising morality and worship's purity, the Church has lost ground. Instead of resisting, compromise has weakened the authoritative and powerful worship God entrusted to us. Marxism now advances like an uncontested coup through governments, schools and even churches.

You may disagree, but I believe the music adopted by the Church in the 1980s significantly contributed to this cultural war, as our compromise rendered us impotent to resist the Marxist infiltration in universities and government.

> *By dismissing Marxism's threat and compromising morality and worship's purity, the Church has lost ground.*

That's why, post-revival, we've lost a generation, and a few good hymns along the way.

Where to Now? War Over Tabernacle of David

By the mercy of God, in response to travail and prayer, the Lord is moving in another generation. Let us not squander another move of God, nor be ignorant of the enemy's tactics. The war is fierce.

It is time to learn, repent and reclaim in prayer. Let us discern and wisely implement the Lord's plan for music and the arts. It is clear in scripture as revealed to King David and implemented in his tabernacle and the subsequent temple.

At one of few conferences I have attended, Chuck Pierce spoke in Brisbane, Australia in 2015. His words, recorded and noted by me, were: 'How the tabernacle of David is raised up in a nation determines how the nation goes.' He had tried to bring this message a decade earlier, but there was such upheaval he could not fully deliver the message. It took him a decade to return and deliver the message.

I was relieved we had not been at that first gathering, as it was in the early days of our ministry as a tabernacle of David, and it might have been too big a discouragement if we had witnessed the mayhem. Suffice to say, his story confirmed that the restoration of the tabernacle of David is subject to major warfare. (Volume 3 will focus on the restored tabernacle of David.)

Questions to Ponder

There are lessons to be learned, and tests to endure, to ensure we are in correct position when the Lord confronts the gods, as He did between the Ark and Dagon. As we head into Part Two, consider these questions before we hop into the origins of music and the cosmic war through it.

- Was a great revival squandered by not teaching Biblical worship but turning worship into something that benefited us rather than God?

- Did we invite the music of culture into our midst, and with it, the gods of culture?
- Did music contribute to the serious decline in the West?
- How should we disciple our young worship leaders and musicians?
- What should we be preaching from the pulpits regarding worship?
- What should intercessors be praying for this to turn around?

ENDNOTES - PART 1

1. https://economictimes.indiatimes.com/news/defence/were-in-battle-of-civilisation-against-barbarism-netanyahu-to-dutch-pm/articleshow/104659855.cms?utm_source=contentofinterest&utm_medium=text&utm_campaign=cppst, 23 Oct 2023, accessed 4 Sept 24.
2. 'Hells Bells' video.
3. https://www.laphamsquarterly.org/music/emperors-new-music.
4. https://www.smithsonianmag.com/smart-news/what-happened-canary-coal-mine-story-how-real-life-animal-helper-became-just-metaphor-180961570/.
5. Check out my article on escalating anti-Semitism: https://www.tabernacleofdavid.org.au/israel/430-escalating-tide-global-antisemitism-impact-on-next-gen.html.
6. Pogroms are Jewish persecution through Russia and Europe in 19th and 20th centuries. Anti-Semitism and replacement theology topics are huge. I have completed multiple programs on radio. To study further, look for the series, 'Romans 9–11 Why Israel?' on our YouTube channel: www.youtube.com/@TabernacleofDavidBendigo. Also, 'Replacement Theology, Has it empowered Hamas?', https://youtu.be/XuA2UcZrPwk?si=ljsXkuY0avPn0hWK.
7. Murray, Douglas. *On Democracies and Death Cults: Israel, Hamas and the Future of the West*, HarperCollins, Gt Britain, 2025, p. 209.
8. Romans 3:2, 9:4.
9. Luke 1:32–34, Isaiah 9:6–7.
10. Isaiah 51:17, 22, 23.
11. 1 Peter 4:17.
12. Genesis 41:46, 2 Samuel 5:4, Luke 3:23
13. https://www.theguardian.com/world/ng-interactive/2021/jan/25/how-the-arab-spring-unfolded-a-visualisation.
14. Matthew 24:6–8.
15. Psalm 68:8.
16. Do yourself a favour and read and compare Psalm 68: 8–35 and Hebrews 12: 18–29. The distinction between the two mountains is given.
17. Lindley, Bruce. *A Whole New Era: emerging apostles and prophets,* 2020, p. 12.
18. ibid, pp. 41–42.
19. Hebrews 12:28 TPT.
20. Revelation 8.
21. 1 Corinthians 15:52.
22. Revelation 1:10, 4:1.
23. Revelation 12:8–12.
24. John 4:24.
25. Incorporate the use of all percussion instruments, as well as drum kit.

Orchestral percussion provides a broader range of sounds than a kit alone. Electronic drum kits can duplicate a lot of options for exactly this purpose.

26. 2 Samuel 6:6–7.
27. Insurance companies recommend hearing protection above 85 decibels. Severe hearing loss occurs around 80 decibels.
28. Romans 11:1–24.
29. 'But Ruth said: "Entreat me not to leave you, Or to turn back from following after you; For wherever you go, I will go; And wherever you lodge, I will lodge; Your people shall be my people, And your God, my God"' (Ruth 1:16).
30. 2 Chronicles 18, 19:2.
31. Genesis 14:7 names Amalekites and Amorites at the town Hazezon Tamar, the earlier name of En Gedi.
32. Strong's Concordance, H7812.
33. Strong's Concordance, G4352.
34. Despite my best efforts, I have not been able to locate the date or title of the documentary.
35. https://www.nasa.gov/gallery/stars/.
36. https://redeemercitytocity.com/articles-stories/evangelistic-worship.
37. 1 Chronicles 16:31–33.
38. Cahn, Jonathan. *The Return of the Gods,* Frontline, NY, 2022, p. 181.
39. ibid. p. 177.
40. Webb, Ruth. 'Holy One', https://www.tabernacleofdavid.org.au/shop/digital/holy-one-digital.html
41. More information in the Chapter 5, 'Don't Touch the Ark', and Volume *Two: Spirit of Rock in the Church* (to be released).
42. https://youtu.be/o3gcb4c_Fig?si=uhP_11u7cKyVoSzS.
43. https://www.arizonachristian.edu/wp-content/uploads/2022/05/AWVI2022_Release05_Digital.pdf.
44. https://templeinstitute.org/temple-mount-liberation-1967/
https://templeinstitute.org/about-us/.
45. https://lancewallnau.com/7-mountain-strategy/.
46. Greg Sheridan interview, June 2024. https://youtu.be/OxhSk-gkDvQ?si=zVqRIsA7iaWYtMBM.

PART TWO
MUSIC AND COSMIC WARFARE
God Created – Lucifer Stole

*Listen to what YAHWEH, the Holy One of Israel ... has to say ... 'I created the earth ... I spread out the cosmos ... made it [earth] ... orderly and beautiful for its inhabitants ... **I am YAHWEH, and there is no other god.**' (Isaiah 45:1-12, 18 TPT)*

*Sing to the LORD a new song! ... For the LORD is great ... **He is to be feared above all gods.** For all the gods of the peoples are **idols,** But the LORD made the heavens. (Psalm 96:1, 4-5 NKJV)*

For Yours is the kingdom and the power and the glory forever. (Matthew 6:13 NKJV)

Jesus made a public spectacle of all the powers and principalities of darkness, stripping away ... every weapon and all their spiritual authority and power ... by the power of the cross ... (Colossians 2:15 TPT)

Be exalted, O God, above the heavens; Let Your glory be above all the earth. (Psalm 57:11 NKJV)

PART TWO: PROPHETIC SNAPSHOT

The cosmic war between God and Satan is, in truth, no contest. Jesus triumphed at the cross, and Michael and his angels cast the dragon out of heaven.

Yet as this ancient conflict nears its climax, we stand at a time gate of convergence. Throughout history, this battle has often been fought through music and sound – created by God to fill the atmosphere of heaven and earth with perfect praise. Yahweh placed that creative gift in Lucifer, in angels, in us and even in creation. NASA confirms this truth in its recordings of stars and planets singing. Scientific research reveals the profound impact of music on the human body and soul.

But Lucifer, once heaven's chief musician, turned his gift towards rebellion. Barred from heaven, his music was corrupted. He knows, and fears, the pure sounds of glory that flow from God's throne.

So the deceiver wages war against true worship and seeks to destroy those near and dear to the heart of God – both Israel and the Church. As in ancient Israel, he seeks to silence our voices and songs of praise – by the 'rivers of [Mystery] Babylon'. With the venom of the serpent, he tries to poison and pervert the sound of glorious praises.

To discern true from deceiving sounds, we must understand the origin of music, and its connection to His Glory and the cosmic war. For it is the sound of heaven, released through the bridal Church, that penetrate darkness and announces the King's return.

CHAPTER NINE

Music at Creation

In the beginning God created the heavens and the earth. (Genesis 1:1)

All things were made through Him, and without Him nothing was made that was made. In Him was life, and the life was the light of men. (John 1:3–4)

In the Beginning …

ALL QUESTIONS AND DISCUSSIONS of music must start here.

God created all things.[1] Our Creator is the greatest artist! He has the most genius creative 'gene' ever. For those of us who are artistic, we appreciate creation through sound, colour and movement. But creation can be understood through science, mathematics, theology and by all who appreciate the sheer beauty of nature.

He created everything, including music and the arts. Nothing is left to chance. Creation by God's hand is *creatio ex nihilo*: that is, out of nothing. It is totally miraculous. The living God created out of Himself. And from Himself came sound, the raw material of music.

> *For by Him all things were created that are in heaven and that are on earth, visible and invisible, whether thrones or dominions or principalities or powers. All things were created through Him and for Him. And He is before all things, and in Him all things consist. (Colossians 1:16-17)*

The Creator of heaven and earth gave a specific role for each creation, including music. Genesis 1 identifies specific roles for parts of creation: sun to rule the day, moon and stars to rule the night. Music and the arts have a different role to the rest of creation – but they have a unique and specific function.

Creator Made Sound

Genesis 1:1 begins with the Hebrew words, *Elohim bara*. These two words identify the Creator, His creative process and His superiority and rulership over all of creation. This is a vital foundational truth to establish before considering the *war* over worship.

Elohim specifically means 'the supreme God', the strongest or only God. It can also refer to other gods, magistrates or judges. When the Bible was written, it was understood there were other elohim; these are the other gods who war against Almighty God. It is these gods referred to by Jonathan Cahn, and it is these gods who war through music. That is why many civilisations have counterfeit creation stories and false creators, each vying and contending for rulership of the earth.

As reiterated throughout scripture, Yahweh, *El Shaddai*, is the one and only supreme God. There is no one else like Him. He is the all-powerful, the strongest, the mightiest, the Holy One who judges all, the Creator of everything. As Moses told Israel:

> ... *The Lord Himself is God in heaven above and on the earth beneath; there is no other. (Deuteronomy 4:39)*

The other Hebrew word in Genesis 1:1 is *bara*, and simply means 'to create'. The reference is to an artistic sculptor who takes a block of wood, stone or even ice, and with their tools of choice, carves or chisels out amazing creations. This is the word used to describe the way the Lord God Almighty created the heavens and earth. He is the master craftsman.

He is also a singer.

God is a Singer!

Do you realise God sings? Is it shocking to think that God is the universe's chief musician?

> *The Lord your God in your midst ... He will rejoice over you with gladness, He will quiet you with His love, He will rejoice over you with singing. (Zephaniah 3:17)*

He sings in the midst of the congregation.[2] The Creator of the universe sings over Israel, and He sings over you. Everything comes from Him, so if the Creator cannot sing, where does your voice come from? We sing because He sings.

What is more, His song was first heard at creation!

Sound, Movement: Shift to the New

At creation, the Spirit of God moved over nothingness and chaos, stirring up vibrations and sound.

> *The earth was without form, and void; and darkness was on the face of the deep. And the Spirit of God was hovering over the face of the waters. (Genesis 1:2)*

Many Christians hear the word vibration or frequency and immediately say it's New Age. No, it's the language of physics of sound stolen by New Age! Beginning my music career as a secondary school music teacher, I defined music for my students with a simplified version of the physics of sound. Movement of a string or air through a tube creates a vibration. Vibrations create sound. Music is ordered sound.

At creation, the Holy Spirit moved, shook, hovered, brooded and fluttered over the darkness and chaos. The Spirit of God, or *rûach* in Hebrew, is literally God's breath or wind. Even the way *rûach* is pronounced, *roo'-akh*, produces a breathy sound. The Spirit hovering is reminiscent of a helicopter hovering above persons in an act of rescue or deliverance. The Spirit fluttering and brooding over darkness and chaos is akin to a mother hen incubating eggs ready for chicks to be birthed. The moving of the Spirit's breath was preparing a miracle.

There is a process between the breath of God being released and the actual creation. As the breath of the Holy Spirit moved upon the darkness, a sound from heaven was released. This sound penetrated, separated and removed the darkness. Some scholars attribute the darkness and chaos to the fall of Lucifer. Whether this is the moment of Lucifer's fall or not, we do know God's breath dissipates the worst darkness – even that of the anti-Christ! The breath of God's mouth combined with the light of His Glory will destroy the 'lawless one' (2 Thessalonians 2:8), often considered to be the anti-Christ.

> *One breath of His mouth can change everything!*

Listen to the wind words. What is the Spirit saying? It is a powerful prayer strategy to ask the Holy Spirit to breathe over any dark and chaotic circumstances in our lives, and our family's lives. One breath of His mouth can change everything! I did this over a tough family circumstance together with declaring light, and within ten days, there was a mighty breakthrough and the situation changed dramatically. Songs from the Holy Spirit are powerful over darkness.

God's breath is powerfully demonstrated through the Biblical trumpet, the shofar (see Chapter 3, 'Beating War Drums'). At creation, God used His breath to create and establish. God's breath has and continues to take out His enemies, whether through wind or taking of breath. At Mt Sinai and at the last trumpet, God breathes on His people. He calls them to life and to meet Him. If God's breath is so amazing, what happens when He joins it with light and sound?

Let There Be Light!

Many scholars believe that when God said, 'Let there be light', He was actually singing creation into existence. This fits with the scriptures above that reveal God as a singer.

The late Rabbi Sacks wrote an article in 2013 in which he spoke of the Jewish perspective of singing the Word of God:

> *Music is central to the Judaic experience. We do not pray ... we sing the words ... Nor do we read the Torah; instead we chant the weekly portion ... though the Torah was given once, it must be received many times, as each of us, through our study and practice, strives to recapture the* **pristine voice heard at Mount Sinai.** *That requires emotion, not just intellect. It means treating Torah not just as words read, but also* **as a melody sung**. *The Torah is God's libretto, and we, the Jewish people, are His choir, the performers of His choral symphony. And though, when Jews speak they often argue, when*

they sing, they sing in harmony, as the Israelites did at the Red Sea, because music is the language of the soul, and at the level of the soul Jews enter the unity of the Divine which transcends the oppositions of lower worlds. The Torah is God's song, and we collectively are its singers.[3]

The Jews consider the Torah to be God's song and they are simply the choir. It is for good reasons that many of the world's best singers and musicians are Christians or Jews, largely because they believe in the Creator and His call to worship Him. Because of these beliefs, they have exercised their voices in praise and given themselves opportunity to develop their potential. Even many who have left the faith began their music development in church or synagogue choirs. Conversely, some denomination and religions ban music. For example, the Greek Orthodox do not allow musical instruments, but singing only.

The Lord told Moses that His word was to be passed from generation to generation, most often through song. The song of Moses is one of these. It was sung at the Red Sea and is sung again in overcoming the dragon in Revelation 15.

> ... **write down this song** ... *and teach it to the children of Israel ... that **this song** may be a **witness for Me** against the children of Israel. (Deuteronomy 31:19)*

Light, Sound and Creative Miracles

When God created light, calling it into existence, He also created sound. Physics tells us that light and sound are part of the same substance: light has higher frequencies, whereas sound has lower and slower frequencies. Hence, the speed of light is much faster than the speed of sound.

Depending on what it travels through, light travels around 1.08 billion kilometres per hour (671 million miles per hour), whereas sound travels about 1,235 kilometres per hour (767 miles per hour). Light is roughly 880,000 to 900,000 times faster than sound; hence, you see lightning before hearing thunder, even though they occur at the same time.

Scripture often speaks of the Lord's voice as lightning and thunder – light and sound;[4] hence the term 'sound and light show'. Many believe His voice brought creation into existence; not just spoken words, but actually *sung*. The voice of God is powerful, majestic, creative and authoritative (Psalm 29). Within His voice are frequencies of the glory. Frequencies carry both light and sound, though they travel at different speeds.

> *In the beginning, God's voice and God's song produced a monumental creative miracle.*

In the beginning, God's voice and God's song produced a monumental creative miracle. When the Spirit of God hovered over darkness, He produced an incubating sound. Sound began the process. When God proclaimed light, it was a different sound. His authority and power, combined with His breath and song, released the miracle – God created the world *through* sound! The psalmist describes God's voice as 'powerful and full of majesty' (Psalm 29:4).

> *By the word of the Lord the heavens were made,*
> *And all the host of them by the breath of His mouth.*
> *For He spoke, and it was done ... He spoke, and it came into being ... (Psalm 33:4–9)*

It is this sound and authority that keeps us alive and holds the universe in place. His voice holds us secure and creates further miracles when needed.

> *He holds the universe together and expands it by the mighty power of His spoken word. (Hebrews 1:3b TPT)*

God did not use light and sound for an entertaining show – though I am sure it was a magnificent spectacle! At creation, light and sound obeyed His authority and power as He called all things into existence for the first time.[5] God uses His breath and voice to rule and reign over all of creation. The disciples of Yeshua were flabbergasted that even the winds and the sea obeyed him![6] Ezekiel was commanded by the Lord to speak or prophesy to the four winds.[7] How can the wind and sea obey if they cannot hear the command?

When we believers understand the mechanism of sound and light and listen to and align with the throne and voice of God, we too will see the creative miracles in our darkening world. There is an authoritative sound that goes way beyond just singing songs. When churches, leaders, psalmists and singers can grab hold of this critical truth, then in this hour of darkness and chaotic situations, the sounds of heaven will be released on earth and dire situations will become creative beauties beyond our wildest imagination!

Science is catching up with the Bible. Creative miracles can be and often are released through sound. Sound waves are even being used in industry and medicine. There was a time when I had sound wave (shockwave) therapy on my shoulders to prevent surgery which enabled me to keep making music.

Made in His Image, We Create!

The pinnacle of creation was when God made mankind in His own image.[8] The ability to create music (and all arts) is only possible because we are made in the image of God. We create because the Creator made us in His image. All creativity comes from His divine imprint. Because God is the greatest artist ever, and we possess His likeness, His creativity flows through our veins. We sing because our Creator sings. We paint and sculptor, dance and make music because He is the great Creator. You may not be a musician, painter or dancer, but creativity has many varied expressions.

When God created out of *nothing*, it was out of *Himself*, not something external. When we create something, we can only re-create from what He already made. We only have the capability to shape, organise or create out of that which already exists. For example, God took the dust which He made and created Adam. We now take that same dust, add water to it (another creation of God) and produce paint or mud. We can reshape God's raw materials to produce a landscaped garden, a mud brick house, pottery or even an idol. Man can only shape the raw materials God has already created from Himself. We do not have the capability to produce a new substance from nothing.

Likewise, a composer takes the raw materials that God has created and produces some new patterns of sound. Pitch, tone colour and rhythm were all created by God as raw material for us to assemble into various patterns.

Wind blowing through objects like trees or hollowed logs create sounds. Man first discovered string instruments when a hunter's bow rested against a tree, and the wind blew and vibrated the string, creating sounds. Man then found that if he put his hand on the middle of the string, he got a great variety of tones; in fact, all the tones of natural harmony. One of the earliest instruments was a ram's horn (the predecessor of today's brass family), and by blowing in a particular way, all the basic tones of the harmonic system could be produced.

Song was put into all of creation at the beginning of time. Birds were created with beautiful singing voices, and even more creative is the voice that man was created with. We even speak with certain tones. The Chinese language has at least four distinct tones that give totally different words depending on the tone.

We make music because He first created sound and sings His song over us. Made in His image, every one of us has been given by God, a voice to express that love and devotion. We can use that voice to echo back His song, singing it back to Him, all while He conducts the universal orchestra!

Some of you will protest. Many people think their voice sounds terrible or out of tune. Medically speaking, the percentage of people who are genuinely tone-deaf is minimal – between one and four per cent of the population. You may not have the voice of a recording artist, but you have a voice. Actually, the contention for your voice is a part of the war for true worship.

Whether you recognise it or not, every human on the planet, including you, is born with a musical gift within them. God has given *you* a unique voice! It is attached to your DNA, so that, like fingerprints, even technology can use it as a security password. There is much you can do with your voice and its unique sound. Every believer can release sounds, songs and art works in agreement with what God has already decreed. When we do this, our prophetic words and songs can call into existence those promises He has made before they become reality!

Every believer is called to sing praises. Singing isn't just about being a professional with a superstar voice; it is about responding to the Creator with the unique sound He has placed within you. Regardless of age, race or creed, every person is born with a need for God and to worship Him. Anointed sounds and songs come from Holy Spirit brooding over us. As we embrace the fact that God used singing, light and sound to create all things, including you and me and our voices, we should be inspired to align with the throne of God, and lift our voice in praise.

Music in the Garden of Eden

In the Garden of Eden, Adam and Eve had sweet and intimate fellowship with God. They heard the sound of the Lord walking in the garden. They heard His footsteps and His voice. But there were other sounds as well.

Did you know music was in the Garden of Eden, that it was filled with songs? When Isaiah compared Zion with the Garden of Eden, he revealed to us what was heard in Eden.

> ... *He will make her (Zion's) wilderness like Eden ... like the **garden of the LORD**; Joy and gladness will be found in it, **Thanksgiving and the voice of melody.** (Isaiah 51:3)*

Eden was a place of joy, and melodic songs of thanksgiving. Joy is associated with melodies and singable tunes. It does not refer to Eden having beautiful harmony or a good beat but a melody sung by creation.

Music was meant to fill earth with the most beautiful environment, reflecting who God is, perfect to sustain His image bearers. Sounds reflecting His character and nature filled heaven and earth with glory, majesty, beauty and joy. Music is ordered sound made up of frequencies, rhythms, harmonies and tone colours. These sounds originate from God Himself, holy and beautiful. These contain the frequencies of glory; literally, the light and sound of God! Remember, Jesus is the light.

The environment of His Presence is constantly filled with pure music. Where He is, the atmosphere is filled with love, life, peace, contentment and great beauty. In His wisdom, God created music as a unique and beautiful vehicle for His Glory. It is a gift and a perfect implement for worship. It is a unique way to express love, thanks, praise and honour to our Creator. It is a perfect instrument to exalt the Lord. A glimpse of the original quality and purpose of music is found in key scriptures[9] like this one:

> *The twenty-four elders fell facedown before … the throne and they … surrendered their crowns before the throne, singing: 'You are worthy, our Lord and God, to receive glory, honor, and power, for **you created all things**, and **for your pleasure** they were created and exist.' (Revelation 4:10–11 TPT)*

God intended music to be a means for His created beings to express the inexpressible, the greatness, majesty and awesomeness of our God. Heaven is a 24/7 praise centre. God intended for earth to be the same.

CHAPTER TEN

Sounds of Eternity

Music for the Glory of God

EACH SUNDAY, JOHANN SEBASTIAN Bach conducted a freshly written cantata. His choir sang his new compositions written to Biblical texts. You can visit that church in Leipzig any Sunday morning and still hear and enjoy one of the beautiful cantatas. What an amazing feat to write and rehearse a complete cantata each week – and all without the help of computers! At the bottom of each cantata, he wrote three letters: SDG – *Sol Deo Gloria*. In Latin, it says, 'To God's Glory Alone'. Bach wrote his music to give glory to the Lord.

Glory Sounds of Eternity

All of God's creation – including music and arts – were created for His purposes: His Glory and honour. All creation is a testimony of His goodness, kindness, majesty, glory and power.

> *All things were created **through Him** and **for Him** ... (Colossians 1:16–17)*

The psalmist reminds us that the heavens declare the glory of the Lord, revealing His handiwork.[10] Paul told the Roman church that creation shows the Lord's *invisible* attributes. He said mankind has no excuses because creation testifies to the eternal power of the godhead.[11]

At significant times when God has interacted with man, His Glory has been accompanied by a sound from heaven. The following list is not exhaustive, but a few key moments provide a glimpse and overview of this point.

- Creation was brought into existence by the sound of God's voice.
- The rebellion of Lucifer was called chaos. The Lord's voice stilled the chaos, and His Glory and sounds brought order out of chaos.[12]
- Israel met with God at Mt Sinai. His Glory appeared above the mountain, and God Himself blew the shofar, which became louder and louder.[13]
- The Ark of the Covenant on earth is a replica of what is in heaven. It represents the presence and *shekinah* glory of God. King David brought it into Jerusalem accompanied by prophetic songs.
- Isaiah saw heaven open up. He saw the glory of the Lord, and heard angels singing 'holy, holy, holy'. The sound of the angelic voices was so powerful it shook the doorposts, one of the strongest parts of a building![14]
- Angels announced the birth of Jesus to the shepherds watching their flocks. Scripture says 'the **glory of the Lord** shone around them'. Angelic choirs sang, 'Glory to God in the highest, and on earth peace, goodwill to all men.'[15]
- Jesus was resurrected from the dead by the glory of the Father.[16] What was the sound? A great earthquake and a powerful light.[17]

- On the day of Pentecost, a sound came from heaven. It was heard all over Jerusalem. It accompanied the fullness of the Spirit to birth the Church.[18]
- The book of Revelation opens a significant window into the sounds of worship in heaven. John described what he saw and the many sounds he heard. Reading the book, I see more of heaven's worship than the activity of anti-Christ. In fact, I see a distinct interaction between the worship of heaven and earth accompanying the Lord as the final war with the ancient serpent, dragon or devil.
- Jesus (Yeshua) is coming again – soon. God Himself will sound a shofar![19]

So many times, the glory of God has changed history and been accompanied by sounds of exuberant praise and passionate worship.

Prophetically, in this new era, there are glory sounds that need to be, and are in the process of being released from heaven and through us on the earth. In alignment with the trumpets and worship of heaven, these will prepare the way for the King of Glory as He returns to earth. These sounds will release and accompany the armies of heaven as they transfer the kingdoms of this world into the hands of Messiah – King Jesus!

> *So many times, the glory of God has changed history and been accompanied by sounds of exuberant praise and passionate worship.*

> *Then the seventh angel sounded ... 'The kingdoms of this world have become the kingdoms of our Lord and of His Christ, and He shall reign forever*

and ever!' And the twenty-four elders ... fell on their faces and worshiped God. (Revelation 11:15–16)

Creation Responds: Stars and Icebergs Sing!

In the beginning, when darkness was infused by God's powerful sound, creation responded with its own song. In music, we call this an antiphonal song; one choir sings, and then another choir (often in an opposite loft in a cathedral) replies with a different song.

Job discovered this when he and God had a heart-to-heart chat. God asked Job to consider the moment of creation.

> *Where were you when I laid the foundations of the earth? ... When the morning* **stars sang together***, And all the sons of God shouted for joy? (Job 38: 4–7)*

As the stars in the universe celebrated creation – they sang a song of joy in harmony together. In several psalms, King David calls stars, moon and mountains to sing praise.

> *Praise ye him, sun and moon: praise him, all ye stars of light. Praise him, ye heavens of heavens, and ye waters that be above the heavens. (Psalm 148: 19)*

Isaiah also calls the earth, the mountains and trees to sing praise and trees to clap their hands![20] We used to think this was poetic and figurative language. Not anymore. NASA has provided proof that God was speaking literally! At the end of the twentieth century, science started discovering sounds in space. The Hubble telescope has not only sent amazing pictures of the planets but also the sounds.

> *Sound cannot travel in space, but sonifications provide a new way of experiencing and conceptualizing data.*[21]

The list is too long to discuss here, but there are myriads of articles to be found. Some writers call the sounds 'spooky', but probably because it challenges our Western mindsets about creation.[22] You can listen to some sounds recorded by NASA if you go to their website.[23]

- Icebergs sing. Sometimes they sound like cooing or whining.[24]
- Black holes in space have a sound that is so low it only hits earth every 10,000 years – and scientists tell us it is here now! Very low frequencies can be quite damaging.[25]
- The sun's atmosphere sings. Its solar flares hit the corona belt like a guitar string.[26] Stars, planets and moons all communicate, including Earth!
- Whales have a different song for different seasons, and these help them navigate to get to the same spot each season.
- Dolphins apparently call each other different names. Many animals and sea creatures either make or can hear subsonic sounds that we humans cannot, but they communicate by it.

Yes, all of creation worships the Creator. An inspirational work confirming this is Louie Giglio's *Symphony*. Louie took some NASA cosmic sounds and overlayed them as a worship team sang 'How Great is Our God'.

We should not be shocked. The psalmist told us in detail in Psalm 19 'the heavens declare the glory of God'. The

Hebrew word for declare is *sâphar* which means to speak, tell, scribe, recount, celebrate. In verse two, David suggests that day and night echo each other and speak to one another like shift workers handing over to the next team on duty. Imagine day 1 speaks to day 2 and reports all the happenings, and night one shares its knowledge with night two. Bizarre? Have another read of Psalm 19.

If stars, moons and day and night do not have language, how do they communicate? The psalmist wrote: 'Their sound has gone out into the entire world, their message to the ends of the earth' (Psalm 19:4 GW). The King James Bible uses the word 'line' instead of 'sound', but that is even more insightful. The Hebrew word *quav* refers to a line like a musical string. The heavens are communicating God's glory in a way that is akin to a guitar or harp string!

Isaiah and Jeremiah called the earth to heed the voice of God. 'Listen, heaven, and pay attention, earth! The LORD has spoken ... (Isaiah 1:2, Jeremiah 6:19)'. The word used for 'listen' is *shama* and means to hear intelligently! The prophets are calling the earth to hear God's Word with perception.

In Revelation 5:13, John says that *every* creature worships God.

> *And every creature which is in heaven and on the earth ... I heard saying: 'Blessing and honor and glory and power Be to Him who sits on the throne, And to the Lamb, forever and ever!' (Rev 5:13)*

Every creature, including the four living creatures around the throne, is heard worshipping the Lord.[27] The Greek word calls them a live animal, a beast. Job encourages us to 'ask the animals, and they will teach you. Ask the birds, and they will tell you. Or speak with the earth, and it will teach you' (Job 12:7–8).

It may seem strange to our Western mindset, but *all* of creation can hear sound, respond to sound and *produce* sound! Even if we know Dr Doolittle talking to animals is fiction, these scriptures suggest that perhaps they are not all allegorical. Some theologians consider this capacity was lost at the Fall.

Why can all creation make sounds? It is not beyond God who made them, and everything finds its completion in worshipping Him. The earth and the heavens were created to be a massive worship centre, resounding with exuberant praises to the King of glory. Perhaps heaven and earth were meant to be, and will become, like those two antiphonal choirs – each echoing the other.

Resonance

Isaiah calls the ends of the earth to sing new songs of praise that will echo all the way to Jerusalem. The 'ends of the earth' is where we live. A colloquial term for this area is 'down under'. The prophetic description for Australia, New Zealand and the South Pacific islands is 'south lands of the Holy Spirit'. Songs of praise from Oceania are to reverberate around the globe back to Jerusalem. (More in Part Four, 'Prophetic Snapshot'.)

> *Isaiah calls the ends of the earth to sing new songs of praise that will echo all the way to Jerusalem.*

> *Sing to YAHWEH a brand-new song!* **Sing his praise until it echoes from the ends of the earth!** *Sailors and sea creatures, praise him! Islands and all their inhabitants, sing his praise! Let them give YAHWEH the*

glorious praise he deserves and declare his praise in the islands! (Isaiah 42:10, 12 TPT)

Resonance is when a sound is being prolonged by vibrating in synchronicity to a nearby object. It causes the sound to recur and continue.

When someone want to get attention or is lost in the Australian bush, especially between the mountains, we give a sharp shrill shout of 'coo-ee'. The sound reverberates, echoes, repeats, resonates, to be heard on the next hills.

Singing His eternal praises full of glory is not a finite, static activity. Our praises resonate through the spirit realm to register in heaven.

*And **my praises will fill the heavens forever**, fulfilling my vow to make every day a love-gift to you! (Psalm 61:8 TPT)*

Pure praises, registered in heaven for eternity, resonates with the praises in heaven! They will echo as the Lord needs and directs. His sound resonates throughout creation, and throughout eternity. His eternal word and voice keeps Earth in position.

> **Pure praises, registered in heaven for eternity, resonates with the praises in heaven!**

Standing firm in the heavens and fastened to eternity is the Word of God. (Psalm 119:89 TPT)

Groaning Earth

The earth itself is groaning.[28] Sin has caused earth to heave and groan, staggering like a drunkard. The groaning of the earth manifests in the increase of earthquakes, tsunamis, cyclones and hurricanes. Sensitive microphones are now detecting unusual frequencies coming from the earth. Men attribute global warming theory to poor stewardship. Perhaps they need to consider that the earth is primarily groaning in response to bloodshed upon bloodshed and curse upon curse, as humanity mocks the Creator and Redeemer. Perhaps scientists and governments should put a tax on sin instead of carbon!

We humans are animated dirt – and there are plenty of groans being heard from that quarter! Medical and scientific researchers have discovered that our human cells and organs make specific sounds. Biologist and author Professor Brian Ford localised the sound of neuron cells communicating, or 'talking to each other', in a frequency similar to the human voice![29] Healthy cells make a different sound to diseased cells. The suggestion is that soon a sound monitor will be able to diagnose serious illnesses rather than having invasive blood tests and biopsies. Bring that one on!

Blood has its own frequency. The Lord said to Cain, 'Your brother's blood is crying out to me from the ground.'[30] Hebrews 12:24 says that Yeshua's blood 'speaks a better message than Abel's'. The Greek word for 'speaks' means to talk or utter words, to preach. The word that Abel's blood speaks from the ground is revenge. But the blood of Jesus (Yeshua) speaks mercy and forgiveness. The blood of Jesus is a sound that resonates into the earth. (See Chapter 30, 'Sound of the Blood…')

Earth, earth, hear the sound of the blood of the Lamb!
Earth, earth, hear the voice of the Lord!

CHAPTER ELEVEN

Music and the Glory

THERE ARE HISTORICAL EVENTS when heaven and earth have aligned with powerful songs and sounds. We should pay attention to sounds that mark, accompany and even contribute to significant shifts in history. Do not ignore them. When they are from heaven, we should investigate thoroughly, seek to align with them and as much as possible replicate them. When sounds are *not* from heaven, we should quickly discern their source and act accordingly, and where possible remove them or at least declare the decrees found in Chapter 36 "Silencing Babylon…"

There are many significant moments in scripture when the glory of God has aligned with sounds from heaven and music. We will highlight just three: the Ark, Pentecost and the Book of Revelation. Each deserve complete chapters and books![31] But for now, these quick examples are to highlight the alignment between the glory and sound, to whet your appetite, and inspire you to dig deeper into His word.

The Glory, The Ark and Sound

The Lord gave Moses very detailed instructions on how to build a tabernacle with all its dimensions and furniture. These were to be copies of what is in heaven.[32] The Ark of the Covenant was covered with gold. Cherubim were carved and placed on each end. The lid of the Ark is the mercy seat, where in heaven, Jesus placed His pure blood for atonement.[33]

The Ark was a representation of God's awesome presence and *shekinah* glory. It is obvious God cannot be put into a box, though too often we try! The Ark made by Moses was a powerful representation of the Ark in heaven, and it represented God on earth, perhaps like an ambassador does. Reminding Israel of God's holy presence, the earthly Ark was still holy, and thus strict protocols were enforced – Uzzah died when he touched it. When Jesus came to earth in human flesh, He embodied the glory of the Father.

> *And the Word became flesh and dwelt among us, and we beheld His Glory, the glory as of the only begotten of the Father, full of grace and truth. (John 1:14)*

The tragic history of Israel's relationship with God corresponds with what happened to the Ark, including being captured by the Philistines. David became king, and despite his flaws and failure, he loved God and treasured the Ark. Though it took two attempts, King David persevered and he finally brought the Ark into Jerusalem. Both times, the transfer featured songs of praise accompanying its journey. The first attempt, anyone and everyone played their instruments, like a big jam session. (Not unlike many churches!) But when David got the divine order correct at the second attempt, he appointed specific musicians as psalmists to release prophetic songs.

After the Ark arrived in Jerusalem, King David established these prophet psalmists and musicians to minister to the Lord 24/7. This was just a shadow of what was already happening in heaven, as the creatures, angels and elders worshipped and declared the holiness of God day and night.

David established a complete order of inter-generational prophet psalmists. He created four thousand instruments under the inspiration of the Holy Spirit! Historically, these temple musicians are referred to as Levitical guilds.

As long as Israel remained faithful to God, the Ark was central, glorious praises surrounded it and the kingdom of Israel was in peace from her enemies. Right there is a powerful lesson for both Israel and the Church today.

When Solomon built and dedicated the temple, he transferred the Ark from the tabernacle of David into the temple accompanied by a new generation of prophet psalmists. When the shofar players, musicians and singers made one sound to praise the Lord, His Glory fell.

> *... the house of the Lord was filled a cloud, so that the priests could not continue ministering ... for the glory filled the house of God. (2 Chronicles 6:13)*

Pentecost: Sound of Heaven

The day of Pentecost began with a sound that was not manufactured by man. It was sudden and unexpected, an arresting sound from heaven. It grabbed the attention of the disciples in the upper room and the Jews leaving the temple.

> *And **suddenly** there came **a sound from heaven** as of a rushing mighty wind, and it filled all the house where they were sitting. And they were all filled with the Holy Ghost, and began to speak with other tongues ... (Acts 2:2-4)*

It was the Feast of Shavuot, so Jews were visiting from many nations. In the temple, they had just read from the Torah:

> *... as I prophesied, there was a **noise**, and behold a shaking, and the bones came together ... So I*

> *prophesied as He commanded me, and the **breath** came into them, and they lived, and stood up upon their feet, an exceeding great army. (Ezekiel 37:10)*

Imagine the shock or wonderment of the devout Jews leaving the temple. Suddenly they are enveloped by a noise reminiscent of Ezekiel's prophecy! The sound was literally a sign and a wonder to confirm the scriptures just read. God had their attention! This new sound was God's Spirit bringing spiritual breath into the religious dead bones of Israel.

For the disciples in the upper room, Jesus had told them to wait until Holy Spirit came upon them, so they were expecting something to happen. How often do we, too, expect the Holy Spirit to show up, but when He does, it is not always how we expected?

There were two sounds heard that day.

The first sound was from heaven 'like a mighty wind'. The Greek words suggest the sound was a roar of a forceful, violent wind. If you have lived through a hurricane, cyclone or tornado, you know that kind of wind roars like a freight train or jet taking off.

In May 2013, the Lord gave us a little taste of that intense sound. We had been in Jerusalem for the Feast of Shavuot (Pentecost). While in Israel, we joined others to prophetically call forth a new Pentecost in the earth. With a company of apostles, prophets, worshippers and intercessors, we asked the Lord for a fresh wind of the Spirit to pick up where the early Church had left off. A week later, we were asleep in our hotel room at Haifa. Suddenly there was a roar. I was not sure if it was jets scrambling or a strong wind. Being only twenty-five kilometres from the Lebanon border and a bit further to the Syrian border, it is not unusual to hear jets screaming overhead.

CHAPTER ELEVEN

We got up and looked out the window. A single cloud was racing towards our window as the wind howled. Was this a cloud of glory, we wondered. It took all our strength to hold the window closed. There was no damage, but it was a roaring wind, not a wind you could sleep through!

One can only imagine the intensity of the wind of the Spirit blowing at the first Pentecost. It shook centuries of religious strongholds and changed history. This wind had announced and released the extraordinary supernatural event whereby the disciples in the upper room were empowered and transformed by the fullness of the Holy Spirit. Seven flames of fire are before the throne of God, and these represent the seven spirits of God as clarified in Isaiah 11:2.[34] The sound heard was the tongues of fire travelling supersonically from the throne room to the upper room in Jerusalem. Landing on the disciples, they were instantly and supernaturally transformed.

The second sound at Pentecost was from the earth, because of the sound from heaven. The empowered disciples began speaking in tongues. They spoke in the different dialects and languages[35] spoken by the Jews who had travelled from other nations for the Feast. Everyone heard the disciples praising God for His wonderful miracles.[36] Without diverting too much, tongues release perfect praise from man to God. Our human flesh does not gravitate to give God the praise and glory He deserves. Tongues is a heavenly language, bypassing our human frailties and resistances. When whole congregations sing in tongues, I describe it as the most exquisite sound on earth. (See Chapter 31, 'Exquisite Governing Sound: Wait for Weighty Glory?')

Hearing the two sounds from heaven and earth, three thousand astounded Jews from the nations encountered the Lord and were born again. Ezekiel's army began to stand to its feet.

Worship in the Book of Revelation

Amid scary symbols and judgements, the Book of Revelation reveals heaven reverberating with spectacular worship. Revelation 1:3 says there is a *blessing* for everyone who reads the book! I encourage you to read the book of Revelation with fresh eyes. 'Revelation' in Greek is *apokalupsis*, which means to disclose truth, to lift a veil. Yet most people, even Christians, think 'apocalypse' is the destruction of life on earth, fearing demonic exploits. Revelation is actually the *unveiling* of Jesus, the triumphant King of kings – not just timelines, dragons, beasts or anti-Christ!

I would like to suggest the book of Revelation contains more insight into worship that we should aspire to than anywhere else I know. The book is not about the victory of the anti-Christ, but about his defeat!

Firstly, Jesus is revealed in the fullness of His Glory. The sight was so overwhelming John fainted, falling like a dead man. John had been best friends with Jesus on earth. At the Mount of Transfiguration, John witnessed Jesus in a glorious state. Yet this unveiled view of Jesus left him breathless.

> *I would like to suggest the book of Revelation contains more insight into worship that we should aspire to than anywhere else I know.*

After receiving instructions for the seven churches, John is taken up to see the throne room, powerfully described in Revelation 4. The interrelation between worship and the Lord releasing His full authority upon the earth, and wickedness in the spirit realm, all start to be revealed in Revelation 5. John saw all ranks of angels in worship. There are elders with harps and bowls, representing worship and intercession. They also have crowns, representing royalty and ruling. Their songs intermingle with those of angels and creatures and people on the earth.[37]

> *Without stopping day or night they were singing, 'Holy, holy, holy is the Lord God Almighty, who was, who is, and who is coming.' (Revelation 4:8 GW)*

The songs accompanying the opening of the seals will be considered in a later chapter about songs being like a nuclear warhead. But the rest of the book of Revelation reveals a powerful correlation between glorious worship and, simultaneously, God dealing with the wicked. There is a constant interchange between worship and judgements.

Sounds of Heaven on Earth

Jesus taught us in the Lord's prayer:

> *Your kingdom come. Your will be done on earth as it is in heaven. (Matthew 6:10)*

Correct alignment between heaven and earth is not just possible, but Jesus told us to pray for it! When King David successfully brought the Ark into Jerusalem, prophetic songs surrounded the procession. It was an alignment of protocols and sounds of heaven being brought into earth.

On the Day of Atonement (Yom Kippur), Orthodox Jews spend the day fasting and repenting of sin to ensure they are written in the book of life. The next day, they begin to build the booths ready for Feast of Tabernacles. In this way, some see themselves as having been in 'heavenly places' and immediately begin preparations to bring heaven to earth.

In this significant time of history, the Lord is calling the church to come higher, and take our place as His *Ekklesia*; i.e. His governing body on earth. We need to be ready to release

His decrees and songs and thus operate in the dominion given to us in the Garden of Eden. We are not called to be spectators who just try to work out the timeline when it will all be over. No, we are called and given the privilege to be active participants, to call forth His will on earth as it is in heaven.

In the late 1970s, the Lord gave me a vision of Holy Spirit fire spreading throughout the nation of Australia. At the time, I didn't really understand the vision, but I knew that revival started with an ember that Holy Spirit breathed on. I knew that somehow music and worship were intertwined. Since then, the Lord has provided understanding that true worship has an important and central role to play in spreading the Holy Spirit flame. There is something about singing His song in the realms of glory. It is not our song; it is His song. When we sing His song, it should have sounds reminiscent of the Lion and the Lamb. Heaven's decrees and angel armies will respond and be activated.

> *The Holy Spirit is stirring us to echo, replicate and create the atmosphere of heaven on the earth.*

Corporate Anointing

Shofars are sounding, calling the Lord's army on earth to arise. A fresh Pentecost *is* coming to the earth. God is again releasing a sound from heaven. Watch. Listen. Be in position.

The Holy Spirit is stirring us to echo, replicate and create the atmosphere of heaven on the earth. The Lord wants His song released on the earth. His sound is released through *all* His people, not just those skilled in music. Every person carries a unique sound that needs to be heard. There is a sound that can only be released in the earth through *corporate* worship.

Corporate worship is the sound of all the voices of the lovers of God releasing a sound from the Spirit. It is your voice linked with the voices of His people around you. It is a corporate sound, not the sound of a particular worship leader or worship team.

The job of psalmists is to facilitate and guide the corporate praises by providing a solid foundation which enables the whole body to be as one voice. A unique sound comes when skilled, called and anointed prophet psalmists follow the Holy Spirit and can bring everyone with them. This causes a congregation to ascend and soar beyond previous experiences, even of a particular song.

'Sound' does not necessarily need words – it can be a hum or 'ooh', a shofar, a bell, a triangle, a harp string. The sound of the Lord is a tone or frequency that originates in heaven and corresponds with a sound from deep in our spirits.

There is a sound that goes beyond unity, a singular 'one sound'. Such a sound was heard at the dedication of the temple.[38] A 'one sound' comes from submitted, yielded, cleansed and tested hearts. Only then can we authentically amplify adoration and praises to Him.

Such sounds do not belong to any particular culture except the kingdom of God. This sound causes us to rise above wicked sounds. More importantly it releases hosts of heaven to arise on our behalf.

In the midst of great darkness on the earth, and everything being shaken, God has been preparing

> *The vital sounds of this season are to prepare the highway of holiness and accompany the return of the King of Glory – in a way, similar to the Ark being accompanied by prophet psalmists into Jerusalem.*

and starting to release those psalmists and sounds. As we align and engage with heaven, this sound will cause a great roar in the ears of religious establishments, the traditions of man and the enemy. This will shake the dry bones sitting in churches, pubs, bars and clubs. And the light of its sound will shatter kingdoms of darkness in the Middle East and around the globe. The vital sounds of this season are to prepare the highway of holiness and accompany the return of the King of Glory – in a way, similar to the Ark being accompanied by prophet psalmists into Jerusalem.

When the storm raged on Lake Galilee, Jesus lifted His voice to the wind and said, 'Be still.' The authority and sound of His voice subdued the raging enemy. There are storms on earth that need His powerful voice. As His song brought divine order at the beginning of time, so too it will be at the end of time.

CHAPTER TWELVE

Frequencies of the Glory

SCRIPTURE IS FULL OF exhortations about singing, music and sound. Science provides insight into the amazing world of sound. When scripture and science are put together, it builds faith. We may not understand how sound works, and we may even cringe at the sound of our own voice, but when scripture exhorts us to sing His songs, it is for *everyone*, not just those we think of as having a magnificent voice. These things are important to encourage us because the enemy frequently tells us our songs of praise are not achieving anything.

There are two keys to grasp: the frequencies of the glory and sympathetic sound. Though our human knowledge is limited, understanding these natural principles provides insight into the power of anointed sound. Let these encourage you to go beyond prior experience and align with His Glory sounds.

Frequencies of His Glory

Frequencies of the glory are not some spooky New Age concepts. They are real, beautiful and very necessary in this time of great darkness covering the earth.

Every musical note has a measurable frequency. Watch a string vibrate on a guitar, violin or piano. A frequency is literally the number of cycles a string vibrates per second. The higher the pitch, the more cycles per second. The lower the pitch, the fewer cycles per second. The scientific measurement for these frequency cycles is hertz (Hz). The human ear cannot hear every frequency. Angels sing in higher frequencies than we can hear or reproduce. Animals can detect frequencies we cannot. Thunder and lightning have distinct frequencies.

When the anointing of the Holy Spirit touches us and affects our music, the sound changes, as in a corporate worship setting when you detect a shift like changing gears or a plane climbing to a much high altitude. As we align more with the Spirit of God, our sound becomes sweeter and more alive. It penetrates more. One sound engineer I worked with observed the times when the anointing was strong, the sound changed so much it impacted the dials on his mixer and he was limited in what he could do. The pre-service sound check became obsolete!

In the Hebrew language, the Glory of God is described by the word *kabod*. The glory is something that is heavy, weighty, consequential, solemn. The Lord's Glory contains His brightness, beauty, majesty, dignity, order, reputation, the bliss of heaven. It comes with the full weight of the Lord Himself. The glory is the full array of who God is – His lovingkindness, His patience with us, His beauty, majesty and His power. We must treat His Glory with respect. When He came to earth, Jesus revealed the glory of the Father to us.[39]

Frequency of His Voice

The glory has a sound because the Lord Himself has a voice. His voice is often described as light, lightning, thunder, even a trumpet.[40] When God spoke creation into being, He called it forth with the sound of His voice. Light and sound contain different measurable frequencies, as discussed in the earlier chapter.

Though the frequencies of trumpets and light can be measured, scripture comparing the Lord's voice to trumpets and light is using a metaphor. What scientific instrument could ever measure the frequency of the Lord's powerful voice, His breath or His footsteps? When His voice shakes the earth, seismometers can measure earthquakes as the earth shakes in response. However, if He truly roared, our best equipment would not cope – maybe fried!

It is beyond our capability to comprehend or attempt to measure the dynamic range of sound coming from His Glory. The best we can grasp are the scriptures that describe His sound and the consequences of it. Isaiah 40 simply asks if we can compare the Lord to anyone else?[41] Psalm 29 aligns the thundering voice of God with His Glory. His voice is powerful and filled with majesty.

> *The voice of the LORD is over the waters; The God of glory thunders; The voice of the LORD is powerful; The voice of the LORD is full of majesty.* (Psalm 29:3–4)

Other scriptures describe the power of His voice laying bare the foundations of the earth, creating the world, scattering schemes of nations and dealing with the lawless one.

> *Then with **his mighty roar** he laid bare the foundations of the earth ... The hidden depths of land and sea were exposed by the **blast of his hot breath**.* (Psalm 18:15 TPT)

> *By the **word of the LORD** the heavens were made, And all the host of them **by the breath of His mouth**.* (Psalm 33:6 NKJV)

> *With **His breath he scatters the schemes of nations** who oppose him; they will never succeed. (Psalm 33:10 TPT)*

> *And then the lawless one will be revealed, whom the Lord will **consume with the breath of His mouth** and destroy with the **brightness of His coming**. (2 Thessalonians 2:8 NKJV)*

The Lord also has quiet sounds. After running from Jezebel, Elijah heard the Lord's still small voice. This redirected Elijah and got him up out of his cave of depression. The Lord's voice can heal us.

In one of our throne room worship gatherings, we were singing about the Lord being the Creator. One worshipper present was prostrate before the Lord and later shared what occurred.

> *It felt like the frequency of each musical note was moving and resounding through my physical body. The Lord revealed the frequency of the sound of His voice brings healing into our bodies!*[42]

His voice, whether quiet or loud, goes right through us, touching our whole being. It is from Him alone that we receive healing and intervention. Yet this testimony also suggests there was a sound in our worship here on earth that resonated with His voice, and that together, His voice released healing.

Many have indicated the sound of the shofar is also a sound that goes right through their whole being. Imagine what it does when God Himself blows the shofar!

Songs Tuned to the Glory

The psalmist says we should tune our songs to the glory.

> *Sing **your songs tuned to his glory**! Tell the world how wonderful he is. (Psalm 66:2 TPT)*

The New King James version uses the word 'honour', which is the Hebrew word *kabod* as discussed above. How do we get in tune with the glory?

The psalmist suggests we do this by our praises that enunciate His wonderful attributes and works. Our melodies, lyrics and lifestyle give testimony to who Yahweh is.

Some people think we can tune into the glory by finding an exact measurable frequency. I am not convinced we can.[43] But I *am* convinced our hearts and lives need to be tuned to His Glory before we worry about a natural frequency. However, considering how musicians literally tune their instruments is a great example of the process to tune our hearts and songs to His Glory. Like string instruments that are susceptible to lose pitch depending on weather and time, so our hearts can lose pitch by pressures of life, no longer in tune with God's Glory. A tuning fork provides a standard frequency to tune each string; the Lord's plumbline is our tuning fork.

When properly tuned instruments play together, they are in perfect harmony with each other. Instruments not tuned accurately cause dissonance to occur. This is a powerful spiritual principle which Paul alludes to in 1 Corinthians 14:7–8.

Sympathetic Sound

The principle of sympathetic resonance is a well-known phenomenon in physics, mentioned earlier re marching around Jericho. It occurs when a sound produced in one object causes another object to vibrate or make a sound because they have a similar frequency.

Sympathetic sounds, resonances or vibrations are harmonic phenomena of music. They cause sounds to be repeated, prolonged or intensified. When a sound resonates with another sound, it actually increases that sound. When our worship is fully aligned with heaven, it echoes, resonates and provides a sympathetic sound to the worship in heaven. The havoc this sound creates on the enemy is akin to a nuclear weapon! Note that Hebrews 12 calls it 'pure worship'. To be aligned with and seek to replicate the worship of heaven, it must be pure rather than the worldly worship often experienced on earth.

At the right pitch and frequency, a singer can cause glass to shatter. When I play certain notes on the piano, if a nearby snare drum has been left tight, even though it is not being played, it will rattle in time to my playing, like a phantom drummer. String instruments have many techniques that exploit sympathetic sounds; a favourite is called harmonics.[44] In a recording studio, sound technicians seek to identify rogue or offensive frequencies that otherwise create distortion or clashes.

Deaf Student Heard the Trumpet

Rowan was a beautiful Christian teenager who was not only profoundly deaf but had other physical handicaps. Rowan spent most of his time at a school for deaf children, but authorities felt it would be good for him to interact with students without disabilities. He came into my music classes. Sadly, he died quite young, but I was so blessed to meet him, and I will never forget what I learned.

At a school camp, and for a bit of fun, I would wake the students by playing 'Reveille' on my trumpet. I will never forget the day Rowan came running towards with me with great excitement and joy. He yelled, 'I heard the trumpet, I heard the trumpet.' I cannot convey to you my shock nor his excitement!

How could Rowan hear the trumpet when he could not physically hear anything? Though the audiology of his ear could not pick up the sound, his body could feel and hear the vibration from the trumpet frequencies bouncing off the water, the hills around us and the building he had been in.

In a similar way, we can tune our spiritual ears to hear the sounds originating at God's throne. God's voice causes structures (including us) to vibrate and shake. As we hear His sounds and obediently respond to them (worship and prophecies), His sound is amplified. When our worship on earth is in total sync with God's voice speaking from heaven, His message is confirmed, consolidated and reinforced. The right song, sound or word at the right time resonates deeply in the Spirit. This can add to the shaking His sound is already creating.

Echo and Resonate

> *Sing to YAHWEH a brand-new song!* **Sing his praise until it echoes** *from the ends of the earth!* (Isaiah 42:10 TPT)

The Lord is calling us to sing His song until it echoes around the earth. We in Australia, New Zealand and the South Pacific islands are literally at the ends of the earth compared to most of the world's population. This scripture specifically is about a song from the ends of the earth that echoes across the globe and back to Jerusalem. For a song to echo, it needs to reverberate in the spirit realm.

There are certain hills not far from Sydney where, in certain atmospheric conditions, your voice will repeat and repeat as it echoes across the valleys. The Lord is calling forth songs and sounds originating from His throne, through our hearts and mouths, that then echo around the globe.

Where there is resistance to His voice and His songs, as with political, financial and demonic systems, as we repeat the sounds of heaven, our echo and repetition reinforce His sound. When we do this, we are not only encouraged, but our sound echoes and adds to the shaking God is already doing to demonic structures. When His voice and our worship align over a specific target, things shift.

The challenge for us is to hear His voice. Obey His voice. Flow with the Holy Spirit to enable our praises to echo His voice.

When we align with His sound through cleansed hearts and pure worship, the sound produced pierces and shatters unseen realms of darkness. Our songs that are tuned into the glory add to those of heaven and reverberate around the earth.

In the spiritual climate in the world today, there is an urgency for the Body of Christ (Messiah) to leave behind the models of entertainment and press into His pure glory sounds. The earth and all its inhabitants need to hear these sounds.

When we align with His sound through cleansed hearts and pure worship, the sound produced pierces and shatters unseen realms of darkness.

Anna Mendez in Australia: Sound to Shatter Glass

The sound that shatters glass is due to sympathetic sound. This principle was important in a prophetic act done in Australia when Ana Mendez Ferrell (a prophetess from Mexico) came to Melbourne, Australia for the first time, 2–4 August 2013.

The Lord had shown her a maze of mirrors as a stronghold over Melbourne, ruled by the kingdom of darkness. Many building exteriors are made of glass, looking big and glamorous, but this is deceptive. The reality she saw was dark alleys filled with dragons. The Lord gave her insight that the reality behind the fragile façade of glass was dragons. We cannot deal with what is masquerading over our nations unless we deal with the reality of the façade of demonic thrones and religion. If we want a shift, we must be in the reality of truth and in the integrity of the Spirit.

The Lord gave her the strategy for a prophetic act, which was to release the sound of heaven into the structure of Melbourne at a pitch that will break the structure of glass! After sharing all this revelation, we went back into worship. It took a while for the sound to reach the required pitch and intensity for the congregation to reach a oneness of singing in the Spirit in tongues. Once this level of worship was reached, Ana Mendez placed a wine glass inside a cloth and smashed it prophetically.

Ana Mendez said she saw the angel of Melbourne and the angel of Australia. These angels were echoing the sound of worship coming from us in the meeting and it was going out across Australia. This sound was reaching beyond the walls and opening doors in cities and towns right across the nation. She said her husband Emerson had sung in a tongue and she received the interpretation: 'That which was barren will be made green. Life will be brought to the desert.'

The Lord showed her a major key to Australia is the bloodshed on the goldfields. The Lord had my attention with the mention of goldfields, dragons and a sound to break through the façade – this is where I live! Later, I got to meet and share with her, and she gave me a portion of the glass to bury in our city.

How Do We Resonate with Frequencies of His Glory?

How do we engage, align and be in tune with the frequencies of His Glory? His strategies are often simple, though not necessarily easy to implement. Sympathetic sound gives us great insight into how our sounds can align with, be tuned to and echo His sounds.

Producing sounds that resonate with His Glory requires a right condition of our heart, as our lives are transformed to reflect His Glory. It is a work of the Holy Spirit bringing change within us.

> *... And with no veil we all become like mirrors who brightly **reflect the glory of the Lord** Jesus. We are being transfigured into his very image as we move from one brighter level of glory to another. (2 Corinthians 3:18 TPT)*

Where His Glory is, all the fruits of the Spirit are manifested. These reveal His beauty His majesty, His divine order. As our hearts align more with His Glory, I believe our songs can also musically reproduce these features.[45]

Will we be carriers of the glory who accompany and resonate His Glory sounds? Will we align with the Presence of God as Joshua and King David did when they followed the Ark? Or will we be like others in scripture who disobeyed, compromised with other gods around them and soon discovered the severe side of the glory?

Anointed Sound Changes Things!

Regardless of how much or how little you understand of the physics of sound, know this – there is a sound from the Lord that can resonate into the world around us. And a lot of it is to do with your walk and your voice – the voice created *in* you! Tune our lives and songs to His Glory.

Align with Glory: obedience

Approaching Jericho, Joshua had obeyed every instruction from the Lord, including circumcision and celebrating Passover before going to war. They circumnavigated Jericho while carrying the Ark correctly and sounding shofars. At the Lord's command, they shouted to the Lord. Obedience brought alignment between God and man. Only the Lord knows exactly how He responded at that moment. However, I suggest to you, the frequencies of the glory contributed to the shattering of those walls that terrified not just the people of Jericho but many of their neighbouring enemies!

Their obedience and trust honoured the Glory of the Lord, as represented by the Ark. This is a unique and encouraging picture for us. What happens when we obediently worship the Lord in the glory realms during a time of war or great conflict? When we ascend in the Spirit and align our worship with the sound of heaven, we activate the frequencies of glory. It is a weighty sound. It carries His light and life. Tuning into the frequencies of His Glory helps to break discouragement and unbelief.

Align with Glory: honour and trust

One meaning of glory is 'honour'. How we honour the Lord's Glory is really crucial. It becomes even more critical in times of trouble, distress and especially in a time of war with the Lord's enemies.

We are on the precipice of a major confrontation between the glory of the Lord and the gods of this world. There is not really a contest from the Lord's point of view, but it is from our point of view because we are involved. But are we ready?

- Are we prepared to fulfil whatever role He asks of us?
- Are we positioned and ready for the Lord's glory waves to roll in?
- Are we ready for the major confrontation with the gods in our nations?
- Are we ready to flow in the glory sound that terrifies the enemy?

Honour and Sing: in a day of trouble

In a time of trouble, how do we respond? Will we sing His song while eyeballing those intimidatory enemies? When the trials and tests come through the various curve balls of life, how do we honour the glory of the Lord?

> **Honor me by trusting in me in your day of trouble.** *Cry aloud to me, and I will be there to rescue you. (Psalm 50:15 TPT)*

> *I'm left with one conclusion: my only hope is to hope in You alone! (Psalm 39:7b TPT)*

Though it is challenging to trust the Lord in times of great distress, it brings great honour to His name. It gladdens His heart that we recognise and depend on Him as our only hope, refuge, strength and hiding place. Trusting Him in difficult times honours Him and activates supernatural help.

King David realised the safest place in troubled times is not just hide in the Lord's Presence, but to *sing* there. Praises sung from troubled hearts produce a very different sound to ordinary singing. When our hearts are breaking but we still choose to sing, it releases a weighty sound. This song carries conviction, authority and glory. Rote learning cannot produce the authenticity of this sound.

It is not easy to physically sing when you are upset and have a lump in your throat. It is also difficult to choose to sing. But when we make that choice, and even as the tears flow, it is where we find comfort, strength and especially victory and breakthrough amid the fiercest battles.

> *For in the time of trouble He shall hide me in His pavilion; In the secret place of His tabernacle He shall hide me ... And now my head shall be lifted up above my enemies all around me; Therefore I will offer sacrifices of joy in His tabernacle; I will sing, yes, I will sing praises to the LORD. (Psalm 27:5-6)*

Everyone, regardless of their vocal ability, can sing weighty songs in His Presence. This is for *every* lover of God. And the sound coming from the lovers of God hiding in His Presence is so different to those who give in to sorrow and self-pity. It is even more contrasted with those who blame God with fist-pumping rants or who in disappointment turn to other gods.

When our hearts are breaking but we still choose to sing, it releases a weighty sound. This song carries conviction, authority and glory.

The more we become one with Him and allow His transforming work to take us from 'glory to glory', the more we manifest His Glory. To be a carrier of His Glory is totally challenging to our flesh, but an enormous privilege.

CHAPTER THIRTEEN

Heaven's First Worship Leader – Mutiny!

GOD'S INTENTION FOR MUSIC was for it to bless all of creation with His Glory. Earth was meant to have the same atmosphere as heaven – love, joy, peace, harmony, and fruitfulness. It was never the intention of God that music would be used for self-glory, harmful gains or to be set in an environment of destruction. Death was never a part of the original plan. But sin marred all of God's original creation, including music.

Sadly, what was meant to glorify God was stolen for other gods. It began with a huge betrayal by heaven's first worship leader! In this tragic episode we are reminded of the sheer awe, holiness, majesty and power of God.

Discovering the truth about the first worship leader in heaven is shocking and disturbing, but also informative and insightful. It should result in a greater fear of the Lord as we consider the implications and challenges for ourselves.

Perfect Beauty and Skill

He was the most beautiful creature. He was the seal of perfection, filled with wisdom and perfect in beauty. His magnificence was dazzling for he was covered with every precious stone, from diamonds and sapphires to gold. He not only looked beautiful, but he also sounded beautiful, for he was given a unique gift of music.

He was not only a skilled musician, but he was created with music *in* him. This special creature was created with string instruments, flutes or panpipes and tambourines *within* his body! This description can challenge our imaginations. Think of it this way: we too were created with an instrument within us – our voice. With it, we can speak or sing. We simply choose to activate the singing voice; we rarely think about it; we just do it.

In a similar way, heaven's first worship leader was like a walking orchestra, and his instruments were activated by choice. As he moved, music flowed out of him. He communicated with music. Those around him were also beautiful and communicated with music.

This most beautiful and talented one was a cherub.

> *You were the anointed cherub who covers; I established you; You were on the holy mountain of God. (Ezekiel 28:14)*

Cherubs were guardians in Eden, and they flanked God's throne in heaven. Two cherubim guarded the Ark, symbolising their task of covering the throne.

> *And the cherubim shall stretch out their wings above, covering the mercy seat with their wings, and they shall face one another; the faces of the cherubim shall be toward the mercy seat. (Exodus 25:20)*

This anointed cherub dwelt in the holy mountain of God. Who was this beautiful creature? Lucifer.

Created by God, he is described as the son of the morning.[46] Lucifer was close to the throne of God, and in fact as a cherub, his task was to surround or cover the throne.

Was the sound coming out of Lucifer intertwined with his role of covering the throne of the Great and Mighty One? Lucifer's music, and that of other worship angels, was to give glory to the Creator of all things – Elohim, Yahweh, *El Shaddai*, the Holy One. The majestic sounds covered the throne of God day and night. In this way, the One Who created all things was honoured. Such beauty mere mortals can only imagine or hope to hear.

It was entirely God's idea that this beautiful creature was created with music *within* him. Who are we to question or understand the wisdom of God? In His wisdom, God created music as a unique and beautiful vehicle for His Glory. Music is a gift given to mankind to express our love, thanksgiving, praise and worship to our Creator.

Music was God's idea. The atmosphere of heaven resonates with non-stop glorious praise music.

> *The four living creatures... they do not rest day or night, saying: 'Holy, holy, holy, Lord God Almighty, Who was and is and is to come!' ... the twenty-four elders fall down before Him who sits on the throne and worship Him who lives forever and ever, and cast their crowns before the throne, saying: 'You are worthy, O Lord, To receive glory and honor and power; For You created all things ...' (Revelation 4:8, 10–11)*

God intended music to be holy, beautiful and a means for His created beings to express the inexpressible, the greatness, majesty and awesomeness of our God. The atmosphere of heaven is filled with such glorious sounds. Here, there is no curse, sickness, or death. Instead, there are all the fruits of the Spirit, great contentment and beauty. The music of God reflects His character and nature.

Confusing Bible Translations About Lucifer

How do we know Lucifer was the first worship leader, as I have described above? Variations in Bible translations have caused some confusion. We can find the scriptural references for the fall of Lucifer in Ezekiel 28:12-19 and Isaiah 14:12. The key verses about his ministry are in Ezekiel 28:12-14:

> *Thus says the Lord GOD: 'You were the seal of perfection, Full of wisdom and perfect in beauty. You were in Eden, the garden of God;* ***Every precious stone was your covering:*** *The sardius, topaz, and diamond, Beryl, onyx, and jasper, Sapphire, turquoise, and emerald with gold.* ***The workmanship of your timbrels and pipes Was prepared for you on the day you were created.*** *"You were the anointed cherub who covers; I established you; You were on the holy mountain of God; You walked back and forth in the midst of fiery stones.' (Ezekiel 28:12-14 NKJV)*

Yet you can read these same verses, especially Ezekiel 28:13b in other translations and there is no mention of musical instruments, only gemstones and gold settings.

> *... And the gold, the workmanship of your settings and your sockets, Was in you. They were prepared On the day that you were created. (Ezekiel 28:13 AMP)*

Why the discrepancy? Answers are found in the Hebrew words.

Lucifer's Ministry: Musician or High Priest?

The English word 'workmanship' shows that Lucifer had a ministry. Occupation, work, service or ministry are what the Hebrew word *melakah*[47] signifies. The root of the word is *malak*[48] and means messenger or angel. It is to dispatch as a deputy or ambassador for God. So, this person in Ezekiel 28 is an angelic being with a ministry around the throne. Now what was this ministry?

Some translations render Ezekiel 28:13 as 'settings for gemstones', as per the breastplate of the high priest. Other translations render the verse as musical instruments, as in tabrets and pipes, or tambourines and flutes. Let us consider both options.

a. Musical Instruments

The Bibles that translate this verse as 'tabrets and pipes' are the King James, New King James Version, Darby's New Translation, American Standard Version and Interlinear Bible (a direct translation of Hebrew for the Old Testament, and Greek for the New Testament). These render the musical instruments, tabrets and pipes, were prepared for him and *in* him, as per my description above.

> *You have been in Eden the garden of God; every precious stone was your covering ... The workmanship of your tabrets and of your pipes **in** you – in the day you were created, they were prepared. (Ezekiel 28:13 Interlinear Bible)*

According to these translations, Lucifer's created purpose was to exude sound to the Glory of God. Because of Lucifer's position around the throne as a cherub, it signifies his role as a ministry in music and worship – a chief musician.

b. Gemstones

Other translations or paraphrases interpret it as the 'mountings and settings of gold'. These translations are The New International Version, Revised Standard Version, The Amplified, The Living Bible, The Passion Translation and many others. The NIV reads:

> *You were in Eden, the garden of God; every precious stone adorned you: ...* ***Your settings*** *and* ***mountings were made of gold****; on the day you were created they were prepared. (Ezekiel 28:13)*

Musical Instruments or Gold Settings for Gemstones?

Why are all translations not in agreement? Why the apparent contradictory translations? How should we read it? Is it 'tabrets and pipes' (i.e. tambourines and wind instruments) or is it 'gold mountings for gemstones'?

I spoke with a professor of Hebrew at Melbourne University about this dilemma. He told me that the original Hebrew has *both* meanings!

The Hebrew word that is the source of the two different interpretations is *toph*.[49] The root of the word is *taphaph*[50] which means play upon or beat a drum, sound the timbrel or tabret (tambourine). However, it also means 'thy settings and thy sockets', referring to the gemstones.

The professor told me that most commentators say it could be either a musical instrument or the setting for the precious stone. He felt the meaning is not clear; therefore, it needs to be left open to questioning.

If it is 'tabret', then my opening comment about heaven's worship leader is accurate. If it is about gold settings, the gold could apply to other passages which refer to Lucifer losing his position because of his abundance of trading. (Refer to Part Three where gold is used for idols and greed.)

Another Hebrew scholar I spoke with agreed that the word *toph* could be either the musical instruments or a gemstone. However, this person thought in this context, the more accurate translation was 'tabret'.

On the surface, gemstones and musical instruments seem to have no relationship whatever. But do they? As I have spent much time praying and pondering, I wondered if there is also another possibility.

Dualism: Greek or Hebrew thinking? Worship and Intercession

Hebrew thinking is different to Greek thinking. Greek thinking is black and white; it is either this or that. Hebraic thinking is happy to have more than one answer, as revealed by my discussion with the Hebrew Professor. I have learned that the Lord often speaks on several layers at once. How often does the Lord address physical and spiritual issues with one quote?

In all translations, the first part of Ezekiel 28:13 lists nine gemstones which have a close correlation with the sockets of gold and gemstones on the high priest's ephod and the breastplate. The ephod had two gemstones, one on each shoulder, and the breastplate had twelve gemstones, four rows of three stones.[51] Both sets of gemstones were

> *Lucifer, having musical instruments in him as well as priestly gemstones, would explain the fierce opposition and intense warfare for worship and intercession operating together, and for the nation of Israel.*

engraved with the names of the twelve tribes of Israel. These represented the way the high priest would bring the twelve tribes of Israel 'as a memorial' before the Lord in prayer. However, in these verses there are only nine gemstones instead of twelve. I have often pondered on this and wondered if there is some hidden mystery or clue in these verses in regard to the Dragon's rage toward Israel?

Is there a priestly role to the cherub's ministry before the throne? Those translations that interpret the Hebrew as 'settings and mountings of gold' would simply be highlighting the gemstones on the high priest's ephod and breastplate, and only to the ministry of intercession, but without worship.

Is it possible the dualism of this verse, of gemstones *and* musical instruments, is pointing to the ministry of *both* worship and intercession? They almost always intertwine in the throne room. A priestly ministry would wear the gemstones bearing the names of the twelve tribes of Israel on the ephod and in this way intercede for the nation of Israel in the holy place on earth. If the priest also had music *within* him, it would present the duality of ministry, as seen in Revelation where twenty-four elders had both harps and bowls in their hands.

Lucifer, having musical instruments in him as well as priestly gemstones, would explain the fierce opposition and intense warfare for worship and intercession operating together, and for the nation of Israel.

Lucifer's Five-Point Manifesto: 'I Will,' Not 'I Do'

Contrasting the humility and subservience of Jesus saying, 'I do the Father's will', Lucifer did the opposite. Five times he rebelliously stated, 'I will'. He placed his own will above God's. Spoken in the future tense, it is like his mission statement, his manifesto. They reveal his ambitions, intentions, objectives and aims.

From serving God at His throne, Lucifer had a severe demotion.

> *How you are fallen from heaven, O Lucifer, son of the morning! How you are cut down to the ground, You who weakened the nations! (Isaiah 14:12)*

> *By the abundance of your trading You became filled with violence within, And you sinned; Therefore I cast you as a profane thing Out of the mountain of God; And I destroyed you, O covering cherub, From the midst of the fiery stones. (Ezekiel 28:16)*

Lucifer was removed from his place of honour in heaven. His manifesto was not just an idle threat; it weakened the nations of the world! So, what did Lucifer say that could undermine and destabilise nations?

> *For you have said in your heart: 'I will ascend into heaven, I will exalt my throne above the stars of God; I will also sit on the mount of the congregation. On the farthest sides of the north; I will ascend above the heights of the clouds, I will be like the Most High.' Yet you shall be brought down to Sheol, To the lowest depths of the Pit. (Isaiah 14:13–16)*

Each statement pinpoints significant places where God's power, authority and glory are proven. In each statement, Lucifer reveals his pride and rebellion. He thinks he is greater than God! Therefore, he seeks to overthrow or replace God.

1. Heaven: 'I Will Ascend into Heaven'

Lucifer wanted to ascend into heaven. But when he made those statements, he was still in heaven! He was the cherub that protected and covered the throne. His removal from heaven was after he had spoken these words, and the rebellion had taken place. If he is already in heaven, why does he say he will ascend into heaven? Because heaven is God's home.

> *Thus says the LORD: 'Heaven is My throne, And earth is My footstool.' (Isaiah 66:1)*

> *'The LORD has established His throne in heaven, And His kingdom rules over all' (Psalm 11:4)*

Lucifer wanted control of heaven. The desire to ascend is about rising to a higher position in heaven. He doesn't want to be guarding the throne; he wants to be *on* the throne! He is not satisfied with being present in heaven; he wants to be the decision maker, the final authority. He wants things done his way. In other words, he wants to take God's place.

Some words in a beautiful song about Jesus the High Priest are, 'We place You in the highest place'. Songs like this enforce the defeat of Satan's lustful plans.

2. Above the Stars of God: 'I Will Exalt my Throne above the Stars of God'

Lucifer wanted to be known as the Creator! Many cultures have creation stories, often alluding to some form of snake. In Australia, the Indigenous dreamtime creator is a rainbow serpent. In the Garden of Eden, the devil is represented as a snake. The fallen Lucifer continually seeks to convince people that he is the creator who should be worshipped. The false creator is a very strong deception. Western culture has also fallen for the false creator through evolution. Whatever tale or myths are supported, Lucifer's aim is for the throne.

3. Zion: 'I Will also Sit on the Mount of the Congregation. On the Farthest Sides of the North ...'

Psalm 48 identifies Zion as the 'mount of the congregation' with its 'sides of the north'. Zion is the Lord's holy mountain.

> *The city of our God ... is **Mount Zion** on the **sides of the north**, the city of the great King ... (Psalm 48:1-2)*

> *... the LORD has chosen Zion; He has desired it for His dwelling place: 'This is My resting place forever, Here I will dwell.' (Psalm 132:13-14)*

Lucifer wants to sit on his throne in the place where God has chosen to live on earth. King David brought the Ark of the Covenant to Zion and established his tabernacle on Mt Zion. King David ruled from Mt Zion. Solomon built the temple just up the hill from Mt Zion. It is another term for the New Jerusalem.[52] Lucifer is saying he will usurp God from Zion and instead, he will rule from God's chosen city. The place where Jesus said would be a House of Prayer for all nations is what Lucifer wants.

The prophecy over Jesus states:

> *He will be great, and will be called the Son of the Highest; and the Lord God will give Him the **throne** of His father **David**. (Luke 1:32)*

Therefore, Jerusalem is the most fiercely contested piece of real estate on the planet. It is the focal point for every major principality and every major religion. They all want Jerusalem! It is the focal point on earth for major conflict – in history and in the end-times. Hence we are called to pray for the peace of Jerusalem.

4. Clouds: 'I Will Ascend Above the Heights of the Clouds'

Yah is the cloud rider. He rides upon the clouds to help His people.[53] Clouds are the dust of His feet.[54] He sits in the clouds. Clouds often represent His Presence.[55] God's presence in the clouds protected Israel as they left Egypt.[56] Jesus is returning on the clouds. Ezekiel saw the day of the LORD as being 'a day of clouds'.[57] Jesus said, 'They will see the Son of Man coming on the clouds of heaven with power and great glory.'[58]

The major pagan gods like Baal and Zeus are often called the 'cloud rider'; Lucifer wanted to be the cloud rider! Where God is content to be camouflaged in or on the clouds, Lucifer wants to be clearly visible for all to see. He simply wants to outdo God. But he cannot. (More in Chapter 35, 'Ark Defeats Dagon …')

Every eye will see Jesus as He comes on the clouds, and consequently, *all* will tremble when they see Him in His Glory and majesty. Every knee will bow and every tongue will confess Yeshua is Messiah, King of kings.

5. God's Quintessence: 'I Will be Like the Most High'

Although wanting to be like the Most High may sound almost honourable, as believers, you and I should seek to be more like Him and less like our fallen sinful state.

In aspiring to be like God, Lucifer uses the description of the 'Most High'. Ezekiel spoke about 'the day he was created' (Ezekiel 28:13). Lucifer was a created cherub. Lucifer was dissatisfied with his cherub status. He no longer wanted to take orders; he wanted to give them. He wanted the same status, essence and authority as God.

As wonderful and amazing as angels are, they are lower than God. Putting it bluntly, they take orders; they don't give them!

> *Jesus Christ, who has gone into heaven and is at the right hand of God, **angels and authorities and powers having been made subject to Him**.* (1 Peter 3:22)

Tragic End

Although originally perfect, Lucifer became proud. He was no longer content to direct heaven's beautiful songs of praise. He wanted the worship of heaven for himself. His amazing perfection, beauty, musical gift and privileged position were corrupted by pride, selfish ambition, rebellion, greed and covetousness.

The disturbance and anguish in heaven must have been so enormous, it is almost unfathomable for us humans. I know emotion in heaven is handled very differently to emotion on earth. But in various ways, the pain felt on earth today is incomprehensible but the consequences for Israel, for the Church and all nations is a grief every day.

In Part One, I spoke of the tragedy of what occurred in our churches music department. Though it was nothing compared to the chaos created in heaven, the sorrow I experienced gave me a slight inkling of the disturbance in heaven and on the earth when Lucifer fell and tried to steal the sound of glory. It took me years to recover. Only God knows how much earth has been traumatised by Satan's rebellion.

The good news is that God is not defeated by such loss. He is the master craftsman who can take broken pieces and make something new and beautiful out of them. He is into total restoration.

CHAPTER THIRTEEN

Restoring All Things

To restore something means to repair or return it to its original state after it has become ruined, marred or has lost its function.

Years ago, when visiting some friends, I noticed their beautiful antique looking dresser. Laurence remembered a similar piece of furniture was at his family farm. We went looking. We found it in a back shed covered in dirt. Someone had painted it, and it was storing paint cans. After permission from my father-in-law, we brought it home, had the paint removed and restored it to its original beauty. Today, this valuable piece of furniture, a family heirloom, is in our dining room and holds precious dinnerware.

> **The Lord will restore all things.**

All of creation was impacted by the fall, as Biblical history and our own lives testify. Our dresser is a picture of what God is doing for all of creation. Piece by piece, He is restoring each life that is surrendered to Him.

After His ascension, scripture says that Jesus stays in heaven until … until when?

> *For he must remain in heaven **until the restoration of all things** has taken place … (Acts 3:21 TPT)*

Until the restoration of all things. Restoration has a process. Go back two verses; it begins with a response from us – repentance. Repentance precedes refreshment from His presence, then restoration of all things, and then Jesus can return!

> *Repent … so that times of refreshing may come from the presence of the Lord … (Acts 3:19 NKJV)*

> *And he will send you Jesus, the Messiah ... For he must remain in heaven until the restoration of all things has taken place, fulfilling **everything** that God said long ago ... (Acts 3:20, 21 TPT)*

The Lord will restore all things. Everything stolen, devoured or destroyed will be restored. 'And by the blood of his cross, everything in heaven and earth is brought back to Himself – back to its original intent, restored to innocence again!' (Colossians 1:20 TPT).

Restoration began with the Father sending Jesus to earth. He came in humility, in the opposite spirit to which Lucifer left heaven. The death and resurrection of Jesus reinstated fellowship between God and man. Restoration of worship is by His blood granting us entrance to the Holy of Holies and enabling us to worship Him in Spirit and truth.

He created everything and is now in the process of restoring it all. The need to restore true worship, including the musical and artistic components, is because of what happened with heaven's first worship leader, not just what happened that caused him to be evicted but all the damage caused since by his revenge and hatred.

> **To repair the unique and powerful contribution music makes to honouring God, we must consider the Lord's original intent for music**

To repair the unique and powerful contribution music makes to honouring God, we must consider the Lord's original intent for music (and the arts), how we strayed from that and how we can realign with his original purposes. We must let Him do the work required in our hearts.

CHAPTER FOURTEEN

Why Lucifer Had to Go

HOW MANY CHRISTIANS TODAY would want to appease Lucifer and keep him on as worship leader? 'Oh, it's unloving to be rid of him.' Sentimental human love would ask how a loving and merciful God could evict one of his most beautiful creatures from heaven. Could not God just convince him to repent or restore him, instead of preparing flames in hell? Such sentiment does not understand the true nature of God, nor the depth of Lucifer's iniquity.

There are three key reasons why Lucifer was evicted from heaven.

Wanted Top Job of Supreme Ruler

God is the Creator. He will not, and cannot, share His Glory. God has no equal. The Creator is infinitely more powerful, intelligent and creative than those he created. Not one created being can come anywhere near the status of the Creator.

> I am YAHWEH; that is my name. I will **not** give (share) my glory to another god nor my renown to idols. (Isaiah 42:8 TPT)

> Thus says the Lord, the King of Israel, And His Redeemer; the Lord of hosts; 'I am the First and the Last; besides Me there is no God.' (Isaiah 44:6 NKJV)

> *... so my name will not be dishonored. I will **not yield my glory to another**. I am the One and Only, the First and the Last. With my mighty hand I laid the foundation of the earth; with the span of my right hand I spread out the cosmos. And when I speak to them, they both stand at attention. (Isaiah 48:11–13 TPT)*

Moses did not want to share the glory; he just wanted a peek. In response to his prayer, 'Please show me Your glory,'[59] the Lord only allowed Moses to see His goodness, i.e. His back. No man can cope with seeing the fullness of the glory, let alone share in His Glory!

Lucifer wanted the glory and supremacy. Deceived by his own beauty, Lucifer had delusions of grandeur. He was no longer willing to bow and worship God. He wanted it for himself. Instead of being faithful and loving in servitude, Lucifer's heart was filled with pride, greed, and violence, ending in a rebellious coup.[60]

At the cross, Jesus defeated *all* the works of the devil. After His resurrection, God raised Jesus to the highest authority in the heavenly realm.

> *And now he is exalted as **first** above **every** ruler, authority, government, and realm of power in existence! He is gloriously enthroned over every name that is ever praised, not only in this age, but in the age that is coming! (Ephesians 1:20–21 TPT)*

Jesus is King above every king. His throne and name are above all others. Reminding Lucifer, the dragon, serpent, devil of these scriptural truths; these facts make powerful decrees to sing and declare.

CHAPTER FOURTEEN

God is Holy

God does not just do holy things – He is holy. Holiness is as much a part of God's nature as love. There are good reasons angels sing 'holy, holy, holy' rather than 'love, love, love'. Nothing unclean or unholy can survive near His holiness. God does not destroy unclean things because of any sort of contempt or unrighteous anger. The very holy nature of God actually destroys unholy things.

Think of the nature of fire. Put anything flammable in the vicinity of a flame, it burns. The flame is not being subjectively unkind, unloving or hateful towards a particular article. It is the nature of flames to burn flammable items like paper. So too with anything unholy. The blood of Jesus is our fire blanket, our robe of righteousness, to protect our fallen nature from His all-consuming fire. His blood is pure and is the only way we can get safely come near His holy Presence.

In the New Jerusalem, the city of God, what we call heaven, nothing unholy is allowed. It is the home of Yahweh and filled with His majesty and glory. Nothing unholy can safely be in His dwelling place.

> There shall by no means enter it anything that defiles, or causes an abomination or a lie, but only those who are written in the Lamb's Book of Life. (Revelation 21:27 NKJV)

> ... Those not permitted to enter are outside: the malicious hypocrites, the sexually immoral, sorcerers, murderers, idolaters, and every lover of lies. (Revelation 22:15 TPT)

The five 'I will' statements of Lucifer exposed his heart – everything he wanted is forbidden in heaven. Lucifer had to go.

> *Lucifer, the son of the morning was cast out of the mountain of God as a profane thing. (Ezekiel 28:16)*

What a sobering lesson for us. God is holy. Heaven can only be filled with holy things. The music of heaven is holy.

Holiness, walking in the Spirit, and worshipping in Spirit and truth are inseparable. We should ask for a fresh encounter with our most 'Holy, Holy, Holy, God'. As the old song says, as we look into the face of Jesus, 'the things of earth grow strangely dim, in the light of His Glory and grace'.[61] We each need an encounter similar to Isaiah's.

When Isaiah saw the holiness of God, he was undone! Any sense of righteousness disappeared. He realised he had unclean and unholy lips. He saw the unrighteousness around him and was willing to do the will of the Father.[62]

When we look into the holiness of God, we see things as they really are, not how we think they are. Contentious issues dissolve, differences melt and fears are allayed. We bow low. As the world gets darker, the Holy Spirit is wooing us to look afresh into the face of Jesus. All eyes on Jesus, and align with the angelic hosts, singing, 'Holy, Holy, Holy, the Lord God Almighty, Who was and is and is to come' (Revelation 4:8).

Failed Coup, Bitter Usurper

God's law for leprosy was one of separation from the rest of the community. This was not meant to punish the individual. Separation from loved ones was painful. It was essential because the disease was highly infectious and needed to be contained rather than wipe out an entire community. Though tough, it was an act of mercy and love.

Lucifer's attempted coup failed. God is supreme ruler because He *is*, and there is none equivalent to Him. Lucifer sought to usurp the throne of God. He not only rebelled himself, but he led a rebellion within the heavenly hosts. He had to be removed, not only because sin could not survive in heaven but also to stop the spread of rebellion. It was nothing personal, but Lucifer could not stay.

Rebellion and sin are contagious. They easily spread like wildfire. Sin is like a disease that infects with bitterness. We are exhorted to:

> ... *run swiftly toward holiness, for those who are not holy will not see the Lord ... And make sure* **no one lives with a root of bitterness** *sprouting within them which will only cause trouble and* **poison the hearts of many**. *(Hebrews 12:14-15 TPT)*

To avoid bitterness, we must run towards holiness. Bitterness and holiness are opposites.

Some suggest, and I tend to agree, the angels that joined the rebellion were probably worship angels under Lucifer's jurisdiction. The consequences for the ministry of worship are huge. Worship was the one ministry in heaven that was violated and interrupted. This is key when considering the need for music and worship to be restored. Lucifer still seeks to usurp the throne of God – in our hearts, in Israel, in the church – and that is our warfare today. It is especially prevalent over music and worship teams

> **Worship was the one ministry in heaven that was violated and interrupted.**

Jesus and Satan Spar Over Worship

Fallen Lucifer became known as the Satan, which means to attack, accuse, be an adversary, an opponent. Face to face with Jesus in the wilderness, Satan tried to lure Jesus into the 'I will' statements. The devil tried to get Jesus, the Son of God, to bow to him in worship! It was a ludicrous attempt to turn the tables on Who is to be worshipped. Jesus reminded the adversary of Who is to be the subject of all worship: 'You shall worship the Lord your God, and Him only shall you serve' (Luke 4:8).

Later, Jesus revealed the Father's call as He looks for true worshippers in the earth. Speaking to the Samaritan lady, He said:

> But the hour is coming, and now is, when the true worshippers will worship the Father in spirit and truth; for **the Father is seeking such to worship Him**. (John 4:24)

It is God's will for heaven and earth to be filled with true worshippers. But the original plan was disrupted. So, what happened when God expelled Lucifer from heaven and removed him from his role as worship leader?

Worship Music Corrupted and Hijacked

As a result of Lucifer's expulsion, Ezekiel wrote, 'You have become a horror' (Ezekiel 28:18-19). Prior to the five 'I will statements', Isaiah revealed Lucifer as a spiritual King of Babylon,[63] demoted to hell. The Passion Translation makes it clear the underworld is excited to welcome Lucifer.

> ... it rouses the spirits of the dead to greet you! All the former tyrants and despots rise from their thrones! One and all will say to you: 'Look at you! You've become as weak as we are. Now you're just like us!' (Isaiah 14:9-10 TPT)

Pride corrupted and devastated this originally magnificent creature, and his gifting. Pride, rebellion and an attempted to coup in heaven meant he could not stay in heaven; instead, was destined for hell. His music is also cursed.

> *Your pomp is brought down to Sheol, and the sound of your string instruments. The maggot is spread under you and worms cover you. (Isaiah 14:11 KJV)*

These evocative descriptions indicate what has happened to music created by Satan ever since. Maggots and worms eat away at original goodness and beauty. Deterioration, decay and death are all that remain. There is much music on earth today that contains the stench of death, destruction and hell, clearly revealing maggots have eaten away goodness and left a rotting mess. Satan's music is filled with poison. It reflects his character and nature: fear, manipulation, lies, rampant immorality, drug abuse, abortion, divorce, murder, suicide and deadly diseases.

> **Though it was God who created music as a unique gift, and a vessel for God's people to corporately worship the Lord, Lucifer hijacked it.**

God did not intend for man to be subjected to deathly, defiling sounds. Yet these sounds are not only a reflection of Satan's fallen nature and character, but this music is being used by Satan to draw masses into hell with him. Such music is like the front door of the house of the anti-Christ, luring multitudes into his dark kingdom. This is the cosmic battle over worship and the Glory of God.

Music and Worship Stolen for the 'gods': Marx and Cultural Revolution

In a blasphemous turn of events, it is like Lucifer stole the music of heaven for his own benefit and to prop up his own kingdom. Though it was God who created music as a unique gift, and a vessel for God's people to corporately worship the Lord, Lucifer hijacked it. He now uses his music gift to:

1. destroy God's creation, especially mankind
2. seduce those who should be worshipping God to exalt self
3. expand the kingdom of darkness by the worship of Satan and other gods.

With his eviction, Lucifer trashed the heavenly sound, like a spoiled child smashing its toys when it does not get its own way. A spiritual war invaded the earth. Satan wars against God and anything and anyone that contains the stamp of God.

I want to suggest that where Eden was filled with sweet melodies, where there are fingerprints of Satan's corrupted sound, it lacks melody and instead ramps up thumping rhythms.

Marxism: Root of Culture Wars

Chapter 8, 'Music, Marx and Recycling the Gods' explored Marx's attitude and the vision of Marxism. The god behind Marxism, Lucifer, is definitely recycled and returned in the twentieth century. Richard Wurmbrand (recorded in *Tortured for Christ*) experienced the fury of Marxism and communism. He suggested the ultimate aim of communism is not to conquer countries or to establish social or economic systems, but to mock God and praise Satan.

CHAPTER FOURTEEN

> ... [Marxists] hated God in whom they believed. They challenged not His existence but His supremacy. When the revolution broke out in Paris in 1871, the Communist Flourene declared, "Our enemy is God. Hatred of God is the beginning of wisdom."[64]

They believed in God, but they hated Him! They hate His supremacy and reign. The closer it gets to the return and reign of Jesus as king, the more intense is the reaction against God and His people. Regardless of the philosophical tag, the real war is to dethrone Almighty God. French poet Charles Baudelaire wrote, 'Race of Cain, ascend to heaven, And throw God to earth.'[65]

God haters identify with Cain. The first murder in scripture was over worship! God accepted Abel's worship but did not accept Cain's offering of worship. The true worshipper was murdered – let that sink in! The spirit of Cain is in the earth again, and Marxists want it to rule.

Yuval Noah Harari, an influential Israeli historian professor and World Economic Forum advisor, has expressed contempt for religion, especially for the God of his fathers. He suggests the Hebrew God only created organic matter! He suggests we may look back and identify the Covid pandemic as the moment a new regime of surveillance began, especially surveillance under the skin. In 2020, he boasted at the World Economic Forum at its annual meeting in Davos Swtizerland about the capabilities of AI technology.

> In the past, many governments and tyrants wanted to do it, but nobody understood biology well enough and nobody had enough computing power and data to hack millions of people. Neither the Gestapo nor the KGB could do it. But soon at least some corporations and governments will be able

> *to systematically hack all the people. We humans should get used to the idea that we are no longer mysterious souls – we are now hackable animals ... In the coming decades, AI and biotechnology will give us godlike abilities to reengineer life, and even to create completely new life-forms.*[66]

What audacity of man! Psalm 2 comes to mind. Jesus said the devil is the father of lies who seeks to rob, kill and destroy. Being a liar and deceiver is his nature. His music is now used to seduce and destroy. It is the forefront of Western death culture. He knows he has limited time and power, so his anger is intensified, especially against the Body of Christ. But the real church need not fear.

> *The God of peace will soon crush Satan under your feet. (Romans 16:20).*

> *Jesus said, 'I will build my church [Ekklesia], and the gates of hell shall not prevail against it.' (Matthew 16:16)*

Ludicrous Hyper-grace

Did Lucifer really think he could continue leading worship in heaven while leading a rebellion against God? What about us? Saul lost his throne because of rebellion. Do we think we can deliberately sin and God will wink at it? There have been some dangerous teachings circulating the Body of Christ that interpret grace as the condoning of sinful practices, especially sexual ones. Furthermore, there are too many testimonies of witches seeking to infiltrate intercession groups and slither into leading worship. Discernment is desperately needed.

How do we see the lifestyle standards for our worship departments on earth compared with heaven? To answer that question, we must consider the words of Jesus, and the standards of heaven.

In the Lord's prayer, Jesus praying to His Father said, 'Your will be done on earth as it is in heaven.'[67] How often do we pray for the Father's will in heaven be replicated in the earth? And what responsibilities do we have for this?

Jesus said to His disciples that they, the *Ekklesia*, have authority to forbid what is not allowed in heaven.[68] What is forbidden in heaven? Despite what we often do, it is not for us to arbitrarily make up a list of what we can forbid! Rather, the list of forbidden things is clearly stated in Galatians 5:18-21, 1 Corinthians 6:9, 10, Revelation 21:8, 27 and Revelation 22:15. In summary, what is not allowed in heaven is sorcery (drugs, occult, witchcraft), sexual immorality (including pornography and perversion), murder (false testimony, slander, gossip), idolatry, lies, cowardice, unbelief (insincerity), unforgiveness … nothing impure!

How do we compare to the standards in heaven? What about our worship teams? If we are to worship on earth as it is in heaven, do we adhere to these standards of heaven or do we tolerate vile offences against the holiness of God?

Do we really think our worship is honourable if our hearts are in rebellion to Him? Jesus warned not to honour Him with lip service while our hearts are far from Him. He called it vain worship! Such worship is futile because hearts are elsewhere, even compromised with other gods. Mixed worship is serious before God.

We are living in critical times in the history of the world. Pray to discern and understand. Let Holy Spirit reveal any unholy issues that need addressing. We can perish for lack of knowledge. Too easily, we can get caught presuming we are worshipping in Spirit and in truth, when in reality we may be idolaters!

CHAPTER FIFTEEN

Battle For Worship

THERE IS BOTH A war *for* worship, and a war fought *through* worship. Worship is both what the enemy wants to destroy, and also what defeats him! The enemy's goal is to divert our devotion and pollute our sound, but true worship realigns our hearts to God's throne and releases His sound and authority into the battle. Though there is a battle over worship, the battle is won through worship.

Root of all Battles: Lucifer's Eviction

Scratch deep enough and you discover that the root of every war, whether on earth or in the heavens above, is ultimately a battle over worship. From Lucifer's fall to historical wars and divisions, today's culture wars and especially the end-time battle, the question persists: who will we bow to – God the Creator, or Satan the deceiver?

Beginning with his expulsion from heaven, Lucifer's rage targets God's image bearers. He targets those who represent God on earth – Jews and Christians. He especially targets worshippers.

Satan's delusion drives him to compete for what belongs to the Creator alone. It is no contest, but over millenia, there have been too many casualties. God alone is worthy of worship; Satan demands worship. God desires fellowship;

Satan demands servitude. This ancient battle underpins all conflict, but the outcome is certain – God prevails.

Light Vs Darkness

Light and darkness are natural phenomena measured in frequencies, but they are also spiritual entities. Jesus is the light of the world. Lucifer, whose name means 'light bearer', is called an angel of light. Jesus is the true light. Lucifer was originally supposed to reflect the true light, just like the moon reflects the sun. But his light turned to darkness, and he now manifests as a counterfeit angel of light to deceive as many as possible.

After God called forth light at creation, He separated the light from darkness. Light eliminates darkness.

> *And God saw the light as pleasing and beautiful; he used the light to **dispel** the darkness. (Genesis 1:4 TPT)*

Amid spiritual battles, it is powerful to sing and decree 'let there be light', and ask the Lord to again separate the light from darkness. Jesus, the light, frees us from the kingdom of darkness.

> *He has delivered us from the **power of darkness** and conveyed us into the kingdom of the Son of His love ... (Colossians 1:13 NKJV)*

One reason for the war over worship is that light is both a sound, and it is God Himself. To win this battle, it is essential for our worship to be filled with His Prescence, and in tune with His Glory light.

Revenge, Jealousy, Anger, Hatred

Lucifer's story is a stark warning. Gifted with beauty and a role as heaven's worship leader, he wasn't content. His jealousy and pride fuelled a rebellious desire for more, turning servitude into a vitriolic, murderous plot. His fall from heaven shows the destructive power of unchecked emotions like jealousy and covetousness, which can spiral into rage and revenge.

How often do we feel dissatisfied with our God-given gifts, appearance or circumstances? We may see our looks, abilities or roles as inadequate, echoing Lucifer's discontent. His eviction from heaven cost him his position as a covering angel and worship leader, leaving a void. Similarly, when we lose a job, possessions or relationships, emotions like rejection or envy can surface, threatening to derail us.

The story of Cain and Abel illustrates this further. Their conflict arose over worship – whose offering God accepted or rejected.[69] Cain's jealousy and sense of rejection led to murder, costing him his destiny. God warned Cain to master his emotions, but he failed. This shows that worship, when driven by fleshly motives, can be *rejected* by God. Jesus cautioned when He spoke of vain worship, honouring God with lips while hearts are distant from Him (Matthew 15:7-9).

Bitter jealousy fuelled the religious leaders to betray Jesus, handing Him to the Roman authorities to be crucified.[70] James warns us to guard against bitter jealousy lurking in our hearts.[71] Paul says jealousy comes about by comparing ourselves with others and leads to strife and division.[72] Proverbs warns jealousy can rot our bones; some translations say cancer![73]

Jealousy can be especially true for those with unique gifts – either against them or towards others. This is especially true for musicians, singers and worship leaders, where envy over talent can breed division. Left unchecked, these emotions can undermine true worship and lead to spiritual consequences.

There are jokes about the artistic temperament. But overcoming these issues is no laughing matter.

Your Voice: Vacancy in Heaven's Worship Department

When Lucifer, heaven's worship leader, was cast out, did a vacancy open in the heavenly choir? Revelation shows myriads of angels and the redeemed from all nations filling heaven with worship.[74] The call of the Spirit is for us to join this chorus and to echo heaven's sound. Our highest praises and deepest worship impact the whole spirit realm.

> *I will praise You with my whole heart;* **before the gods** *I will* **sing praises to You.** *(Psalm 138:1)*

Hearing the redeemed sing to the worthy Lamb, and joining the angelic choirs he once led, Lucifer and his cohort's rage with jealousy. Sitting in dust and ashes, Lucifer is angry with God and jealous of his victims as they get delivered, transformed by the blood of the Lamb and fill his vacated space.

Obedient lovers of God produce a unique and exquisite sound that Lucifer once helped to produce. As the sound of worship grows, rising like incense, it glorifies God and provokes Satan's fury. As your praises rise to heaven, they remind Lucifer of his past and future, fuelling his fury.

> **As your praises rise to heaven, they remind Lucifer of his past and future, fuelling his fury.**

True worship faces fierce contention because it disrupts Lucifer's schemes and exalts the Lamb of God. Lucifer knows what pure heavenly worship sounds like, its effectiveness, and what is needed to produce it. Therefore, he intentionally targets those things to shut them down.

Your Voice: DNA and Identity

Your voice, like your fingerprints, carries your unique DNA and identity. Your voice is a powerful gift from God. The enemy seeks to silence it, especially in praise, using lies to make you doubt its value. Many feel embarrassed by their voice, often because of harsh words from authority figures like parents or teachers – 'Your voice is terrible'. Words like this can lodge deeply, especially in the heart of a child, remaining for a lifetime. Or maybe it's straight from the enemy into your mind. Wherever they originate, agreement with lies about our voice is damaging.

In Chapter 1, 'Mum's Canaries to Global Landmines', I spoke of a workshop to teach folk to sing scripture. We discovered deep wounds requiring prayer to break curses spoken against their voices. To reclaim your voice:

1. forgive those who spoke negatively.
2. break agreement with lies, recognising them as curses, and bring them to the cross, where Jesus became the curse for us.
3. give thanks to the Father for your unique voice and use it to praise Him.
4. remember, your voice in worship can drown out Satan's lies!
5. persist in prayer to heal emotional scars and secure your identity in the One who created you.[75]

God created Lucifer with built-in instruments – flutes, tambourines, strings – but within mankind, He placed a voice! Our voices are our instruments of praise. Your voice, with its unique timbre, is *exactly* right for you, designed by Father for His choir, not to win acclaim or competitions. When the voices of the lovers of God unite in His praises, the corporate sound is like the cluster of grapes, rich unique flavour not found anywhere else.

This sound is powerful to align with the glory, shift darkness and bring glorious victory. Hence this is a battleground. Lucifer's bitter jealousy targets worshippers who would dare to replace him. There is special venom for your voice, and for worship leaders and psalmists who unite God's people in song. Revelation 12:11 reminds us to be overcomers.

> *And they **overcame him by the blood of the Lamb** and by the word of their testimony, and they did not love their lives to the death. (Revelation 12:11)*

Apply the blood of the Lamb over every attack on your voice or worship gifts. The blood of Jesus has a sound. When you sing of His blood, your voice aligns with heaven, reminding Satan of his defeat and enforcing victory through praise.

Overcoming Sabotage

If the saints have impenetrable spiritual weapons, how can the devil sabotage our worship? True worship is one of the most potent weapons in the spiritual arsenal, fiercely targeted by the enemy through sabotage, deception, division and counterfeits.

Military forces guard their arsenal under tight security. Personnel undergo strict and disciplined training, with stock accountability being paramount. The spiritual army must be wiser in protecting the gift of worship. There have been too many casualties in worship ministries. In one situation, a leader pleaded with me, having recognised they had insufficient intercessors as armour bearers. In another instance, when I enquired about prayer backing for the person, I got a strange look as if they did not know what I was talking about, or I had asked an inappropriate question.

Sometimes casualties occur due to:

- insufficient prayer support
- ignorance or denial of the battle for worship
- mishandling of spiritual weapons through presumption or lack of training
- using worship for our own benefit instead of for His

It is easy to point the finger, criticise and take offence. The enemy will use whoever he can to help destroy ministries and callings. Will we listen to gossip and add fuel to demonic fires, or will we contend in prayer instead?

To overcome demonic sabotage:

1. Recognise worship's power

Lucifer, a roaring lion, seeks to discredit and devour worshippers, especially those with great anointing (1 Peter 5:8). We must understand the weapon that worship is. We must reject the lie that worship is trivial or the battle won effortlessly. We must reject 'Christian ease' which says, 'Jesus won the battle. Done. I don't have to do anything. Sing a song. Done.'

> *We must reject the lie that worship is trivial or the battle won effortlessly.*

Jesus' victory empowers us, but we must enforce it over our calling and unresolved issues. And we must not be afraid of the enemy but be assured of whose we are.

2. Strengthen prayer support

Worship attracts spiritual warfare. Contention in the spirit realm can operate during worship itself. Worship teams need intercessors as armour bearers to discern and counter enemy tactics, both in daily life and during meetings.

3. Embrace accountability

Worshippers need trusted confidants for sharing struggles and to pray through healing for deep wounds or generational curses. Jesus defeated Satan because there was nothing in the soul of Jesus that the ruler of darkness could hook into and legally accuse Jesus. There was no dirt in him to exploit.

> *I won't speak with you much longer, for the ruler of this dark world is coming. But he has no power over me, for he has **nothing to use against me**. (John 14:30 TPT)*
>
> *... **nothing in Me**. (John 14:30 NKJV)*

The battle for true worship is won as our hearts bow in awe of the Creator, and through the blood of the Lamb, arise in holiness. We overcome sabotage as we bow in awe of Him and choose gratitude to overflow into musical and artistic expressions; worshipping 'in the beauty of holiness'.

Four Lies That Deceive and Undermine Worship

To restore true worship, we must expose the lies that weaken and contaminate it. From Eden to the wilderness, the devil has always twisted God's words to deceive us. Jesus overcame by answering with the Word – and so must we.

In my journey, I've identified four key distortions that subtly corrupt worship. They often sound reasonable but are incomplete truths or just excuses to justify questionable music.

1. Music is neutral
This suggests any music can be used for worship, ignoring its origins or spiritual impact.

2. Focus on lyrics
It is right to want lyrics to be scripturally accurate. However, this argument quietly embraces the neutral argument and dismisses what music itself carries. Ignoring the music itself removes the call to prophesy through instruments and its benefits to body, soul and spirit.

3. The right heart
Absolutely, the heart of the musician and songwriter must be right with God. However, some ministries claim that as long as the heart is right, the music doesn't matter. This reasoning quietly embraces the lie that music is neutral. Scripture warns that 'the heart is deceitful above all things'. The danger with deception is that we rarely recognise it. A right heart is vital, but only when it is continually being transformed by the Holy Spirit through repentance, healing and deliverance. Assuming our hearts are right simply because we are 'saved' is faulty. Only God truly knows the heart.

4. Stages replace altars
If music is neutral and God's will for heavenly worship is ignored, churches are turned into entertainment venues like disco halls, and stages replace altars of true worship.

In the next three chapters, I will examine three of the lies with scientific data, testimonies and scripture to uncover the truth of God's design.

CHAPTER SIXTEEN

Why Music: Divine Mystique or Neutral?

MANY PEOPLE RESPONSIBLE FOR making choices of Christian music, worship leaders, pastors, Christian media, those hosting Christian events would evaluate their choice of songs based predominantly on the lyrics. For many people, the music is not so relevant so long as they *like* it. People seldom understand that music itself also carries a message. For this reason, since the 1980s, many have embraced secular music with the rationale to attract non-believers. Leaders have justified the use of worldly genres, rationalising that music is neutral or amoral. Sadly, some also denied the possibility that demonic realms could impact Christian music itself so long as there were scriptural words present. On this basis, some dubious music was okayed for the church.

What is Music? Please Explain!

Is music just a neutral object, explained only by structure and form, or is it an unexplainable mystery? What about aesthetics, beauty, emotional and especially spiritual connections?

> 'For two thousand years, philosophers have tried to solve the mystery of music ...'[76]

Great thinkers, from Plato to Jordan Peterson, have concluded that the mystery of music almost defies explanation. Each of them has tried. Some of their quotes are in this chapter. Peterson turned his thoughts into a geometric 4D piece of art that includes the spiritual dimension. He called it *The meaning of music*.

German composer Robert Schumann made a stark observation about the origin of music:

> In **no other field** is the proof of the fundamentals as **difficult as it is in music**. Science uses mathematics and logic, to poetry belongs the decisive, golden word; other arts have taken nature, whose art forms they borrow as an arbiter. Music, however, **is a poor orphan** whose father and mother no one can name ...[77]

A poor orphan? Hardly! But many have subscribed to that notion; hence, our need to emphasise that music bears the Creator's fingerprints. If its origins elude us, is it because society recoils from God as Creator of music? Is music rationalised as neutral, amoral and powerless as a way to demean and camouflage its real potency?

Mystical, Unique Gift of Creation

Encapsulating Chapter 9, 'Music at Creation', Yahweh, Elohim, the Creator of heaven and earth, is the source of all things, including music. It is *from* Him *to* Him and *through* Him. Music is a gift from loving Father.

In its pure form, music radiates Him. Without demonic or fleshy interference, music intersects with His voice, beauty and joy. It carries the frequencies of His Glory and a part of His light.

His voice manifests the glory. It is not just a sound, a frequency, a timbre, a pitch or certain words. His voice embodies who He is and carries His love, majesty, authority, beauty and creativity. His voice and our voices carry DNA and identity. Anointed music connects us to His Glory, enabling us to hear His voice. Anointed sound sparkles with eternity. It is a mystery difficult to quantify with words.

There is a certain tension because music is mystical, yet it is also accessible to every human. In addition, it has a unique unifying capability when we align with others to play in an orchestra, sing in a choir or congregation or dance to its rhythm.

> *Anointed music connects us to His Glory, enabling us to hear His voice. Anointed sound sparkles with eternity.*

Yet increasingly, society denies or seeks to remove the Creator from life. Modernism and postmodernism have tried to shut down beauty in music and reduce it to form and genres. But God is raising up some unexpected voices to call us back to appreciate the Lord's magnificence in sound. Despite great darkness, there is hope.

Chaos to Order: His Glory, Voice and Music

In a dream, I heard the Lord speak emphatically: 'The Glory sets things in order.' His Glory brought divine order to creation, turning chaos into functional beauty, through the sound of His voice.

> *Chaos once challenged you ... Yet at the **sound of your voice** they were all stilled by your might. What a majestic King ... (Psalm 93:3–4)*

The glory sets in order – broken bodies, hearts and creation. The Father's heart of love establishes order in orphan hearts. The glory sets in order broken relationships and chaos from hate and dysfunction.

Glory (Hebrew: *kabod*), God's weighty fullness, fills heaven with non-stop thunderous worship. Creation's majesty – roaring oceans, starlit skies – evokes awe, revealing the Creator's order.

How does music correlate with the glory? As mentioned before, I taught my students that music is organised sound, echoing the *Harvard Dictionary of Music*: 'the art of collecting and combining sounds into a pattern pleasing to the ear'.[78]

Is there some connection between the glory setting things in order and music being ordered sound? Order belongs to both. They contain sequence, pattern, creativity, beauty and functional structures, all given by the Creator's command.

Since the fall, not all music is from the glory, but when music is orderly and anointed by the Holy Spirit, there is a heavenly inspired beauty. Anointed music flows in His river and releases His eternal glory – sounds to inspire believers and assist in activating voices in praise.

Has the Church Lost Music's Mystique?

From antiquity to modernity, philosophers have grappled with music's mystery, *never* deeming it neutral. Yet, in the late 1980s, I was stunned when church leaders, despite affirming God as Creator, claimed music is just genre and form – neutral (from the Latin *neuter*, meaning 'neither'.) Ironically, today's sharpest minds, often sympathetic to Christianity, celebrate music's divine mystique, while some Christian leaders strip it of sacred power. Has the church forgotten the Creator's design, reducing His gift to mere structure?

Why does this matter? In Babylon, Israel hung up their harps. The atmosphere of Babylon stifled the Lord's song. Since God removed Lucifer from his position in heaven, worship music has been a battleground. Reducing music to form and genre and removing its divine origins effectively denies the Creator and separates the glory from music and sound. This is an attempt to stifle the authority of the Lord's song. Yet today's world desperately needs His authority in sound.

Music's Purpose and Power: Awaken Souls and Shift Atmospheres

If music is neutral and has no unique properties, why do we use it for advertising, films and waiting rooms, and why is the music industry one of the wealthiest? The essence of music is that it can uniquely move us, spiritually, physically, socially, psychologically. It has the capability of touching something deep inside of us. Dr Howard Hanson, Professor of Music and former director of the Eastman School of Music, University of Rochester says:

> *Music is a curiously subtle art ... It is made up of many ingredients and, according to the proportions of these components, it can be soothing or invigorating, ennobling or vulgarizing, philosophical or orgiastic. It has powers for evil as well as for good.*[79]

Who among us has not felt moved when listening to stirring music? If music is neither positive or negative, why spend money and time to listen to it? Prayer meetings can be dry, hard work without the flow of prophetic song.

At award ceremonies, athletes weep as their national anthem resounds, the music and national flag weaving joy and pride into an unforgettable moment. Without music, reciting lyrics alone falls flat. Why does even secular music stir emotions so deeply?

I'm acutely aware of music's power – good and evil – whether in concerts or everyday settings like shopping centres. Lyrics are not always needed; instrumental music alone can move us profoundly. And music wields heaven's glory or hell's darkness. Here are four examples:

1. At a Melbourne Symphony Orchestra concert, a purely instrumental piece, despite flawless musicianship, felt intently evil.[80] An icy chill gripped me, urging me to flee the oppressive sound. No lyrics – just the music created that dark atmosphere. Evil was tangible and creepy.

2. Mahler's Second Symphony, *The Resurrection*, performed by a doubled orchestra, brass band and double choirs, overwhelmed me. At its glorious crescendo, I physically felt pushed back in my seat. Mahler, born Jewish, baptised Catholic, believed in the Creator and the resurrection. As the music concluded, the auditorium fell silent in awe – there was a reverential hush. A friend said the choir director, overwhelmed, got drunk post-performance. I concluded he was unable to process the music's divine power without knowing God personally.

3. Vile, thumping music invaded our neighbourhood day and night for months. Its low frequencies made me want to move house. The perpetrator's mistreatment became personal. The Lord gave me revelation of a very strong witchcraft assignment at work. With advice and agreement from a trusted pastor, we prayed to forbid it, per Matthew 16's authority, and the person soon left the neighbourhood. This reveals

music's spiritual battleground, and our need to step into our God-given authority.

4. Handel's *Messiah* at Melbourne Town Hall was electrifying. It was the most extraordinary rendition I have ever heard. During the 'Hallelujah Chorus', I was standing as per custom. I felt as if heaven was open, as Handel reportedly saw while composing it. The anointed music lifted my heart bursting in praise, wondering if this was how the Rapture would begin!

Dr Jordan Peterson: Music the Highest Form of Art

Across various lectures and interviews, Dr Jordan Peterson expressed his belief that music has a deeper impact on individuals and society than we realise. His comments are insightful and helpful in an age when respect for God has diminished. He sees the arts as an expression of the eternal, even of the kingdom of God! Peterson believes music is 'an imperishable art' that plays a powerful role in our culture because it speaks meaning to us whether we understand it or not – and it is beyond rational critique.[81]

Music is not random, like evolutionists say about humans and earth. Music has a structure based on many patterns, as per all of creation. Without order, there is chaos and no recognition of the Creator. Speaking with Joe Rogan, Dr Peterson said:

> *Music is layered patterns. These patterns have a harmonious interplay and represent the patterns of the world. It is something we need in the modern age.*[82]

When you violate God's order within creation, there is anarchy in society. The responsibility of the Church and worship team is to reflect our Creator's order and structure in music.

Showing Dr Oz his office and artwork, Dr Peterson described the layered geometric art he produced to describe the meaning of music.[83]

> *[Music] is like layered geometric forms. It is a struggle between ideology and realism ... Music is the **most** representational art form, rather than the least ... Music moves out from the void toward us, and represents the structure of experience itself. Music cannot be destroyed by rational criticism or critique. Something we need in the modern age.*

If even vicious critics cannot destroy music, then it must contain a powerful eternal substance. Peterson advocates the arts even express the kingdom of God. No wonder they flourish in the Church when encouraged.

In another podcast, Peterson says:

> *Music represents a harmonious and ideal society. In a nihilistic and atheistic society, music fills the void left by the death of God! Music speaks to you of meaning. It is difficult to transform meaning into articulated explanation. **The role of artists is to articulate the unknown.** No matter how cynical you are, you cannot toss it aside.*[84]

When society says no to God, music subtly reminds us of His Presence!

What a profound statement. Read it again!

When society says no to God, music subtly reminds us of His Presence! Effectively, Peterson says artists help bring understanding of unseen realms of the supernatural and of the kingdom of God. It is reminiscent of Romans 1:20 where creation causes us to perceive the Lord's invisible attributes.

> *For since the creation of the world His invisible attributes are clearly seen ... even His eternal power* **and** *Godhead, so that* **they are without excuse** *... (Romans 1:20)*

Biblically, music starts and ends with God. In a conversation with Douglas Murray, Dr Peterson discussed the importance of aesthetics and beauty as represented by music and the arts including literature, poetry, the fine arts.

> **Murray:** *'A beautiful thing is not just beautiful; it is telling you something. Therefore, you must change your life.'*
>
> **Peterson:** *'That is why people are terrified of beauty. They are terrified in proportion to the distance your life is from what is beautiful. Because it is a judge. It exposes your own life.'*[85]

Modernism and postmodernism reduce art to form, stripping away divine beauty. A godless society becomes an empty shell. Beauty in music or art can convict painfully, leading some to reject God rather than accept His judgement.

Historical Views on Music

Philosophers of antiquity believed music had its origins in the state, the universe or in God. The 17th century considered music and the arts as expressions of human temperament, passion and mood.[86]

- Pythagoras (550 BC) explained music as the expression of that universal harmony which is also realised in arithmetic and astronomy.
- Plato (400 BC): music seemed the best way for social and political education.
- Plotinus (d. 270 BC): interpreted music as a mystic and occult power.
- Kepler (1571-1630): correlated musical sounds with movements of the planets.
- Leibnitz (1646-1716): music is an unconscious exercise in arithmetic.
- A. Schopenhauer (1788-1860): considered music the purest recitation of the will and the expression of human feelings (love, joy, horror) in their abstract interpretation as metaphysical ideas.
- H. Kretzschmar: a German musicologist (1848-1924), saw music as a language which although it had less clarity than words, had finer shades and deeper effects than ordinary speech.

Modernism and Postmodernism[87]

Modernism, also called liberalism and secularism, approximately covers the period of the 20th century which included two world wars, the Holocaust and recessions. Some, like Jews after the Holocaust, felt abandoned by God. 20th century music reflected the pain of the earth.

Denying divine beauty is easier than wrestling with inexplicable pain. Reducing music to neutral form, stripped of sacredness, mirrors this trauma, reflecting inner voids rather than celebrating God's glory. Sometimes the arts reflect inner trauma rather than celebrating sheer beauty! Reducing music to a neutral, amoral, structure would be much easier to handle emotionally.

People sought an ideal world of utopia in rational thought, Eastern mysticism and Marxism. God was dead and creation was replaced by evolution.

As Europe struggled to rebuild, Western society increased in rebellion against authority. Music became influenced by hedonism, drugs and the occult. Morality regarding sexuality affected the church. Lawlessness surged as people became more sceptical and suspicious of reason as individual truth replaced God's truth.

> ... postmodernism broke the established rules about style, it introduced a new era of freedom and a sense that 'anything goes'.[88]

Heart Vs Postmodern Straitjacket

At university, studying composition under a renowned Australian classical composer, I unknowingly collided with modernism and postmodernism. My early compositions were deemed 'too romantic', clashing with a 20th-century ethos that shunned emotion and beauty for form and structure. As an evangelical from Melbourne's heartland, this was jarring. I faced a choice: abandon the course or conform. I chose to endure, reducing composition to an intellectual exercise. Serial[89] and electronic music, with their rigid scales and limited notes, stifled the creativity God stirred in my soul. When classes ended, my postmodern straitjacket was removed and I freely and joyfully resumed writing songs to the Lord from my heart.

1980s Church Mantra: Music is Neutral

Encountering postmodernism at university in the 1970s was unsurprising, but its echo in the church by the late 1980s was disturbing. Some argued music was neutral, amoral, without inherent power, like a gun wielded for good or evil based on the musician or lyrics. This view, tied to genre and taste, justified adopting rock and other secular styles in worship, reshaping it dramatically. Demonic influences even crept into worship teams (a topic for Volume 2).

This remains a strong mindset in the church, influencing criteria for worship music. Is this belief a way of justifying desires and avoiding scrutiny? If music is not part of the cosmic war, and music is neutral, then Christians are free to use whatever music they want. Their own desires become the criteria.

> *If music has no benefit to you, try living without it for a day or two.*

Neutral implies no movement forward or backward. A car in neutral idles, unmoved, regardless of fuel or driver. In electricity, neutral is neither positive nor negative; in conflict, it's impartiality. How does your experience of music fit this definition? Does music leave you unmoved?

Try removing music from your life, as I challenged my students. If music has no benefit to you, stop downloading tracks. Try living without it for a day or two. If music is neutral, why invest time and money in it? No one, Christian nor secular, suggests abolishing music. The music industry, Christian and secular, thrives as one of the wealthiest sectors.

CHAPTER SIXTEEN

'Houston, We Have a Problem' – What, With the Creator?

Calling music neutral denies God's creative design, ignoring its power to reveal the divine. When people struggle with God as Creator, some turn to humanism, evolution or atheism, crafting alternative narratives. Many ancient cultures even claim a snake as creator! Yet, Psalm 2 reveals the absurdity:

> *Look at how the power brokers of the world rise up ... as the rulers scheme and confer together **against YAHWEH** and his Anointed King, saying: 'Let's come together and **break away from the Creator** ... God-Enthroned merely laughs at them ...'(Psalm 2:2–4 TPT)*

It is clearly prideful rebellion against God's sovereignty and their own lust for power. Romans 1:19–20 (TPT) affirms

> *... the truth of God is known instinctively, for God has embedded this knowledge inside **every** human heart ... **seeing the visible makes us understand the invisible.** So then, this leaves everyone without excuse. (Romans 1:19–20 TPT)*

Creation, including music, unveils the spiritual realm, leaving us accountable to God. For the church, this means we are responsible to honour His gift of music and recognise our responsibility to steward it carefully for worship and revelation. Denying this accountability risks muting God's voice in our midst.

Living in a regional area, I marvel at star-filled skies and the Milky Way. Such a view brings reality and perspective to our place in the universe.

> *Lift up your eyes to the sky and see for yourself. Who do you think created the cosmos? He lit every shining star and formed every glowing galaxy, and stationed them all where they belong. He has numbered, counted, and given each one a name. They shine because of God's incredible power and awesome might; not one fails to appear!* (Isaiah 40:26 TPT)

Such awe of the Creator sparks true worship, humbling pride and reveals His vast love.

Conflict of Christians Advocating Music is Neutral

Calling music neutral denies the Creator. But most Christians believe God is the Creator. So how do these contradictions fit together? The contradiction deepens when we call music neutral, yet at the same time expect it to draw the unsaved or usher us into His Presence in worship.

How can music be powerless yet stir souls towards the Lord? These positions cannot coexist. Music cannot be stationary and able to move us at the same time.

Denying the Creator's purpose for music diminishes a powerful gift full of His Glory, which releases His authority and shifts atmospheres from havoc to order. What leads a Christian to suggest music is neutral? It is a way of justifying our own desires. Three influences stand out:

1. *Postmodernism's impact*

Has postmodernism affected the church? Likely. Metamorphic reshaping of society over decades has had a definitive influence.

2. Resisting call to crucify flesh

Christians do not reject creation per se. Rather, recognising music as God's creation demands accountability. Claiming it is neutral justifies using it to indulge the flesh. If we like music because it stirs up our flesh, it is easier to say it has no power rather than deny the flesh being stirred up. Some argue redemption also sanctifies the sound, yet sanctification is a lifelong process. Junk in our trunk taints our music. We must choose – our way or the cross?

3. Denying demonic influence

Some Christians struggle to accept that demons can affect believers, especially worship teams. Denying this possibility avoids accountability, as it's easier to dismiss the devil's access to our sound than to confront it with courage and close the door to the enemy. It is also easier to deny the devil's influence on the relationship between music and culture than confront the evil he brings.

There is a fourth influence, to be considered in the next chapter. When we consider songs without words, we discover the power of music through instrumental prophecy, songs of deliverance and healing.

CHAPTER SEVENTEEN

Songs Without Words: Prophesy on Your Instrument!

CONCLUDING THE LAST CHAPTER, we considered why some people oscillate between the belief that music can move us but simultaneously be neutral. We identified confusion from postmodernism, our flesh and the denial of demonic influence on music. Now I want to present a fourth reason – and this has to do with instrumental prophetic songs when there are no words.

Criteria for Evaluating Worship Music: Lyrics or Music?

Most people evaluate worship music by the lyrics. Of course, sound, Bible-based lyrics are essential. But what about the *music* that carries the lyrics? Do we evaluate songs by the actual music, or do we lack understanding of the power and language of music? Hosea says God's people are 'destroyed for lack of knowledge' (Hosea 4:6).

It could be an attitude that words are more important than the music. Or maybe critiquing music is more difficult, especially as it is often subjective – and everyone has their own opinion! (See Chapter 27 'Our Sacred Cows')

Music and words are like a good marriage – they must not be unequally yoked but a divine match! (Volume 4 will explore how music reflects the character of God.)

Music Breaks Open Dark Sayings

The writings of King David give us extraordinary insight into the Lord's DNA embedded in music.

> *I will incline my ear to a proverb; I will **disclose my dark saying** on the **harp**. (Psalm 49:4 NKJV)*

> *I will **break open mysteries with my music**, and my song will release riddles solved. (Psalm 49:4 TPT)*

Dark sayings and proverbs are the mysteries of the wisdom of God. Music breaks these open. Music goes deep into the eternal realm and releases things way beyond words. That is why we often call it 'songs without words'.

When the Church does not understand or ignores the potential of music, we are missing out on important wisdom and revelation from God. In this time of cosmic war, we need His insight and revelation more than ever. If we fail to embrace music as a conduit for divine revelation, are we omitting a powerful gift from the Lord needed to outwit the enemy?

If we fail to embrace music as a conduit for divine revelation, are we omitting a powerful gift from the Lord needed to outwit the enemy?

Music, like words, can be good or evil, and powerfully so. The only reason that music has power is because God made it that way.

Without the understanding that music itself contains a message, we can never ascend to prophesy on our instruments as King David exhorted.

Prophesy Without Words – How?

After he brought the Ark into Jerusalem, King David established the tabernacle. To prepare for building the temple, he organised the priests, Levites and musicians. Three worship teams were established under Asaph, Heman and Jeduthun. They were appointed to prophesy on their *instruments.*

> *Moreover, David and the captains of the army **separated** for the service some of the sons of Asaph, of Heman, and of Jeduthun,* **who should prophesy with harps, stringed instruments, and cymbals.**
> (1 Chronicles 25:1)

Reading these passages in my Green Bible was both enthralling and scary. It sounded wonderful. I could feel the tug of the Holy Spirit. A sung prophecy with words is tricky enough, but without words? The idea of prophesying was scary enough, but prophesying on a piano, harp, violin, guitar or cymbals on an instrument? This was a real stretch. I saw it in scripture but had never seen it in practice.

I remember sharing this revelation with the music team, both the insight and the fearful challenge of going into such unknown. Yet, the Lord had prepared me in what may seem a bizarre way. Sometimes while practising Beethoven or Liszt, I would get tired, lose concentration, and mentally wander. I began to improvise and create something entirely new. It was a bit like being transported somewhere else and keeping on creating music in the same flow! After a while, it was like awakening out of a dream and I'd go back to playing the music Beethoven and Liszt had written.

Years later, we were in our home group meeting. During worship, I felt the creativity of the Holy Spirit come upon me. As everyone else finished singing in the Spirit, I kept playing. There was a new piece of music bubbling up from deep in my spirit, which I created spontaneously. When I had finished, a lady in the group who often prophesied gave an interpretation to the music I had played. She said, 'This is the word of the Lord you just played on the piano …'

> **This is the word of the Lord you just played on the piano ...**

I was totally shocked. I had not sung any words; it was piano playing only. I don't remember the specific word spoken. But for me, the vital realisation was I had just prophesied on the piano! It felt supernaturally natural, even normal. It was not weird. It was just I had not seen it modelled before. Nor had anyone taught me, explained it or highlighted the scripture. It was just the Lord who had trained me. It was not 'jamming' or improvisation but a brand new song.

Exploring Realms of Spirit and Sound

I had discovered what it meant to prophesy on my instrument with no words being sung. The interpretation simply revealed what the Holy Spirit was doing in that moment. As I played, the Holy Spirit had moved, as Psalm 49:4 says, breaking open 'the mysteries of the Spirit' through music.

Sometimes the Lord's ministry to our soul surpasses words, embedding truths too deep for speech. Like a national anthem at a medal ceremony, music stirs beyond what lyrics alone can achieve. Yet, the church has barely tapped into this divine gift and potential. Have we truly pursued music that 'releases riddles solved' (Psalm 49:4 TPT)?

We must empower young musicians to explore this realm. While some churches encourage prophetic singing, they also need to foster instrumental prophecy. The starting place is learning to flow musically in the Spirit. Creating new spontaneous songs is the foundation of instrumental prophecy and demands skill, faith, and bold encouragement. This is what David appointed the temple musicians to do. Neglecting this causes a void, a gaping hole in our worship.

> *Sometimes the Lord's ministry to our soul surpasses words, embedding truths too deep for speech.*

Have we tried too hard to emulate secular music for worship because we have undervalued music's spiritual power and failed to cultivate prophetic, wordless songs? Anointed musicians, created in the Creator's image, should produce vibrant music that can shift atmospheres by tapping into the mind of the One who shaped creation. Yet rigid mindsets and bondage to the clock often shackle our freedom to explore the realms of Spirit and sound.

Music to Release Prophets

Israel had many prophets. When Jehoshaphat, King of Judah, saw Israel was about to be attacked by Moab, he called Elisha to bring the word of the Lord. Elisha first called for a musician. He needed the anointing of the prophetic psalmist to stir up the gift and help him hear what the Holy Spirit was saying.

> *Elisha said, 'Now bring me a musician', And it happened, when the musician played, that the word of the Lord came upon him and he said, 'Thus says the Lord …' (2 Kings 3:15)*

Anointed musicians will release prophets, prophetic words, intercession, artwork, dance and visions, or the 'dark sayings'. When the clock, church frameworks or old mindsets do ***not*** restrict our worship times, the Holy Spirit will take us on a powerful and creative prophetic journey.

When there is a crisis, we must rise above the noise of the enemy. Anointed music is the environment of heaven. Prophetic music and worship help us quickly ascend into the realms of glory to hear how heaven is responding to the situation. Anointed psalmists will either create a prophetic word without words or can stimulate and facilitate spoken or sung prophecy. They may flow together or from one to the other.

I do not know how this all works, except that it is powerful and defies the notion that somehow music could be neutral with no influence or ability to move us. We need to tap into the mysteries of God through prophetic music, even *without* words.

Schools of the Prophets Included Psalmists

It was not an unusual thing for Elisha to call on a musician. Samuel had begun a school of prophets[90], which Elijah and Elisha continued. These schools existed in Bethel, Jericho and Gilgal. Musicians belonged to the prophetic company. Music and prophecy have a long Biblical connection.

In the flourishing of the prophetic today, where are the prophet psalmists? Why are they not included? Too often, we gather and end up with a talk fest, and prophetic worship is squeezed out. I witnessed this at a major conference. Delegates were given the 'option' to attend worship, which was in a back room! And we wonder why we lack insight and power!

Prophetic Atmospheres Transform

When Samuel anointed King Saul, he told him that he would meet up with some prophets and musicians who would be prophesying.

> *Then the spirit of the Lord will come upon you and you will prophesy with them and be **turned into another man.**" (1 Samuel 10:5–6)*

After this occurred, people asked if Saul had become one of the prophets! Knowing the end of his story, that seems astonishing. The point is, Saul was affected by the mantle of the prophets and prophet psalmists. It changed his character enough to fulfil his calling as king. Even though he had a tragic end, he served as the Lord's anointed.

I have seen people come into the atmosphere of prophetic worship who are delivered, healed and transformed. Not all have become all the Lord intended; nevertheless, they have shifted significantly after having encounters with the Lord in the atmosphere of prophetic worship.

Songs of Deliverance

Late 2008, we had booked to pass through Bangkok airport enroute to Phuket for a worship conference. Bangkok was experiencing violent protests, that spilled out to the large international airport. After bombs went off, the unthinkable happened – the main Bangkok airport shut down! We looked at alternative travel, but we both felt the Lord say, 'No plan B!' So I prayed at the piano. Suddenly I began to sing and play: 'Open up the gates, open up the gates of praise. Open up the gates, open up the gates. Open up the gates to the King of glory. Open up the gates, open up the gates to the King of praise!' Each day I sat at the piano; it was a test of faith. I continued to sing, 'Open up the gates …'

CHAPTER SEVENTEEN

Bangkok airport reopened the day before our flight. I have never seen that airport sooo quiet! Amazingly, as we went through customs, an officer was concerned about our shofars. Were they really musical instruments? One of our team proved it by blowing it. Brian strategically blew the shofar in the major gateway into Asia! 'Open up the gates', a song of deliverance, has been sung in many different nations![91]

> *You are my hiding place; You shall preserve me from trouble; You shall surround me with* **songs of deliverance.** *(Psalm 32:7)*

After the Spirit of God departed from King Saul, the Lord sent a distressing spirit to trouble him. Saul's servants sought a skilled harp player to calm him. It must have been general knowledge that music could be an effective healing agent. David, the young shepherd psalmist, played his harp. It worked until fits of jealousy and rage rose up, and Saul started chucking spears at David. The Lord released songs of deliverance, for both David and Saul.

Even non-Christians cite David's harp as the earliest music therapy, a recognised profession today that uses music to heal mental, emotional or physical ailments. If the world values this, how much more should the Church?

Anointed music has the power to liberate individuals from demonic bondages and sicknesses. I have witnessed this during worship. Without people being specifically prayed for, I have frequently seen people being delivered of severe demonic oppression. There is a sound that not only soothes a troubled soul but displaces the evil entity that has brought confusion and distress.

When we have experienced severe warfare, pushing through in praise has kept us sane; the Lord gave us songs of deliverance. I believe the church has a vast untapped resource in this area. As God's people learn to really worship the Lord, lives are touched and transformed. Can such effect be labelled neutral?

The word of the Lord can come through Elisha's voice, modern prophets or anointed songs. They all require at times a heavenly sound in music, which the church has not always comprehended or embraced. How we need the prophetic sound today.

Can Anointed Music Help Society?

One of my nephews was born prematurely because his mum had pre-eclampsia. After much trauma, they both made it home. I had just released my first instrumental album, *Be Still*. The only way they could get the baby to feed properly, and for him and his sister to get to sleep, was to play my instrumental music over them.

Is there something God has placed within music that touches us not just spiritually but also psychologically and physically? Has He wired us to respond to His creative sounds? What if prophetic worship can touch the rest of society as it changed Saul? Does prophetic music and the arts have a capacity to shape society positively, or are we happy to allow secular musicians to reflect and affect society's existing values?

Philosophers note music's societal impact, and scientific research increasingly shows its profound effects on the brain – spiritually, physically, physiologically and socially – proving music is far from neutral.

Sociological Effects of Music: Education, Politics and Culture

Before modern technology, music primarily reflected society's values, with composers like Bach often only gaining fame posthumously. Today, with the internet, music can reach global audiences instantly, actively shaping societal beliefs and values rather than just mirroring them.

Art, architecture, and music both mirror and influence culture. A new building in our city, designed to look like it's collapsing, reflects a crumbling society. Climate fears and rising immorality signal a society in decline, crying out for revival. No wonder Gen Z males are flocking towards the Lord.

Aristotle believed music shapes character, a view echoed in ancient Greece where music and gymnastics were as vital as reading and writing.

I witnessed this firsthand in 1980–81 while teaching music at a government school. Tasked with streaming new students by musical ability, I assessed them and passed the data to the class coordinator. We formed three music classes and three non-music classes to increase the effectiveness of the music program. The unintended result was striking: music classes were filled with obedient, high-achieving students who excelled in English, maths and physical education. In contrast, non-music classes had disruptive, poorly behaved students who struggled academically and lacked coordination. This unplanned outcome vividly demonstrated music's profound impact on character and academic success. I also had regular phone calls from parents wanting their children shifted into a music class.

Music can shape the core of society for good or evil.

- Plato noted in *The Laws*, '… styles of music are never disturbed without affecting the most important political institutions.'[92]
- Richard Wagner purposely used opera to fuel revolution; his anti-Semitic works inspired Hitler.

- Vladimir Lenin claimed, 'One quick way to destroy a society is through its music.'
- At the 1946 'Arts as a Weapon' symposium in New York, communist leaders like William Foster and Dalton Trumbo declared art a revolutionary tool. J Edgar Hoover observed, *'The war between communism and the free world is not fought with bombs ... the greatest concentration of Communist workers has been found in three fields – education, union, entertainment.'*
- David Noebel's *The Marxist Minstrels* argues communists use music to create neurotic, unstable youth.[93] Jerry Rubin in *Do It!* stated, *'Rock n' roll marked the beginning of the revolution ... We've combined youth, music, sex, drugs and rebellion with treason – and that's a combination hard to beat.'*[94]

Since the 20th century, music reflecting godless ideologies – evolution, humanism, consumerism, hedonism – has fed anxiety and hopelessness. When music shapes these values, it endangers society's spiritual and emotional health.

Physiological

> *Sensitivity to beauty and the making of beauty comprise one of man's most distinguishing characteristics. Without beauty man is ... sick or handicapped. The use of music for man's health, happiness, and comfort is universal. This universal need is not ephemeral – it is a physiological component of man's well-being.*[95]

We all respond to music, some more than others. Often, we are not conscious of our responses – some are spontaneous; others just a reflex.

Advances in technology and neuroscience have helped identify our physical responses:

1. Beat response: people unconsciously nod their heads or tap their feet to music's rhythm.

2. Vital signs: breathing and heart rate shift with tempo changes, affecting blood circulation.

3. Eye reactions: eyelid and pupil movements adjust to musical dynamics.

4. Nervous system: Music can heighten tension or induce relaxation. Abrupt volume, pitch, or speed shifts overstimulate nerves, potentially causing pain or digestive issues, even triggering seizures in prone individuals.

5. Muscle action: Rhythmic music stimulates movement, aiding productivity in factories or gyms and helping those with physical disabilities. Dr John Diamond found heavy rock music reduces muscle strength by two-thirds in ninety per cent of listeners, worsened by high decibels, and overstimulation causes collapse.[96]

6. Chemical balance: low bass and driving rhythms boost adrenaline and sex hormones, depleting brain blood sugar and impairing decision making.

7. Hearing damage: the inner ear regulates posture, muscle tone, breathing, heartbeat, blood pressure, nausea and eye reflexes.[97] Sounds over 85dB, like at rock concerts (120–140dB), risk deafness compared to orchestras (80dB) or conversations (70dB). The physiological impact of extreme volume such as loud drumming in rituals, like Moloch ceremonies, numbs

pain and induces exhaustion or possession, overloading the nervous system.[98]
8. Brain rhythms: Andrew Neher's 1962 study found bass-heavy drumming drives brain alpha rhythms, triggering trances or convulsions without ear damage.[99]

Neuroscience Reveals Music's Effect on Brain

Neuroscience reveals music's impact on the brain. A special sized cello has even been developed to fit inside an MRI to measure a musician's brain while they play music!

Dr Ellen Winner notes:

> *There are about five different areas where the brains of musicians are larger structurally, but we don't know if they were born that way or if that's growth because of all the use and development.*[100]

TED Ed reports:

> *Neuroscientists have observed musicians' brains while they play hooked to EEGs and seen vibrant activity in the visual cortex, as well as the auditory and motor cortices ... Music-making engages both halves of the brain equally ... musicians build a strong corpus callosum ... As a result, musicians are more likely to be inventive problem-solvers.*[101]

The Music and The Brain Foundation (2014) advocates music for brain disorder treatment.[102] Daniel J Levitin's 2017 book, *This is Your Brain on Music*, states, 'Music is fundamental to our species, perhaps even *more* so than *language*.'[103]

Though music is considered a 'language', the essential nature of music to humanity could be more vital than language. That is a huge call!

Music contributes significantly to brain plasticity. To play an instrument activates the parts of the brain involved in memory, listening, language, fine motor skills and many more. Reports of music's effect on humans, water, plants, and animals are confirmed and measurable with modern research. Before such technology, Dorothy Retallack's 1973 book, *The Sound of Music and Plants*, documented experiments at Temple Buell College showing plants exposed to devotional music flourished, leaning towards speakers, while classical music plants grew moderately, and rock music plants shrivelled and died.[104]

In 2004, Dr Masaru Emoto's *Hidden Messages in Water* used high-speed photography to capture water crystals responding to words and music. The human body is around sixty per cent water, and we depend on water for life. His hypothesis is that water responds to positive or negative words and hence our bodies. Though not fully scientific, his work is interesting, though having inferences of New Age.[105]

For all the positive examples, there are also many negative ones where music has been used by the occult and also by the military in war zones.

Colonel Aquino, a Satanist, in articles on music that kills, describes a Russian multi-wave oscillator exciting biological levels, noting: 'An independent researcher ... reports that everything went black and he had to break off the experiment so as not to lose consciousness'. He adds that binaural beats, where 'the perception of such a beat can disorient an individual and render him, or her, highly suggestible'.[106]

In other words, musical rhythms can be employed to deliberately manipulate people, even society!

Psychological

In nearly all cultures, music and religion go hand in hand as a defence against fear and aloneness ...

> *Its peculiar quality also seems to make it a fit means to reach or influence that which is thought to be supernatural.*[107]

Nowhere do we see a more positive or powerful effect of music than in the Bible and in the Christian Church.

Music profoundly impacts the mind and spirit, blending psychological and spiritual effects. It shapes emotions, thoughts and behaviours, helping combat fear and loneliness. Music reduces stress and anxiety, as seen in doctors' waiting rooms or supermarkets where it relaxes shoppers to boost sales.

I've witnessed music aid recovery from fatigue syndrome, car accident injuries and nerve issues. Singing from our congregation comforted hospitalised friends. When our two-year-old suffered ear pain, softly singing 'Jesus loves me' calmed her instantly. Music also expresses joy and celebration, inspiring jubilation.

Conversely, music can evoke fear, as in the movie *Jaws*, where ominous tones signal danger despite a calm visual. If music were neutral, it could not achieve this. Filmmakers and advertisers lucratively exploit music's power to convey fear, sensuality, success or sadness, manipulating emotions and choices.

Satan, aware of music's divine power in God's kingdom, perverts it to subtly infiltrate the Church by promoting the lie that music is neutral. By corrupting this sacred tool, he aims to weaken the saints, hinder God's unleashed power and build an anti-Christ kingdom and apostate church. Christians must discern music's spiritual impact, reject deception and restore true worship to unleash God's glory against the enemy's schemes.

CHAPTER SEVENTEEN

Response to God's Mercy: Holy Living and Worship

In Romans 9–11, Paul summarises the unique calls of Gentiles and Jews. Immediately in Chapter 12, he asks, what is the appropriate response to the Lord's mercies to Jew or Gentile? His answer?

> ... *to surrender yourselves to God to be his sacred, living sacrifices. And* **live in holiness** ... *For* **this becomes your genuine expression of worship. Stop imitating the ideals and opinions of the culture around you,** *but be inwardly transformed by the Holy Spirit through a total reformation of how you think. (Romans 12:1–2 TPT)*

The loving mercies of God are eternal and undeserved. Our response should be:

- surrendered holy lives expressed in genuine worship
- not imitating the values and opinions of the culture around us
- allowing the Holy Spirit to transform us.

Be brave to ask the Holy Spirit of understanding of where you may have embraced the ideals, opinions and even music of the culture.

As we appreciate what music can do, allow the Holy Spirit's transformation in our soul to seep into our music. Can we allow His blood and His Spirit, both of which have a voice and breath, to flow into our musical expressions? Such praise distinguishes God-inhabited music from music under Satan's influence. Music is never neutral, but to be beneficial, it hinges on His holy presence.

CHAPTER EIGHTEEN

When Entertainment Supplants His Glory

Father's Sorrow: Lightweight Worship

IN A DREAM IN early 2024, I heard and felt the Lord's anguish and heartbreak. In the dream, He said that too much worship from His people is superficial, shallow, lightweight entertainment. And it broke His heart. As I awoke, I was overwhelmed by His sorrow, even grief.

As I pondered, the *weight* of this became clear: entertainment entertains man but is lightweight. By contrast, true worship is about the glory, and the glory, *kabod*, is *heavy*.

Entertainment is without depth or deep roots. It is superficial, shallow, limited, frivolous. Entertainment seems real or important, but it doesn't last. For God's people, giving a mere appearance of worship but lacking substance is lightweight entertainment that prioritises the present over eternity.

True worship leads to character transformation as deep calls to deep. Psalm 1 contrasts those who follow God's ways and those who do not. Deep rooted folks are contrasted with those that are like chaff – lightweight and blown by wind.

> *He will be standing firm like a flourishing tree planted by God's design,* **deeply rooted** *by the*

brooks of bliss, bearing fruit in every season of life. He is never dry, never fainting, ever blessed, ever prosperous. But how different are the wicked. They are like chaff blown away by the wind. (Psalm 1:3–4 TPT)

The *Merriam-Webster Dictionary* defines entertainment as 'an amusement or diversion provided especially by performers'. Basically, entertainment is an activity or performance that provides pleasure, a distraction, diversion, play, mirth, recreation, gratification, fun, a good time.

In a time of war, musicians entertain the troops to give them a light-hearted reprieve or distraction from the horrors. However, entertainment, like alcohol, only provide temporary relief, they do not resolve PTSD or take out any enemies.

Remember, the Lord spoke in the dream about entertainment-based worship.

Kabod: Weight of Glory

While entertainment is lightweight, the glory of God is heavy, and it is about His honour. The Hebrew word *kabod* is from the root word *kabed*, and *Strong's Concordance* says it is used two hundred times in scripture.

Dr Annechiena Sneller-Vrolijk writes:

> *The Hebrew verb כבד 'kabed' which – starting from a basic meaning of 'being heavy or weighty' – has the meaning of: to honor, to deem respectful, to deem high. As a noun, 'kabod' has two aspects of meaning: First, 'kabod' can be translated as: weight, strength, power, ability. Second, 'kabod' means honor, glory, magnificence, dignity, splendor.*

> *In this second aspect of meaning, 'kabod' occurs mainly with regard to the Lord God Himself, his Divinity, Word, his name, works, sanctuary, and city.*[108]

Kabod is used to describe the full sum of who God is. It signifies His reputation. The One who created the heavens and the earth and sustains it by His word is definitely weighty! It also refers to His abundant riches. Often the word is linked with worship, calling for us to give Him reverence and honour. After all, worship is about our response to who He is.

> *Give unto the LORD the glory due to His name; Worship the LORD in the beauty of holiness.*
> *(Psalm 29:2)*

We used this scripture on the logo of our ministry for the first edition of this book. The exhortation to give glory to the Lord is this Hebrew word, *kabod*. The way we honour His name and character is to worship in the beauty of holiness. True worship is weighty; entertainment is lightweight.

If *kabod* is aligned with true worship and gives all glory and honour to the Lord, then what does entertainment do? It grieves the Lord – and may I suggest, dishonours Him.

This understanding of the superficiality of entertainment fits with my disquiet at university about developing musical skills just to entertain people.

Show me a scripture that encourages entertainment in worship and I will revoke this book. Is the golden calf incident the Biblical version of our contemporary entertainment? If so, the consequences before God are serious.

Stages or Altars?

Has the Lord called us to build altars or stages? Are we called to enter nightclubs or the Holy of Holies? Study scripture and the answer is obvious. Perhaps we need a harsh reality to see through a fog of deception and confusion.

Stages are about us; altars are about God. Building an altar of the Lord is a selfless act. Reality is, stages are selfish. Church activities based on stages must meet our needs, wants and comforts.

> *Stages are about us; altars are about God.*

Scripture is clear that altars are places of worship to the Lord. Done righteously, the Lord's name and blessing are on those places where altars are raised. But there are conditions how to build the Lord's altar – and it is the opposite of building stages! The instructions to Moses say:

> *An altar of earth you shall make for Me, and you shall **sacrifice** on it your burnt offerings and your peace offerings ... In **every place** where I **record My** name I will come to you, and I will bless you. And if you **make Me an altar of stone**, you shall not build it of hewn stone; for if you use your tool on it, you have profaned it. Nor shall you go up by steps to My altar, that your nakedness may not be exposed on it. (Exodus 20:24–26)*

First, altars are places where sacrifices are to be offered to the Lord. When an altar is pleasing to Him, He says He will place His name in that place and release blessing.

Altars were made with stones. To shape them to size, man-made tools are forbidden. In the New Testament, *we* are the living stones, and we are to offer sacrifices of praise through our lips.[109] As living stones, we must not use man-made processes or tools to prepare ourselves for worship. Such contributions would cause the altar to be defiled! It is the work of

Holy Spirit alone to shape, mould and place us into position for His altar of worship.

> *... you also, as living stones, are being built up a spiritual house, a holy priesthood, to offer up spiritual sacrifices acceptable to God through Jesus Christ ... But you are a chosen generation, a royal priesthood, a holy nation, His own special people, that you may* **proclaim the praises of Him** *who called you out of darkness into His marvelous light.* (1 Peter 2:5, 9)

The last requirement for the altar in Exodus 20 is that it must not have steps to go higher than the ground. Stages have steps – altars do not. Sometimes churches use one or two steps to make viewing easier. That is different from platforms that are about giving people a prime or influential position. The Lord warns about putting steps on altars. He says that would cause the worshipper to be 'exposed'. Figuratively, the Hebrew word means to be disgraced, shamed, expose improper behaviour, to be unclean. This is serious.

Stages cause man to go higher and be the focus. Pride goes up, whereas humility means going lower. How many times are stages of entertainment, even within God's house, exposed because of shameful and ungodly behaviour?

The Lord requires sacrifices to be offered on altars. Hebrews 13:15 reminds us the sacrifices today are the fruit of our lips, to give thanks. The psalmist too links altars of worship with songs.

> *When I* **come to your altar***, YAHWEH ... approaching* **with songs of thanksgiving***, singing songs of your mighty miracles.* (Psalm 26:6–7 TPT)

CHAPTER EIGHTEEN

> *... I will come closer to **your very altar** ... I will praise you with the **harp that plays in my heart to you** ... my magnificent God! (Psalm 43:4 TPT)*

The Lord's response to altars of worship is to record His name and to bless that place.[110] He does not place His name on stages, only on altars!

Raise Up Altars of True Worship Above Strongholds

As related in Chapter 5, 'Don't Touch the Ark! My steep learning curve', our personal call in a city renowned for gold and dragons and many other idols is to raise up an altar of true worship above all the strongholds. This understanding of His raising up His altar is not only our current ministry mandate, but it also came after we had witnessed the devastation of stages replacing altars. There is such a big difference between stages and altars – there is no comparison. True worship is only found on altars, not stages.

> *True worship is only found on altars, not stages.*

Night Club or Holy of Holies?

Are we committed to hosting the Presence of the Lord as per the Holy of Holies, or are we more likely to replicate a night club with stages?

Fog machines are a poor and blasphemous imitation of the smoke of incense that arises from the combination of intercession and worship at the altar of incense. The detail about how the ingredients for godly incense is collected and put together is a large subject for elsewhere. But it is all about sanctification and brokenness before the Lord.

Drum cages (perspex screens around drums) are loved by sound engineers to get a cleaner sound by stopping any bleed spilling into the mix. Personally, I detest them for musical and spiritual reasons. A drum cage separates the drummer from the rest of the worship team. Prophetic worship requires a strong physical and spiritual connection to see and hear what each other is doing. Separation of physical space places a barrier between the worship team members and limits the creative expression between them. Unity is vital, musically and spiritually. The perspex surround disconnects and separates a drummer from the rest of the team. In my opinion, this stifles Holy Spirit creativity and contributes to poor musicianship.

> *It is critical to have an anointed drummer who can pick up the heartbeat of the Father, not just establish the beat of a song.*

Without a drum cage, a musician has to play with restraint and discipline rather than bashing the skins. It is critical to have an *anointed* drummer who can pick up the heartbeat of the Father, not just establish the beat of a song.

Theatrical lighting is a terrible counterfeit to the true light of God. After the launch of the first edition of this book, we noticed a church trend was to paint their walls black, cover windows with black curtains, and then install theatrical lights. The phrase 'lights, camera, action' comes to mind. Many consider it easier to control the environment for filming. What is the message of black walls and coloured lights?

Contrast this with the lighting of the tabernacle or temple. In the outer court, the lighting is natural from the sun, moon or stars. In the holy place, the lighting is from the seven-branched *menorah*. Priests trimmed the wicks daily to ensure the lamp kept burning. Fresh oil of Holy Spirit is needed each day to keep the lights burning. In Revelation 1, Jesus stands in the middle of the *menorah*, symbolising the seven churches mentioned in Revelation 2-3.

The Holy of Holies is an enclosed space, with *no* lighting – well, none that man can contribute towards! The only light is the *shekinah* glory. Man cannot safely enter there without following strict protocol. The only safe way for us to enter is by the blood of Jesus. The mercy seat on the Ark holds His blood. His blood speaks, is life and is powerful.[111]

Jesus is the true light-revealing the glory of the Father.[112]

The Holy of Holies is dependent upon the Presence and Glory of God being manifested – this is not something we can orchestrate or mimic. We can only position ourselves according to His word; the rest is up to Him. Do we want His Glory or a counterfeit?

Mimicking the Real: Doodads and Fairy Floss

When life is tough, do we want gimmicks or the real McCoy? Fairy floss may be fun at a circus, but there comes a time when hunger kicks in and we long for something more substantial, like steak and veggies.

Entertainment or superficial worship may attempt to mimic the real, but it is nothing more than doodads and fairy floss. It is impossible to mimic heaven's worship, because our flesh wars against the Spirit. You cannot imitate the glory and weight of God. It is dangerous to try. Counterfeits have consequences.

Superficial worship may be sincere but sincerely wrong. It can be filled with passion but lack roots. Weightiness comes by putting our roots down deep into the river of God. This comes through trials, even crushing, and being tested in fire. Weighty worship, when expressed in music, is not just words sung and tunes played. It comes from the depths of experience, forged from intimacy in His Presence – and produces a weighty sound, full of beauty.

Regardless of how great or how small we consider our musical gift, our use of music in worship is an overflow of our walk with God. Regardless of our musical skills, we cannot go deep in worship if the culture of the world, our own indulgences or self-importance pollutes the springs of our inner life.

We can rationalise using entertainment by saying, 'But my heart is right', 'My heart is bowing down to the Lord'. In the context of us putting our roots into the Lord's river, Jeremiah reminds us the heart is rather fickle. 'The heart is deceitful above all things' (Jeremiah 17:9). If our hearts are aligned with the Glory of God, why would we want music that is frivolous?

Some, even spiritual leaders, have tried to tell me it is more important to have a 'heart of worship' than musical skills. That is not the attitude of King David. The musicians accompanying the Ark were required to be musically skilled *and* totally consecrated to the Lord. To say otherwise is like suggesting we must have the Spirit but disregard the word. No, we must have the word and the Spirit. And we must have musically skilled psalmists who also have circumcised and consecrated hearts.

Some musicians who got saved during the *Jesus Revolution* changed their lifestyles but kept their old music. Some just added scripture lyrics to their old music.

Our walk with the Lord should also affect our music choices, whether as a musician or as one listening. In my journey, the Lord revealed some music genres and attitudes I needed to renounce and pray into. (More in Volume 2.) Transformation of our hearts should flow into our sound. When it does, a glorious sound is released.

CHAPTER EIGHTEEN

A few clarifying points:

- Not all worship music brings glory to the Lord.
- Musicians who are Christian do not automatically play music aligned with heaven.
- Not all Christian musicians have the call of God to facilitate worship or accompany His Glory.
- When worship music is entertainment, it will not draw us closer to the Lord. The audience is man, not God.
- Some music is actually worship to other gods. Be discerning.

ENDNOTES – PART 2

1. According to John 1:1, Colossians 1: 15–16 and Proverbs 8, Jesus participated in creation.
2. Hebrews 2:12, Psalm 22:22.
3. Rabbi Sacks: 'The Torah as God's Song', 26 August 2013. http://www.rabbisacks.org/nitzavin-vayelech-the-torah-as-gods-song/.
4. Job 37:2, 'thunder of his voice'; Psalm 104:7, 'voice of Your thunder'.
5. As Abraham did in Romans 4:17.
6. Matthew 8:27.
7. Ezekiel 37:9.
8. Genesis 1:26.
9. Isaiah 6, Revelation 4, 5, 7, 11, 15, and 19.
10. Psalm 19:1, Psalm 97:6.
11. Romans 1:20–21.
12. Psalm 93:3 (TPT).
13. Exodus 19–20.
14. Isaiah 6.
15. Luke 2:1–14.
16. Romans 6:4.
17. Matthew 28:1–4.
18. Acts 2:2–4.
19. 1 Corinthians 15:52, 1 Thessalonians 4:15–18.
20. Isaiah 44:23, 49:13, 55:12.
21. https://science.nasa.gov/mission/hubble/multimedia/sonifications/#:~:text=Hubble.
22. http://nasasearch.nasa.gov/search?query=sounds+of+space&affiliate=nasa&utf8=✓; http://canyouactually.com/nasa-actually-recorded-sound-in-space-and-its-absolutely-chilling/.
23. https://science.nasa.gov/mission/hubble/multimedia/sonifications/.
24. http://www.livescience.com/24303-spooky-science-unexplained-ocean-sounds.html.
25. https://www.astronomy.com/science/is-there-any-sound-in-space-an-astronomer-explains/.
26. In 2015, Craig DeForest, a leading heliophysicist from the Southwest Research Institute's Department of Space Studies, answered a question about how loud the sun would be if sound could hypothetically travel through space as it does through the atmosphere of Earth. After some calculations, he explained that the sun would theoretically blare out a noise of around 100 decibels, almost as loud as standing next to a speaker at a rock concert or busy nightclub. 'The sound waves are so deep they are normally at frequencies that are far too low for the

human ear to pick up. It is also not a singular tone, but an intensely complex pattern of acoustical waves, a bit like a bell. To make the sounds audible to our ears, scientists must speed them up by tens of thousands of times, compressing weeks of vibrations into a few seconds.' https://www.iflscience.com/what-does-the-sun-sound-like-immensely-noisy-apparently-69087.

27. Revelation 4:7, 8:19.
28. Romans 8:19.
29. http://news.bbc.co.uk/today/hi/today/newsid_7679000/7679354.stm.
30. Genesis 4:10.
31. In *Restoring True Worship* (edition), I wrote a couple of paragraphs about the Tabernacle of David. Having now pioneered a ministry under that banner for two decades, this subject will be Volume 3 in this series.
32. Hebrews 8:5.
33. Hebrews 9:3–8, Hebrews 10:19.
34. Revelation 4:5.
35. Act 2:6.
36. Acts 2:11.
37. Revelation 5:11–14.
38. 2 Chronicles 5:13.
39. John 1:14.
40. Revelation 1:10, Revelation 4:11.
41. Isaiah 40:18, 25.
42. My personal notes for the Clarion Call 2009. These are not for publication. 'Clarion Call' was a pamphlet for the attendees of TOD and contained testimonies from previous meetings.
43. The standard tuning frequency today is A440. There are some who suggest A444 is more godly or a FQ of His Glory. I have yet to be convinced of the arguments presented so far. Tunings of instruments have developed over the centuries in alignment with the development of the instruments themselves.
44. When parts of the strings resonate at their fundamental or overtone frequencies when other strings are sounded. For example, an A string at 440 Hz will cause an E string at 330 Hz to resonate, because they share an overtone of 1320 Hz.
45. I am currently preparing an online course with practical musical suggestions, help and information to be in Volume 4.
46. 'How you are fallen from heaven, O Lucifer, son of the morning! How you are cut down to the ground, You who weakened the nations!' (Isaiah 14:12)
47. Strong's Concordance, H4399.
48. ibid, H4397.
49. ibid, H8596.
50. ibid, H8608.
51. Exodus 28:8–12, 15–30.
52. Revelation 21:9–27.

53. Deuteronomy 33:26, Psalm 68:4, 104:3.
54. Nahum 1:3.
55. Exodus 24:14, Job 22:14, Psalm 18:11, 97:1.
56. Exodus 14:19.
57. Ezekiel 30:3
58. Matthew 24: 3.
59. Exodus 33:18–20.
60. Ezekiel 28:16–17.
61. 'Turn your eyes upon Jesus', written by Helen H Lemmel in 1918, after becoming blind and her husband leaving her. https://enjoyingthejourney.org/hymn-history-turn-your-eyes-upon-jesus/.
62. Isaiah 6:3–8.
63. Isaiah 14:9.
64. Wurmbrand, Richard. *Marx and Satan*, Crossways, NY, 1976, p, 29.
65. ibid, p. 8.
66. https://www.weforum.org/agenda/2020/01/yuval-hararis-warning-davos-speech-future-predications/.
67. Matthew 6:10.
68. Matthew 16:19.
69. Genesis 4:7.
70. Matthew 27:18.
71. James 3:14.
72. 1 Corinthians 3:3.
73. Proverbs 14:30.
74. Revelation 15:4.
75. Psalm 139.
76. Apel, Willi. *Harvard Dictionary of Music*, 'Aesthetics of Music', p. 14.
77. ibid.
78. ibid. A collection of sounds is organised into a pattern or an 'arrangement of, or the art of combining or putting together, sounds that please the ear'.
79. Hanson, Howard. *The American Journal of Psychiatry*, Vol. 99, p. 137.
80. I do not recall the name of the composer or piece played.
81. 17 Oct 2018, 'The Meaning of Music', https://www.youtube.com/watch?v=LssAdBWhuJ0.
82. 'Jordan Peterson on Music', interviewed by Joe Rogan, 26 January 26 2022, https://youtu.be/jCd6ifFdKvk.
83. 'Oz Talk With Jordan Peterson: Jordan Peterson's Office Tour', 26 Feb 2024. https://www.youtube.com/watch?v=nP716jWeVU0.
84. 'Jordan Peterson – How MUSIC can LITERALLY save YOUR LIFE: Chaos and Order', 26 May 2022, https://youtu.be/9uBBiqcHGck',

85. Jordan Peterson and Douglas Murray, 'Furnish Your Mental Furniture", 7 September 2024, https://www.youtube.com/watch?v=KcAViSGtGkk.
86. This belief was called the 'doctrine of affections'.
87. https://www.libertyparkmusic.com/the-postmodern-period/#:~:text=A%20 common%20theme%20throughout%20postmodern,Total%20Serialism%20 and%20Electronic%20Music, accessed 7 Sept 2024.
88. https://www.tate.org.uk/art/art-terms/p/postmodernism#:~:text=While%20 modernism%20was%20based%20on,are%20universal%20certainties%20or%20 truths.
89. Serial music was a rigid composition technique of twelve tones.
90. 1 Samuel 7:17, 19:20.
91. 'Open up the gates to the King of Glory', https://dashboard.dittomusic.com/releases/view/941500/details.
92. Noebel, David. *The Marxist Minstrels: a Handbook on* Communist Subversion of Music, American Christian College Press, p. 4.
93. ibid, p. iii.
94. Ibid, p. iv.
95. Gaston, E Thayor. Music in Therapy, Colliwe Macmillan, NY, 1968, p. 22.
96. Rouget, Gilbert. Music and Trance – A Theory of the Relations Between Music and Possession p. 76f.
97. Rouget, p. 171.
98. Rouget, p. 176.
99. Rouget, p. 173.
100. The Brains of Musicians - Dr. Ellen Winner on Neuroplasticity https://www.youtube.com/watch?v=QMYQHTbPTVA.
101. https://www.mic.com/articles/96150.
102. https://www.musicandthebrain.org.au/.
103. https://www.amazon.com.au/dp/0452288525.
104. https://www.goodreads.com/book/show2098330.The_Sound_of_Music_and_Plants.
105. https://thewellnessenterprise.com/emoto/. His work hints at spiritual connections, though not Christian.
106. *The New Citizen,* Sept–Oct–Nov 1991.
107. Gaston, ibid, p. 23.
108. https://www.biblword.net/biblical-vocabulary-gods-honor-and-glory-part-1/
109. Hebrews 13:15.
110. Exodus 20:22–26.
111. Hebrews 9:12, 10:19–22.
112. John 1:4–5, 9, 14, John 8:12.

PART THREE
GOLD FOR WORSHIPPING THE KING
Crafted Into a Calf

When they ... saw the young child with Mary, his mother, they fell to the ground at his feet and worshiped him. Then they opened their treasure chests full of gifts and presented him with gold, frankincense, and myrrh. (Matthew 2:11 TPT)

They made an idol of a calf at Sinai and bowed to worship their man-made statue. They preferred the image of a grass-eating ox to the presence of the glory-filled God. (Psalm 106:19–20 TPT)

And do not become idolaters as were some of them. As it is written, 'The people sat down to eat and drink, and rose up to play.' (1 Corinthians 10:7)

How dare the nations plan a rebellion ... the power brokers of the world rise up to hold their summit as the rulers scheme... against YAHWEH and his Anointed King, saying: 'Let's ... break away from the Creator...' (Psalm 2:1–3 TPT)

... people everywhere see God's glory in the sky! ... **For all the supernatural powers once worshiped the true and living God.** *For you are the Most High God over all the earth. You are exalted above every supernatural power!(Psalm 97:6–7, 9, 12 TPT)*

PART THREE: PROPHETIC SNAPSHOT

The cosmic battle is won or lost in our hearts according to the issues raised in this section. Satan targets God's image bearers. The redeemed in God's kingdom are tempted and targeted with seducing and defiling actions – especially to do with worship.

Gold first appeared in scripture beside the river flowing out of Eden, reflecting the glory of the King of kings – meant for pure worship to Him alone. But the jealous serpent twisted and perverted it, luring Israel to fashion it into an idol. Yet the church, too, has its sacred cows – idols of opinions, covetousness, celebrity and much more.

Our city was built on gold; its veins still glint beneath our feet. Yet it is also home to the largest dragon in the southern hemisphere. This dragon is an effigy connected to Chinese culture, made from paper maché and mirrors, and paraded through our streets each Easter. Yet, in the spirit realm, it connects strongly to the cosmic war of Revelation 12. It is said, where there is gold, there are dragons – an apt metaphor for the cosmic war over pure worship.

Therefore, in Revelation 3:18, the Lord counsels us to:

> ... buy from Me **gold refined in the fire**, that you may be rich; and white garments, that you may be clothed ... and anoint your eyes with eye salve, that you may see. (Revelation 3:18)

Pure worship that is refined in His fire carries the weight of His throne. Aligned with heaven, such sounds shake thrones on earth and in unseen realms of darkness.

> He will purify the Levites, refining his priests until they are **like pure gold** and fine silver. Then I, YAHWEH, will have those who bring me offerings in righteousness. (Malachi 3:3 TPT)

CHAPTER NINETEEN

Are You Paying Attention?

THREE TIMES THE HOLY Spirit spoke to me about the golden calf incident, a warning to purify worship in this time of cosmic war. The first time was in answer to a question. The second time was a dream. The third time was 7 October 2023.

When the Lord speaks once, listen. When He speaks twice and three times – pay attention, it's important. Sometimes He speaks *and* shakes.

> See that you do not refuse Him who speaks. (Hebrews 12:25)

Sinai to Zion: Listen to His voice

Hebrews 12:18-29 is a key *now* text. The call is to listen to His voice. The presence of the Lord was on both Mt Sinai and Mt Zion. His voice caused both mountains to shake.[1] Israel and music provide warning bells for civilisation and for the Church. His warnings are for redemption and restoration. Are we paying attention?

The Lord says He is now bringing us to Mt Zion. He wants to shift Israel and the Church from the issues of Sinai and bring us to the realms of Zion. Zion can represent both the earthly and the heavenly Jerusalem.

To bring His Church from Sinai to Zion, the Lord has to violently shake every foundation so we can inherit His unshakeable kingdom. The heavenly Jerusalem contains: Father God, the righteous judge, Jesus whose blood is upon the mercy seat, the seven Spirits of God and innumerable angels. Like Pentecost, heaven sends a sound and a ferocious wind to shake the earth. Blowing on us are winds of revival, colliding with winds of anarchy and perversion.

Any who have not resolved the shakings from Mt Sinai will struggle to survive the shakings approaching Mt Zion. Any residue of unresolved 'golden calf' issues will be a great hindrance on Mt Zion. Hebrews 12 concludes with these words:

> *Since we are receiving our rights to an unshakable kingdom we should be **extremely thankful and offer God the purest worship that delights his heart** as we lay down our lives in absolute surrender, filled with awe. For our God is a holy, devouring fire!* (Hebrews 12:28–29 TPT)

When we are in awe of God, the purest worship comes forth, bringing great delight to His heart. This is the redemptive purpose of the shakings and why any lingering attachments to sacred cows *must* go. May we all heed what the Spirit is saying.

I carry this message with the burden of an intercessor's heart. Come join my journey with the Lord as He repeatedly spoke about the issues encountered on Mt Sinai.

Nine-fold Multiplication

In the first edition of *Restoring True Worship*, I had one chapter on the golden calf. This edition has nine! Why? The

Lord keeps emphasising this episode and has expanded the revelation since 1993.

The chapter in the first edition resulted from my questions to the Lord amid the severe upheaval in our church and the music department. On discovering the consequences of adopting the music of the sexual revolution, and Holy Spirit speaking the phrase, 'the spirit of rock has entered the church', I asked the Lord this question: were there any incidents in the Bible akin to this? I thought it was an absurd question, not expecting an answer. Almost immediately, He drew my attention to the golden calf incident in Exodus 32.

Obviously, the Bible does not use the more recent terms 'rock music' or 'sexual revolution'. Israel did not have amplifiers and guitars in the desert – but there was revelry.

However, Exodus 32 contains characteristics and heart attitudes that align with what we have witnessed since the sexual revolution.

Watching the Golden Calf from Heaven's Grandstand

On 13 April 2023, we flew to Israel for the Spirit of Elijah Summit being held at Mt Carmel. The Bible portrays Mt Carmel as the site of Elijah's confrontation with Jezebel's prophets of Baal, where Elijah called on Israel to stop flip-flopping between the true God and false gods.

The summit we were attending was an important gathering of global intercessors, apostles, prophets and leaders to seek the Lord in a critical time as prophets of Baal are in our faces again.

Just prior to the Israel trip, I had commenced work on this new edition, but was not thinking about the golden calf per se, although I was praying about the need for a new Elijah mantle to heal families and the Body of Christ from consequences of incorporating other gods into our midst.

The night before leaving Australia, I had a dream about the golden calf. To say the dream shocked me is an understatement.

In the dream, it was as if I were sitting beside the Lord in a grandstand. We were watching and discussing the golden calf episode as if it were happening in real time. As we watched, I heard the Lord speak. Over and over and over, He kept saying, 'And all Israel rose up to play, and all Israel rose up to play …'

With the background of the upcoming conference and the re-write of *Restoring True Worship*, the Lord had my full and undivided attention!

His words thundered and reverberated in my ears, not just in my dream but also on the long flight to Israel and throughout our visit.

This was our sixth ministry journey into Israel, and the air over the land was thick with division and foreboding. Several times I mentioned this dream to Messianic friends in the land and asked if this was an accurate word. Each time, the answer I received was a sorrowful 'Oh, yes'. I was told about the many Eastern gods that are celebrated, especially in the north-west coastal regions of Israel.

One day at the Mediterranean Sea, I felt a deep sadness that prompted me to do a live post on Facebook. Many young people seemed to be carefree and enjoying the beach in the sun. Yet, there was a heaviness and foreboding in the air. How many of these young people would soon be at war? How many would survive? Were these young people making the most of their time in the sun before war? Though picking these sentiments up in the Spirit and praying, none of us could imagine the worst nightmare that was about to descend on the land.

Massacre at Supernova

Six months after my dream, the historic marker that Israel will never forget – 7 October 2023.

A friend from Australia had been in Israel a week earlier and had discerned a horrid atmosphere of idolatry in the land, an atmosphere not discerned before. Was this connected to my dream?

When Israel danced around the golden calf after leaving Egypt, some three thousand died because they forsook the Lord.

The biggest Jewish massacre since the Holocaust was certainly on 7 October. Some twelve hundred[2] people died at forty sites during the massacre after five thousand six hundred Hamas terrorists invaded Israel. On the Gaza border, the Supernova music festival had been in full swing where thousands of young people had been having an all-night techno dance rave party. These were among the first to be killed that fateful day. The festival site is now a memorial to the three hundred and sixty-five who died there. Shock and trauma continue in Israel, beyond the statistics of the twelve hundred people killed and two hundred and fifty hostages taken into Gaza.[3] Considering the size of Israel's population and the numbers killed, this event was ten times larger than 9/11 – as if forty to fifty thousand Americans had died in New York!

> *The Hamas terrorist attack on Israel on October 7, 2023, will go down as one of the worst terrorist attacks in history … is the deadliest per capita terrorist attack since the Global Terrorism Database started data collection in 1970, with a rate of slightly over one person killed per every 10,000 Israelis. This metric adds context for the national impact of the attack and sense of loss for Israel …*[4]

What does this tragedy have to do with the golden calf? Sadly, a lot.

The heartbreaking loss of life and trauma on 7 October has a tragic resemblance to when ancient Israel danced around the golden calf where there was also substantial loss of life.

Advertised as a fun festival, as we drill down into the nature of the festival and its occurrence at Succoth or Feasts of Tabernacles, the spiritual tragedy becomes clear. Was this festival an open door to the enemy? (Answers are found in Chapter 23, 'Supernova Sukkot'.) I have heard of Israeli musicians who love Jesus who can no longer take part in such music festivals because of a strong environment of other gods.

Blessings or Curses?

The wind of the Spirit is propelling a restoration of true worship. However, evil winds are seeking to seduce God's people to compromise. Disastrous deception says we can add other gods to the mix. *The enemy prefers us to play than pray.* When the world is increasingly hostile to Christianity, any mixture within the Church is dangerous.

> **The enemy prefers us to play than pray.**

Blessings and curses are attached to worship responses. Love and worship only Him and He will bless and protect you from enemies, but serving other gods exposes you to defeat and destruction. This principle is not for Israel alone. There are many similar disturbing instances of such festivals in many nations and, horror of horrors, some also within the Church.

> Israel deserted YAHWEH...who had rescued them from Egypt. They found **new gods to worship** – the gods of the people around them. They caused

> *the anger of YAHWEH to be kindled against Israel ... **He surrendered them to their enemies...** (Judges 2:11–15 TPT)*
>
> *Because you have abandoned me to serve false gods, I am no longer coming to your rescue! (Judges 10:13 TPT)*

While we were flying home from attending the World Prayer Assembly in Perth, tragic events in Israel were unfolding. The Lord kept impressing three words on my heart: opendoor, betrayal and infiltration. Somehow, the shocking events of 7 October and the dream six months earlier confirmed the original golden calf message written in 1993. Though thirty years separated these events, it felt they all melted into one loud message.

As we dive into the depths of this episode, consider these questions:

- Why did a calf made of gold make the situation worse?
- Why do such events grieve the heart of God so badly?

Before you go further, be encouraged and remember the Lord's amazing mercy and grace. Despite the golden calf and repeated failures, for forty years the Lord supernaturally provided for Israel in the wilderness: food, water, health, protection by a wall of fire and a cloud of His Presence. He tabernacled with them in the wilderness – and their shoes and clothes did not wear out!

Let conviction and grace give you courage to deal with any issues Holy Spirit highlights in these next chapters, but also know His mercies are new each day.

CHAPTER TWENTY

Betrothal to Betrayal

Jilted at the Altar

Have you ever wondered why the golden calf incident was so outrageous? Yes, it violated the first of the Ten Commandments. It is also referred to repeatedly through scripture, and the Lord spoke to me about it three times. Why was it such an outrageous offence?

Was it just a lack of gratitude for supernatural deliverance from Egypt? Or was it something more serious?

Fifty days after their Passover and miraculous escape from Egypt, Israel arrived at Sinai. The Lord had carried them on eagles' wings and offered them a promise. Israel would become 'a kingdom of priests and a holy nation' (Exodus 19:4, 6).

Israel accepted the offer. So, the Lord called them to a meeting, requiring them to be cleaned up and ready. This was no ordinary meeting. The preparation sounded like getting ready for a wedding, dressed in their cleanest and best!

It was essentially a *marriage betrothal*. The equivalence in our Western culture would be somewhere between an engagement party and a wedding. Sadly, this engagement party turned into an orgy!

Wedding *Chuppah* (Canopy)

Jewish weddings generally take place under a *chuppah*, or wedding canopy, supported by four poles. It represents the new home the couple will build together. Spiritually, a *chuppah* represents the Presence of God to cover the marriage covenant.

At Mt Sinai, the Presence of the Lord covered the mountain like a *chuppah*!

> *Now the **glory** of the LORD rested on Mount Sinai, and the cloud covered it six days ... The **sight of the glory** of the LORD was like a **consuming fire** on the top of the mountain in the eyes of the children of Israel. (Exodus 24:16–17)*

The glory of the Lord above Mt Sinai must have been quite scary! The mountain shook. The Lord's trumpet (shofar) got louder and louder. The Israelites trembled and 'stood afar off' (Exodus 20:18). They withdrew and asked for only Moses to speak, fearing the voice of God would kill them.

For good reasons, we need the blood of Jesus to safely come near His Presence. Being in awe of Him is the starting place of wisdom, and true worship.

Jewish Wedding: *Ketubah*

In ancient Jewish wedding culture, betrothal occurs after the couple agree to some conditions that are put into a document called a *ketubah*. A *ketubah* is a legally binding marriage covenant, and therefore, breaking it provides grounds for divorce.

In a *ketubah* ceremony, the groom tells the bride what he will give her in the marriage. He then tells her what he expects of her. She has to say yes or no. God promised Israel:

> *... if you will indeed obey My voice and keep My covenant, then you shall be a special treasure to Me above all people; for all the earth is Mine. And you shall be to Me a kingdom of priests and a holy nation. (Exodus 19:5-6)*

Israel said yes.[5]

Exodus 20-23 lays out all the conditions God would expect from Israel. The conditions include the Ten Commandments (Exodus 20), the law of the altar, moral and ceremonial laws, issues of justice and the requirement to meet Him three times a year at the feasts. Information was also given about where they would meet (i.e. the tabernacle) and where they would live (i.e. the Promised Land).

Once the woman agrees to the terms, the couple shares bread and wine or a blood sacrifice to make the *ketubah* legal. Five times in the conditions, God stipulated Israel must have 'no other gods'.

> *And **all** the people answered with one voice and said, 'All the **words** which the LORD has said **we will do**.' (Exodus 24:3)*

Moses wrote down all the words of the Lord, as agreed to by Israel, and then *built an altar* at the foot of the mountain.

> *Then he took the **Book of the Covenant** and read in the hearing of the people. And they said, "**All that the Lord has said we will do, and be obedient**." And Moses took the blood, sprinkled it on the people, and said, 'This is the blood of the covenant which the Lord has made with you...' (Exodus 24:7-8)*

Thus, the first covenant was established – with blood. At this point in a Jewish wedding, a couple is legally married, but they do not consummate the relationship until the marriage supper, when their home is ready to be occupied.

If a woman is unfaithful during this time, her husband could divorce her. Hence, when Joseph discovered Mary was pregnant, he thought about divorcing her because they were already betrothed. He could have legally divorced her on grounds of adultery, except the angel intervened, revealing a supernatural conception rather than infidelity. For this same reason, God repeatedly calls Israel out for her harlotry and says He would thus issue a certificate of divorce.

Creating the golden calf was not just a minor error, slip up or miscalculation. The blood had hardly dried on the covenant when Israel desecrated it. Actually, Moses was on top of the mountain as the finger of God was engraving the covenant in permanent stone when they broke the agreement.

Israel repeatedly said yes to God in the betrothal process. Creating the golden calf violated the covenant. It would be like a bride running off with the best man at her wedding – or worse. The engagement party became an orgy! The language and description around the phrase '… and Israel rose up to play', made this evident. Betrothal shifted from a potential celebration to a horrendous betrayal. On every level, it was treacherous and disloyal. It reveals an insincere and unfaithful heart.

No wonder God was angry.

But it gets worse …

Wedding Ring Traded for an Idol

Yahweh shared with Ezekiel profound insight into His heart over the broken marriage covenant. This included everything that He had given to her, such as wedding garments and jewellery.

CHAPTER TWENTY

> '... I swore an oath to you and entered into a covenant with you, and you became Mine,' says the Lord GOD ... 'And I put a jewel in your nose, earrings in your ears, and a beautiful crown on your head. Thus you were adorned with gold and silver ...' (Ezekiel 16:8, 12-13)

It was these gold earrings that Aaron gathered from the women and children, melted and used them to create a golden calf. Insult upon insult. Trade your wedding ring in and turn it into an alternative husband! Through Ezekiel, Yahweh bluntly told Israel, 'you have broken your marriage covenant and despised your promises to me' (Ezekiel 16:59 TPT).

God, who is eternally patient and faithful, saw His betrothed go find another lover, while He was still giving Moses all the details of the tabernacle. This is a further insult. Why?

Having provided detailed instructions for the tabernacle in Exodus 25, the Lord said to Moses, 'And there I will meet with you, and I will speak with you from above the mercy seat ...' (Exodus 25:22).

The Hebrew word for 'meet you' could be like an appointment, but it also contains the meaning of betrothal! The tabernacle is the shadow of the bridal home they would dwell in together. Israel not only trashed the covenant and melted the bridal gifts into an idol, but they did this while the Lord was giving instructions to build the place where they could dwell together. The earthly home would be a shadow of the home in heaven!

The pain felt by the Lord at Mt Sinai can be understood by those who have gone through a broken engagement, been jilted at the altar or been betrayed through adultery. If this was an earthly lover's tiff, a woman trashing all her man had done for her, words would fail for the level of betrayal and anguish he would experience. Such an episode in the natural would lead to such immense harm. Domestic violence is tragically common in society. For anyone who has walked through such betrayal and trauma knows recovery can be difficult and a lengthy process. Yet, God's mercy is beyond measure.

Idolatry is Adultery: Bride Has Another Lover!

Covenant is serious. Blood seals it, signifying it is unto death. The Lord treats it seriously. Mt Sinai being like a marriage covenant is very clear in many passages of scripture where the Lord speaks to Israel about her infidelity.

> *Does a young woman disregard her engagement ring, or does a bride forget about her wedding dress? Yet, my people have continually forgotten me.* (Jeremiah 2:32 TPT)

In the next chapter, Jeremiah links idolatry to adultery, and the Lord gives Israel a certificate of divorce – something He hates.

The pain felt by the Lord at Mt Sinai can be understood by those who have gone through a broken engagement, been jilted at the altar or been betrayed through adultery.

> *YAHWEH asked me, 'Did you see what unfaithful Israel has done?* **Like an adulterous wife,** *she has turned away from me. In every high place and under every green tree, she has* **prostituted herself to worship other gods.**' (Jeremiah 3:6 TPT)

> *Then I saw that for all the causes for which backsliding Israel had* **committed adultery,** *I had put*

> her away and given her a **certificate of divorce**... (Jeremiah 3:8 NKJV)

> She **polluted the land** and committed adultery by worshiping idolatrous stone and wood pillars. (Jeremiah 3:9 TPT)

The Church must also take heed of these warnings. When adultery is in the spiritual realm, it easily shifts to the natural realm and slides into physical adultery. I mentioned earlier the high numbers of divorces in the church we were in, and only the Lord knows how many adulteries. Sexual immorality in the Church is rampant and a serious issue.

Consider the call of Hosea – to marry a prostitute! The prophetic message through Hosea was his life. His 'marriage' was to show Israel how God saw them. Yet Hosea was to love Gomer and woo her back. The names of their children indicated the stages in that process!

Breaking a covenant has severe consequences – death. Faithfulness to covenant has immense blessings – life.

We can read and understand the Mt Sinai encounter as a marriage covenant yet still continue to see Israel as the only offender. How much of the Church understands the gravity and enormity of the New Covenant? The writer of Hebrews reminds the reader of the punishment under the old covenant and then says violating the New Covenant has *greater* punishment!

> *Of how much worse punishment, do you suppose ... who has trampled the Son of God underfoot, counted the blood of the covenant by which he was sanctified a common thing, and insulted the Spirit of grace?* (Hebrews 10:29)

How much of the Church grasps the seriousness of dishonouring the blood of Jesus, and the connection between idolatry and adultery? Are we open to the Holy Spirit revealing and dealing with any ungodly traditions or sacred cows we have brought into our relationship with God, even into worship services?

Pentecost: Has the Church Rejected the Bridal Gift?

God does not do things randomly. He speaks and acts at strategic times according to His own calendar. The death and resurrection of Jesus fulfilled the first Passover, and the day of Pentecost (Shavuot) fulfilled Mt Sinai.

Both Mt Sinai and Pentecost were fifty days after Passover. Like Mt Sinai, Pentecost was also a bridal occasion. This time, it was for the *New* Covenant.

In our culture, the woman is given an engagement ring. In Jewish culture, at the time of betrothal, she is given gifts. At Pentecost, God gave gifts of the Spirit to believers. These were bridal gifts!

We may criticise Israel for surrendering her earrings to be turned into an idol, but what about when we in the Church refuse the gifts of the Spirit? Are we any different? For me, this was an enormous battle. For some reason, I had believed the lie that the gifts of the Spirit, especially tongues, were of the devil! I speak about my resistance, struggle and breakthrough in Chapter 31, 'Exquisite Sound Beyond Description'.

Many religious spirits try to prevent us from seeing the gifts of the Spirit for what they really are. First, they are a gift from God! Do we refuse His gifts? Second, they are to set us apart for Him. Just like when I received my engagement ring, it sent a message – 'I am taken, I am preparing for marriage'. Third, the gifts of the Spirit help His Bride to be sanctified, without spot or wrinkle, prepared for the marriage supper of the Lamb. The early Church only exploded when the fullness of the Holy Spirit fell on them and deposited His gifts.

Without the fullness of the Holy Spirit, including His gifts, true worship cannot be restored. The gifts of the Spirit are a distinguishing element in the restoration of true worship. Pure worship by the bride of the New Covenant (Jew and Gentile of Ephesians 2) depends on the gifts of the Spirit, including singing in tongues.[6]

Are we no different to Israel at Mt Sinai when we sing songs that stir up the flesh instead of singing as led by the Holy Spirit? Are we, like Israel at Mt Sinai, allowing the systems of the world, the flesh and the devil to interfere with God's work through neglect, curses, mockery and blasphemy?

Idols Render Us Unfit for Worship!

Idolatry has severe consequences. The Lord showed Ezekiel that Israel had become defiled by idolatry and had 'made herself unfit for My presence by worshipping all the idols...' (Ezekiel 23:7 TPT).

The defilement made Israel *unfit* for worship! Having broken the Lord's commandments, Israel chased after idols but descended into bloodshed.

> *... because they sacrificed their firstborn children in the fire, I declared them **defiled** and **unfit to worship Me**. (Ezekiel 20:26 TPT)*

What about the idols of our hearts? These make us unfit for worship too! Idols of the heart *disqualify us from true worship.* No wonder I had to deal with the idol in my heart before being released into my calling in worship.

By creating the golden calf, Israel broke the betrothal covenant. Moses broke the covenant tablets and God issued a divorce. God hates divorce. Israel did experience violence at the hands of their enemies because of exile.

Bloodshed today comes through abortion and divorce. Malachi 2:16 says divorce brings a covering of violence. Too often, divorce leads to children being harmed, even sacrificed.

Without repentance, idols defile us, create substantial damage and render us unfit to worship God in His Presence. This is not just a problem for Israel; it is a serious problem for the Church. Because the blood of Jesus ratified the New Covenant, the consequence of idolatry is even more severe for us.

> *Idols of our hearts make us unfit for worship, disqualify us from true worship.*

Paul told the Ephesian church that idolatrous greed, along with immorality, would keep us out of the kingdom of God!

*… the kingdom of God **cannot** be accessed by anyone who is guilty of sexual sin, or who is impure or greedy – for greed is the essence of idolatry. How could they expect to have an inheritance in Christ's kingdom while doing those things? (Ephesians 5:5)*

John said idolatry is one of the things that will exclude you from the holy city, the New Jerusalem, or what we refer to as eternal life in heaven.

> *Those not permitted to enter are outside: the malicious hypocrites, the sexually immoral, sorcerers, murderers, **idolaters**, and every lover of lies. (Revelation 22:15 TPT)*

While idolatry is not the only sin referred to by Paul and John, it follows the pattern of the slippery slope. Once hearts have turned away from the Lord, sexual sins and bloodshed soon follow.

Idolatry is extremely serious for us all. It is not only the antithesis of true worship; it is also the greatest nemesis.

CHAPTER TWENTY-ONE

Excuses, Excuses: This Calf Came Out by Itself!

HUMANS OFTEN INVENT WILD excuses to dodge trouble. As a former schoolteacher, I've heard hilarious homework justifications that could fill a comedy book. My mother loved sharing a childhood story: when corporal punishment was godly wisdom, she asked my older sister about a missing strap. The reply? 'The rooster took it!' Months later, Mum found it melted under the copper washing machine!

Aaron's excuse ranks among the best (or worst). He claimed that when the gold melted down, amazingly, out of the fire came a calf – all by itself! Even though Exodus 32:4 says he 'fashioned it with an engraving tool'!

I wonder if Eve told herself, 'It's just a small bite. It won't hurt'. We all know how that turned out!

We hear the enemy's seductive voice in our self-talk: 'It's only a small sin. It looks so good, it can't hurt.' The enemy always appeals to our desires, weaknesses and our natural minds. A telltale sign are non-scriptural excuses.

Where is Moses?

Despite having seen God's supernatural deliverance from Egypt, Israel's faith was not strong. They grumbled about food, water and Moses' leadership. They even thought it might be better back in Egypt than the Promised Land full of giants!

Moses was up the mountain again. He had been gone forty days, and Israel was restless. Would Moses even return? Has he gone for good?

> *When the people saw **how long** it was taking Moses to come back down the mountain, they gathered around Aaron. 'Come on,' they said, **'make us some gods** who can lead us. We don't know what happened to this fellow Moses …' (Exodus 32:1 NLT)*

With a mix of impatience and unbelief, they conspired to get Aaron to help them violate the covenant they had just agreed to. They asked Aaron to make them 'some gods who can lead us'. Had they considered the missing Moses, who had been leading them, their 'god'?

Need a God We Can See?

Bakers Encyclopedia of the Bible says:

> *The tendency of Israel towards idolatry was in part the expression of the universal human longing for a god one can see and know through the physical senses.*[7]

Doubts and fears get tested by an invisible God and the unseen realm. It is easier to worship a God we can *see* and touch in the now.

Moses was God's representative, not their god. How often do we treat spiritual leaders as if they are God, and then wonder why we get disappointed upon discovering they are human? Idolatry of spiritual leaders is a red flag. Shifting gaze from the Lord to a leader is problematic. Any time we get overly infatuated or critical with leaders, beware. Obsession can quickly turn from love to hate. The first to betray are often those previously enamoured by your gift or call. In Numbers 12, Aaron and his sister Miriam criticised Moses. The Lord rebuked them.

We must honour and respect a leader for the position God has given them, but they are *not* God. God created us with an inbuilt need to worship, but it is for *Him*, not an alternative!

Impatient Waiting for God?

In a world of instant gratification, celebrity culture and entitlement, we, like the prodigal son, rush for destiny and want inheritance now. Are we too impatient to wait for God's timing? Moses waited seven days in the glory cloud *before* God spoke, and the disciples waited ten days for the Spirit's outpouring. How long will we endure for His promises?

What about waiting forty days or even forty years? Forty represents testing. Before I wrote *Grumble Fast*, our team fasted from grumbling for forty days. It was difficult, and it exposed hidden self-talk and habitual complaints. Moses waited forty days for the Ten Commandments, tabernacle blueprints, priesthood and daily life regulations. But forty days was too much for Israel when the Presence of God was at a distance, so they built their own god. Did Israel's forty-day trial foreshadow their forty years in the wilderness?

Jesus endured forty days in the wilderness, exemplifying how to conquer the temptations of the devil and the weakness of the flesh; it was vital for true worship. Where Israel failed by trying to supply their own needs and by trusting other gods, Jesus succeeded by trusting His Father and His word.

After waiting for the Holy Spirit, the early church received the sound and fire of heaven, the fullness of the Spirit, which turned fear into boldness and birthed the church.

Will we wait for the fullness of the Spirit, the fire of God, the glory cloud, or check our watches if we think worship is too long or we have other plans? Do we as leadership limit the glory realms by our schedules, or prefer big name speakers, or like Aaron pander to complaints and noise of the multitudes? Can we resist manufacturing revival, fulfil our own destinies or chasing other gods? Waiting for God takes perseverance, trust and courage.

After breaking the first tablets, Moses went up the mountain and waited another forty days. This time, Israel endured, and he descended not angry and upset, but with the glory radiating from his face so brightly he needed a veil.

The Lord extended our forty-day grumble fast to another forty days, yielding a major breakthrough. Sometimes it can take a double forty-day fast to come into His Glory realms. Waiting for God can test us, even painfully. But God's ways are best, and they work.

Why Did Aaron Comply?

Aaron should have known better. He had earlier feasted in the presence of the Lord on top of the mountain. He heard the instructions. Still, he surrendered to the demands of the people. Why? Was he complicit? Or was he afraid of the mob stoning him?

Elijah ran from Jezebel's threats, despite being victorious over the prophets of Baal. Intimidation by the crowd or witchcraft threats are real and dangerous. Baal worship is in our culture. Globalist agendas, fuelled by Baal worship, become more vulgar in media, music and entertainment. Intimidation against God's people escalates, especially against the prophetic.

The Covid pandemic exposed fear, confusion, disinformation, intimidation and threats against individuals, workers and those wanting to worship corporately. Cancel culture targets any opposing views. Issues of gender fluidity, redefining marriage and sexual perversion have legislation targeting and censoring Christian values. Anti-Semitism, which has ramped up since 7 October, is frightening and sickening. The heinous assassination of Charlie Kirk confirms this spiritual war.

Fear of man is a terrible obstacle to true worship. Faced with threats or intimidation, the fear of the Lord must become greater than the fear of man. The fear of the Lord brings wisdom, courage and a willingness to obey, regardless of the cost. A fresh vision of the message of the cross is the only way to die to self and overcome such pressures. Failing to embrace the cross, we compromise, even bowing to the mob and their idols.

This 'God' Delivered from Egypt?

Upon seeing the gold calf, Aaron had made, the people excitedly uttered a most damning statement.

> *O Israel, these are the gods who brought you out of the land of Egypt! (Exodus 32:4 NLT)*

Did they not remember the plagues of Egypt?[8] How could this calf god – that could not hear, see, smell or think – rescue Israel from Pharaoh? How could a gold replica of the already judged Egyptian cow god be capable of miraculously splitting open the Red Sea? It was an absurd insult – yet this is how the enemy twists and perverts our thinking. He blinds us to the truth and makes us believe ridiculous things. Intimidation, sorcery and witchcraft defy logic, and common sense becomes less common.

Based on my experiences, I am going to ask a hard-hitting question: has some contemporary worship music become our golden calf, lifted as our deliverer? Some well-meaning and sincere leaders have told me that rock music and other genres attached to culture are necessary to reach the youth. Yet, are we, like Aaron saying, 'This is your god … that brought you out of the land of Egypt', trusting music – or politicians, elites or celebrities – to save nations?

It is *only* the message of the cross that contains the power of God to save and deliver.[9]

Replacing the Word and Spirit with flesh, faith with unbelief and obedience with rebellion invites trouble, not blessings. A wind of holiness now uproots what our Father didn't plant.

> *Has some contemporary worship music become our golden calf, lifted as our deliverer?*

Aaron Built an Altar

> *Aaron saw how excited the people were, so he **built an altar** in **front of the calf**. Then he announced, 'Tomorrow will be a festival (feast) to the Lord!' The people got up early the next morning to sacrifice burnt offerings and peace offerings. After this, they celebrated with feasting and drinking, and they **indulged in pagan revelry**. (Exodus 32:4–6 NLT)*

Immediately after giving the Ten Commandments, including to not have other gods, the Lord specifically instructed them how to build His altar of worship.[10] Altars were exclusively for the worship of the Lord. Everywhere true altars of worship were raised, the Lord said He would place His name in that region.

> *An altar of earth you shall make for Me...In every place where I record My name I will come to you, and I will bless you. (Exodus 20:24)*

The huge subject of altars is close to my heart, as this was the call of the Lord to us to 'raise up the altar of true worship above all the idolatry in your city'.

What altars are we establishing? Remember, Aaron was not an occult priest – he was the High Priest of Israel! He not only built the golden calf and declared it a god, but now he built an altar, enabling Israel to offer sacrifices to a false god. The altar Aaron built in front of the calf blatantly violated the Lord's instructions.

Let us ask Father for forgiveness for anywhere we have tolerated such compromise or supposedly worshipped at such an altar. May we be like Elijah who gathered God's people to confront the worship and prophets of Baal.

> *He **rebuilt Yahweh's altar** that had been torn down. (1 Kings 18:30)*

Depending on the translation you read, Elijah rebuilt, repaired or healed the Lord's altar that had been broken, torn or damaged by Israel's mixed worship.

Mixture and Syncretism

Mixed and adulterated worship is insidious. Syncretism combines and merges different religions or 'systems of thought or belief'.[11] It tries to crossbreed good and evil but produces a mongrel. God's people become spiritual adulterers, and true worship is destroyed.

Things deteriorated badly as Aaron called a feast *to the Lord* but *with* their calf god![12] Their lips and actions were contradictory. No wonder the Lord and Moses were angry at the vile syncretism.

Aaron was the High Priest yet blatantly facilitated mixed worship. This is a warning to all Christian leaders – worship leaders, apostles, prophets, pastors and whatever title they carry. The biggest danger for God's people is mixed worship.

> *... because you are lukewarm, and neither cold nor hot, I will vomit you out of My mouth. (Revelation 3:16)*

Mixture, Counterfeits and Confusion

Mixed worship, harder to detect than blatant paganism, poses a greater danger than a clear enemy. Soldiers in the Vietnam war faced unsure foes – children or combatants. In Gaza, Hamas hides in tunnels under schools and hospitals being shielded by women and children. Like thieves, counterfeits are the hallmark of Satan whose goal is to sabotage true worship.

At Sinai, Israel, fresh from God's Presence, embraced a counterfeit. From the glory to a counterfeit was quick. The Lord had told Israel *not* to copy the cultures around them. Ancient civilisations of Mesopotamia and Canaan all practised animal sacrifices, food and drink offerings and burning incense. The *Eerdmans Bible Dictionary* notes that pagan rituals[13] had some resemblance to Israel's sacrificial system, except who they were offered to. This similarity possibly fuelled Israel's frequent descent into idolatry, even human sacrifice: 'They sacrificed their sons and daughters to demons ... and the land was polluted with blood (Psalm 106:37–38)'.

Confused or not, they were seduced by the enemy. God had made it clear He hates mixture.

Amos condemned Israel's idolatry, corruption and oppression of the poor yet pretending to worship like King David.[14]

> *I hate, I despise your feast days ... Though you offer Me burnt offerings and your grain offerings,*

EXCUSES, EXCUSES: THIS CALF CAME OUT BY ITSELF!

> ***I will not accept them**... Take away from Me the noise of your songs, for I will not hear the melody of your stringed instruments. (Amos 5:21-23)*

Israel had adulterated Davidic worship with drunkenness and ignored the suffering of the people. God hated their singing and dancing – to Him it was noisy, seductive and sensuous.

Melody Green's biography of her husband Keith reveals his challenge at a flesh-indulgent Christian festival. While Keith was weeping under the piano, a girl came to their caravan door with a slip of paper. On it was written Amos 5:21-23. Keith had just been asking the Lord where to find that very scripture. He went on stage and challenged the crowd: 'Take away from Me the noise of your songs, for I will not hear the melody of your string instruments.'

> ***Take away from Me the noise of your songs.***

The Lord was rejecting their songs. Though He originally ordained them, now they were defiled! The call is for *changed hearts, not the absence of music*!

> *Hate evil, love good ... Establish justice in the gate. (Amos 5:14-15)*

Israel's songs to the Lord were used to also accompany them carrying the tabernacle of Moloch and statue of Chiun, thought to be Baal Peor.[15] This involved prostitution and child sacrifice and mirrors today's pornography, premarital sex and abortion

> ***The call is for changed hearts, not the absence of music!***

among Christians, burdening Keith at the 'Christian' music festival, as it did for Amos so long ago.

Offering sacrifices 'to the Lord' is no guarantee He will accept them. Israel convinced themselves they were worshipping God. Deception can be sincere but sincerely and devastatingly wrong. The danger area for all God's people is mixed worship. We can think we are right with God. We can worship Him with good intentions, yet undealt-with sin or unhealed wounds can lead us astray.

Tolerance is reckless and dangerous. It endorses imitating pagan worship when we are told to destroy counterfeit worship systems. This warning applies to ancient Israel, modern Israel and the Church: mixed worship is perilous.

Mixed worship sends confusing mixed messages. Follow Jesus, follow Baal, follow Buddha, follow Muhammad, take your pick …

No! Jesus is the *only* way to the Father. Have no other gods. Worship must be holy like Him – holy hearts, holy words, holy music, holy musicians.

To discern counterfeits, soak in His glorious presence. The true light of Jesus exposes the counterfeit angel of light. (2 Corinthians 11:14–15). When you have experienced the glory realms in worship, you are spoiled for the ordinary and dissatisfied with anything less.

Yes … No … Make Up Your Mind!

Elijah confronted Israel about Baal worship. Their divided hearts were exposed. A tug of war was going on. One minute they worshipped God, the next it was Baal. Their response to God was a hesitant 'Yes … no'. They were not completely convinced of Yah being the great I AM, the only true God.

The *Complete Jewish Bible* says, 'How long are you going to jump back and forth between two positions?' (1 Kings 18:21).

It is possible we can say yes to God, but when the crunch comes, say no. We may say yes to God but say no to His ways. We may like the idea of being in fellowship with God, but when it gets costly, and the heat intensifies, we back off.

> *When you are half-hearted and wavering it leaves you unstable. Can you really expect to receive anything from the Lord when you're in that condition? (James 1:7–8 TPT)*

21st–Century Syncretism

The following tragic examples are for awareness and intercession, so that the Church grows in discernment and wisdom.

1. It is suggested the song that launched the Beatles in the US was an imitation of popular gospel songs sung in America. 'My Sweet Lord' praised Krishna, not Jesus as many thought, introducing transcendental meditation into mainstream culture. How many believers brought their music into church, even though much was inspired by drugs and demons?

2. In December 2018, Hillsong Sweden's 'This is Christmas' featured elements of Hindu music and dancing and a lotus flower backdrop.[16] The lotus flower is a symbol of rebirth and spiritual awakening in Buddhism and Hinduism.

3. In September 2022, Pope Francis signed the 'Human Fraternity Document' with Grand Imam Al-Azhar. The Vatican's aim is tolerance, coexistence and to prevent religious wars. Some call it 'Chrislam', the joining of Christianity and Islam, the start of a One World Religion.[17] Yet, some Muslim countries have

enacted laws making it illegal for Muslim-background Christians to meet for fellowship.[18]

Have we, like Israel with its golden calf, created man-made saviours? Leaders push rock music to reach youth, but does this elevate it as a delivering god?

In our desperation to see people delivered from spiritual Egypt, have we also created a man-made saviour? Have we likewise attempted to worship the Lord with a golden calf? By imitating music from the sexual revolution, have we been like ancient Israel and lifted it up as the god that delivers us?

After leaving our original church, several churches asked me to mentor and/or lead their worship departments. Each time I was upfront about my position and the revelation in this book. One pastor suggested 'the music did not matter, so long as hearts are right'.

Jeremiah warns 'the heart is deceitful … and desperately wicked. Who can know it' (Jeremiah 17:9)? When busily serving the Lord, I thought my heart was fine. But God said, 'No, there are idols in your heart.' Jesus taught that what comes out of our mouth, the fruit of the heart (words and songs) reveals what is in the heart.[19] Incidentally, I never filled any of the mentoring or worship positions mentioned above.

Jesus cautioned our worship is vain if our lips honour Him but our hearts are far from Him.[20] Mixed worship, even if sincere, dishonours Him. Deception is habitually, sincerely and devastatingly wrong.

Generational Consequences

At Sinai, men squandered their inheritance by taking gold earrings from the women and children for the calf. The Spirit of Elijah is about reconciling parents and children. Elijah had to deal with Baal and Asherah, the demonic powers that cause division between generations.

Once embedded in society, government or church, to rid the strongman of Baal requires a major intervention of God – our current reality.

When the sexual revolution occurred in the 1960s, little was understood about the consequences of fatherlessness. Nor was the church aware that sophisticated demons were manipulating things behind the scenes.

Oral Roberts' Melbourne healing tent being burned by communists mirrors the spirit of Marxism now invading schools, where drag queens read to kids and teens change gender without parental consent. Music stars sanitise, endorse and promote sexual perversion and the occult. It is time to wake up, rise up and say no!

What if we followed the example of Moses? The Lord told him to grind the calf to powder for the people to drink (Exodus 32:20) and 'utterly destroy them and smash their sacred pillars' (Deuteronomy 12:3).

To restore true worship, we must first eradicate Baal from our own lives and generations before tackling Baal worship in society. Ask the Holy Spirit to reveal any evil practices from our culture that need removing from your household.

CHAPTER TWENTY-TWO

What is the Worst Sin? It is Poisonous!

OF THE SEVEN DEADLY sins, is there one worse than the others?

All sin violates the glory of God. Sin causes us to fall short of His Glory. Without diminishing the seriousness of *any* sin, is there one that acts like a gatekeeper, opening the floodgate to all others? What singular sin set us on a slippery slope, releasing a poisonous root of bitterness and evoking God's jealousy?

Consider the teachings of Jesus, the Law of Moses, the evaluation of Israel's good and bad kings, the list of things heaven allows and disallows. Is there a common thread?

No Other Gods

The first of the Ten Commandments begins with a proclamation:

> *I am the LORD your God, who brought you out of the land of Egypt, out of the house of bondage.* "You shall have **no other gods before Me.** *(Exodus 20:2–3)*

Many prophets confirmed these words.[21] Israel was not to even *mention* the names of other gods, let alone copy worship practices of surrounding cultures.[22] When asked what the most important law was, Jesus summed up every law (all six hundred and thirty-one!) into just two:[23]

1. love God with all your heart – one hundred per cent
2. love one another and yourself.

Addressing just the first point, we were created to worship – but *only* our Creator. It is a covenantal commitment to Him.

> *I am making this covenant with you so that **no one** among you-no man, woman, clan, or tribe-will turn away from the LORD our God to worship these gods of other nations, and **so that** no **root** among you **bears bitter and poisonous fruit**. (Deuteronomy 29:18 NLT)*

Worshipping other gods distorts the image of God and poisons our souls. Devastation comes not so much because of an external judgement from God but because it kills us on the inside. It destroys our walk with God and relationship with others. It is poisonous fruit.

Spiritual Dehydration While Active in Worship Team

In Australia's vast hot outback, dehydration can kill. On my first trip to Alice Springs, one afternoon I underestimated my water needs and arrived desperate for water and gasping. Years later, I faced worse – spiritual dehydration. Our bodies need water; losing sufficient of it can sneak up on you and is deadly!

Though active on our church's worship team, I was dying inside. I had put our pastor on a pedestal, and I was bowing down, as noted in Chapter 5, 'Don't Touch the Ark'. The Lord showed me I was treating my musical gift as an idol. I was shocked and horrified to learn how easily idols can enter. There is such a fine line between honouring leaders and those with exceptional gifts and anointing or bowing to them. They are *not* God and treating them as gods has severe consequences.

Spiritually dying, and with His fire extinguished and joy gone, yet I continued in the worship team and attended every meeting. How can one keep participating in worship in that condition? It was sad and scary to realise I had relied on habit, skill and duty, not the Holy Spirit's anointing! There is no replacement for intimacy with God.

> ***Worshipping other gods distorts the image of God and poisons our souls.***

> *My people have committed two evils: They have **forsaken Me**, the fountain of living waters, And **hewn themselves cisterns**-broken cisterns that can hold no water. (Jeremiah 2:13)*

Like Jeremiah's prophecy, I too had a broken cistern, I'd forsaken the Lord and my soul was dry. Worship was no longer flowing in the river of Holy Spirit; intimacy with God had evaporated.

Once the heart of worship is gutted, songs become a hollow charade. With no living water, worship becomes entertainment, relying on gimmicks to mimic anointing. Compromise and secularisation affect everything.

> ***Once the heart of worship is gutted, songs become a hollow charade.***

Our church mirrored Israel's decline, with sexual sin and broken marriages. Idols of the heart destroy covenant. A marriage-breaking spirit was active. God's grace preserved my marriage after we reclaimed submission to each other.

Losing my role on the worship team was a redeeming wake-up call, like Israel's exiles. Many left the faith, but through God's mercy, He exposed the idols in my heart, and after repentance, restored my calling.

Idolatry: Hidden Root of Spiritual Abuse

I realised our church community was in pain, suffering from spiritual abuse and control. When honour due the Lord shifts to humans and things, it brings trauma to individuals, families and ministries.

When respect and esteem of people become subservient idolatry, control and manipulation flourish – it's the basis of cultic environments. Spiritual abuse increases, going into emotional, financial or sexual abuse. We might protest, but idolatry plagues too many Western churches. It stems from trusting people above our heavenly Father, filling the void in an orphan's heart. If we comply with abuse, our compliance actually sustains an abusive environment. If we forsake the Lord and help dig broken cisterns, we share some responsibility, even though that system hurt us. Yet, resisting spiritual abuse takes courage and even miracles to break free.

Idolatry breaks Father's heart, betraying His love. It kills us on the inside, devastates relationships, extinguishes passion for God and desecrates the altar of true worship. As quoted earlier, Deuteronomy 29:18 warns of the devastating consequences when *any* person (man, woman, family or tribe) diverts their heart and mind to other gods – it is the source of bitter poison.

> *... turns from **Yahweh** our **Elohim** to worship the gods of those nations ... is the **source** of this kind of **bitter poison**. (Deuteronomy 29:18 NOG)*

> *lest there should be among you a [poisonous] root that bears gall and wormwood (Deuteronomy 29:18 AMPC)*

Bitterness and resentment spread like a contagious plague – they kill.[24]

Trading Jesus for Another God

Having other gods before our Redeemer is an insult to the lover of our soul. We dishonour Him and lower our esteem of Him when in fact He deserves the highest honour. It is not possible to love God with our whole heart and also have other gods at the same time. Both Jeremiah and Jesus put it bluntly:

> *Has a nation ever traded in its gods (even though they are not really gods)? But my people have **bartered away their glory** in exchange for gods who do nothing. (Jeremiah 2:11 TPT)*

> *Jesus said: 'How could you worship two gods at the same time? You will have to hate one and love the other ...' (Matthew 6:24 TPT)*

If we need Jesus plus somebody or something else to save us, we have more than one master. Jesus said it is impossible to serve two masters. The kingdom of God does not have dual citizenship!

The late Michael Heiser wrote in his book *Supernatural*:

> *Whether in the Old Testament or the New, salvation is never earned, or even deserved. It's given by the grace of God in response to faith ... [The]*

*Israelites had to believe their God was the God of all gods, trusting that He made them His people. They alone had access to the God of gods. The law was not how Israelites achieved salvation – it was how they showed **loyalty** to the God they believed in. Salvation for an Israelite was about faith in the promises and character of the God of gods, and about **refusing to worship another god.** It was about belief and loyalty from the heart, not earning brownie points with God.*

King David did awful things like commit adultery and arrange a murder. According to the law, he was a lawbreaker and deserved to die for his crimes. Even so, he never waivered in his belief in Yahweh as the Most High God. He never switched his loyalty to another god. And God was merciful to him.

*The same is true in the New Testament. Believing the gospel means believing that the God of Israel came to earth as a man, voluntarily died on the cross as a sacrifice for our sins, and rose again on the third day. We must embrace that by faith and then **show our loyalty to Jesus by forsaking all other gods**. Regardless of what those other gods may say about salvation, the Bible tells us there is **no salvation in any other name than Jesus** and that faith must remain intact. **Personal failure is not the same as trading Jesus for another god–** and God can tell the difference.*[25]

The lie of idolatry is a false narrative. It subtly says other gods are more powerful and do more for us than the Most High God. It suggests other gods are:

- more powerful than the Creator of the universe
- better comforters and carers than the Creator who knows every hair on our head
- greater providers than the one who died for us.

The insult of spiritual adultery is that it steals our heart from the One who is worthy of our affection.

> *For only a fool would **trade** the unfading splendor of the immortal God to worship the fading image of other humans, idols ... (Romans 1:23 TPT)*

How could a true Christian substitute Jesus for another god? When life is tough, is God our refuge and strength or do we turn to false comforters? When life's curveballs hit – disappointment, betrayal, especially from natural or church family – do we blame God or praise Him?

There are too many examples in history of despots who started off in church. Some wanted to be poets or musicians; disillusioned, they turned to witchcraft and Satanism. Karl Marx and Hitler are glaring examples.

> **The lie of idolatry is a false narrative. It subtly says other gods are more powerful than the Most High God.**

Oops, There Are Demons!

Scratch below the surface of idolatry and you discover why it is the worst sin of all – and why the golden calf at Sinai was so serious. What lurks behind the gold and stone statues? Demons.

> *They provoked Him to jealousy with foreign gods ... They sacrificed **to demons**, not to God ... (Deuteronomy 32:16-17)*[26]

When Rehoboam set up the golden calves, the Levites went to seek the Lord. But what accompanied the golden calves? Demons!

> *Then he appointed for himself priests for the high places, for the **demons**, and the calf idols which he had made. (2 Chronicles 11:15)*

Paul warns that worshipping other gods is, in reality, worshipping demons.

> *... the things which the Gentiles sacrifice they **sacrifice to demons** and not to God, and I do not want you to have fellowship with demons. You **cannot drink the cup of the Lord and the cup of demons;** you cannot partake of the Lord's table and of the table of demons. Or do we provoke the Lord to jealousy? (1 Corinthians 10:20-22)*

We cannot have fellowship with demons and the Lord at the same time. The church cannot feast at the table of the Lord and the table of Jezebel and her demonic entourage. Nor can we treat it like a smorgasbord and wander from table to table. Worst of all, the reality would be trading Jesus for a demon!

Today the various gods show up in so many parts of life that appear good. These deceive and seduce believers and non-believers alike. Many are blinded to the reality of demons behind some exercises like yoga and secret societies like freemasonry. Paul warned we must not have any fellowship with demons.

Slippery Slope

Forsaking the Lord opens a door to the enemy, setting us on a risky path to destruction, regardless of who we are – ancient or modern Israel, the Church or civilisation. Idolatry is a downward spiral of lies, deception and devastation. It is toxic.

Israel's history shows the tragic pattern. They obeyed God for a time. Then they worshipped other gods. They lost their moral compass. Devastation followed.

1. Idolatry: hearts turn away from the Lord
2. Sexual sins: immorality and perversion
3. Bloodshed: child sacrifice, murders or wars
4. Exile, captivity or defeat by enemies

Idolatry is a slippery slope; it leads to sexual and social disorder, bringing judgement and death.[27] The Lord said the land itself would 'vomit' Israel for the sin of idolatry.[28] God gave the Ten Commandments to protect and bless us.

Don't Point the Finger at Israel!

Do not accuse Israel! With increasing anti-Semitism, it is too easy to join the chorus of those criticising Israel. Christians must not forget their Hebrew roots. We must pay attention to Paul's stiff warning to the church:

> ... ***beware*** *if you think it could never happen to you, lest your pride becomes your downfall.* (1 Corinthians 10:12 TPT)

The Church risks an episode like Israel at Sinai because of pride, the same sin that caused Lucifer to lose his position in heaven!

The phrase the Holy Spirit highlighted in my dream is repeated in a warning Paul gave to the Church. Various translations interpret, 'The people … rose up to play' (1 Corinthians 10:7) as 'unrestrained revelry', 'a feast turned into an orgy', 'became wildly out of control', or 'indulged in revelry'.

Prior to his murder, Stephen spoke of Israel's history, including the golden calf, and bluntly told the Jewish leaders they had resisted the Holy Spirit![29] Why does the golden calf incident stir up a fanatical, murderous spirit? Stephen's message thunders across millennia, challenging believers to fear the Lord and confront sacred cows opposing true worship.

Despite our own vulnerabilities, we too easily judge Israel. Reading the scriptures, I had wondered why Israel's propensity for idolatry and why they did not just obey the word of God. My inner talk was not complimentary until the Lord rebuked me: 'You are no different!' Ouch!

Paul urges us to learn from Israel's history: *'Flee* from idolatry'.[30]

The Israelites built a golden calf within days of their deliverance from Egypt. Our salvation from spiritual slavery mirrors Israel's deliverance. It is too easy for us to forsake the Lord in subtle ways, insulting our Redeemer and risking bondage to a Christianised Pharaoh!

Amid rising anti-Semitism, it is vital to remember that Israel is an *example* for the Church to learn from. A seductive spirit is seeking to divide believers from Israel, aiming to ultimately stop Jesus from physically sitting on the throne of David in Jerusalem.

Idolatry Our Default

Theologian John Calvin is credited with the famous quote, 'The human heart is a perpetual idol factory'.

Timothy Keller defined an idol as 'anything that absorbs your heart and imagination more than God, anything you seek to give you what only God can give'.[31]

There are four areas of vulnerability: money, sex, power and approval. Satan exploits these, seeking to seduce and lure every person to worship him – including Jesus! The devil offered Jesus *every* kingdom. The price? Bow and worship Satan.

> Jesus answered and said to him, 'Get behind Me, Satan! For it is written, "You shall worship the LORD your God, and Him only you shall serve."' (Luke 4:8)

Jesus would inherit all the kingdoms of the world, but it would come via the cross, not by bowing to Satan. In the end-times, the devil will not just tempt people to worship him; he will demand it! Hence, it is critical for the Church to resolve all matters of idolatry.

We are *all* vulnerable to having other gods. Idolatry is the default state of every human heart, identified as a work of the flesh![32] Our flesh and the devil work in partnership against God. Witchcraft and sorcery are listed in Galatians 5:20 not as occult activities but as works of the flesh!

James suggests that wisdom from the world and flesh lead to demonic and occult activities.

> ... *if you have bitter envy and self-seeking in your hearts, do not boast and lie against the truth. This wisdom does not descend from above, but is earthly, sensual,* **demonic**. *For where envy and self-seeking exist, confusion and every evil thing will be there.* (James 3:15–16)

Operating in the soulish or sensual realms opens the door to demonic activity. Indulging in fleshly desires – whether through lifestyle, speech or music – aligns us with these forces, inviting demonic influence.

We may try to excuse the flesh, but God does not. What begins as earthly and sensual – like self-gratification and *bitter envy* – can become demonic.[33] Pandering to our flesh opposes the Holy Spirit and gravitates to the demonic. Crucifying our flesh allows us to walk in the Spirit and defeat the demonic.

The only solution is to crucify the flesh![34]

Assessment of Idolatry: Good and Bad Kings

God assessed every king of Israel and Judah by whether they were faithful to Him or worshipped other gods. If they encouraged idolatry in the nation, they were a bad king. If they removed idols and restored true worship, they were good.

Despite his failures, David, the sweet psalmist of Israel, is said to have a heart after God. He never built altars to other gods or served them. David's heart remained loyal to the Lord.

> *David did **what was right in the eyes of the LORD**, and had not turned aside from anything that He commanded him all the days of his life, **except** in the matter of **Uriah the Hittite**. (1 Kings 15:1–5)*

Unlike his son Solomon, who despite having built the temple, worshipped other gods. David warned his son, and all of us, the consequences of idolatry are terrible. 'Those who abandon the worship of God **will perish**' (Psalm 73:27 TPT).

Azariah followed and worshipped the Lord in every way 'except that the high places were not removed' (2 Kings 15:3–4). His heart was not one hundred per cent for the Lord.

Manasseh rebuilt the high places, erected altars to Baal and Asherah, worshipped the stars (astrology), sacrificed his sons in the fire, practised sorcery, and 'seduced the people to do **more evil than the pagan nations** whom the Lord had destroyed before the children of Israel' (2 Kings 21:9 NLT).

Then came Josiah. He humbly wept, heartbroken over Israel's condition. The heading for 2 Kings 23 is 'Josiah Restores True Worship'.[35] Josiah burned all pagan altars, removed pagan priests and temple prostitutes, made child sacrifices impossible and got rid of all mediums and household gods. He read the Book of the Covenant to the people, and they returned to the Lord.

God's assessment of good and bad kings reveals He is deeply concerned about worship. *How* we worship *is* important! If we do not worship God in Spirit and in truth, we leave ourselves open to the flesh and demonic interference. Such actions contaminate, pollute and even destroy our worship of God.

At this historical moment, God is calling those like Josiah and David. He needs those who will weep over idols in the heart. He is calling for Gideons who will destroy pagan altars, first in their own lives and then in nations.

Prophets Concerned with True Worship

> *One of the chief concerns of the prophets, such as Isaiah, Jeremiah, and Amos, was the sincerity and purity of worship ... Isaiah is most explicit in his prophetic condemnation of corrupt worship.*[36]

Joshua told Israel, '... choose for yourselves this day, whom you will serve ... But as for me and my house, we will serve the Lord' (Joshua 24:14, 15). Elijah reminded Israel, 'How long will you falter between two opinions? If the LORD is God, follow Him; but if Baal, follow him' (1 Kings 18:21).

As Jonathan Cahn contends in *Return of the Gods*, the worship of Baal, Ishtar and Moloch has been reactivated in Western civilisation. A choice needs to be made, among God's own people first. The war over worship is intense. Holy Spirit is sounding the trumpet call: 'Who will we worship and serve?'

The fierceness of the battle for worship in the end-times will challenge us all. Israel tried to be faithful but got pulled off course. For believers, idolatry can be a simple alteration of focus. We can start well, but if foundational heart issues are amiss, we can end in tragedy.

Jesus alone must be Lord! The only safe place is, as Jesus said, 'Seek **first** the kingdom of God' (Matthew 6:33) – with undivided hearts.

> *Idolatry is the default state of every human heart*

Families are God's idea and a blessing from Him. When we put the Lord first, marriages and families come into divine order. Advice from coworkers and peers is essential, but not co-dependency – our dependence must be on the Lord. Talent is a wonderful gift from God, but it is not our identity – that is completed in Him. We need possessions and wealth for ministry and life, but all our needs are met in the glory and by seeking first His kingdom.

Idolatry makes us unfit to worship in Spirit and truth. Outward appearance is not enough. We must worship with sincere and pure hearts.

God will continue to shake the church until every high place and every pagan altar has gone. Though the awakening that leads to repentance is confronting, it is liberating.

> 'Your own wickedness will correct you, And your backslidings will rebuke you. Know therefore and see that it is an evil and bitter thing That you have forsaken the Lord your God, And the fear of Me is not in you,' says the Lord God of hosts. (Jeremiah 2:19)

CHAPTER TWENTY-TWO

Worship tests the motivation of our hearts. Presuming your heart is right with God is perilous. Restoring true worship involves giving permission to the Holy Spirit to do His deep work in us. The blessing of true worship flows as we repent, crucify the flesh, commune with Him and obediently walk with Him.

CHAPTER TWENTY-THREE

Supernova Sukkot

THE SAVAGE MURDERS AT the Supernova festival on 7 October 2023 are deeply heartbreaking, making this hard to write about. The loss of life is devastating. Does this tragic event fulfil the golden calf dream I had six months prior, of 'all Israel arose to play'?

In presenting this material, I am trying to present the facts of the event through a heavenly lens. God has not forsaken Israel! He is drawing her closer, shaking her, as He is with the Church and the nations. Despite the material you will read, still His 'mercy triumphs over judgement' (James 2:13).

Miraculously, an even greater catastrophe was averted. Israeli Defense Forces soldiers uncovered plans in Lebanon's tunnels for a coordinated and simultaneous attack by Hezbollah, Houthis and Hamas throughout all Israel. Hamas acted prematurely, seeking glory, and the hand of the Lord spared Israel from an even greater disaster.

Global Supernova Festivals

There are many name-brand techno music festivals, sometimes related to the country of origin. Some examples are 'Tomorrowland', 'Awakenings', 'The Street Parade' and many more. Supernova is one of these and refers to a massive explosion of a star, causing a burst of light. NASA has observed many such explosions, which are among the most energetic events in the universe. Tragically, 7 October was a colossal explosion at the Supernova festival, but not as expected.

Supernova festivals are a global phenomenon. They have elaborate stage designs and provide a carnival atmosphere. The focus is the techno artists, DJs, and space to dance and party day and night.

Rolling Stone magazine of 15 October 2023, tells us the story about the festival held at Re'im.

> Between 3,000 and 4,000 attendees flocked to an open-air space – about three miles from the Gaza border – where 16 DJs from around the world were set to spin in darkness and light for 15 hours straight … Officially called "**Supernova Sukkot Gathering**," … The all-night party was … Woodstock with electronic music. It's … a hippie culture, but the music is different." **The headline of the story was:** 'They Wanted to Dance in Peace. And They Got Slaughtered'. Israel's Supernova festival celebrated music and unity. It turned into the deadliest concert attack in history.[37]

Confusion: Music or Gunfire?

At 6:30 am, as rockets, gunfire and sirens erupted, Supernova festival attendees did not initially notice the mayhem. Familiar with Gaza rockets or under the influence, many mistook the chaos for music. The Guardian reported, 'at first the rocket noise sounded like it was part of the music. The beat of the music became confused with gunfire'.[38] Only when the music stopped did reality dawn. Panic ensued as concertgoers and DJs fought to survive.

Tragically, the music masked the danger, blending with gunfire. Similarly, when God sent Moses and Joshua to stop the idolatrous party at Sinai, Joshua asked, 'What is this sound I hear?' Is it the sound of music or war?[39]

In a dream some thirty years ago, I witnessed loud music fuelling an orgy. Adjusting the volume did nothing. Finally, the Lord said, 'Pull the plug.' The power source had to be removed!

Sometimes we need to find the power source, turn the music off and uproot it. There are times we must silence distractions to discern reality and thus stop substantial harm. Perhaps the Church and society should turn off some music to grasp reality and to hear what the Holy Spirit is saying.

Mystical Music Genre: 'Supernova Psytrance'

Supernova psytrance, linked to psychedelic trance and electronic music, emerged in the 1990s, coinciding with the first edition of this book.[40] Originating in India's Goa trance scene, it blends hypnotic beats, fast tempos suitable for dance (a hundred and thirty to a hundred and fifty beats per minute) and tribal melodies to induce an 'altered state of consciousness'. Some label this music as a 'glimpse into the mystical music genre'.[41]

The *Rolling Stone* article continued:

> The [Supernova] festival reflected ... Israel's history with **musical escapism**. In Israel, mandatory military service starts at 18. In the 1980s, post-service soldiers travelled to Goa, immersing in techno, culture, and drugs, bringing psytrance back home. "[Psytrance] is up-tempo, four-on-the-floor dance music," says Freeland. "The minimum tempo [in dance music] is 130 beats per minute, but [psytrance] is up to 150. It's what we used to

*describe as acid house but sped up." This influence shaped the **Hindu-inspired tents and decor at Supernova.*** [42]

Supernova, Hindu Shiva and the Pantheon of 'gods'

A TikTok video confirmed what *Rolling Stone* hinted: a giant Shiva statue loomed over the festival stage.

Messianic musicians in Israel who had once played at such events have left the scene because of the rampant idolatry and witchcraft.

Eastern religions worship a pantheon of gods. Hinduism has many gods. Shiva is their supreme god – creator, protector of the universe and god of destruction. The presence of Shiva above the stage aligns with the 'Hindu-inspired' elements and the destruction unleashed on 7 October 2023.

Initially, I mistook the image on TikTok for a Buddha, as Hindu gods influence some Buddhist branches, like Tibetan Buddhism, which has a major temple in our city. Young Israelis frequently finish their army training and travel to Asian countries to immerse themselves in Eastern religions. This reflects a misdirected spiritual hunger. An Israeli friend nearly became a Buddhist nun before Jesus rescued her.[43]

In 2008 in post-tsunami Phuket, a pastor invited us to conduct a worship conference and to worship over the beaches touched by the spirit of death. The pastor hosting our worship conference said that nearly thirty souls were saved weekly in this Buddhist stronghold. I asked how this worked. His answer was telling. He explained that locals, accustomed to hundreds of gods, initially viewed Jesus as another god to add to their existing collection. Only about one-third of converts renounce the other gods to follow Jesus alone.

In one of our meetings, the Holy Spirit led me to challenge attendees to choose Jesus as the only way to the Father. True disciples of Jesus must bow to Him as the only supreme God, Creator and Redeemer.

Moses and Joshua warned Israel against adopting the gods of other nations. Israel was to be different – a light to the nations. Similarly, spiritually hungry Israelis, Australians and others must encounter and connect with the living God, not ritualistic religion, to find true salvation.

Supernova Sukkot, Feast of Tabernacles

The full name and timing of Israel's Supernova festival carry a stark prophetic message. Sukkot, the Feast of Tabernacles, prophesies the end-times when God will dwell with humanity forever. In 2023, Supernova aligned with Sukkot (September 29–October 6), incorporating the feast's name and timing.

While holding up the golden calf, Aaron proclaimed a 'feast to the Lord' (Exodus 32). In 2023, a Hindu god loomed above the stage as Israelis danced before it during the 'feast of the Lord'. This haunting echo of the golden calf is unmistakable and heartbreaking.

To prepare for Sukkot, Jewish families build sukkahs – like gazebos but with roofs of natural materials like palm fronds. Families live and eat in these booths for a week of joy, remembering God's presence during forty wilderness years in tents. But it also foreshadows the future.

> *Behold, the tabernacle of God is with men, and he will dwell with them, and they shall be his people, and God himself shall be with them, and be their God. (Revelation 21:3)*

On the last day of Sukkot, they pray for rain for the coming agricultural season. This occurred when Jesus was at the Temple. While priests prayed for rain and poured out water, Jesus poignantly invited all who were thirsty to drink from Him, the living water.[44]

The eighth day, Simchat Torah ('Joy of the Torah'), celebrates completing the yearly Torah reading cycle (Genesis to Deuteronomy plus prophets). To celebrate this cycle, and before the new one starts, they dance holding the Torah scrolls – literally dancing with God's word. In some ways, they show greater reverence for scripture than many Gentile Christians!

Dancing with Torah or Golden Calf?

At Mt Sinai, Moses received the Torah while Israel danced, not with the Torah, but the golden calf, violating the covenant. Moses shattered the tablets, symbolising the broken covenant. The Supernova Sukkot Gathering, held on Simchat Torah, coincided with Hamas's attack on Israel. Observant Jews danced with the Torah in synagogues, but festival attendees danced before a stage with Shiva, the Hindu god of destruction. Instead of dancing with Torah, thousands of young Israelis danced before Shiva, figuratively a modern golden calf.

My heart sank. I wept – and recalled the 12 April dream that had warned 'And all Israel rose up to play'. Did dancing before the god of destruction, especially on the day of Simchat Torah, give permission to the demonic realm to wreak such havoc? Was this serious breach before the Lord akin to Israel's sin at Sinai, betraying Israel's covenantal call?

'And Israel Rose Up to Play': Revelry

> *Israel ate, they drank, they danced, they sang, and they rose up to play ... (Exodus 32:6)*

This phrase is the crux of the episode, as highlighted in my dream, providing insight into the Supernova festival and some practices even within the Church.

The mix of alcohol, song and dance soon descended into sensual and sexual revelry. Most drinking parties follow the same descent, ending in licentious immorality. The Hebrew word for 'play' is *tsâchaq* and means to laugh outright in merriment or scorn. The implication is to mock, to jest, to sport!

Other Bible translations add insight.

- The Amplified Bible: 'they got up to play' (without moral restraint).
- The Complete Jewish Bible: 'then they got up to **indulge** in revelry'.
- Names of God Bible: 'Afterward, they sat down to a feast, which turned into an orgy'.

It is clear ancient Israel had a drunken orgy before a foreign god. Wild partying typically follows rebellion and defiance against God. The Supernova music festival had a false god, an altar (stage), plenty of alcohol, psychedelic drugs, dancing, and likely promiscuity and orgies.

In the quotes from *Rolling Stone*, it refers to the Supernova as 'musical escapism'. How often is music used like a drug to anaesthetise pain or as a false comforter to deliver us from whatever ails us, rather than going to the Lord for comfort? Anne Hamilton calls them 'false refuges'.[45]

God's pure worship involves singing and dancing, resulting in joy, gladness and blessings. Mixed worship inevitably exhibits a partying spirit and a mocking spirit. Sadly, we have witnessed this even within the church. Mixed and idolatrous worship results in hedonistic singing and dancing, taking on a partying spirit. In this context, hedonism confuses what is of God and what is of the flesh. What begins as revelry often leads to loss of moral restraint.

Has immorality become an issue in the house of God? If you think so, then check the music. Wherever such practices are found, His holy name is often mocked.

Was my dream six months earlier a severe prophetic warning? Let Israel and the Church heed His warnings. Do not let mockery rise in our ranks against Him! Paul warned God will not tolerate mockery.

> *Do not be deceived, God is not mocked; for whatever a man sows, that he will also reap. For he who sows to his flesh will of the flesh reap corruption, but he who sows to the Spirit will of the Spirit reap everlasting life. (Galatians 6:7–8)*

We live in a critical and defining moment in history. For the Holy Spirit to be highlighting this phrase suggests we must have a problem that needs addressing. This is as much a call to prayer as a warning to heed – for the modern state of Israel *and* the Church.

If we sow to the flesh, we will reap corruption. And 'rising up to play' is a sowing to the flesh. Have we in any way, shape or form mocked the New Covenant? Or do we think God just turns a blind eye?

Singing and the Noise of War

When Joshua descended Mt Sinai, he was unsure if he heard the sound of war or music. 'There is a **noise of war** in the camp' (Exodus 32:17). Moses replied, 'It is not the noise of the shout of victory, nor the noise of the cry of defeat, but the **sound of singing** I hear' (Exodus 32:18).

Was it war? Was it singing? Who was right?

They both were.

The Hebrew word for 'singing' used here is *anah*,[46] which means to browbeat, depress, afflict, defile or force – unlike other Hebrew words for singing that denote praise and thanksgiving to God.

Israel's singing around the golden calf was a war against God, akin to battle cries, fuelling idolatrous revelry, drunkenness and defilement. Drunken singing with its lack of inhibition can expose the heart – and in this case, it was not towards the Lord. To further understand the choice of word *anah*, it was used in 2 Samuel 13:12 where Tamar tried to resist rape. It expresses a sound of destruction, of violence, abuse or worse. How often does intoxication and wild music at parties result in rape, fights breaking out, even fuelling murder?

The sound Joshua heard was an act of war against God! Their songs of merriment were mocking their Deliverer and sounded like people fighting in a battle. This was not a spiritual war to defeat demons but to help them. Joshua perceived the destroyer at work in this hostile revelry, a hallmark of idolatrous bacchanalia. When music strays from glorifying God and instead accompanies idol worship, it can open doors to demonic oppression, causing physical, emotional and spiritual harm. People become defiled and vexed.

Some music can open doors to demonic oppression and even possession. Lucifer's fall changed his music from glorious praise to a sound of war against God. Instead of glory, death and destruction covered his beauty and music.

> *Your pomp is brought down to Sheol, and the sound of your stringed instruments; the maggot is spread under you, and worms cover you.* (Isaiah 14:11)

Similarly, when churches adopt music from the sexual revolution, the spirit of rock or attached to any other gods, it can bring aggression and division, not spiritual victory. Not all singing by God's people exalts Him! Sadly, there are times that it actually wars against Him – especially if our hearts stray.

True worship, led by the Holy Spirit, is a powerful weapon in spiritual warfare, even strong and robust, but carnal singing – marked by *anah* – afflicts and divides God's people.

I have witnessed warfare music in churches driven more by the flesh than the Spirit, invading the people of God rather than the gates of hell. Musical bombardment and defilement frequently occur in spiritually abusive environments. After such an experience, an ordained prophet told me he 'no longer believed in spiritual warfare!' The issue was with carnal weapons. If you observe immorality, division or abuse, ask the Lord about the music.

Sadly, the music from the sexual revolution brought a sound of war between the generations, even in the Church. One of the saddest consequences I have seen has been the spiritual abuse, divisions and dishonour of older believers. Too often, churches make musical choices based on being 'relevant' to youth, dismissing the needs of others, even suggesting headphones for those bothered by loud music.

> *Music from the sexual revolution brought a sound of war between the generations, even in the Church.*

This insensitivity and dishonour strengthen and aid demonic schisms between generations, contrary to the prayer of Jesus for unity. These things ought not to be.

Destruction

In the natural, we secure our homes and systems against thieves, intruders, hackers and terrorists with locks, bars, alarms and firewalls to seal every entry point. The spiritual realm requires similar vigilance.

David, in Psalms 27 and 91, found safety hiding under the shadow of the Almighty. Thus, he sang praises to the Rock of salvation:

> *For in the time of trouble He shall hide me in His pavilion; In the secret place of His tabernacle He shall hide me ... (Psalm 27:5)*

Hiding in God offers protection. David's songs contrasted sharply with the destructive songs at Mt Sinai.

Scripture repeatedly warns that forsaking God for idols brings devastating consequences. At Mt Sinai, three thousand of Israel's finest were killed for mocking God in their idolatrous orgy. Similarly, on 7 October 2023, Hamas hang-glided into Israel, first attacking those at the Supernova Sukkot Gathering.

> *Idolatry opens a spiritual door for the destroyer.*

They killed more in this one place where young Israelis had danced before Shiva, the Hindu god of destruction. The result was tragic: loss of life, innocence, immeasurable sorrow and a surge in global anti-Semitism.

Idolatry opens a spiritual door for the destroyer. The Church, too, has suffered devastation as it embraced the music of other gods in our culture. Scandals, eagerly exploited by the media, reflect this devastation. After three months travelling Australia to release the first edition of *Restoring True Worship*, I observed a troubling apathy and compromise in the Australian Church. If we ignore these lessons, will we face similar persecution?

Powerful Promises to Israel

Betrayal, infiltration and open doors to the enemy, like those seen at the Supernova festival and the 7 October 2023 attacks, are not Israel's end. They signal birth pangs for restoration and greater glory. The Lord says when they are back in their land, He will wash them clean from the pollution of all their idols. This is His promise. And He is faithful to His word!

> *For I will take you from among the nations,* ***gather you out of all countries, and bring you into your own land****... I will* ***cleanse*** *you from all your filthiness and* ***from all your idols****. (Ezekiel 36:24–25)*

This wonderful prophecy is unfolding. In the wake of the Holocaust, in 1948, Israel's miraculous rebirth occurred. Jews continue returning from the nations in growing numbers, despite ongoing wars and threats. As they return, the Lord says He will cleanse them of their idols. Though the monumental change is gradual, a few statistics in recent history show what the Lord is doing.

In 1948, there was just a handful of Jewish people who believed Jesus, Yeshua, was their Jewish Messiah.

In 1967, after the Six-Day War reunited Jerusalem, the Jesus Revolution broke out. Many who were involved were Jewish hippies who embraced Yeshua as Messiah. Messianic congregations in Israel multiplied, reaching about thirty thousand believers by 2017. Growth continues, though precise numbers are hard to verify.

Post 7 October trauma has deepened spiritual hunger. The Lord is wooing them back to His heart. Many Israelis, especially in kibbutzim hit by the massacre, recognise that giving away His land does not bring peace and that attackers targeted them just for being Jewish. Jewish identity, battered by pogroms and the Holocaust, is reviving.

Spiritual hunger is growing. 'Yeshua' is Israel's most Googled term, and online Jewish testimonies garner millions of views, surpassing the number of Hebrew speakers![47] Even if inflated by bots, a spiritual stirring is undeniable.

As so many prayed for the hostages, visions were seen of the Lord dispatching angels to minister His Presence to them in the Gaza tunnels. Some former hostages are now sharing their stories of encountering Him in captivity, prompting previously secular Jews to pray, attend synagogue and honour Adonai. His promise to cleanse and restore Israel is active – He is faithful.

CHAPTER TWENTY-FOUR

Gold For Royalty and Worship, Not Idols

'The silver is Mine, and the gold is Mine,' says the LORD of hosts. 'The glory of this latter temple shall be greater than the former,' says the LORD of hosts. 'And in this place I will give peace,' says the LORD of hosts. (Haggai 2:8–9)

Gold Represents Royalty: Worship the King of Glory

IN A PROPHECY TO encourage building the second temple, Haggai said the gold and silver belong to God. Gold represents His Glory, reflecting the magnificence of the great King. Gold represents the atmosphere of pure worship surrounding the throne and filling the kingdom of Almighty God.

The Bible first mentions gold at creation. A river flowed from the Garden of Eden, and there was gold – pure gold!

The first river, Overflowing Increase (Pishon), encircles the gold-laden land of Havilah. The gold of that land is pure... (Genesis 2:11–12 TPT)

- Gold adorned the tabernacle and temple, including the furniture.
- The wise men brought gifts of gold, frankincense and myrrh to worship the newborn King of the Jews.
- The bridal garment of the King's bride is embroidered with gold.[48]
- Gold represents pure hearts refined in the fire of God.
- Gold paves the streets of the New Jerusalem.

Wealth of Abraham and King David: Fund Building the Temple

Abraham, called to father the nation of Israel and other descendants by faith, was wealthy, with much livestock, silver, and gold.[49]

After the golden calf fiasco, the Lord gave Israel instructions for the tabernacle. They were to bring what was necessary, including gold they had plundered from the Egyptians.

> From what you have, take an offering for the Lord. Everyone who is willing... bring... an offering of gold, silver and bronze ... (Exodus 35:5)

The list also included linen, yarn, lambskins, wood, olive oil, spices and gemstones. It might be hard to believe, but they had to tell the people to stop giving – they had more than they needed![50]

But they had to tell the people to stop giving – they had more than they needed!

Though King David desperately wanted to build the temple, the Lord said, 'No, your son Solomon will.' But David provided the designs and an extraordinary amount of gold, silver and treasures.

CHAPTER TWENTY-FOUR

> *With all my resources I have provided for the temple of my God – gold for the gold work, silver... bronze ... iron ... and wood ... as well as ... all kinds of fine stone and marble – all of these in **large quantities**. (1 Chronicles 29:2 NIV)*

King David contributed approximately 3862.6 tons of gold and 37,762 tons of silver, equivalent roughly to more than $450 billion (calculated in mid-2025). Most of this was from Israel's treasury, but a staggering amount was from David's own pocket: 112 tons of the gold and about 262 tons of silver. And that is before the bronze, wood, marble, stones and gemstones.[51]

Inspired by the King's generosity, the people all gave.

Add the letter 'l' to God and you have the word gold. When it is just God and gold, it is magnificent. The description of the New Jerusalem in Revelation 21 is stunning:

> *... He showed me the holy city, Jerusalem, descending out of heaven from God. It was infused with the **glory of God,** and its **radiance** was **like** that of a very **rare jewel** ... The angel ... had a **gold measuring rod** to measure the city, its gates and walls. The **city** was **pure gold** ... The city has no need for the sun or moon to shine, for the **glory of God is its light**, and its lamp is the Lamb. (Revelation 21:10-23 TPT)*

The resplendence of gold reflects the glory and the magnificence of the King and His kingdom.

Problems come when dragons and men want the gold intended for the worship of the King of Glory! Finances and worship to the Lord become a fierce battle zone to prepare the way for the return of the King of kings to earth. We must cleanse the desecration of gold. Our praises establish a golden pathway worthy of His sacred and scarred footsteps.

Hence, the Lord gave explicit instructions that gold and silver were only for His house – not other worship houses!

> *The resplendence of gold reflects the magnificence of the King and His kingdom.*

Never make any gods of silver or gold for yourselves. Never worship them. (Exodus 20:23 GW)

While Moses had been in the Presence of the Lord receiving the blueprints for the tabernacle, including the gold needed for worship, that is when Aaron created the golden calf. No wonder God and Moses were so angry. Israel had 'made gods out of gold **for themselves**' (Exodus 32:31 GW).

Gold and Dragons: Bendigo

Where there is gold, there are dragons. This can be spiritually, psychologically or naturally.

The major Australian gold rush of the mid-1800s led to the creation of our city of Bendigo, two hours north-west of Melbourne. During the gold rush, Bendigo yielded over 700 tons of gold. There is nearly as much gold still in the ground, but it is difficult to reach. The wealth of the gold fields (Bendigo, Ballarat and Beechworth, to name a few towns) built Melbourne and helped to pay the debt of the United Kingdom.

Reflecting the legacy of the many Chinese on the goldfields, Bendigo has the largest imperial dragon in the southern hemisphere. An imperial dragon is a symbol of the emperor or the king, as Chinese culture considers emperors descendants of dragons. Bendigo's first Chinese dragon, Loong, took part in the procession in Melbourne to celebrate Federation in 1901.[52] Government grants now sustain the dragon museum.

Living in a city of 'gold and dragons' and raising up a worship ministry, Tabernacle of David, over twenty years is a message in itself! The topic definitely reflects our life story.

People believed that dragons, or *drakon* in Greek mythology, guarded gold because they were the most fearsome creatures that could deter potential thieves. Dragons in Chinese culture are symbols of 'luck', power and authority. Akin to Baal, they have control over storms, rain and floods.

Jordan Peterson said, 'Dragons hoard gold because the thing you most need is always found where you least want to look.'[53] He warns, 'You don't get the gold without the dragon!' Peterson uses the dragon and gold analogy as a warning of psychological problems when we leave too many problems unchecked, which leads to excessive chaos.

Biblically, the dragon is the thief who Jesus said robs, kills and destroys,[54] and is the father of lies.[55] Revelation 12:9–10 identifies him as 'the great dragon, serpent of old, called the Devil and Satan, who deceives the whole world … the accuser of the brethren.'

Because gold belongs to God, represents His Glory and is a picture of pure worship, the dragon wants it. Scripture, history, mythology and psychology all agree that dragons show up to steal physical, spiritual and emotional gold wherever they find it.

Because the Lord specified gold for building His house, the devil seeks to contaminate true worship and the glory either through financial insufficiency or scandals in the house of the Lord. He steals what belongs to God for his own benefit or to counterfeit or contaminate true worship – whatever is most effective.

How easily do people find money to build temples for other gods while houses of true worship struggle financially? How much money is available for worship stages of false gods?

Contention for Glory: Gold and Dragons

In the year 2000, the Australian Prayer Network came to Bendigo to pray. Global watchmen, prophets and intercessors had identified Bendigo as vital to Australia regarding a spiritual war over the dragon. They saw the body of the dragon winding through Asia, with its tail ending over Bendigo.

By this time, we had already published the first edition of this book and established a prayer group for Israel. But I was ready to leave the city because it was so tough. We put our house on the market. As the Australian Prayer Network came in, they said, 'What God's wanting to do is like trying to dig gold out of this ground. It's all rock, it's hard rock, and you just want to give up before finding the seams of gold.' But God was saying, 'Keep digging, keep digging! Because "there's gold in "them there hills"!' So we stayed!

After gold is found and extracted, it then proceeds to the refining stage, separating it from the dirt. In our city, they used cyanide, a poison. The Lord spoke to us and said, 'Sometimes there's poison in your life.' But He allows it to bring the dross to the surface to get the pure gold.

An intercessor from England visiting Bendigo gave this prophecy.

> *I just saw Bendigo, the centre of gold rush Australia, and as I saw this, I heard the Spirit whisper. There is going to be such a gold rush in Bendigo, but instead of gold, people will be rushing after the presence of God. Unlike the gold, God's presence will not run out and 'prospectors' will not compete for space; worshippers will rise up, teaching and living God's*

presence, spreading His Glory throughout this land and exporting the fire to the rest of the world. I see fire and gold, the fire that refines, and the worshippers here will be like refined gold, pure and malleable by the Spirit of God. Bendigo's past was in man's riches, but its future is in God's riches. Revival fire, fall! Amen.[56]

This encouraging word has enabled many to continue. Living in the atmosphere of a city affected by gold and dragons is how the Lord has taught me what interferes with true worship and how to restore true worship. In this environment, He has taught me the priority of throne room worship in warfare and the need to contend for the glory.

Gold, Greed and Mayhem

Wealth itself is not evil. Greed is the problem. When gold, silver, money and wealth are not used to worship and give glory to the Lord as intended, then trouble is on the horizon. Turning gold and silver into idols is a demonic snare that tests the heart. Paul warned Timothy:

> *… the **love** of money is a root of all kinds of evil, for which some have strayed from the faith in their greediness, and pierced themselves through with many sorrows. (1 Timothy 6:10)*

Greed shifts focus from God to self, corrupting gold and wealth, opening floodgates to the enemy. Paul warned the church at Ephesus 'greed is the essence of idolatry' (Ephesians 5:5 TPT). (See Chapter 27, 'Our Sacred Cows'.)

Many movies have depicted the havoc wrought by greed during gold rushes – murder, racism, riots, prostitution and alcohol abuse. In Victoria, Australia, the government exploited miners through unjust taxes, sparking further trouble, even bloodshed at Ballarat's Eureka Stockade. Amid it all, Bendigo had some revivals.

Ana Mendez (see Chapter 12, 'Frequencies of the Glory') saw the bloodshed on the goldfields as a key to revival in Australia but hindered by a glass facade which dragons hide behind. The Lord's sound is key to breaking the glass facade.

Gold exposes greed and corruption. To discover those responsible for scandals, whether in politics, business, or church, follow the money!

> *There is a battle for true worship that manifests in gold and in dragons.*

Many rock musicians who sold their souls to the devil for fame and fortune have faced misery and premature death. A *British Medical Journal* study says many rock and pop stars die young – average age of forty-five years in the US and thirty-nine in Europe –from drug overdoses, AIDS or drink-driving accidents.[57]

> *Bloodthirsty and deceitful men shall not live out half their days. (Psalm 55:23)*

There is a battle for true worship that manifests in gold and in dragons. Israel's gold calf replaced the true God of Abraham, Isaac and Jacob, polluting the glory. Do we create gods of gold? Ministries must guard against gold, glory and sexual lust. Ironically, old gold towns like Bendigo often have high rates of poverty.

Building Our House Before His: Haggai

After Nebuchadnezzar destroyed the first temple and took hostages, exiled Jews returned from Babylon to rebuild. Yet, true to form, the outraged enemy unleashed cunning tactics to halt its completion. In this context, Haggai prophesied the Lord owns the gold and silver and a greater glory would be seen in the second temple.

> *The people of the land tried to discourage the people of Judah. They troubled them in building, and hired counselors against them to frustrate their purpose ... (Ezra 4:4–5)*

Eventually, accusations, spies and lawfare worked – work stopped for some ten years! 'Thus the work of the house of God which is at Jerusalem ceased ...' (Ezra 4:24).

Building a house of prayer for all nations is very difficult. It might sound as if God's plan should be straightforward. I can assure you it is not! Trouble comes from within and without.

Whether we think about the Christian houses of prayer, or the third temple to be rebuilt in Jerusalem, opposition is fierce! The reason? They provide a clear choice over *who* is to be worshipped. The Temple Mount in Jerusalem is a demonic flashpoint. Many have had visions of the dragon trying to occupy it. A house of prayer on Temple Mount is a battle over whether the God of Israel or the god of Islam (Allah) will be worshipped. In 2014, we were in Jerusalem for three days of worship. On the second day, there was a 'day of rage' called, and the old city was closed down. The Holy Spirit led Laurence to bind Luciferian spirits around the Temple Mount. His first attempts were choked off. With persistence, he finally could mouth the words and pray it. The third day saw a major breakthrough.

Construction of the second temple resumed some ten years later after it was stopped (the second year of King Darius' reign). It was the prophecies of Haggai and Zechariah that got them back to work.

> *Then the prophet Haggai and Zechariah ... prophesied to the Jews who were in Judah and Jerusalem ... So Zerubbabel ... rose up and began to build the house of God which is in Jerusalem; and the prophets of God were with them, helping them.* (Ezra 5:1-2)

Haggai's first word was a stinging challenge to the people of God to get back to work and build the house of God. Having been discouraged and idle for ten years, they had devoted their energy and resources to building their own houses. Haggai told God's people they were living in their own expensive panelled houses, while the house of the Lord was in ruins.

The Hebrew word implies their houses had wainscoted panels used for exclusive feature walls or a trim to insulate and decorate.

This is what the LORD of Armies says: 'Carefully consider your ways! My house lies in ruins while each of you is busy working on your own house'. (Haggai 1:7, 9 GW)

The Lord was calling for His people to get their priorities straight – His house before their own. It was in this context He identified gold and silver as belonging to the Lord. Though the second temple was not as grand as Solomon's temple, He said,

> 'The latter glory of this house will be greater than the former,' says the Lord of hosts, 'and in this place I shall give [the ultimate] peace and prosperity,' declares the Lord of hosts. (Haggai 2:9)

The dragon will steal the gold intended for God's house to ruin, delay, discourage and stop the building of the house of God. We need the voice of the true prophets to encourage God's people to finish building His house. The finishing anointing is needed for the houses of prayer and true worship. Building our own houses can also refer to building our own ministries ahead of what He wants built for His kingdom. Finish corporate houses of prayer and worship for all nations before focusing on our own ministries.

Buy Gold From the Lord!

There is a greater glory coming, one that goes beyond a physical temple. In 70 AD, Titus destroyed the second temple, about forty years after Jesus warned of its destruction. Through the sacrifice of Jesus, believers are now the living stones of the temple. Our bodies are the temple of the Holy Spirit.[58]

> *... like living stones, be yourselves built [into] a spiritual house (1 Peter 2:5 AMPC)*

> *You are rising like the perfectly fitted stones of the temple. (Ephesians 2:20 TPT)*

There is a greater glory in this temple because Yeshua, the cornerstone, is the foundation of our lives. Human hands cannot build this temple. As He transforms and sanctifies us, we become the gold refined in His fire.

> *He will sit as a refiner and a purifier of silver; He will **purify the sons of Levi, And purge them as gold and silver,** That they may **offer to the LORD An offering** in righteousness. (Malachi 3:3)*

It is this gold that adorns His temple – a greater glory. We, as human beings, become the carriers of His Glory! The process requires His gold. The Lord counsels us through His word to the lukewarm Church of Laodicea:

> *I counsel you to **buy from Me gold refined in the fire,** that you may be rich; and **white garments, that you may be clothed**, that the shame*

of your nakedness may not be revealed; and anoint your eyes with eye salve, that you may see. (Revelation 3:18)

As we embrace His fire, He refines our hearts to be pure gold and set apart to worship Him. There is a beautiful picture of this process of redemption and refining in Japanese art whereby broken pottery pieces are repaired, and the cracks filled with gold. This process is called kintsugi, which turns broken pieces, like our lives, into something even more beautiful. We become His workmanship or His poetry.[59]

That refined gold represents pure worship to the Lord.

If we do not purchase His gold from His fire, then instead of gold being purified hearts worshipping the Lord, gold will be turned into idols for the worship of other gods.

He is removing the garments of shame from His bride. His bride's garments are pure, white and embroidered with gold. Clothed in His royal garments, He enables us to offer heart-generated praises and give Him pure worship He alone deserves.

2023 Word to Watchman at Mt Carmel

As a spontaneous prophetic act, I took some small pieces of gold from Bendigo to Israel in 2023. In preparation for prayer for the Elijah summit on Mt Carmel, the Lord said He was mining treasures on Mt Carmel and going deep into the foundations. I presented the gold to the leadership team after sharing my brief testimony as in this chapter and proclaimed that refined gold represents pure worship to the Lord.

Based on what I prayed at that gathering, pray this prayer for yourself, and the Body of Messiah worldwide.

CHAPTER TWENTY-FOUR

Thank you, Lord, that you are calling forth worshippers in Spirit and in truth; a company You are refining in Your holy fire. Your fire purifies and cleanses, to bring forth worshippers who are like the purest of gold. Though at times You allow 'poisons' to cause the dross to come to the surface, it is to ensure there is no mixture or contaminates left. Thank you, Lord, that you desire our hearts to be the purest of gold, so that from the nations comes forth Your pure, holy priesthood, dressed in royal robes adorned with gold. Like Zadok the priest, and as Your Melchizedek priesthood, we present our bodies as living sacrifices to bring forth the praises You alone deserve – pure, holy worship to Almighty God, King of kings, Messiah. Amen.

CHAPTER TWENTY-FIVE

The Ark or Golden Calf?

Two Icons

THE ARK OF THE Covenant and the golden calf can be metaphors representing the battle for true worship. Both are found at Mt Sinai as the Lord betrothed Himself to Israel, and the contrast between them could not be greater.

You may wonder where the Ark was on Mt Sinai. While on top of the mountain, God gave Moses the detailed blueprint of the Ark and commissioned him to build it.

Though a shadow at that point, the Ark revealed on Sinai foreshadowed what was to come and provides a powerful message that resonates through the ages. The Ark of the Covenant manifests the glory, the fullness of who God is, like every facet of a complete diamond glistening in the light. This revelation foreshadows how all His goodness, severity, majesty, authority and power will play out in history.

Purpose of the Ark

The Ark of the Covenant was the first piece of furniture God instructed Moses to build with all its specifications. What was its function?

> And there **I will meet with you**, and **I will speak with you** from **above the mercy seat,** from between

the two cherubim which are on the ark of the Testimony ... (Exodus 25:22)

The Ark is a meeting place, and the seat is His mercy. Once built, the glory descended on the tabernacle and 'the LORD spoke to Moses face to face, as a man speaks to his friend' (Exodus 33:11).

The Ark is important in the death and resurrection of Jesus. He placed His blood on the mercy seat, in heaven. The mercy seat is effectively the lid of the Ark.

*... we have come to Jesus who established a new covenant **with his blood sprinkled upon the mercy seat.** (Hebrews 12:24 TPT)*

Hence, the mercy seat is our hope. It is where we obtain mercy and hear God.

*Our **anchor of hope** is fastened to the mercy seat in the heavenly realm beyond the sacred threshold ... (Hebrews 6:19 TPT)*

Ever since the Garden of Eden, the Lord's intention was to establish a place on earth where God and humanity could safely meet for sweet and intimate fellowship. The Lord wanted a place where He could dwell and commune with His image bearers. The Creator of the universe wanted a habitation with humans. Extraordinary! Right there is the love and mercy of 'God so loved the world ...'

The Ark is the point where heaven and earth meet, a place where Almighty God can have reverential communion with those in covenant with Him. The Ark, the glory, is a place of immense privilege, awe and responsibility. Here, God speaks to His people. Those who honour His covenant will hear the thunderous yet tender voice of Almighty God as He reveals the secrets of His heart.

The Lord gave Moses meticulous instructions from Exodus 25 to 31, beginning with the Ark of the Covenant, the rest of the tabernacle furniture and the clothing and orders for the priests officiating within the sacred space.

Top of Sinai: His Glory and the Ark

The glory of the Lord rested on the top of Sinai. After seven days, the Lord invited Moses to enter the glory cloud.

> *The sight of the glory of the LORD was like a consuming fire on the **top** of the mountain ... So Moses **went into the midst** of the **cloud** ... (Exodus 24:17–18)*

Moses was on top of the mountain *within* the glory cloud. The glory totally engulfed him. While there, Moses witnessed the Lord engrave His laws (Torah) onto tablets of stone and then Moses received the blueprints for the tabernacle and all its furniture, beginning with the Ark.

God instructed Moses to build according to the pattern *already* established. The earthly tabernacle and Ark are replicas of the original in heaven.

> **... make Me a sanctuary, that I may dwell among them...** the **pattern of the tabernacle** and the pattern of **all its furnishings** ... (Exodus 25:8–9)

> *The priests on earth serve in a temple that is but* ***a copy modeled after the heavenly sanctuary;*** *a shadow of the reality. For when Moses began to construct the tabernacle God warned him and said, 'You must **precisely** follow the pattern I revealed to you on Mount Sinai.' (Hebrews 8:5 TPT)*

The original real tabernacle and Ark are in heaven!

The Ark Opened After Seventh Trumpet

At the end of days, the real Ark in heaven will be opened.

The symbolic Ark was vital to Israel's history, and we His people are carriers of the glory. However, the real Ark in heaven will be actively involved in end-time events when all kingdoms on earth will finally bow to King Jesus. The golden calf and every other idol will become like Dagon – shattered before the Ark. Regardless of what nation has what god, they will all fall before the Presence of the Lord.

In Revelation 11, the seventh trumpet sounds; the clash of kingdoms comes to a final climax. Previously, the kingdoms of the world had railed against Jesus the Messiah. Now, all kingdoms come under the rule and authority of King Jesus.

> *Then the seventh angel sounded … 'The kingdoms of this world have become the kingdoms of our Lord and of His Christ, and He shall reign forever and ever!' … Then the* **temple** *of God was* **opened** *in heaven, and* **the ark of His covenant was seen in His temple***. And there were lightnings, noises, thunderings, an earthquake, and great hail. (Revelation 11:15, 19)*

When the Ark in heaven is opened, the Lord releases His full stop and exclamation mark on history and the war for worship. Hail removes the refuge of lies as the covenant with death is annulled (Isaiah 28:17). His voice and glory sound like thunder (Psalm 29:3–5).

> *Listen to the roar of God's voice, to the rumbling that comes from his mouth. He flashes* **his lightning everywhere***... It is followed by the* **roar of his voice***. He thunders with his majestic voice. He doesn't hold the lightning back when his thunder*

is heard. El's voice thunders in miraculous ways. It does great things that we cannot understand. (Job 37:2–5 NOG)

The Lord has the final say. There is only one rightful king with a claim to the throne. True worshippers of all nations, tribes and tongues are called to His mountain to bow and worship before Him.

Base of Sinai: Revelry

Such a contrast between the top of Sinai and the base of it! While Moses was with God on the peak, Israel was at the base of the same mountain making an idol out of gold. While Moses communed with God *inside* the glory cloud, Israel danced before the golden calf, epitomising the battle for true worship.

We either go up the mountain of the Lord and learn of His ways or stay at the bottom of the mountain and end up creating and bowing to our sacred cows. It is true, at this point, that the Lord had not allowed Israel up the mountain, but how do we handle the positions the Lord assigns us? Are we faithful and willing to wait, or disloyal and impatient?

> *While Moses communed with God inside the glory cloud, Israel danced before the golden calf, epitomising the battle for true worship.*

There is a tug of war for every heart. These two diametrically opposed icons, as well as the two contrasting positions on the mountain, clearly illustrate the struggle and war for our heart in worship.

Contrasting Dances

The contrast between the Ark and the golden calf is manifested in music and dance.

When King David successfully brought the Ark into Jerusalem, he danced with all his might, joyfully accompanying the Ark. Contrasted with King David's dance is the dancing that took place at the base of Mt Sinai, and more recently, at the Supernova festival near Gaza. Both ended in tragedy.

The dance before the Ark is victorious and joyful. The dance before the golden calf mocks God, bringing defeat, division and great sadness.

When David danced before the Ark, it set judgemental tongues wagging. Tragically, David's wife Michal became barren (2 Samuel 6:14–17).

A Picture of Worship: Holy of Holies or Outer Court?

The Holy of Holies where the Ark dwells is akin to climbing the glory-covered mountain of the Lord. Where His Presence is tangible, it encompasses and transforms those who go there.

The outer court of the tabernacle resembles the base of the allegorical mountain; God's Presence is in the distance.

Where Moses was inside the glory cloud, it did not touch Israel.

Where Moses was *inside* the glory cloud, Israel could only observe the glory in the distance. The glory enveloped Moses: it did not touch Israel. Either the glory will engulf and saturate us, or we will be spectators of it. Gazing at the glory from a distance makes us even more vulnerable to being seduced by other gods.

We can worship God at the outer court, but it is not wise to stay there. At the outer court, the distance from the glory is greater, with a higher risk of mixed worship. In Revelation 11:2, John was told to measure the temple but not the outer court, because the Gentiles had permission to trample it.

Worshipping in the Holy of Holies is being engulfed in His Glory, set apart from earthly tugs. Remember, Ezekiel says compromised worship restricted the Levites to the outer court, and only Zadok's priesthood were permitted in the Holy of Holies because they had remained faithful.

> *We can worship God at the outer court, but it is not wise to stay there.*

Though God did not permit the nation of Israel at the top of Mt Sinai, this changed when Jesus went to the cross. Jesus opened a way for *all* to come to the peak of His mountain, into the Holy of Holies. As Jesus died, the veil was torn.

> *... having boldness to enter the Holiest by the blood of Jesus, by a new and living way which He consecrated for us, through the veil, that is, His flesh ... (Hebrews 10:19–20)*

We no longer have to stay at the base of the mountain. In fact, it is an affront to do so. Jesus paid the price, so we can all come up the mountain of the Lord and enter His Glory realms. Since Jesus ascended to the right hand of the Father, it is actually risky to stay at the base or outer court.

Last Days House of God: Top of the Mountain

Isaiah expressly says the call to come up higher is in the last days. The Lord establishes His house at the *top* of the mountain, not at the base.

> ... *in **the latter days** ... the LORD's house Shall be established on the **top of the mountains** ... And **all nations shall flow to it**... 'Come, and **let us go up to the mountain of the LORD**, To the house of the God of Jacob; He will teach us His ways, And we shall walk in His paths. For out of Zion shall go forth the law, And the word of the LORD from Jerusalem.' (Isaiah 2:2-3)*

In the last days, the Lord is calling all nations to come to the top of His mountain to learn of His ways. The call is to journey upwards, to ascend, climb – not stay at base camp! You can discern the difference.

1. Either you will ascend in the realm of Holy Spirit, or you will stay down immersed in the world, the flesh and the devil.
2. You will either be immersed in the glory of the Lord's presence or just see the glory from a distance, on others but not on you.
3. Your music and dance will be filled with frequencies of the glory, or the sound Joshua heard as he descended the mountain, a sound akin to war and caused depression and death.
4. Your music and dance will either exude joy and victory or it will be sensuous to gratify the flesh, opening a door to division, sexual sin, barrenness or death.

Climbing the Mountain of Suffering Love

Much more effort, care and discipline are required to climb to the top of a mountain than to stay at its base. It takes perseverance, commitment and courage to climb into His Presence.

In the Song of Solomon, the bride had to leave behind shadows and fears to climb the mountain of suffering love. But she had to choose to do so. It was not easy – it was a bridal choice.

> *I've made up my mind. Until the darkness disappears and the dawn has fully come,* **in spite of shadows and fears, I will go to the mountaintop** *with you –* **the mountain of suffering love** *and the hill of burning incense. Yes,* **I will be your bride***.* (Song of Songs 4:6 TPT)

The hill of burning incense is a picture of the altar of incense of worship and prayer. But she had to overcome dark shadows, fears, threats, wrong beliefs. Humility and brokenness before the cross are essential ingredients to climb up, as we overcome temptation, rejection, shame and suffering.

Once the Shulamite bride had overcome her fears and climbed up, the heavenly Bridegroom met her at the top and, together, they waged war against the real enemies rather than just shadows.

> *'Now you are ready, my bride, to come with me as we* **climb the highest peaks together.** *Come with me through the archway of trust. We will look down from the crest of the glistening mounts and from the summit of our sublime sanctuary, from the lion's den and the leopard's lair.'* (Song of Songs 4:8 TPT)

Together, they deal with the lions and leopards in their dangerous lair, a place wild animals use for refuge, birthing and nurturing cubs. Mama and papa lions are vicious. It is such a picture of spiritual war; it is only safe to do warfare from the top of the mountain, together with Him in His Glory. The psalmist had a similar revelation.

> Through you I ascend to the highest peaks ... You've trained me with the **weapons of warfare-worship**; *my arms can bend a bow of bronze. You empower me for victory with your ... presence. (Psalm 18:33–35 TPT)*

Being *with* Him at the *top* of the mountain provides a different perspective to being *without* Him at the *base* of the mountain! It is easy to think we are talking about non-Christians at the bottom of the mountain, but remember, it was *God's* people at Sinai. This message is an end-time warning and call to the Church to come out of mixture, be His bride and come with Him to the top of His mountain.

Habitation For the Glory

When a king is about to visit, people make exorbitant preparations to welcome him. When King Jesus returns to earth, He will have a place prepared for Him. We must make these preparations – first, within our hearts.

> *Who may ascend into the hill of the LORD? He who has clean hands and a pure heart, Who has not lifted up his soul to an idol ... (Psalm 24:3–4)*

Psalm 24 boldly declares the heart preparation to welcome the King of Glory:

> *Lift up your heads, you doorways of eternity! Welcome the King of Glory, for he is about to come **through you**. (Psalm 24:7 TPT)*

The second place prepared for Him are all the places where altars of true worship have been raised up around the earth, places prepared for Him to inhabit. In the midst of the encounter at Mt Sinai, the Lord gave this promise:

> *An altar of earth you shall make for Me ... In **every place where I record My name I will come to you**, and I will bless you. (Exodus 20:24)*

Wherever people raise up altars of true worship to exalt Him, He records His name.

> *'For from the rising of the sun, even to its going down, My name shall be great among the Gentiles; In every place incense shall be offered to My name, And a pure offering ...' says the LORD of hosts. (Malachi 1:11)*

Revival is good; habitation is better.

Revival is good; habitation is better. Are we raising up altars of true worship, so His name is registered? Are we preparing hearts and places to welcome the King of Glory?

CHAPTER TWENTY-SIX

Cute and Cuddly Lamb or Cow?

Passover Lamb

The Bible honours the Passover Lamb; Baal worship honours a bull. Ancient Egypt and Hinduism exalts cows.

While in Egypt, Israel observed Egyptian worship of bovine deities. They also witnessed God judge the cattle gods in the fifth plague. As the Lord prepared to deliver Israel from Egypt, He demonstrated the difference between the lamb and the cow.

Though Egyptians despised shepherds (Genesis 46:33), Israel was delivered from death and slavery by applying the blood of the Passover Lamb to their doorways. Prophetic of Yeshua whose blood delivers us from spiritual slavery and eternal death, Hebrews 9 & 10 clarifies the distinction between sacrificing a lamb or cow.

The blood of bulls and goats cannot remove sin (Hebrews 10:4), nor can it cleanse and renew the conscience of worshippers. It is only the blood of Yeshua that can purge, cleanse and purify our conscience from 'dead works' or the guilt and shame caused by sin. This is necessary to enable us to worship in Spirit and truth. (Hebrews 9:14)

Demons exploit guilt and shame with torment. It is why they fear the blood of the Passover Lamb. Sadly, too many believers receive forgiveness yet remain tortured by guilt and shame. The light of Yeshua exposes sin so we can be cleansed by His blood. (1 John 1:7-9) This was my experience when He convicted me of idolatry and of bitterness. Though forgiven, it was only when I worshipped the Lamb, my conscience was cleansed and restored, enabling true worship. No wonder saints and angels declare: "Worthy is the Lamb who was slain…" (Revelation 5:12–13).

Heaven honours the Lamb. Hell honours bulls and calves.

Psalm 22 speaks prophetically of Jesus on the cross, and the bulls of Bashan encircling Him. Biblically, Bashan has definite associations with demonic hordes, including the giant King Og. It is the region on the Golan Heights where Jeroboam established calf worship. As Jesus hung on the cross, it was these demonic bulls that tormented Him.

> *Heaven honours the Lamb. Hell honours bulls and calves.*

> *I'm surrounded by many violent foes like bulls; forces of evil encircle me like the strong bulls of Bashan. (Psalm 22:12 TPT)*

Jesus overcame and defeated death and every demon represented by a bull or calf.

> *Jesus made a public spectacle of **all** the powers and principalities of darkness, stripping away from them **every** weapon and all their spiritual authority and power to accuse us. And by the power of the cross, Jesus led them around as prisoners in a procession of triumph. He was not their prisoner; they were his! (Colossians 2:15 TPT)*

We overcome the devil, the dragon, the ancient snake, by the blood of the *Lamb*.⁶⁰

Getting Egypt Out of Israel

It is often said: Israel escaped Egypt, but Egypt remained in Israel.

> *They did not all cast away the abominations which were before their eyes, nor did they forsake the idols of Egypt. (Ezekiel 20:8)*
>
> *She (Israel) has never given up her harlotry brought from Egypt. (Ezekiel 23:8)*

When we are born again, do we remove old idols, mindsets, habits, attitudes and yes, even music of our past, or do we carry them into our walk with God? Compromising with evil practices is counterproductive. The Lord instructs us to cast them away from us and 'utterly destroy them' from our midst.⁶¹

Bull Vs Calf Worship

Baal worship, represented by a bull, and calf worship, are not the same. They are different. A small verse about King Jehu highlights this distinction.

> *Jehu destroyed every trace of Baal worship from Israel. He **did not, however, destroy the gold calves** at Bethel and Dan, with which Jeroboam had caused Israel to sin. (2 Kings 10:28-29 NLT)*

Jehu spared the gold calves. Why? In short, it's political!

If Baal and calf worship were identical, Jehu's eradication of Baal worship from the northern kingdom would have included the calves. Yet Jehu spared the gold calves. Why? In short, it's political!

King Jeroboam introduced calf worship to protect his own throne! He was afraid that allowing worship in Jerusalem would lead his people to defect to the King of Judah. He set up golden calves in Bethel and Dan to keep them home. But he repeated history and invoked the memory of Mt Sinai by declaring, 'Here are your gods, Israel, who brought you up out of Egypt.' (1 Kings 12:26–30). Like Aaron, Jeroboam ordained a counterfeit feast, sacrificed to the calves and appointed priests for the high places.[62]

Calf worship mimicked Egypt's bovine worship. Externally, sacrificing a calf or bull to YHWH or a false god might appear similar, but they were distinct. Similar worship practices of neighbouring pagans, and demonic coercion, often enticed Israel into idolatry. The Lord gave clear instructions:

> *You must **not** worship the gods of these nations … **or imitate** their evil practices. Instead, you must utterly **destroy them**.." (Exodus 23:24 NLT)*
>
> *… make **no covenant** … with their gods. (Exodus 23:32 NKJV)*

Israel made the calf soon after leaving Egypt, causing some to view it as belonging to Israel, as part of their identity. Not in God's eyes! Baal, however, was a foreign god, the supreme deity of the Phoenicians from Lebanon and Syria. Princess Jezebel, daughter of King Ithobaal I (a former priest of Astarte, or Ashtoreth, in Sidonia, Lebanon), entrenched Baal

How often do idolatry and politics collude and intertwine to shape a nation, influence the church?

worship in Israel through her marriage to Israel's King Ahab in a political alliance.

Jeroboam initiated calf worship for political gain; Jehu preserved it for similar reasons. During Jehu's reign, Israel remained a divided kingdom at war with Judah. Removing Baal or bull worship was not so dangerous politically. Removing calf worship would have required realigning with Judah to worship in Jerusalem, which Jehu avoided. Politics fuelled both the creation and persistence of calf worship.

How often do idolatry and politics collude and intertwine to shape a nation? How often does idolatry and politics influence the Church? In this time gate, the Lord is dealing with both idolatry and the political spirit.

There's another distinction between calves and bulls – natural and spiritual.

Cute and Cuddly

In the world of cattle, a bull is a mature father; a calf is its offspring. This emphasises the need to uproot all false worship altars. Baal worship, symbolised by a mature bull, is a demonic 'father', virulently reproducing evil through its prophets and evangelists. The vileness and depravity of the mature Baal worship system is evident. Jesus called the devil the father of lies.[63] Calf worship, however, represents an immature idolatrous system. Though not yet reproductive, it carries the DNA and potential of the dangerous bull.

Egypt's bovine worship, tied to fertility and pharaohs, was judged by God in the fifth plague.[64] Israel, having observed this and heard the words of YHWH – 'have no other gods' – yet still adopted calf worship at Mount Sinai. This is the first instance of Israel doing so, and for Israel, worshipping cattle was in its infancy!

Repeatedly, YHWH made it clear this was not acceptable.

At Sinai, Israel engaged in calf worship. By the time Elijah confronted them at Mt Carmel, it had 'matured' to bull worship. Baal worship, endorsed by Queen Jezebel and King Ahab, was funded by taxpayers – let that sink in! Taxpayers financed the sophisticated and entrenched bull worship, which the Lord says needs uprooting.

Don't Dismiss Cute Sins

Babies and baby animals are cute and cuddly, but they grow. Toddler mischief, being naughty but cute, may amuse, but the same behaviour in adults is not funny. We easily perceive fully blown demonic worship systems but often overlook or are blinded to noticing embryonic idols and demons, dismissing them as trivial. Yet small mustard seeds grow into mighty trees. Do we excuse practices that seem innocent, yet have demons behind them?

When occult heavy metal music is blatant, most believers reject it, but what if the sexual revolution's music and culture were a worship system in embryonic form, and thus harder to detect? To see a baby in uterus requires special ultrasound equipment. To detect a worship system in embryo requires Holy Spirit discernment, and a willingness to face truth.

At the 2023 Grammys, even non-believers criticised the mixing of satanic acts and music as trans artists Sam Smith and Kim Petras performed a song entitled 'Unholy' while dressed as the devil (see Chapter 29, 'End-time Battle of Bands'). The point here is that this vile act was not an act in its infancy, but it was the mature fruit of the rebellion, music and drugs planted in the 1960s. Such diabolical acts are the bitter fruit from the bitter roots of a tree planted when churches embraced the music and culture of the sexual revolution. All justified as a 'small bite' of something 'cute and cuddly'.

If rock's spirit was merely about musical taste and genre choice, it wouldn't have shifted attitudes towards sexuality and marriage in the Church. Yet many Christians, influenced by this spirit, have compromised biblical principles – living together before marriage, having abortions or endorsing homosexuality, even within the house of God.

A prominent Australian worship leader once advocated for worship music to be more culturally relevant to reach the unreached, which contributed to negative changes in our church. Later, after some serious issues, he admitted on a podcast to no longer identifying as Christian. Thankfully, his faith was restored. Sadly, this is not an isolated case; others have walked away, some claiming to now be atheists.

As we reflect on these heartbreaking examples, consider the words of Jesus: good trees produce good fruit. Trees grow from seeds. The warning of Jesus is this: His axe is ready to cut the *root* of trees with bad fruit.[65]

Nip Them in the Bud

Sin, when mature, harms us and our children. James says it even releases murder!

> *Evil desires give birth to evil actions. And when sin is fully mature, it can murder you! (James 1:15 TPT)*

Jonathan Cahn brilliantly argues that Baal worship is evident in Western society. Addressing serious sin early prevents it from taking root. Like cancer, sin is easier to eradicate early than when advanced. Sadly, we often delay action until pain and loss compels us.

When the Lord commanded Saul to destroy every Amalekite and their flocks, it was to prevent corruption of future generations. Saul's disobedience cost him his crown. Generations later, an Amalekite descendant, Haman, nearly annihilated the Jews in Persia. It took the bravery of Esther and Mordecai to eradicate the Amalekite seed.

Will we, like Saul, cling to 'cute and cuddly' or what we deem to be 'beneficial' idols? Or will we, like Esther and Mordecai, courageously expose them so they can be uprooted? The 'cute' sacred cows we cherish are often the hardest to identify and remove. As kingdoms clash, it manifests between the Lamb and the bull.

CHAPTER TWENTY-SEVEN

Our Sacred Cows

IT IS MUCH EASIER to identify Israel's golden calf than our own sacred cows! As Jesus said, don't point at the splinter in someone else's eye while there is a plank in your own.

Christians who follow Jesus and have made Him Lord do not usually set up idols in their homes or hearts. Yet as we consider what scripture says about idols of the heart, is it possible we could do so inadvertently and not realise until disaster hits?

Unknowingly Crossing a Line

On 1 September 1983, a passenger 747 aeroplane enroute from Anchorage to Seoul was shot down by the Russians. The flight began apparently on target, but a slight navigational error put into the computers was unnoticed, not creating a problem until further along the trajectory. They ended up off course and strayed into Soviet prohibited airspace. Two hundred and sixty-nine passengers and crew died.[66]

Even if we do not understand why the airliner strayed off course, or in similar circumstances that can occur to us all, scripture gives us strong warnings with dire consequences. Ephesians 5:1–5 first encourages us to stay in the love of the Father. Then give thanks and let worship fill our hearts.

Simultaneously, avoid immorality, lust, greed, obscenities and filthy speech. Some excellent suggestions? It's much stronger than that.

> ... *the kingdom of God cannot be accessed by anyone who is guilty of sexual sin, or who is impure or greedy – for greed is the essence of idolatry.* (Ephesians 5:5 TPT)

True worship of God is with an undivided heart. Idols of the heart divide the heart and take us off course. The Lord's Church needs to awaken to the reality that *how* we worship really matters. It is not a 'Ruth rant'. It can be life and death. Just because we have seen major advancements in worship, and think we understand the subject, does not mean the Lord is not calling for a greater shift again. He needs us on the right flight path. He is calling us higher.

> ***True worship of God is with an undivided heart. Idols of the heart divide the heart and take us off course.***

There are seven traps to consider scripturally, though some overlap:

1. our opinions
2. adapting the values of the world
3. greed or covetousness
4. work of our hands
5. things made from gold or silver
6. what is owned
7. what we do

Idolatry is allegiance to or confidence in something other than God. A sacred cow can be those things we do not want to give up but stubbornly want to hold onto as if they are divine.

Aaron knew the golden calf was wrong, but for whatever reason, made it anyway. Sacred cows can be a belief, institution or person that we deem as immune to criticism or questioning. It can be a belief or mindset that is so ingrained, revered or respected that people are reluctant to challenge or change. When these things are *above* the ways and thoughts of the Lord, that challenge and oppose Him, we could be dancing around a sacred cow.

Is it possible we think our sacred cows are harmless, like bad quirks but not really serious?

It is very possible that the values, beliefs and attitudes of our family or society that we have grown up with are so ingrained in us, we don't realise they could be idolatrous traps. They may seem normal to us but are contrary to the Lord.

Our Opinions

A major sacred cow, especially found in the Church, is opinions! You will also find them in pubs, coffee shops, social media and even pulpits.

My friend and colleague on Global Watch Oceania War Room, Karen Wilson, shared some challenging insight into the idol of our opinions (used with permission).

A major sacred cow, especially found in the Church, is opinions!

> *Some years ago, during the challenges brought to the church by the definition of marriage debate, the gender diversity and sexual orientation issues and then the impact of Covid and the differing views on*

vaccination, I was grieved by the level of disunity, judgement, criticism and finger pointing that was taking place within the Christian community, especially being voiced on public media.

I was sitting with the Lord when the voice of the Father suddenly broke in. I felt Him say, 'Karen, anytime you form an opinion, judgement or criticism about a person or a situation without coming to Me first and finding out and submitting to what I say about them, you are committing idolatry. You are putting your opinion above Me. It's time to lay down your right to an opinion and to seek the things above.' This was said in a stern tone.

There are two great questions to ask: Father, what do You want me to know about this and what do You want me to do? Opinions lead to judgement, judgement to criticism and criticism to finger pointing. This is earthly and devilish. So let's cut it off at the head. Lay down your right to an opinion until you have spent time with Jesus and the Father and heard what love has to say about it.[67]

Such wisdom. The Lord said our opinions are idolatry!

Christians can be the most judgemental people around! It is too easy to consider judgemental criticism as discernment, or even normal. But the Lord says, 'No, this is an idol of the heart. It must go.'

Karen mentioned some opinions that troubled her. There are many things we have opinions about, especially pet doctrines: women in ministry, what Bible translation should be used, end-time prophecy, the rapture, worship styles, how to use the arts, are tongues of God or the devil. Is everything we believe a divine truth, or are there some errors mixed in? And what about lifestyle attitudes about sexuality and morality, lewd speech and behaviour, and attitudes to money, business and politics?

The point is, do we seek the Father's heart and allow Him to teach us his ways? Do we seek His way of love in these conflicting positions? Are relationships more important than being right?

It is too easy for us to join with the mindset of cancel culture and political correctness and isolate brethren we disagree with. Love is not easy. Covid rules tested and tore apart many natural and spiritual families. The Lord wants us to be above the storm, not part of it!

Asaph wrote a psalm expressing his distress over the wicked who were flourishing – until he went into the house of the Lord. In worship, he saw the situation from God's perspective. He then writes:

> *When I saw all of this, what turmoil filled my heart, **piercing my opinions** with your **truth**" (Psalm 73:21 TPT)*

The Lord's perspective pierced the opinions even of the psalmist. We too should get into His Presence and allow His truth to pierce and override our opinions.

Adapting Values of the World

Love of the Father and love of the world are incompatible! Jesus spoke of the narrow path, in contrast to the values and pathways of the world. James and John spell out clearly the consequences of Christians adapting the values of the world. James is blunt!

> *Adulterers and adulteresses! Do you not know that friendship with the world is enmity with God?*

> *Whoever therefore wants to be a friend of the world makes himself an enemy of God. (James 4:4 NKJV)*
>
> *And if you ask ... with corrupt motives, seeking only to fulfill your own selfish desires. You have become **spiritual adulterers** who are having an affair, an **unholy relationship with the world**. Don't you know that **flirting with the world's values** places you at odds with God? Whoever chooses to be the world's friend makes himself God's enemy! (James 4:3-4 TPT)*

Those who make friends with the world make themselves enemies of God!

Modern idolatry can be as simple as taking on the world's values and priorities. Or as Paul said, coveting wealth! As John identifies the values of the world, he exhorts us to not set our hearts on such things.

> *Don't set the affections of your heart on this world or in loving the things of the world. The love of the Father and the love of the world are incompatible. For all that the world can offer us – the gratification of our flesh, the allurement of the things of the world, and the obsession with status and importance – none of these things come from the Father but from the world. (1 John 2:15-16 TPT)*

What worldly values are anathema to the Father?

- Gratification of the flesh
- Obsessed with possessions
- Obsession with status and importance

This book raises flesh gratification as a trap, especially in relation to music. In the next point, we will consider obsession with possessions – greed. Being preoccupied with status and importance is linked with pride. We especially see it when folks clamour for titles and positions.

Greed, Covetousness and People on Pedestals

In Ephesians 5:5, quoted previously, Paul spoke of things that would keep us out of the kingdom of God. The last on his list is greed, which he identifies as akin to a sacred cow: 'for greed is the essence of idolatry'. In Colossians 3:5, Paul framed it as 'the desire for wealth is the essence of idol worship'.

Greed and intense desire for wealth are the two things Paul equates with idol worship – sacred cows! This is how the dragon hoarding gold can ensnare us into idolatry.

Greed is by definition an intense, selfish, insatiable desire for something, especially wealth, power, status, position. It is the obsession with possessions. James says it is a value of the world that does not originate with our heavenly Father but can cause a fallout in our relationship with Him.

If greed and ungodly desire for wealth are the intrinsic nature of idolatry, then these have to be part of the 'worst sin', as discussed previously. An issue, Paul says, can keep us out of the kingdom! No wonder Paul told the Corinthian church to 'flee idolatry'![68]

Paul provides us with the answers. First, imitate our Father and surrender to His love in everything we do. Second, avoid sexual sin and greed. Thirdly, 'let worship fill your heart and spill out in your words' (Ephesians 5:1-2 TPT).

True worship is not an optional extra, a good idea or a time slot at church. It is a core response to loving God.

Wealth: Things Made from Gold or Silver

In Chapter 24, we considered that the wealth of gold and silver belongs to God and is for worship. However, it does become part of the war over worship. Where there is gold, there are dragons!

At Sinai, Israel created a 'god of gold'.[69] Likely with that background in mind, King David wrote in Psalm 135:15, 'the idols of the nations are silver and gold, the work of men's hands'.

When Jesus spoke of not being able to have two masters, it was in context of worldly wealth. Luke 16:13 says, 'You cannot serve God and mammon.' Or put another way, choose between God and the wealth of this world.

Not all wealth is bad. It can be used for worshipping God and blessing others.[70] It is the desire, the craving after wealth as a priority, that is a snare to believers.[71]

Our reliance must be on the Lord, not the wealth we create ourselves. He is to be our source.[72] The principle of tithing is a way to show that God is our source. It is also a way to overcome the dragon who wants us destitute. The *dragon* is called a *devourer*. With correct application of tithing, the Lord of Hosts says He will rebuke the devourer so we can have abundance.[73]

A great prayer and words of reassurance for us:

> *Cause my heart to bow before your words of wisdom and not to the wealth of this world ... The words you speak to me are worth more than all the riches and wealth in the whole world!* (Psalm 119:36, 72 TPT)

CHAPTER TWENTY-SEVEN

Work of Our Hands: What We Own, What We Do

The unbelieving nations worship what they make.
They worship their wealth and their work.
They idolize what they own and what they do.
Their possessions will never satisfy... cannot bring life to them!
Their things can't talk to them or answer their prayers... (Psalm 135:15-17 TPT)

The psalmist was specifically speaking of making idols with our hands. In general, what we create with our hands, what we own and our livelihoods are good. But when we look to these for answers, contentment and fulfilment and answered prayer, then their value shifts. Self-indulgence can start to take over. The work of our hands, what we own, what we do can become our sacred cows.

When we drift into trusting in the work of our hands, we become like the walking dead who make and worship idols. And the dead cannot praise God nor give Him glory.

Those who make them (idols) are like them. (Psalm 135:18 NKJV)... everyone who trusts in these powerless, dead things will be just like what they worship – powerless and dead! (Psalm 135:18 TPT)

Idolatry can be as simple as false comforters, false refuges and covetousness.[74] Grumbling and complaining activates idolatry.[75] Whether it's our opinions, careers, livelihood, possessions, investment portfolios, people we love or admire, networks, our skills and talents, ministries – these can all be blessings from God. But it is too easy to get off course, even without being aware. Is loving, worshipping and serving the Lord a higher priority than these good things?

Dealing With Sacred Cows

Moses pulverised the gold calf to dust, put it in the water supply and made Israel drink it! The people were unrestrained, out of control, and naked (Exodus 32:25); their shame was exposed. Then Israel was given a choice – who is on the Lord's side? Three thousand died. Redemption was at Pentecost as three thousand were saved.

The choices are stark: life or death.

The Ten Commandments were given by a loving Father wanting to protect and bless His children. A plague swept through Israel by the end of Exodus 32. The very existence of ancient Israel was endangered by defying the commands of the Lord. We should not wait until disaster strikes to be willing to admit or deal with our sacred cows. Are blessings withheld from us or do we face severe trouble because of sacred cows? This is important to consider when there are so many hostile people in society who actually hate Christians.

> *Restoring true worship is not just what we do, but also what we get rid of.*

Do our sacred cows need pulverising, as Moses did? Restoring true worship is not just what we do, but also what we *get rid of*. We must destroy our sacred cows and grind them to powder!

It is a choice. The consequences of not doing this are severe. Israel did not uproot the idolatry they had learned in Egypt, and they rehashed it.

Restoring Worship: Synergy of Anointing

Both Moses and Elijah gave Israel an ultimatum to choose between the true God, I AM, and the gods of gold and cattle.

Is the Spirit of the Lord giving a similar challenge today? Who is on the Lord's side? Do we fluctuate between two opinions?

In the confrontations requiring Israel to make a choice, both Moses and Elijah released the sword of the Lord against false worshippers. We are in an urgent time that requires us to wield the sword of the Spirit to divide between the Spirit, the realm of the soul and the demonic.

Though Elijah took out the prophets of Baal, it took the anointing of Jehu to deal with the crown of Israel that had fed and permitted Baal worship to flourish. Not only did he instigate the destruction of Jezebel but he also killed the entire household of Ahab, his acquaintances and his priests. Eventually, Jehu eradicated Baal worship from Israel (2 Kings 10:11, 18–28).

Yet for all this, though Jehu removed Baal worship from Israel, he did not remove the golden calves. This is a tragic and graphic reminder for us all. We must make sure the job is done completely and the uprooting is meticulous.

Restoring true worship in our culture and times, requires the synergy of several anointings. We need the anointing of Elijah to deal with the prophets of Baal and to heal and repair the hearts of multi-generations. We need the Jehu anointing to remove Baal worship from the crown, from government and from the people of our nations. But the big warning for us all is this – we must also remove our sacred cows! We need the Josiah anointing to uproot it all.

Are we willing to deal with our own sacred cows? Are we open to the Holy Spirit to uproot ungodly things we have embraced from our culture? We will find them among our desires, like gold and silver and sexual lusts. But we can also find them in good things that divert our time and attention away from the Lord.

In the next chapter, we see the importance of watchman and intercessors standing in the gap, as Moses did, to appeal to the Lord's mercy, for the sake of His name and reputation.

CHAPTER TWENTY-EIGHT

Intercession: Battle at the Gates

Moses Pleaded With God

GOD WAS SO ANGRY. He wanted to eradicate Israel and start again with Moses. But Moses interceded, pleading with the Lord.

> *Why should the Egyptians speak, and say, 'He brought them out to harm them, to kill them ...'* (Exodus 32:11–13)

Moses reminded the Lord that His name and reputation were at stake before Egypt. He invoked God's eternal covenant with Abraham. Covenant matters. God keeps His covenants. Honour of His name matters.

We too, are called to intercede for families and neighbours and churches enslaved to idols of the hearts or ones made from gold and silver.

New Age festivals, often with seductive music, are everywhere, drawing spiritually hungry souls seeking truth and solace. We must intercede for them for the sake of God's name. Like Moses, we intercede by recalling His covenant. Paul urged Timothy to wage warfare with prophetic promises.[76]

In the wake of the 7 October tragedy, locals and others have interceded and repented at the music Supernova festival site. It is now a memorial site among the gum trees (as, like Australia, the area is planted with many of our trees). Intercede for those traumatised by 7 October, and remind the Lord of His promise: 'All Israel will be saved'(Romans 11:26).

May we in the Church not forget – without repentance and intercession for similar spiritual breaches, what happened to Israel could happen to us.

Stand in the Gap

In biblical times, a soldier standing in the gap of a broken city wall stood to repel enemies while repairs were being made – a dangerous yet vital role. Intercession mirrors this. Jesus is the ultimate advocate, Who 'makes intercession for us'.[77]

When we stand in the gap, we stand in the middle of two opposing visions. We face damaging malevolence in governments, corporations, families and even the Church while also beholding the Lord's glory and hearing His directives, warnings or promises.

Intercession can bring distress. When Moses saw the breach of the golden calf, he smashed the tablets, the word written in stone, symbolising a broken covenant. The body of Jesus, the living Word, was also broken to make the New Covenant.

When we stand in the gap, we must stay vigilant. Avoid being overwhelmed or fixated on evil; focus on Jesus, His extraordinary deliverance and redemption. We intercede so His will is done and He is glorified. Without intercessors standing in the gap, tragedy strikes!

> *'I sought for a man among them who would ...* **stand in the gap** *before Me on behalf of the land, that I should not destroy it; but I* **found no one**.*'*

> *Therefore,* God **poured His wrath** *on the nation!*
> *(Ezekiel 22:30)*

What a responsibility! Amid perversion and anti-Christ rhetoric, only those standing in the gap can shift the trajectory and avert disaster.

Nations face complex, heartbreaking issues, yet it would be simpler if they would stop dishonouring the Lord's name and character. He will not tolerate His holy name to be defiled. He will not share His Glory with anyone, visible or invisible.

> *... I will make sure that my holy name is no longer allowed to be profaned. Then the nations will know that I am YAHWEH, the* **Holy One of Israel***.*
> *(Ezekiel 39:7 TPT)*

> *For when Your judgments are in the earth, the inhabitants of the world will learn righteousness.*
> *(Isaiah 26:9b NKJV)*

The Lord is summoning those who will contend for His name to be exalted in the nations. He is summoning those who will contend for worship to be pure and restored to its glorious purpose.

Who is on the Lord's Side?

After Moses destroyed the golden calf, he challenged the people: 'Who is on the Lord's side?' The Levites were the only tribe who answered yes, but their resolve was tested. They were required to wield the sword against rebels, even family and friends.

The Levites were preserved and rewarded by being appointed guardians of worship and the holy things, including the Ark. King David later established them as gatekeepers, singers, and musicians in the tabernacle.

God tests true worshippers regarding idolatry. A faithful heart is the essence of true worship. Family, natural and spiritual, often test our resolve. Overcoming brings a stronger anointing and increased authority. Isaiah, Ezekiel, Jeremiah, Hosea and Amos stood against idolatrous Israel and Judah. The Holy Spirit once challenged me: 'If you were the last person standing on this music and worship issue, would you still stand?'

Will we pay the cost for God's house to be a house of prayer for all nations, filled with pure worship? In Ezekiel 44, those Levites who compromised with other gods were restricted to serve in the outer court. Only faithful Zadok and his sons could minister in the holy place. They were to teach Israel the difference between the holy and the profane (Ezekiel 44:4-23).

The Lord is calling for a priesthood like Zadok (meaning 'righteous'), after the order of Melchizedek (whose name means 'my King is righteous'). There are some who had been faithful in the past, like the Levites at the time of Moses, but have since compromised, like in the time of Ezekiel. They continue to serve but their anointing and effectiveness has declined. The issues raised are not about salvation but acceptable worship in the holy place. Do our sacrifices welcome His Glory and Presence? He seeks to release His glorious sounds through us onto the earth. Let us pray for a faithful generation of pure worshippers and psalmists to arise who are trustworthy to accompany the Ark as the Spirit of God moves afresh.

If the price tag seems too high, remember, idolatry leads to captivity. The church may not get whisked off to physical Babylon, but spiritual Babylon is gaining power in the earth. A division looms for the Body of Christ: compromise or faithfulness. The Holy Spirit asks, 'Who is on the Lord's side?'

While some chase popularity or prosperity, will you crucify personal dreams to do the will of the Father? When others compromise and conform to the crowd, will you be part of the faithful, courageous remnant?

Taking the Sword to Your Relatives – Seriously?

To us, taking the sword to our brethren is drastic Old Testament thinking. But the sword we need to wield is the two-edged word of God. Paul articulates the serious situation we face.

> *You cannot drink the cup of the Lord and the cup of demons; you cannot partake of the Lord's table and of the table of demons. Or do we provoke the Lord to jealousy? Are we stronger than He? (1 Corinthians 10:21–22)*

It is impossible to sit at the Lord's covenantal table at the same time as sitting at the devil's table. We cannot be in covenant with them both. It is one or the other. The Lord says, idol worship is to demons, or entertains and invokes demons.

> *Jeshurun [Israel] ... abandoned the Elohim who made them ... they worshiped worthless idols.* **They sacrificed to demons** *that are not Elohim, to gods they never heard of. These were* **new gods***, who came from nearby ... (Deuteronomy 32:15–18)*

The only way to resolve this serious breach is to wield the sword of the Spirit to divide between soul, spirit and the intents of the heart.

Turn Back the Battle at the Gates

When the Levites chose the Lord's side, they wielded their sword from 'gate to gate' to quell the rebellion (Exodus 32:27). The Israelite camps were organised by tribe, with gates at each entrance. At ancient gates, authorities made decisions and wise counsel was given (Proverbs 1:21). To stop idolatry, Levites fought at each tribe's gate.

Victory requires conquering the gates. Battles are turned back at the gates.[78] The natural and heavenly Jerusalem both have twelve gates, symbolising governmental authority. Jesus gave the authoritative keys of the kingdom while standing at Caesarea Philippi, known as the Gates of Hell! With these keys, Jesus said His church, the *Ekklesia* (legislative body) would defeat the gates of hell.[79] Michael Heisler says we often wrongly see ourselves as fending off the demonic realm, but the reality is,

Closed gates refuse entry to evil; open gates welcome righteousness. There is a special victory as the Lord's people worship at the gates and exert their authority.

> *It is the gates of hell that are under assault – and they will not hold up against the Church. Hell will one day be Satan's tomb.*[80]

Amen! He has given us the keys to open and close gates. Closed gates refuse entry to evil; open gates welcome righteousness. There is a special victory as the Lord's people worship at the gates and exert their authority. Releasing His authority through the sound of worship at gates terrorises the gates of hell.

> *Swing wide, you gates of righteousness, and let me pass through them... to worship only him.* (Psalm 118:19 TPT)

> **This is the gate of the LORD,** *Through which the righteous shall enter.* (Psalm 118:20 NKJV)

CHAPTER TWENTY-EIGHT

The gate of the Lord is righteousness. Praise is the gateway into His Presence, so we worship before Him. 'Enter into His gates with thanksgiving, And into His courts with praise' (Psalm 100:4).

City walls are a metaphor for salvation – solid and immovable. Gates represent praise: their ability to open and close also makes them vulnerable to invading armies. 'You shall call your walls Salvation, And your gates Praise' (Isaiah 60:18).

Gates of praise are the entrance to worshipping the LORD.

> *Stand in the gate of the LORD's house, and proclaim, 'All you of Judah who enter in at these gates to worship the LORD!'*
>
> **Amend your ways** ... *and I will cause you to dwell in this place. (Jeremiah 7:2-3)*

In a time of war, praise can be vulnerable if soulish emotions dominate. The Levites had to overthrow idolaters at the gates. Idols in the hearts of worshippers (especially music teams) can be the weakest, most vulnerable spot. Battles for worship are won or lost at the gates of praise; any idols in the heart ensure defeat. To dwell inside His gates, we must check and amend our ways.

Notably, Isaiah 60:18 states, 'Violence shall no longer be heard in your land'. The Hebrew word for 'violence' is *chamas*, or *hamas*! The message of salvation and praises of the Lord, even over the gates of Gaza, is key to Hamas being uprooted! It is an ancient stronghold and needs Isaiah 60:8 to be appropriated over this gate.

In a time of conflict, worship warriors head to the gates. They carry a sound that is needed to block evil and welcome righteousness. Appropriately, Levites were musicians and gatekeepers in the tabernacle of David.

INTERCESSION: BATTLE AT THE GATES

> *And he set the gatekeepers at the gates of the house of the LORD, so that no one who was in any way unclean should enter. (2 Chronicles 23:19)*

The Lord strengthens those who turn back the battles at the gate (Isaiah 28:6). Ultimately, the King of Glory is welcomed at the gates of praise!

> *Lift up your heads, O you gates! ... And the King of glory shall come in. Who is this King of glory? The LORD of hosts, He is the King of glory. Selah. (Psalm 24:9–10)*

Repair Broken Altars: Judgement to Redemption

As Israel entered the Promised Land, they built altars that represented covenant and worship. Righteous altars bearing God's name were vital to claim His promises and overcome enemies, especially giants in the land. When Israel turned to idols, they blatantly abandoned God's altar and erected demonic ones instead. God gave them, and gives us, a choice.

> *I have set before you today life and good, death and evil ... (Deuteronomy 30:15)*

Choosing life brings prosperity; idolatry leads to destruction. Similarly, honouring purity in and before marriage fosters family; sexual sin defiles it. Choosing life upholds God's image, while rejecting it invites bloodshed or spiritual abuse.

Israel's idolatry defiled the land and themselves, leading to oppression by foreign nations. Yet, when they cried out, God's infinite love moved Him to remember His covenant and show mercy (Psalm 106:36–45). His judgements aim not to destroy but to awaken and redeem.

We intercede at the gates or entry points for our families and nations through repentance, resisting demonic powers, praying for mercy and restoration. God's limitless love ensures mercy triumphs over judgement, redeeming those who cry out to Him.

Uprooting Demonic Altars, Raising God's Altar

When Gideon dismantled his father's pagan altars, it sparked fierce contention. Destroying demonic altars while raising up altars to God always stirs conflict, like a storm where hot and cold air collide. Today, we see this clash unfolding globally. Winds of revival and restoration sweep through Israel, the Middle East and beyond, while icy currents of anarchy and perversion plunge nations into chaos.

A spiritual war rages in the heavens over the Middle East and the West, fought through universities, music and street protests. Yet God is moving powerfully. Though demonic conflict seeks to fracture, the Holy Spirit heals and unites. Paul quotes Habakkuk 1:5 as He encourages the church:

> Look among the nations! See! Be astonished! Wonder! For I am doing something in your days – You would not believe it if you were told. (Acts 13:41)

Holy Spirit is Moving

Before the 2023 war in Israel and Gaza, young Jewish and Arab believers gathered from prayer houses in the land at a prayer camp. They filmed the song 'Raise Us Up'.[81] This anthem of united worship is about being together as one in the battle being fought through prayer and worship. It reflects a growing hunger for God amid ongoing conflict.

In the US, February 2023, the Holy Spirit was poured out at Asbury University, with non-stop prayer and worship affecting thousands. In the UK, it is reported Gen Z males are reversing the downward trend of church attendance, with a forty-five per cent increase in attendance, and seeking the Lord.[82] With each key marker – Covid, 7 October, Charlie Kirk's assassination – there is a move of God sweeping, especially, young people flocking to church, to prayer, to read their Bibles.

Division and Trouble

Tel Aviv, vibrant yet secular, mirrors many modern cities. Known as the city that plays, unlike praying Jerusalem, it promotes itself as the world's gay capital, with 250,000 attending its 2022 pride march. Efforts to extend these marches to Jerusalem, alongside high abortion rates, clash with Israel's value for life. Prior to the war, protests in Tel Aviv against the government, countered by massive pro-government rallies in Jerusalem, revealed deep divisions. Politics are complicated in Israel. A sense of internal 'civil war' makes Israel vulnerable to surrounding nations wanting to wipe her off the map. This traumatised nation often disagrees on how to fight the war and bring back its hostages. The Middle East conflict and rising global anti-Semitism are all symptomatic of a fierce spiritual battle.

Globally, demonic calls to eradicate Jews 'from the river to the sea' or 'finish Hitler's work' echo in cities like Melbourne, Sydney, New York and London, with attacks on synagogues and Jewish businesses. Jewish people are rightly frightened in *every* nation!

We cannot afford to compromise with the enemy in any area.

- The Church must stand uncompromisingly with Israel. A redeemed Israel will unleash resurrection life worldwide (Romans 11:15). It is key to global revival!

- We must embrace pure, righteous lifestyles and worship practices for His name's sake.
- Strategic worship and intercession at the gates will shift nations towards redemption.

Restoring the Altar of True Worship

Paul's exhortation challenges us: 'You say, "I hate idolatry and false gods!" but do you withhold from the true God what is due him' (Romans 2:22 TPT)?

We may despise idols, but are we giving God the pure worship He deserves that belongs to Him alone? It is one thing to avoid doing evil. It is another to do what He says!

'Give unto the LORD the glory **due to His name**' (Psalm 29:2 NKJV). The Passion Translation adds: "… worship him wearing the glory-garments of your holy, priestly calling' (Psalm 29:2b TPT)!

It is a high call and privilege to give God the glory He deserves.

Summary: Consecrate Altars of True Worship

The end-time battle is over worship – who each of us will bow to. We do this by restoring His altars of true worship.

1. Clean hands and hearts

To restore, and to come near to God's altar, we must consecrate ourselves, be clean before Him. It is with pure hearts that songs of thanksgiving can be offered at His altar.

> When I **come to your altar**, YAHWEH, I'll be **clean before you**, approaching with songs of thanksgiving, singing songs of your mighty miracles. (Psalm 26:6–7 TPT)

Access to the Lord's holy mountain is a huge privilege, and dangerous without meeting the pre-conditions: clean hands, pure heart, no idols!

> *Who may ascend into the hill of the LORD? Or who may stand in His holy place? He who has clean hands and a pure heart, Who has not lifted up his soul to an idol, Nor sworn deceitfully. (Psalm 24:3-4 NKJV)*

2. Lay axe to idols, covetousness and immorality

Like Moses interceding for Israel at Sinai or Shadrach, Meshach and Abednego refusing to bow to Nebuchadnezzar's image, we must boldly confront idolatry.

Every sacred cow, idol, gold calf, Baal or Asherah that seeks to replace God's presence must be cut off at the roots.

> *And even now the ax is laid to the root of the trees. Therefore every tree which does not bear good fruit is cut down and thrown into the fire. (Matthew 3:10 NKJV)*

In trials, don't waver – fear the Lord, the beginning of wisdom (Proverbs 9:10). Repent, turn fully to God and obey His commands, as Jesus said: 'If you love Me, keep My commandments (John 14:15). Abide in Him, the true Vine (John 15:4). Get into agreement with what the Lord is saying and doing.

3. Practise gratitude

Regularly thank God for His blessings, acknowledging His sovereignty in all aspects of life. If you haven't done it yet, feast on gratitude by using my book, *Grumble Fast*. The forty-day devotional is changing the lives of seasoned believers across the globe. In a time when negativity is bombarding our minds, this is a powerful strategy to keep your hearts fixed on Him.

4. Live in obedience and holiness

Pursue a life that reflects God's character, aligning actions with His commands that will honour His name. Every time we overcome temptations, we have a fresh, victorious testimony, giving us new authority over the enemy.

5. Offer pure worship, exalt His name

Dedicate time to worship God alone through prayer, song and adoration, free from distractions or worldly influences. Give Him glory by testifying to His work in your life. Don't just honour His name by singing but by demonstrating it when no one is looking!

When prophetic watchmen are not on the wall or are silent, immorality and false worship thrive, robbing the Church of its authority to drive out evil.

It is time to boldly intercede and call forth the restoration of true worship. Arise to turn back the battle at the gates. Prepare the way for the King of Glory in all His dazzling presence. As He comes, He sweeps aside all darkness and fully restores divine order, right relationships and the most glorious sound of worship aligned with heaven!

As we move into the last section, we identify and uncover some glory sounds. Some are surpassingly simple and beautiful. Come join me and see how they are activated in end-time battles for worship.

ENDNOTES - PART 3

1. Hebrews 12:18–22.
2. Suggested figures include six hundred and ninety-five Israeli civilians (including thirty-eight children), seventy-one foreign nationals and three hundred and seventy-three members of the security forces, around two hundred and fifty hostages taken and thousands more injured.
3. https://www.timesofisrael.com/idf-okayed-nova-music-festival-but-didnt-inform-troops-deployed-at-border-probe-finds/
4. https://www.csis.org/analysis/hamass-october-7-attack-visualizing-data.
5. Exodus 19: 8.
6. 1 Corinthians 14:15. See Chapter 31 in Part Four
7. Elwell, Walter; Beitzel, Barry. *BAKER Encyclopedia of the Bible*, Vol. 1, 'Idolatry', Revell, Michigan, 1988, p. 1014.
8. Exodus 9: 1–7.
9. 1 Corinthians 1:18.
10. Exodus 20:22–26.
11. 'Syncretism' vocabulary.com.
12. Exodus 32:5.
13. Burnt offerings: 2 Kings 17:32, 2 Chronicles 28:4. Drink offerings: Isaiah 57:6. Ezekiel 16:19. Incense: 2 Kings 16:4, Ezekiel 6:13.
14. Amos 6:5–7.
15. Amos 5:26.
16. This is Christmas 2018 | Hillsong Church Sweden https://www.youtube.com/watch?v=gdzYR926QFY.
17. There are too many articles to footnote. Research 'Chrislam.'
18. https://www.khaleejtimes.com/uae/up-to-dh3-million-fine-in-uae-new-draft-law-regulating-non-muslim-places-of-worship-approve.
19. 'For out of the abundance of the heart, his mouth speaks' (and sings!) (Luke 6:45).
20. Matthew 15:8–9.
21. Just a few references: Jeremiah 22:9, 25:6, 44:3–15, Ezekiel 20, 22–23, Hosea 3:1.
22. Exodus 23:13, Deuteronomy 6:14.
23. Matthew 22:35–40.
24. Hebrews 12:15.
25. Heisler, Michael S. *Supernatural: what the Bible teaches about the unseen world – and why it matters*, Lexham Press, Michigan, 2015, p. 72–73.
26. Also Leviticus 17:7.
27. Romans 1:18–32.
28. Leviticus 18:25, 28, 20:22.

29. Acts 7:41.
30. 1 Corinthians 10:14.
31. Keller, Timothy. @timkellernyc 6:09 am · 26 Nov 2019.
32. Galatians 5:19–20, 1 Corinthians 5:9–12.
33. James 3:14–15.
34. Galatians 5:24.
35. David compared Jeroboam to David. 1 Kings 14:8–9.
36. Ashcroft, Robert, J. *Worship: A Biblical Survey; an Independent Study Textbook*, International Correspondence Institute, Springfield, 1987, p. 84.
37. Browne, David; Dillon, Nancy; Grow, Kory. 'They Wanted to Dance in Peace. And they got Slaughtered', 15 October 2023, https://www.rollingstone.com/music/music-features/hamas-israel-nova-music-festival-massacre-1234854306/.
38. https://www.theguardian.com/world/2023/oct/09/how-the-hamas-attack-on-the-supernova-festival-in-israel-unfolded.
39. Exodus 32:17–18.
40. Much more on trance music in Volume 2.
41. exronmusic.com.
42. https://www.rollingstone.com/music/music-features/hamas-israel-nova-music-festival-massacre-1234854306/
43. Read Dahlia's testimony, https://zionemet.com/about.
44. John 7:37–39.
45. Hamilton, Anne. *Hidden in the Cleft: True and False Refuges*, Armour Books, Australia, 2019.
46. H6031.
47. https://www.youtube.com/@TreeofLifeMinistriesIsrael.
48. Psalm 45:13.
49. Genesis 13:2.
50. Exodus 36:6–7, 'And so the people were restrained from bringing more, because what they already had was more than enough to do all the work.' (NIV).
51. 1 Chronicles 29:1–9.
52. https://www.anart4life.com/dragons-in-bendigo/.
53. https://jordanpetersonquotes.com/dragons-hoard-gold-quote/.
54. John 10:10.
55. John 8:44.
56. Given by Peter Nicholls, World Prayer Centre, Birmingham, UK, July– August 2001.
57. https://scitechdaily.com/the-reason-why-rock-pop-stars-die-young/
58. 1 Corinthians 6:19.
59. Ephesians 2:10.
60. Revelation 12:11.

61. Exodus 23:24.
62. 1 Kings 12:32.
63. John 8:44.
64. Exodus 9.
65. Matthew 3:10.
66. https://www.history.com/this-day-in-history/korean-airlines-flight-shot-down-by-soviet-union; https://en.wikipedia.org/wiki/Korean_Air_Lines_Flight_007#Alternative_theories.
67. A private conversation, written at the author's request.
68. 1 Corinthians 10:14.
69. Exodus 32:31.
70. Luke 16:9.
71. 1 Timothy 6:9, 17.
72. Psalm 62:10.
73. Malachi 3:10–11, Revelation 12:4.
74. We recommend Anne Hamilton's book, *Hidden in the Cleft: True and False Refuge*.
75. Webb, Ruth, *Grumble Fast: 40-Day Gratitude Feast*, Heart of the Psalmist Inc, Bendigo, 2020.
76. 1 Timothy 1:18.
77. Romans 8:34, Hebrews 7:25.
78. Isaiah 28:6.
79. Matthew 16:18.
80. Heisler, Michael S. *The Unseen Realm*, Lexham Press, Michigan, 2025, p. 285.
81. https://youtu.be/MDSgT0cVtAM?si=cpOSm6-sCzLN1rgm.
82. A YouGov tracker cited by GB News and Breitbart reported that belief in God among eighteen- to twenty-four-year-olds rose from sixteen per cent in August 2021 to forty-five per cent in January 2025, aligning with the Bible Society's findings. While the interest in God has surged, commitment is still being monitored.

PART FOUR
WORSHIP MUSIC TUNED TO THE GLORY
Activate Angels, Dissipate Darkness

*... darkness shall cover the earth ... But the LORD will arise over you, And **His Glory will be seen upon you**. (Isaiah 60:2)*

*... When the trumpeters and singers were **as one, to make one sound** ... saying: 'For He is good, For His mercy endures forever,' that ... the glory of the LORD filled the house of God. (2 Chronicles 5:13–14)*

*For the **earth will be filled** with the knowledge of **the glory of the LORD**, as the waters cover the sea. (Habakkuk 2:14)*

*I heard ... the roar of a great multitude of voices ... 'Hallelujah! Salvation and glory and power to our God! ... For he has judged the great prostitute who corrupted the earth with her sexual immorality ...' Then I heard ... a great multitude, like the sound of a massive waterfall and mighty peals of thunder: 'Hallelujah! For the Lord our God, **the Almighty, reigns!**' (Revelation 19:1-2, 6 TPT)*

PART FOUR: PROPHETIC SNAPSHOT

Glory Wave and Angels from the Ends of the Earth

Australia and the islands of Oceania – known as the 'ends of the earth' – comprise some ten thousand islands with many Christian inhabitants. Yet this region also bears the marks of ancient sea gods and the dragon's influence.

The Lord has declared that songs of praise will rise from this region, echo across the globe and return to Jerusalem.

> *Sing to the LORD a new song, And His praise from the ends of the earth. (Isaiah 42:10)*

Many prophets have spoken of a tsunami wave of glory sweeping from the ends of the earth back to Jerusalem. But the enemy fiercely resists. He is terrified of the glory that shatters darkness.

This final section unveils end-time songs, sounds and decrees tuned to His Glory. When the redeemed on earth align with heavens worship, the cosmic war accelerates as angelic hosts demolish demonic altars. Visions and dreams spanning a decade are now manifesting, revealing glory waves, glory bells and glory angels rising as kingdoms clash.

While at the World Prayer Assembly in Perth on 5 October 2023, two days before the 7 October attack, two visions were shared.

The Lord's Rod Removes Strongholds to Release The Glory

Rick Ridings, Director of Succat Hallel in Jerusalem, shared a vision received during Passover 2014.

Rick saw the Lord standing at the dateline near the Solomon Islands, which would indicate a change of times and seasons. With His rod, the Lord broke down four sea walls the enemy had built to stop the Lord's glory wave. The Lord's rod produced a spiritual tsunami.

> *Satan ... had spent centuries building one sea wall after another ... the principality on each throne had its arms crossed as if to show 'You will never get past me'.*
>
> *But the tsunami wave ... broke down wall after wall and throne after throne!*
>
> *The first wall and throne toppled were the strongholds of Shintoism and idolatry. The second wall and throne represented Buddhism and ancestor worship. The third wall represented Hinduism. Each of these crumbled and fell before the wave, and a great harvest of people were brought into the Kingdom of God.*
>
> *The fourth and final wall was that of Islam ... it had a huge principality on its throne that looked very intimidating. But even that wall fell before this wave.*
>
> *I saw many intercessors and harvesters who began to ride the tsunami wave. They were from the Pacific, especially from New Zealand, Australia the Philippines and Japan ... I heard the voice of the Lord proclaiming loudly, 'I am breaking up the fountains of the deep so that the earth may be covered with the glory of the Lord.'*[1]

In January 2022, the Tongan volcano erupted, sending tsunami waves across the Pacific, Atlantic Caribbean and Mediterranean! This massive explosion in the natural confirmed the vision Rick had received eight years earlier.

Space satellites captured not only vast clouds of ash but also nearly supersonic shockwaves. The eruption caused Earth's atmosphere to 'ring like a bell', circling the globe three times at frequencies too low for human hearing. These 'Lamb' waves, named after their identifier, were comparable in force to nuclear blasts, hundreds of times stronger than Hiroshima's bomb in 1945![2]

In the coming chapters, you will see how the Lord wields His rod of authority *through* music and worship on earth.

Glory Bell

In July and August 2014, I received two significant dreams. In the first, I saw a terrifying tsunami – swirling waters filled with debris and filth. I heard the Spirit say, 'Tsunami of hate, tsunami of hate – anti-Semitism'. A decade later, that wave has reached our streets, and even parts of the Church.

In the second dream, I was climbing a mountain and ringing a glory bell to the nations. Within months, I was literally ringing bells in Malaysia, Germany and Israel, prophetically calling nations to welcome His Glory. In Herrnhut, Germany, where the Moravian hundred-year prayer revival began, I climbed the Jesus Haus belltower and rang their bell. Many church bells had just been returned after Hitler's theft of them. Even our Berlin hotel was named 'Abelle'!

Eight years after ringing the glory bell, the Tongan Lamb shockwaves rang the earth like a *bell*, echoing heaven's message: the Lord's judgement on enemy strongholds through the release of the frequencies of His Glory.

We later rang bells at Israel's northern border town of Metula, targeted by Hezbollah in the 2023–2024 war. Joined by worshippers from many nations, we all rang bells together during worship at Caesarea Philippi where Jesus had declared, 'I will build My church [*Ekklesia*], and the gates of hell shall not prevail'. The glory bells rang out once more with His authority and victory.

Glory Angels

After Rick Ridings shared his vision at the WPA, he invited our friend, Jenny Hagger from Adelaide, to the platform. During worship on the first night of the Prayer Assembly, Jenny had an open vision.

In the spirit, Jenny saw from a heavenly perspective the Oceania region. She heard the words 'changing of the guard'. She heard a swooshing sound as thousands of angels left the region. Horrified, she asked the Lord, 'What is this? We need them!' Jenny then saw multitudes of massive angels with huge golden wings coming in over the region. She asked, 'What are these?' The Lord said, 'These are My glory angels.' Then multitudes of different angels appeared. Again, Jenny asked, 'What are these? The Lord said, 'These are My warrior angels.' The warrior angels were called to protect the glory angels.

That the glory angels needed protection by warrior angels is very telling. Though the Glory itself is so powerful, it is viciously attacked by evil. Like in the Garden of Eden, the Ark in heaven is covered by two cherubim. The end-time Glory wave has a protective escort.

Glory Over Darkness

Like the Ark before Dagon, these visions, dreams, prophetic acts and even the volcano speak of the Lord's authority, angelic hosts and His Glory demolishing demonic sea walls, altars and thrones, and tsunamis of hate.

Darkness and light are both spiritual entities and natural reality. As the light of Jesus confronts the kingdom of darkness, the Lord calls us to release sounds and songs that carry the frequencies of His Glory. The glory terrifies demonic kings but brings freedom, healing and restoration to those once bound by them. The radiant Bride, ready for the marriage supper of the Lamb, will sing exquisite songs to the worthy Lamb.

Let His Glory ring out, filling the globe with our worship aligned with His sceptre and throne of authority.

> *When you arise to intervene, all the nations and kings will be stunned and will fear your awesome name, trembling before your glory! (Psalm 102:15 TPT)*

CHAPTER TWENTY-NINE

End-Time Battle of the Bands

Clash of Kingdoms, Contention for the Airwaves

IN THE END-TIMES, BATTLES will involve not just governments and armies but music and sound. As God prepares His church for the greatest harvest and return of Jesus, so Satan readies the world to accept him as the false Messiah. Music and the arts are at the forefront of the final cosmic showdown between God and Satan.

This 'battle of the bands' is not a competition for the best music, but combat for territory. As kingdoms clash, the battle at the gate of sound is for air supremacy of the airwaves. In Ephesians 2:2, the spirit working to get humans to rebel is 'the prince of the power of the air'. The Passion Translation describes him as 'the dark ruler ... who fills the atmosphere with his authority.

I dislike the term 'band' as it carries worldly connotations, yet it conveys the idea of the battle for the airwaves where sound permeates the atmosphere, influencing people for the Lord or for evil.

Music has been used to heal since David's harp brought peace to Saul (1 Samuel 16:23). Part Two's final chapters cite many positive examples of sound. Anointed music sustains 24/7 prayer rooms globally. The enemy flees when worshippers unite to exalt the name of Jesus, especially for sustained periods like twenty-four and seventy-two hour marathons. We have witnessed amazing breakthroughs after such events.

Yet, sound is also used by the enemy as a weapon of torment. Sound can heal or destroy. In the end-times, demonic music will become more blatant, seductive and shocking. The sounds of godly worship grow sweeter, wielding greater authority as hungry souls press into the Lord's Presence. The sounds of heaven will defeat the sounds of the world, the flesh and the devil!

Do the sounds currently heard in churches repel or attract the enemy?

Music and Cosmic Battle to Dethrone God

> *He [Jesus] has to remain in heaven until the time comes for restoring everything, as God said long ago, when he spoke through the holy prophets. (Acts 3:21 CJB)*

> *... as you have heard that the Anti-Christ is coming, even now many anti-Christs have come, by which we know it is the last hour. (1 John 2:18)*

God is working to restore all things; Satan is working to destroy all things. The role of music rises. Demonic entities work feverishly for a false global saviour, with evil forces aligning to welcome and install this person.

The 20th century saw two world wars, the Cold War, the Korean and Vietnam wars and cultural and moral revolutions. The 21st century faces terrorism, IT and a looming third world war, possibly nuclear. It also faces cancel culture, political correctness and culture wars reflecting Marxism's attempt to eradicate Christianity, and globalism undermining national sovereignty. Karl Marx declared, 'The idea of God is the keynote of a perverted civilization. It must be destroyed.'[3]

In the 20th century, lies like 'God is dead' and evolution denied God's creative existence. In the 21st century, humanity has become its own god, even exalting self above God. Proud elites intimidate citizens to bow to their schemes.

The music of the 1960s and '70s waged war for the souls of the baby boomers, defiling a generation through sexual immorality, illicit drugs and abortion. Yet God intervened with the Jesus Revolution. As the battle intensifies, we see hopeful signs. But we must intercede for the full harvest Jesus died for, to turn back the battle at the gate of sound.

Tormenting Sounds

In 2022, tens of thousands rallied at Canberra's parliament grounds for the freedom truck convoys protesting harsh lockdowns. Laurence, I and various ministries attended with a Bible marathon, a man carrying a cross, evangelism, intercession and Christians who spoke of the need for Jesus. Salvations and baptisms occurred! But there were also some fringe groups present, advocating anarchy.

At one point, police used a Long-Range Acoustic Device (LRAD), sounding like a very loud loudspeaker.

> *Rebel News reported on 22 April 2022, that 'Australian Capital Territory Policing admitted [using] a LRAD during the Canberra Convoy Freedom rallies ... LRADs have been employed in military settings ... and against crowds at the 2009 G20 summit in its weaponised mode, causing serious and permanent injuries ...*[4]

CHAPTER TWENTY-NINE

A parliamentary committee questioned the Australian Federal Police about its LRAD use. Under scrutiny, they admitted owning LRADs with a weapon mode but denied activating them. The sound was painful, ten times louder than the event speakers, such as those used for big concerts. Immediately after this, Laurence became so weak he struggled to walk to our car.

Armies sometimes use music and sound for torture. In the 1991 Gulf War, Western military blasted rock music across the desert to flush out Iraqi soldiers from their rabbit holes. In 1990, the US Army sought to drive General Noriega out of hiding in the papal embassy in Panama by bombarding him with heavy metal music to drive him crazy. EMI and DECCA record companies are 'heavily involved in producing electronic equipment for defence'.[5]

As the spiritual battle for hearts and minds intensifies, the rage against God fuels more destructive noise. As intimacy with the Lord increases, a sweeter, yet more potent, weighty song emerges.

Grammy Award for 'Unholy' Vs Asbury Revival

In February 2023, the world had a three-day peek into the end-time battle of the bands though two-contrasting events.

On 5 February 2023, Sam Smith and Kim Petras took home a Grammy award for their song 'Unholy'. Complete with theatrical fire and devil horns, their performance exalted demons and transgenderism. Afterwards, Kim Petras, told reporters she had 'tried religion, and was not wanted'! Ouch! She was clearly angry and felt judged and rejected by the Church.[6] Traumatic events can open doors to the demonic. Rejection often flows into rebellion and the blatant synergy of music, pornography, perversion and occult practices. The danger is real and blatant. She felt the song 'Unholy' was the perfect vehicle to express her pain.

Three days later on 8 February (yes, the all-important third day), an outpouring of the Holy Spirit broke out at Asbury, spreading to other states and nations. Featuring non-stop worship and prayer, there were no famous worship bands, no lights, no fog machines, no overheads, no restrictions, no agendas, just raw pressing into God. Wherever people were hungry for His Presence, a wave of revival broke out.

On my social media feed, one person summarised the two events: 'Satan takes Hollywood and says, "The world will worship me for five minutes." Three days later, it is like God says, "Nope, I, the Lord God Almighty, the King of all Kings, I [will] have the final say!"'

A friend shared a video of someone nearing Asbury. He said five miles out, the Presence of God hit him in the car; he could not stop weeping. Another person described the 'sweet Presence of God; I can't stop weeping'. Another described it: 'Tranquil! No selfish ambitions, just love and peace.'

The difference between these two events could not be more stark, highlighting the contrast of sounds in this season of war in the unseen realm. Hollywood's sound faded in a few days. Eternity records Asbury's pure revival sounds.

Demonic Music Festivals: False Deities

Two festivals, Tomorrowland and Supernova, both honour a goddess and god of Hinduism, blatantly exacerbating the degeneration of the 1960s sexual revolution. Woodstock's drug-infused festivals have given way to 21st-century festivals blending an addictive mix of electronic dance music (EDM) and occult fantasy, yet promoted as a wholesome, drug-free zone![7] Participants get immersed in a tech-driven fantasy extravaganza with mother earth.

CHAPTER TWENTY-NINE

In Part Three, we discussed the Supernova. Tomorrowland, a leading influential EDM festival, which began in Belgium in 2005, is a vital 'partner' to Supernova, seducing audiences with themes such as 'The Book of Wisdom' – but it's not the book of Proverbs!

> *It's an imaginary world full of energy, shapes and colors, living within a spirit of brotherhood summarized by the motto of Tomorrowland PLUR (Peace, Love, Unity, Respect).*

Be alert. Tomorrowland festivals are in many nations, seducing youth to bow to false deities, through music.

> *On the centre stage of Tomorrowland is a huge slowing spinning replica of the CERN hadron collider gate. On stage is a giant mirror in which the digitally created face of the goddess Kali appears and speaks to the crowds....As helicopters flew overhead, and as beacons of colored lights flashed across the night sky a deep, powerful male voice said: 'People of Tomorrow, as a new chapter unfolds, you will learn about one man, who knew the mysteries of the universe from within.' Because of his vision a great work was completed (CERN). With its sacred key, the machine can forge unique experiences continuously.* **Humanity can be reborn ...**[8]

CERN, a nuclear research centre on the French–Swiss border with a one-hundred-metre underground tunnel, received a Shiva statue from India, as Hindus believe he danced the universe into existence, and will eventually extinguish it![9] That's right, the same god at Supernova in Israel on 7 October.

END-TIME BATTLE OF THE BANDS

In 2016, Switzerland's Gotthard Tunnel was opened with a bizarre ceremony that honoured Baphomet and Kali with occult music. Held underground in Europe's deepest train tunnel, world leaders[10] attended, sparking rumours of connections to CERN two hundred kilometres away, which were denied.

Tomorrowland honours the Hindu goddess Kali, and Supernova honours the Hindu god Shiva, the queen and king of Hinduism. Though these festivals have different names, they align in the spirit. They both drive destruction, seducing young people with psychedelic sounds and lights to dance before these two entities.

Biblically, they align with the Queen of Heaven and the dragon, the two involved in the end-time battle over worship! The Queen of Heaven (Babylon) is the *consort* of the dragon. Despite differing names and variations of culture, Kali and Shiva have the same aim as Mystery Babylon and the dragon – destroy true worship, dethrone God.

A teacher of Karl Marx claimed Christianity was wretched compared to the 'glorious' past of Greek culture, exalting the pantheon of gods in Greek mythology above Jesus! The 2024 Paris Olympics opening certainly continued this theme.[11]

The array of names of false gods can be confusing. Put simply, they change names according to the nation, culture and era. For example, Zeus to the Greeks, Jupiter to the Romans, Baal to the Canaanites, Shiva to the Hindus. Despite slight differences in appearance, these four are the 'highest' god of each culture, with one purpose – to dethrone and replace God Almighty.

Whether it was Lucifer, Nimrod, Baal, Moloch, Osiris, Zeus, Dionysus, Marx, Lenin, Hitler, Kali or ideologies like Buddhism, Freemasonry, socialism, humanism, evolution, yoga, materialism or Beatlemania – every anti-Christ activity aims to dethrone Almighty God. The clash of kingdoms may appear to be for global domination, but it always targets the throne of God, the Creator of the universe.

Demonic Alliances, Counterfeit Marriage

Ephesians 5 compares the marriage of husband and wife to the Messiah's Bride. After Mystery Babylon falls, the marriage supper of the Lamb occurs (Revelation 19).

Demonic liaisons like Shiva and Kali, and Mystery Babylon and the Dragon, are blasphemous *counterfeits* of the heavenly union. These wage war to destroy marriage. Music festivals are the front to seduce another generation into the arms of false gods, a demonic subterfuge to seduce and subvert the foundation of civilisation, God and marriage.

The undermining of faith and marriage wreaks havoc on individuals and nations – so heartbreaking.

Worship the Lamb or the Beast?

Earlier I spoke of the book of Revelation providing a glimpse into the fullness of God's Glory and heaven's spectacular worship. Read Revelation – the Greek word 'apocalypse' is an unveiling, not an annihilation! You will be blessed just to read the book, even if you do not understand all the scary symbols and judgements!

You will also discover the battle of the bands and a display of end-times worship in Revelation. It is an enthralling, eternal sound. It unveils Jesus and the worship for the end-times where heaven and earth are joined in the most powerful sounds. Are we ready?

> I saw **a vast multitude of people** – so huge that no one could count ... **victorious ones** from **every** nation, tribe ... and language. They were all ... standing before the throne and before the Lamb...

> ***with a passionate voice: 'Salvation belongs to our
> God ...' (Revelation 7:9–10 TPT)***

After defeating death and hell, Jesus was resurrected and sits at the Father's right hand. His honoured position to reign over the earth terrifies the demonic realm. His reign, declared in Revelation 11:17, infuriates nations seduced by evil entities who know their time is short. Heaven's end-time language is victorious, not pessimistic! Yes, there are challenges, but like Jesus, He endured the cross for the joy of what would be accomplished (Hebrews 12:2).

Repeatedly, Revelation appears to oscillate between judgement and worship, even though these may seem to be incompatible opposites. God's judgements are righteous; they correct and vindicate those who have suffered, and address evil. His judgements are released from heaven's atmosphere of constant praise.

A pattern emerges in the book of Revelation:

1. A variety of extravagant pure worship is heard.
2. Heaven *and* earth participate in these praises.
3. God's voice thunders, releasing judgements on the wicked.
4. Angels execute the judgements.

What is our role in connecting worship, divine sounds, justice and judgements? Chapter 32, 'Psalm 149: Nuclear Warhead' answers this question.

For now, be encouraged to read Revelation differently!

Worship of the Lamb Vs Babylon

Two end-time 'bands' vie for the hearts of humanity: true worshippers of God and those beguiled by Mystery Babylon's fame, fortune and power.

CHAPTER TWENTY-NINE

Worshippers of Heaven and Earth

- Heavenly worship when reproduced on earth is beautiful, powerful, transformative, and shapes history. Most revivals have been accompanied by specific songs with a unique anointing as ordinary folks have exalted the Lord in praise.
- The sound of God's voice thundered from heaven bringing order out of chaos at creation (Genesis 1).
- The Lord's voice thundered at Mt Sinai, revealing Himself to Israel (Exodus 19–20).
- King David replicated heaven's worship in the tabernacle in Jerusalem (1 Chronicles 16.)
- Solomon's temple continued David's worship pattern (2 Chronicles 5).
- The church was birthed after sounds from heaven shook Jerusalem (Acts 2).
- Revelation shows all God's lovers (heaven and earth) worshipping before His throne (Revelation 5:13).
- Faithful saints sing a unique song. Having overcome the anti-Christ, theirs is a sound of victory (Revelation 15:2–3)!
- A roaring sound of praise fills heaven to announce the Lamb's marriage supper (Revelation 19:4–7).
- Sounds of praise encompass the throne of God 24/7. Sounding like 'many waters', they fill the atmosphere with joy, triumph and life. This is the atmosphere chosen by Almighty God for His eternal home, reflecting who He is (Revelation 14:2; 19:6).

Worshippers of Babylon

In contrast, the sounds of Mystery Babylon are seductive, vile and deadly, like the previously mentioned festivals. Thankfully, they are short-lived! How do we know Mystery Babylon has a band? One judgement is on her musical instruments – they are to be silenced! To be stopped, her instruments must first exist! (See Chapter 36, 'Silencing Babylon: Praise Eruption!')

Seduced: Bowing to Satan

Bowing to and worshipping Satan, as a musician or otherwise, comes at a cost. He even tried to lure Jesus!

> *The devil then said to Jesus, 'All of this, with all its power, authority, and splendor, is mine to give … Simply* **bow down to worship me, and it will be yours!** *You will possess everything!' (Luke 4:6–7 TPT)*

Jesus, though weakened by fasting, rebuked him with the God's word.

> *'Get behind Me, Satan! For it is written, "You shall worship the LORD your God, and Him only you shall serve."' (Luke 4:8 NKJV)*

Jesus knew His reign over all the kingdoms of the world would come through the cross, *not* Satan's offer. If the devil tempted Jesus with power in exchange for worship, he will surely target us too. Many musicians admit to having sold their souls to the devil for fame and fortune only to end in devastation.

Their importance to the devil is to either undermine the kingdom of God or help him build his power base. Like a paper bag, Satan uses people as disposable, discarding them when they have served their purpose. This is the pattern of the spirit of control and abuse. Satan does not respect free will. Rather, he manipulates, intimidates and bludgeons to coerce us to bow, exploiting our flesh.

In total contrast, the Lord values and cherishes His worshippers, blessing us abundantly in this life and the next. He respects free will. Even if we stray, He gently woos us back with His love. Our sacrificial gifts of worship, though big to us, are small compared to our eternal rewards.

The end-time battle over sound hinges on *whom* and *how* we worship. The choices we make manifest in the sounds we make. Our hearts and music must align with heaven's victorious sounds, not Babylon's. Which 'band' influences you? Do you listen to the instruments of Babylon or Heaven? Which chorus will you join?

How Music Shapes Society

Music shapes society much more than we realise. It mirrors the unseen realm through frequencies and songs. Specific instruments, melodies, rhythms and arrangements show which God or god a home or nation welcomes.

All music for the Lord must clearly reflect His nature – love, holiness, *justice, truth* – *to avoid confusing and mixed messages.*

1. *Reflect*

Music that mirrors the environment of the Lord must manifest characteristics matching who He is. Sounds should reflect His love, majesty, joy, *shalom* and beauty. Music reflecting the kingdom of darkness will manifest lies, theft, brutality, and murder and breed fear, hatred, manipulation, death, destruction, betrayal, and ugliness.

2. Exalt

Scripture exhorts us to sing songs of praise to exalt and glorify the name of the Lord. Pagan gods use songs to glorify themselves. Sound will distinguish and publicise the characteristics of each kingdom. The sounds we produce must exalt the Lord's holy name.

3. Propagate

Advertisers know how much music influences culture, so they use it subliminally to influence the masses, and make their fortune. Do not underestimate the magnitude and influence of sound in the spiritual war! Holy Spirit-anointed music repulses and repels Satan's kingdom.

Frequencies, sounds and songs are weapons in spiritual warfare – between Yahweh, the source of sound, and the thief whose ugly sound desecrates all beauty. Lucifer's fallen music, subjected to 'maggots and worms',[12] taints nearly every genre with decay.

Trojan Horse to Worship

Satan aims to steal the worship and glory belonging to God. If that fails, he tries defiling worship with seductive counterfeits and making us unfit for worship. Rather like the Trojan horse or a wolf in sheep's clothing.

As heaven's former worship leader, he knows everything about true worship: how it sounds, what it takes to create it. As the father of lies, he has the best custom-made tactics to damage and disqualify our worship – especially white-anting. If defilement fails, he seeks to kill worshippers.

Three tactics to defile and destroy worship are:

1. Syncretism

True worship is pure, with no mixture. Syncretism fuses truth with lies. Satan seeks to weaken worship through compromise. Part Three, 'Gold for Worshipping the King…' reveals the susceptibility we all face to syncretism, theologically and musically, and its results are devastating.

The push for a one-world religion grows daily. The UAE's Abrahamic Family House (an interfaith complex of a mosque, church and synagogue), is designed to 'provide a common base from which tolerance and understanding can be promoted.'[13]

2. Pamper the flesh

The devil entices us to indulge fleshly desires, to pamper the flesh and to offer worship devoid of sacrifice or obedience. Self-gratification aids his cause. If we, God's people, focus on self rather than Jesus, we do the devil's work for him! How does this honour the Father who gave His only begotten Son? All sowing to the flesh breeds corruption.[14] No exceptions.

3. Persecute, kill true worshippers

If syncretism fails, Satan kills. The 20th century had more Christian martyrs than all previous centuries combined. Open Doors reported:

> *Over 360 million Christians worldwide suffer high levels of persecution and discrimination for their faith – that's a staggering 1 in 7 believers.*[15]

People opting for mixed worship, preferring to pamper their flesh with entertainment, often scorn true worshippers with slander and gossip.

> *Lying about and slandering people are as bad as hitting them with a club, or wounding them with an arrow, or stabbing them with a sword. (Proverbs 25:18 TPT)*

King Saul threw spears at David, even while he was playing his harp (1 Samuel 19:9–10). Saul aimed his jealous rage at the true worshipper. Saul lost his throne because of rebellion and witchcraft. David, the worshipper, replaced him. Saul is quite the picture of Lucifer losing his anointing, being thrown from heaven and attacking true worshippers who would replace him!

We should expect this. 'For the flesh wars against the Spirit' (Galatians 5:17). True worship requires the flesh to be crucified; soulish worship indulges the flesh.

Worship Clashes Intensify in End-Times

The Bible's bookends reveal a fierce clash over worship, escalating in the end-times. It will sort out priorities, sifting true worshippers from pagan and mixed worshippers.

David had to dodge Goliath's taunts and Saul's spears before stepping up to be king. Then David could usher the Ark (the glory) into Jerusalem accompanied by prophetic music and establish the tabernacle. He appointed prophet-psalmists based on heaven's pattern.

It is time for the Church to consolidate the heart of worship and its sound, revitalising the prophet-psalmists who have the Melchizedek call. The audience of such psalmists is the Lord, not people. God's breath is releasing a new sound through prophet-psalmists of all ages. In these end-times, the sound coming from true worshippers aligned with heaven will subdue seducing and destructive sounds.

True worship is neither cheap nor without sacrifice. The first biblical worship involved Abraham's costly obedience with Isaac. David echoed this while seeking to secure the threshing floor from Araunah. David insisted on paying for the land:

> *... nor will I offer burnt offerings to the Lord my God with that which costs me nothing. (2 Samuel 24:22–24)*

CHAPTER THIRTY

Sound of the Blood Needed for His Glory

THE TIMELESS POTENT TRUTH of the gospel is that the power of the blood of Jesus defeated every work of the devil. Not some, but *all* his works – for eternity.

> *The reason the Son of God was made manifest (visible) was to undo (destroy, loosen, and dissolve) the works the devil [has done]. (1 John 3:8 AMPC)*

The message of the cross is the power of God, for complete redemption, salvation, deliverance, healing, restoration and reconciliation.

When Jesus triumphed over death and hell, the voice of His blood was like a nuclear bomb going off in the devil's domain. If the devil and his cohorts had realised, they would not have conspired to kill the King of glory!

> *... which none of the rulers of this age knew; for had they known, they would not have crucified the Lord of glory. (1 Corinthians 2:8)*

The sound from the blood of Jesus is essential in the end-time cosmic war, as revealed in Revelation 12. When the ancient serpent, or dragon, is cast out of heaven, he is *defeated* on earth by *us enforcing* the blood of Jesus, and by declaring *our testimony* of what His blood has done for us. It inflicts a dual blow on the devil's domain in every area he has sought to harm us.

> *So the great dragon was cast out, that serpent of old, called the Devil and Satan, who deceives the whole world; he was cast to the earth, and his angels were cast out with him…And* **they overcame him by the blood of the Lamb** *and by the* **word of their testimony**, *and they* **did not love their lives to the death**. *(Revelation 12:9-11)*

The Blood and the Glory

Where the blood is honoured, the glory comes. The worship of heaven honours the blood of the Lamb. Heaven is filled with His Glory because it is His home. If we want the glory, we must honour the blood of the Lamb. In fact, it is dangerous to pursue the glory without the blood of the Lamb.

In her book, *The Blood and the Glory*, Billye Brim shares her powerful testimony of searching for and preaching about the glory for many years. After some time, she experienced an increase in bizarre demonic attacks. After checking with the Lord, there were no open doors through sin. Continuing to seek the Lord, she discovered the blood must be applied – the blood and the glory go together.

Remember the vision of Jenny Hagger at the start of this fourth section? Glory angels needed warrior angels as a protective escort because of the cosmic conflict, like a president's or prime minister's aeroplane flying in hostile territory needing an escort of fighter jets. We need to enforce the blood of the Lamb to overcome the dragon in his end-time rage and summon the Lord's victorious glory realm. No blood of the Lamb, no glory.

Billye Brim writes:

> *Salvation is not just what we are saved '**from**' – the devil and sin. Salvation is what we are saved '**to**' – God and His Glory! The church is destined to stand before God's face forever, in the presence of His glory (Ephesians 1:4; 3:21). In the last days … God's glory is to be manifested in greater degree in His church. [It is the blood of Jesus] that cleanses us, and covers us, and enables us to stand in His Glory.*[16]

The well-known salvation scripture has more truths than often taught: 'for all have sinned and **fall short of the glory** of God' (Romans 3:23).

Adam and Eve were created in the image of God, with a covering of the glory. This covering is revealed in Psalm 104:1–2 where the Lord Himself is clothed with glory, majesty and light. That is why before sin, Adam and Eve did not see or were unaware of their nakedness – they were covered in glory! Sin separated them and us from the glory. Salvation is about recovering the ability to stand in the glory. It is only by the blood of Jesus we can have confidence to enter the Holy of Holies (Hebrews 10:19).

Decreeing and singing about the blood is vital for worship in the throne room. Sounds attached to the glory always honour the blood of the Lamb.

The Voice of the Blood Speaks!

The blood of Jesus has a *voice*. To our Western mindset, the idea of blood having a voice or a sound may seem bizarre. Yet scripture is clear. Life is in the blood, and the blood of Jesus speaks from the mercy seat in heaven.

> *... to Jesus the Mediator of the new covenant, and to the **blood** of sprinkling that **speaks** better things than that of Abel. (Hebrews 12:24 NKJV)*
>
> ***blood** that continues to **speak from heaven**, 'forgiveness', a better message than Abel's blood that cries from the earth, 'justice'. (Hebrews 12:24 TPT)*

All blood has life and a voice. After Cain killed his brother, the Lord told him his brother's blood was crying from the ground. In Genesis 4:10, the Hebrew word for crying is *tsaaq* and means to shriek, cry out in distress, a loud calling out or crying for help. Abel's blood, and that of any other victim, is a sound crying out for justice. The occult feeds on and is empowered by the shedding of blood, especially of the innocent – murder, war, abortion. Mystery Babylon feeds on the blood of the martyrs.

But the blood of Jesus speaks a better word or message. The Greek word for 'speaks' in this passage is *laleo*, which means to talk, preach, to tell, emit or articulate sounds. The blood of Jesus releases a powerful sound, a frequency. His blood is alive, speaking mercy on our behalf and reverberates in the spirit realm.

Bloodshed defiles land, families and nations. Only the blood of Jesus contains a greater sound and can remove the cry of bloodshed, cleanse the iniquity of murder, heal broken hearts and heal defiled land.

The blood of Jesus is a pure sound from His pure DNA. Its message resonates through time and through lineages. His blood agrees with the Glory of God. He placed His blood on the mercy seat, the lid of the Ark. His blood speaks powerfully on our behalf. No blood, no forgiveness, no mercy, no glory. This is vital in the end-time war over worship.

'Old timers' or early Pentecostals used the term 'I plead the blood' extensively. It is a legal term, invoking the idea of a plea in a law court. The devil is a legalist, accusing us before the throne day and night. Jesus is our advocate. His blood speaks on our behalf. Forgiven, debt paid!

The voice of His blood is indispensable. Decreeing and singing about the blood is a sound needed especially in the end-times.

Reconciliation Dream: 'Oh the Blood' Our National Anthem!

Towards the end of 2020 in our region, we had been in lockdown for a considerable length of time. The uncertainty of life was not just fear of a deadly disease but also from governmental control and wicked schemes by global elites and conglomerates. In that context, I had a dream about the blood of Jesus.

In the dream, I was having a coffee while looking at a newspaper in an outdoor kiosk area. To the north of my seat was a stadium. The page of my newspaper had the medal tally for the swimming events of the Barcelona Olympics. An Olympic swimming pool was on the east side of the coffee shop, and in the stadium the crowd was watching. I was like an observer, rather than being present at the event.

As I read about the medal tally, a medal presentation began. I heard snare drums rolling to announce a national anthem. I was shocked to hear the melody of 'Oh the blood of Jesus'. I didn't realise it was an anthem for any nation! The sound was majestic and powerful. I had never heard it sung that way before.

An older black American man in the middle of the stadium immediately stood to his feet, took his hat off and placed it across his heart. Others joined him. They all sang with great gusto and fervour. It reminded me of how people are when their national anthem plays after winning a gold medal. The song and the atmosphere of those responding to it indicated that the blood of Jesus was active and powerful. It was tangible. I saw such respect and appreciation for the blood of Jesus. The power of the blood was very real.

I awoke with the song resonating in my heart, and three things stood out as I prayed for interpretation.

First, I will not sing that song the same again. It was clearly the anthem of the kingdom of God! Second, in a dream, a swimming pool represents purification or cleansing. To swim in a pool is to be immersed in God. Third, I knew the mention of the Barcelona Olympics was important, but I did not even know if Barcelona had ever hosted the Olympic Games. I was amazed by my research.

The Barcelona Olympics took place in 1992 and was significant for three major geo-political shifts:

1. Apartheid in South Africa was being dismantled, resulting in South Africa taking part in an Olympics for the first time in thirty-two years.
2. In 1989, the Berlin wall had come down, reuniting East and West Germany. This was the first time in fifty-six years that they were competing as a united Germany.
3. In 1991, the Soviet Union had ended. For the first time in some sixty-nine years, twelve of its previous Soviet republics united. They competed for the first time as the Unified Team known as EUN.[17]

Previously, each of these situations had separated people through racism, ethnic hatred, politics or anti-Christ ideology. The song, 'Oh the Blood of Jesus', was the national anthem of the kingdom. The medals of honour, glory and reward belong to the Lord for the work of His blood. I felt my dream was a message of hope regarding fragmented relationships in families, churches and nations.

> *For He Himself is our peace, who has made both one, and has broken down the middle wall of separation. (Ephesians 2:14 NKJV)*

> *Ethnic hatred has been dissolved by the crucifixion of his precious body on the cross...Two have now become one, and we live restored to God and reconciled in the body of Christ. Through his crucifixion, hatred died. (Ephesians 2:15-16 TPT)*

The blood of Jesus reconciles us with God and others. Only the blood of Jesus can cleanse, purify and heal where relationships have been breached, even severed, whether between families, churches, people groups, or nations. It is real.

For a decade or more, this truth has been my prayer for some fragmented relationships in my family. In the last two years, I have experienced the joy of reconciliation by the power of His blood. This is my testimony! The blood of Jesus tangibly proclaims His reconciling power.

In these end-times, as nations and ethnicities rise against one another, let us boldly sing our national anthem, 'Oh the blood of Jesus'.

The Cross is the Power of God

I hear people lament, 'Where is the power in the church?' Let me ask, 'Where is the cross?'

> *For the message of the cross is foolishness to those who are perishing, but to us who are being saved it is **the power of God**. (1 Corinthians 1:18)*

If you want His power, you must have His cross. No cross, no power. In His journey to the cross, Jesus shed His blood in seven places[18]. Each of these can bring great healing and deliverance in our lives if we learn to apply His victory to our specific needs.[19]

1. Gethsemane: Jesus was close to death as He bled through His pores. He was 'crushed with grief' of rejection and betrayal and had to overcome human willpower to surrender to Father's will!
2. Beatings: skin was ripped as His back was scourged. 'By His Stripes we are healed'.[20]
3. Beatings: He had bruises and internal bleeding. 'He was bruised for our iniquities.' Sin is an archery term meaning 'to miss the mark'. Iniquity means you have a crooked bow. Generational curses are deep wounds that need His blood for healing.
4. Crown of thorns: His head bled profusely as they mocked Him. Blood from His head is powerful over our thought life and mental issues, connected to the helmet of salvation.
5. Nails in hands: this frees our conscience from dead works to worship and serve the living God (Hebrews 9:14).
6. Nail in feet: His pierced and bruised feet crushed the head of Satan, bringing peace to our walk.
7. Spear in His side: blood and water signify death but are also present at birth. Jesus fulfilled every jot and tittle as the Passover Lamb. The Hebrew word for finished is *kalah*: 'It is finished, my Bride' (John 19:30 TPT).

The blood of Jesus saves, heals, delivers, restores and disarms every insidious scheme against the lovers of God and their desire to worship in Spirit and truth.

Overcoming End-Time Dragon Accusation: Communion

The modus operandi of the dragon is lies mixed with accusation. But he often does it through us via the spirit of Cain, who murdered his brother *over worship* when they were working in the fields of harvest! It is too easy to hook into the spirit of the dragon. The blood of Jesus is the antidote to the poison, but first we must break agreement with the accuser.

Dean Briggs writes brilliantly on this in *The Great Communion Revival*:

> *Satan is not just an accuser, he is a liar who deceives everyone in the way he accuses … The world is increasingly polarised about everything … Even [our] moral outrage over immoral issues, we are literally feeding the beast … What was once a little snake in the garden is now a mighty dragon … The little snake has been well fed by humanity. He has gorged on our agreement with his values and tactics, and grown huge as a result. We have nursed him from a snake of deception slithering through Eden to the global dragon called, 'Accuser of the Brethren.' With our tongue, we give loyalty, nutrition and attention necessary for accusation to thrive.*[21] *Such is the brilliance of Satan's design, to put so much lethality and poison upon the human tongue. When we claim God's promises, we put God's word in our mouth. When we accuse, we replace it with Satan's. We can't play the accusation game to defeat the great accuser. To the degree that we bring accusation for him* **Satan has access**. *Sadly, we do this all the time. Daily. Constantly … In our families, marriages. Among those with*

> *whom we agree and those with whom we disagree. Against that church across the street, or that pastor we don't like so much ... We speak cursing far more than blessing ... You cannot follow the lamb while sharpening your teeth."*[22]

Jesus defeated the devil through humbling Himself, not by accusing the devil! We humble ourselves to repent and forgive regarding accusations. Every time we are aware of the devil's accusations from us or about us, we need the help of the Holy Spirit. We need His help to stop hooking into the spirit of the dragon by accusing ourselves, others and even God!

The blood of Jesus is not a magic incantation. It must go deep into our wounds, transgressions and bloodlines. We must break agreement with the accuser. Then apply the blood, 'plead the blood', and allow His blood to wash away any residual poison from our emotions and thoughts.

As the dragon's end-time rage intensifies, the language for God's people is for victory over this entity, not defeat! Revelation 12:11 provides three keys for victory:

1. the blood of the Lamb, which has defeated every work of the devil
2. a personal testimony of how Jesus' blood enabled you to overcome, beyond a religious head agreement
3. taking up our cross and our total surrender to the Lord's purposes, regardless of the cost

As we apply and plead the blood of Jesus and speak our testimony, it reminds the devil of his defeat and reverberates powerfully in the earth and in the spirit realm. True worshippers honour the blood of Jesus by defeating the dragon's accusations.

As the Israelites placed the blood of the Passover Lamb on the doorways of their homes, they were protected and gained deliverance. The angel of death had to 'pass-over' them. Pharoah is a prophetic picture of the end-time dragon principality and cosmic war. Pleading the blood of the Passover Lamb over our households is vital in the end-time spiritual battles. The blood of Jesus is the only thing that stands between us and the devil's accusations, deceptions and cruel assignments.

Heaven's Worship Honours the Lamb

Heaven's worship honours the blood of the Lamb – ours must too. Revelation 5 unveils the historic moment when Jesus, the Lion of Judah, is the only one found worthy to open the sealed scroll and release the end-time judgements. He alone has the authority because He prevailed at the cross over sin, death and every power of darkness (Revelation 5:5). (The meaning of the scroll is discussed in Chapter 32, 'Psalm 149: Spiritual Nuclear Warhead'.)

As Jesus, the Lion and the Lamb, takes the scroll from Father's hand, the Ancient of Days, worship erupts in heaven. A new song is sung by four living creatures, the twenty-four elders and angels beyond number. The choir grows as the same song spills onto the earth as eventually every creature in heaven, on earth and in the sea declare:

> *You were slain, And have **redeemed us to God by Your blood** Out of every tribe and tongue and people and nation ...**Worthy is the Lamb who was slain** ... (Revelation 5:9, 12)*

When we sing 'Worthy is the Lamb', we align with the eternal anthem of heaven and prophetically foreshadow what is soon to unfold. It is a powerful song, resonating with the glorious sound of the blood that speaks, and is filled with the frequencies of His Glory.

The cross remains the key to victory, including the battle over worship. To restore true worship, we must decree, sing and apply the blood of the Lamb to every circumstance.

Bush Praise and Battle Hymns: Songs to Make Demons Run

Before we were married, Laurence and I played in a bush band as part of the evangelism team attached to our church. With Australian folk instruments, dressed in pioneering clothes and using pioneering era music, we sang the gospel while the team shared tracts in the city mall.

Spiritual resistance was common. Whenever pressure intensified, we would launch into the old Salvation Army hymn, 'There is power, power, wonder-working power in the blood of the Lamb!' Instantly, the atmosphere shifted. I could sense demons fleeing like a stampede in the spirit. Freedom to minister always followed, with no further hindrance. I have witnessed this scenario repeatedly as I have led worship inside and outside of church buildings.

One time as I sang and played that salvation hymn, a young lady came in off the street to see what was happening and asked if we were drunk! Joy and dancing had broken out in the meeting as we were singing 'Power in the Blood'.

Some of our most powerful worship has come after communion, having enforced the victory Jesus won at the cross. So why are there so few songs about the blood of Jesus in modern worship?

As the end-time battles intensify, we must increase the songs that honour the Lamb and His blood – a sound that speaks life, and the enemy dreads.

Testimony of the Blood

We overcome the dragon with our testimony of what the blood has done for us. When we allow His blood to seep deep into our hearts, our proclamations and songs carry our testimony, the authenticity of truth and sound of authority. We cannot just speak and sing about the blood religiously. It must be our personal testimony.

We recently had a wonderful focus on communion with powerful testimonies shared about the power of the blood:

- to be able to forgive the 'unforgiveable'
- decrees that stopped a murderous thief in Africa
- decrees powerfully resulting in drugged neighbours screaming out of their house, stopping their invasive music in the night and leaving the area.

Other powerful testimonies not shared on that day came from:

- a believer who had no 'safe room' during the Hamas attack. They stood and pleaded the blood over the doorway of their bedrooms. Hamas left and they were unharmed.
- my grandmother who had a visit from a cult. After reading their material, she had a nervous breakdown. A friend shared with her about the blood of Jesus. My grandmother had a vision of a cup full of the blood of Jesus. She was fully restored to a sound mind.

The Lord delivered me from a hindering and debilitating bitter root. In Part One of this book, I spoke of the devastating events in our original congregation, when I stopped playing the piano until the Lord directed me to go and worship Him, with just Him and me. In the early stages of recovery, the only songs I could sing were hymns about the blood and the worthy Lamb of God. Other songs triggered painful memories. Songs to the worthy Lamb released many tears, but pressing into the cross and identifying with the sufferings of Jesus brought much healing. These songs were comforting and put my circumstances into eternal perspective. The result was so tangible, each day when Laurence returned from work, he could discern if I had worshipped the Lord that day or not! He recognised my joy levels plummeted if I had not.

The authority to publicly speak and sing about the blood of Jesus did not come immediately. It required many more victories until it was no longer head knowledge, but it was my deep testimony. That there is power in the blood is not just a song or a cliché. It is truth. A reality. The blood of Jesus is a voice filled with life. The restoration of true worship is dependent upon all of us going deeper and deeper into it.

Applying the Blood Apostolically

In a dream in 2016, the Lord first rebuked us and then said to honour and apply the blood of Jesus 'apostolically'!

The rebuke was that we had got into a rut in the way we were doing prophetic acts. Communion is one of those prophetic activations.[23] In the dream, we had to really press into the Lord to get out of the habitual way of doing things. The Lord revealed we were stuck in a jungle, and the only way out was to use His blood apostolically. A jungle represents the world, trials and complicated journeys.[24] Cosmic war playing out on the earth is like a jungle!

To apply the blood apostolically, we must do so from a kingly position. What do I mean?

We are made kings and priests by the blood of Jesus (Revelation 1:5–6). Priests offer sacrifices for sin. Frequently, our songs about the blood are applied in the priestly realm.

Kings rule with authority. Their decrees must be obeyed. By the blood of Jesus, we reign with the King of kings in heavenly places.

> *and raised us up with him and seated us with him in the heavenly places in Christ Jesus. (Ephesians 2:6 ESV)*

Apostles are 'sent' ones on a mission. Generally, the mission is attached to a vision and with the authority to plant or pioneer that vision. Here, the application of the blood of Jesus is the apostolic 'mission'. It must be done from a ruling, kingly position. This cannot be done religiously, habitually or without faith in it. It requires the wearing of His robe of righteousness and being exactly what we say. Authenticity of our speech comes because we have personally appropriated the blood of Jesus to our inner beings. Only then can we speak and sing the blood with authority into situations on the earth.

Worship has these two streams as well: priestly and kingly. Much of the church worships as priests. It is good and must be done first. We offer the sacrifices of praise from our hearts and lips, blessing and honouring His blood.

Apostolic worship begins with priestly sacrifices and sweet-smelling offerings but then shifts to worshipping in the Holy of Holies, or around His throne. As the shift takes place, we hear His voice and then echo or reproduce His message into situations on earth. Releasing the voice of His blood apostolically is at His direction, as kings releasing His key of authority, to close unrighteous gates and open righteous gates. It is applying His blood over specific gates to ensure they remain closed or open. Release the sound of His blood with authority to ensure victory and breakthrough.

The enemy knows which songs carry the glory. He panics when we sing them. When the Bride lifts the anthem of the Lamb's blood, darkness loses its grip. This is the kind of worship we must restore.

CHAPTER THIRTY-ONE

Exquisite Governing Sound: Wait for Weighty Glory

IN THE 1970S, I heard the most exquisite sound. Despite my musical training, it was not a sound I had heard before, nor was I able to analyse or evaluate it, but it was definitely a sound from heaven. It penetrated my heart and broke through the stiff resistance I had had as a teenager towards the Holy Spirit.

There is a unique sound from heaven that reverses the curse of the tower of Babel where nations and languages were divided. It was a sound heard on the day of Pentecost as heaven's language was restored on earth.

As the Ark was brought into Solomon's temple, the musicians and singers created a 'one sound' which activated the glory. This sound synergises the language of heaven with the frequencies of His Glory. It is a powerful, unifying sound from heaven which the church must urgently recover.

Vietnam War, Charismatic Era: My Resistance Broken

In the 1970s, amid Vietnam War protests on university campuses, including where I was studying music, the Jesus

Revolution and charismatic renewal swept through hippie communities, churches and homes. My conservative evangelical church and family in the 'Bible belt' suburbs of Melbourne were being affected. I was curious, but resistant.

Years earlier, I had a close school friend who was Pentecostal. One day, I emphatically told her to stop talking about the Holy Spirit. She had not really said much; I was just under conviction. I did not want to hear anything! My head was full of arguments. For some unknown reason, I believed tongues had died with the early church, and worse, I feared it was demonic. Sadly, many still believe this. I researched every theological book I could find to disprove the message of tongues. My intellect was satisfied, but conviction persisted.

Two factors broke my resistance.

First, I read *Prison to Praise* by Merlyn Carothers who described miracles of salvation and healings in response to thanksgiving and singing praises to the Lord, including tongues. It resonated with my childhood call to worship ministry. The connection with praise, tongues and miracles was inspirational and stirred my heart. The second breakthrough came after hearing the magnificent sound that relates to Acts 2.

Exquisite Sound Beyond Description

At the height of the charismatic outpouring, about a thousand people gathered at the Camberwell Civic Centre near Melbourne for a night of worship. Every person present sang their own song of praise in tongues, all at the same time! It was unrehearsed, spontaneous. Every person was engaged. There was no visible conductor and no lyrics displayed, yet it was not a cacophony. Rather, there was order, and every voice blended and harmonised. Musically, the harmony was simple, based on a single chord. Nobody was out of tune or out of time. The sound was pure, profound, ethereal, angelic, unlike anything I had heard before.

Bach's genius is legendary. His fugues are masterpieces because multiple melodies are superimposed on each other and blend harmoniously and rhythmically. The sound I heard that night differed from Bach, though reminiscent. Dare I say, greater, or at least on another level than Bach! Here were non-musical people who simultaneously and spontaneously created magnificent melodies that harmonised! It was a heavenly sound. Despite my prior resistance to the Holy Spirit, undeniably His breath was all over the magnificent sound, and He was the conductor.

Unable to analyse the sound, the best description I found is in Revelation.

> *I heard ... the voice of a **great multitude**, as the sound of many waters and as the sound of mighty thunderings, saying, 'Alleluia! For the Lord God Omnipotent reigns!' (Revelation 19:5)*

The Lord had captured my heart with His exquisite beauty. Hearing a sound that transcended my musical and spiritual knowledge, all arguments were gone. I was convinced. Tongues are from God, and they are for today. Only God could create and orchestrate such a beautiful sound.

Return Singing in Tongues to the Church – Urgent Priority!

There is something extraordinary and beautiful when an entire congregation sings His praises with great gusto. But anointed spontaneous singing in tongues by a whole congregation is another level, and gloriously supernatural. Speaking in tongues is powerful, but singing in tongues synergises the language of heaven with the frequencies of the Glory!

CHAPTER THIRTY-ONE

Singing in tongues is one of the most powerful weapons against the enemies of the Lord. The Lord is calling His church to rediscover this exquisite sound. The Lord is calling for a resurgence of congregations singing in the Spirit. It is necessary to meet this era's level of spiritual warfare.

Once you have tasted heaven's glory sounds, nothing else satisfies; you are spoiled for the ordinary. Despite the beauty of singing in tongues in the 1970s, by the late 1980s, many charismatic and Pentecostal churches reduced or even eliminated singing in the Spirit. Many wanted to provide seeker-sensitive environments, including the music of the culture. Entertainment became a higher priority than encouraging congregations to sing in the Spirit.

The church has been robbed. Too often, tongues is misunderstood, underrated and under-used.

In this era of war, deception and trauma, we must recapture the magnificent sound of tongues in corporate worship. We need a resurgent renaissance of singing in the Spirit. For those who have not abandoned it, the Lord is calling to soar higher, explore deeper and engage more intentionally.

Tongues Defeat Babel – Babylon

God cursed the babbling Babel (Babylon): He divided their tongues and stopped their unity and ability to build a name for themselves. The Lord created many languages and scattered them into different nations under various princes or principalities.

El Shaddai then chose Abraham to father the nation of Israel to be His covenant people to worship Him alone. Israel would be distinct from other nations. The gentiles would be subject to demonic rulers, but Israel would be under the jurisdiction of the Holy One of Israel – but they had to choose to worship only Him. Hence, a wrestle would ensue for Israel: to worship the one true God or the gods of the other nations.[25]

At Pentecost, the heavenly language broke the curse of Babylon's divided tongues and brought unity in the Spirit. Jews and Gentiles are united through the blood of Jesus to form the one 'new man'.[26]

Governing Sound

Singing in the Spirit is not just a beautiful sound – it is a governing sound. To align more fully with heaven, and to exercise our authority on the earth, we need this sound.

As kingdoms clash, we face momentous challenges. Singing and praying in tongues is the *purest* and *most powerful* way to give thanks and exercise dominion and authority of the *Ekklesia*. Tongues bypass natural senses and emotional turmoil and negates witchcraft intimidation. It enables us to offer pure, powerful praise regardless of circumstances.

Tim Sheets, in *Governing Authority*,[27] reminds us of the Garden of Eden where God gave Adam (and mankind) dominion, and until the tower of Babel, they all spoke the same language, the language of the Spirit. The language of heaven is infused with dominion, government, and kingdom authority, including creativity, and needed to have dominion.

To pray and sing in tongues is to call forth the will of God rather than ours. It activates agreement between heaven and earth, which is critical when interceding for a region, especially with regard to demonic thrones. Regional breakthroughs require the *Ekklesia* to pray *and* sing in tongues.

> *For then I will change the impure speech of all the people to the **pure speech of praise** so that **all** may **worship my name together** and serve me shoulder to shoulder. (Zephaniah 3:9 TPT)*

The impure language Zephaniah referred to belonged to a culture infested with idol worship. The first thing restored to the church at Pentecost is tongues, a pure supernatural language, free of idolatry, enabling us to give perfect praise. Pure speech only comes through tongues. Pure language is needed for corporate worship of the Lord. No wonder hell fights for this language: the very lie I had swallowed in my teens, 'tongues is not for today'!

Praying in tongues is powerful, but singing in tongues lifts it to a higher dimension. Singing in tongues adds the frequencies of the glory. The human voice is a musical instrument of praise, given to us when we were created. Lucifer was created with flutes and tambourines within him. He was a walking orchestra. We were born with an instrument inside of us too, our voice! Hundreds of scriptures command us to sing praises. Something changes dramatically when we choose to shift gears from speaking to singing. Singing requires more air, especially when holding longer notes – a picture of needing more Holy Spirit. Singing requires pitch, so we must listen more. Singing in tongues brings all these features together: more Holy Spirit, listening to and flowing with Holy Spirit, uncontaminated communications and frequencies of His Glory!

Sounds From Heaven: Singing in Tongues

When Isaiah saw the Lord on His throne, he heard pure singing that was so powerful, the sound shook the most secure part of the building.

> ... I clearly saw the Lord ... on his throne ... The **thunderous voice** of the fiery angels **caused the foundations of the thresholds to tremble** as the cloud of glory filled the temple! (Isaiah 6:1-4 TPT)

In an earthquake, the strongest part of a building and the safest place to shelter is under a doorframe. But the sound of the fiery angels singing 'Holy, holy, holy' caused even the doorframes and the foundations to shake and tremble. The sound of the glory is more intense than any earthquake!

On the day of Pentecost, wind and fire from heaven shook not just Jerusalem but civilisation throughout history.

> *Suddenly they **heard the sound of a violent blast of wind ... from out of the heavenly realm**. **The roar ...** was so **overpowering** it was all anyone could bear! ... a **pillar of fire** appeared ... **separated into tongues of fire** that engulfed each one ... They were all filled ... with the Holy Spirit ... speak in tongues ... in languages they had never learned!* (Acts 2:1–4 TPT)

The ferocious wind that hit Jerusalem was from the throne of God. The fullness of the Holy Spirit, seen in Revelation as seven flames of fire,[28] empowered the hundred and twenty disciples in the upper room. They all spoke proper languages, even though unlearned. It was not garbled gibberish.

Pentecost occurred during the Feast of Shavuot, so crowds of Jews from many countries were in Jerusalem. Pentecost echoed Sinai's marriage covenant. In Jerusalem, the Holy Spirit poured out gifts on the fledging church like a groom giving wedding gifts to His bride.

> *He ... has given us the Holy Spirit like an engagement ring is given to a bride – a down payment of the blessings to come!* (2 Corinthians 1:22 TPT)

Meanwhile, at the temple in Jerusalem, near the upper room, Ezekiel 36 was being read:

> *... as I prophesied, there was a **noise** ... and the bones came together ... He said to me, 'Prophesy to the breath ... Come from the four winds ... and breathe on these slain, that they may live.'* (Ezekiel 37:7, 9)

As the visitors came out of the temple, they heard a sound similar to what they had just read. God had their attention. It was a miracle!

A second miracle occurred when they could understand what the disciples were saying. The disciples supernaturally spoke the foreign languages and dialects of the visitors!

> *They were all filled ... with the Holy Spirit and ... speak in tongues ... **in languages they had never learned!** Yet we hear them **speaking of God's mighty wonders in our own dialects!*** (Acts 2: 4, 11 TPT)

Tongues, the supernatural gift of the Holy Spirit, enabled the disciples to praise God uniquely. The visitors were stunned as praises to the Lord went beyond the disciple's capability and experience.

Heavenly Language and Tongues of Fire

Tongues ushers us into the realm of angels around the throne – perfect praise, or *'rapturous praises in the Spirit'*.[29] The Greek word infers singing *and* musical instruments.

> *Singing in tongues is the most powerful way to give thanks to God. It is a gift from God to help us bypass our natural senses of fraught emotions and confused minds – even demonic torment. It enables us to offer pure, and beautiful praise. It is the language of heaven. When we sing in tongues our*

> *praise originates in heaven, flows through our spirit man and back to the Lord. Thus, singing in tongues is cyclical and releases rapturous praise!*[30]

Post Pentecost, the disciples changed. Once a fearful mob who abandoned Jesus during His arrest, they became courageous preachers and many who were martyred – evidence of the *dunamis* power of the Holy Spirit. The Greek word *dunamis* means miraculous power, to make one excellent of soul! Regardless of feelings or circumstances, the sevenfold Spirit of God miraculously heals our soul, empowers perfect praise and releases a sound that terrifies the enemy. We need to stir up this powerful gift.

Five Truths About Tongues

Jesus said after He ascended, the Holy Spirit would come and bring comfort and help. In 1 Corinthians 14, Paul gives insight into the necessity of tongues:

> *For he who speaks in a tongue does not speak to men **but to God** … in the spirit **he speaks mysteries**. (1 Corinthians 14:2)*

1. Direct access to God

Tongues is a heavenly language. It is our personal, secure, heavenly hotline – undecipherable by the devil. It's a direct line not to the president of the USA or the prime minister of a nation but to the Creator of the universe! This gift bypasses noise, confusion and torment, enabling direct communication with the heavenly Commander-in-Chief.

Speaking with others is great, but communicating directly with the Lord is irreplaceable. Tongues bypass our flesh, so we swiftly ascend into the Spirit.

As kingdoms are clashing and deception is rampant, we desperately need to hear what the Holy Spirit is saying rather than the enemies' words. To bypass the enemies domain of the second heaven, tongues is irreplaceable and should be at the top of our list!

2. Speak and sing mysteries

Ever struggle to know how to pray or what to do? When circumstances are confusing, we are in turmoil or intense spiritual warfare, and it is too easy to be discouraged, want to quit or just unsure of how to pray. We need divine intel or intervention. Perfect praise via tongues gets immediate access to the Holy Spirit to reveal 'dark sayings', riddles, conundrums and mysteries. Gaining divine insight and wisdom into situations ensures we can pray and decree with accuracy and authority.

We may have to wait for answers, but intentionally speaking and singing in tongues brings insight and clarity.

3. Builds up your inner man

'He who speaks in a tongue edifies himself' (1 Corinthians 14:4). The Greek word for 'edify' means to restore or repair a building. Sin, life's stresses and trauma damage our souls, or emotions, thoughts and choices. When we face tough situations, our souls need strengthening, to be rebuilt, repaired, even transformed.

How many Christians struggle with mental and emotional breakdowns because of the stresses of life? Prioritising tongues is vital for the church as it strengthens the innermost being of believers and would save a lot of counselling! We frequently witness people delivered, healed and receiving divine insight into their circumstances while we are in such worship. Tongues enables us to ascend out of grumbling into thanksgiving. Gratitude is an important step in healing. We have many testimonies of major breakthroughs when people have done my *Grumble Fast: 40-Day Gratitude Feast.*[31] Gratitude and thanksgiving align with perfect praise. Praying and singing in tongues edifies the individual and 'you indeed *give thanks well.*'

4. Releases perfect praise

What does it mean to '*give thanks well*' (1 Corinthians 14:17)? The Greek word *kalos*[32] suggests these praises are beautiful, excellent, genuine, precious, pure and comforting. Perfect praise is not entertainment, nor is it driven by our flesh. We cannot give perfect praise to the Lord without the help of the Holy Spirit.

Individual and corporate singing in the Spirit helps us quickly ascend into the throne room. Tongues strengthen us, delivering divine wisdom for spiritual warfare.

> *A warrior filled with wisdom ascends into the high place and releases breakthrough, bringing down the strongholds of the mighty.* (Proverbs 21:22 TPT)

In this era of clashing kingdoms, praying and singing in tongues is vital for His intel and victory.

5. Interpretation

Tongues often precede a prophetic word or interpretation.

> ... *if you speak in a tongue,* **pray for the interpretation** *to* ... **unfold the meaning** *of what you are saying.* (1 Corinthians 14:13 TPT)

Traditionally, an interpretation of tongues may sound like a prophetic word in the native language. But interpretations can vary in presentation, though they should explain the meaning of the tongues.

Sometimes an interpretation can come through a scripture that leaps off the page, or a picture or vision that is dropped into your spirit and spoken with a strong anointing. Gifted individuals may express interpretations through art, dance, poetry or music. Even a small phrase rising in the heart to pray or sing counts when it is inspired and releases a strong unction of the Spirit.

These are all valid interpretations, giving insight to worshippers to understand what the Holy Spirit is saying. If we dismiss the possibility of a variety of interpretations, we can mistakenly think there has been no interpretation.

Diverse interpretations enhance the anointing and flow of throne room worship; hence, tongues should be a significant portion of the worship flow.

Minimising Singing in Tongues

Some churches have minimised singing in tongues because of theological concerns, fear or human wisdom. Regardless of the reasoning, wrong thinking has led to diminishing worship's potential. My battle with tongues suggests a strong demonic resistance. The enemy is rightly afraid, seeking to suppress this potent gift.

1. *Theological*

Some interpret Paul's teaching in 1 Corinthians 14 to say that we should give priority to prophecy over tongues in corporate settings. Yet Acts 2 reveals that heaven sent tongues of fire first; prophecy came later. Tongues is the language of the Spirit which we must not suppress or diminish.

2. Fear

Some fear tongues as if it is spooky or mystical, thus driving people away from the house of God. Yet, crowds flock to New Age and occult festivals, revealing people actually crave genuine supernatural encounters. Suppressing the Holy Spirit's gifts pushes people to seek divine connections elsewhere, and in wrong places.

After addressing controversies in the early church about tongues, Paul exhorted:

> *I will pray with the spirit,* **and** *... with the understanding. I will sing with the spirit,* **and** *... **also** sing with the understanding. (1 Corinthians 14:15)*

It is good and necessary for the church to have prayer and singing both in tongues and with understanding, i.e. our native languages.

Wait For the Weight of Glory

Do you long for the power and miracles of the early church? Jesus gave clear instructions before ascending:

> *Don't leave Jerusalem, but* **wait** *... you will be baptized in the Holy Spirit ... you shall* **receive power** *when the Holy Spirit has come upon you ... (Acts 1:4–5, 8 TPT)*

Jesus told them to *wait*!

In an age of fast food and instant everything, we are not good at waiting. Yet a hundred and twenty disciples obeyed, remaining behind locked doors until the Holy Spirit came.

How many cities today could gather a hundred and twenty people to pray without a set finish time, no agenda, no speaker – just to wait? It was not a prayer meeting for an evangelical outreach or some crisis. The *only* purpose was to wait for the Holy Spirit, not knowing when or how He would come.

When leading worship, waiting is essential. We sensitively tune into the Spirit's ebb and flow like surfers waiting for the right waves. We sing in tongues, staying attentively waiting for the anointed song or word, and then ride the anointed current when it comes. Both in surfing and in worship, we must position ourselves, wait patiently, then soar!

Jesus promised the disciples power from the Holy Spirit, but His power is not for self-promotion. Power for self and without purity becomes witchcraft. Jesus said the Spirit's power would enable them to be 'witnesses' to Him – literally, *martyrs*! This call was not for fame, but faithfulness unto death. That kind of call tests every motive and thins the crowd!

What shifts our sound from being lightweight entertainment to weighty glory? Crushing. Olives must be pressed to release oil. Gethsemane means 'oil press', and it was there Jesus came close to death as blood oozed from His pores. He battled human will verses Father's will. Out of that brokenness flows the anointing that aligns us with His throne and produces the overcomer's song – a sound born of surrender, not ambition.

In these last days, heaven is stirring again. A sound waits to rise on earth as it is in heaven. Will we wait for the weight of His Glory?

Moses waited six days on the mountain before entering the glory cloud. Israel couldn't wait – they made a golden calf.

The disciples waited ten days before Pentecost. When the Spirit came, He came in a windstorm and flames of fire – terrifying yet transforming. They received the gift of tongues and were emboldened. It birthed the church, and many martyrs.

How long will we wait for the weight of His Glory? Will we pay the price for the glory?

Your Voice, Corporate Tongues: Powerful Weapon

> *But I will proclaim the victory of the God of Jacob. My melodies of praise will make him known. My praises will **break the powers of wickedness**, while the righteous will be promoted and become powerful! (Psalm 75:9–10 TPT)*

When humanity colludes with evil, an overcoming strategy is singing in tongues and asking the Lord to 'divide the tongues' of the wicked – the Lord's boomerang on Babel's original judgement.[33]

Because of its potency, the enemy seeks to minimise tongues in corporate worship. He seeks to silence us by lying about our voices. Many believers feel their voices are unworthy and sound bad. But your voice *matters*. Your voice is custom-made by your Creator. Every voice is needed to complete the beautiful sound of every believer singing in tongues. The church urgently needs this sound to triumph – it is like a sonic boom in the spirit realm.

The end-time church *must increase corporate singing* and praying in *tongues* to overcome Mystery Babylon. It is an exquisite, unifying, powerful and governing sound. It penetrates the darkness and seduction of Babylon and releases the strategies and authority from the throne of God. It is vital for victory.

CHAPTER THIRTY-TWO

Psalm 149: Nuclear Warhead

> *Once and for all I will not only shake the systems of the world, but also the unseen powers in the heavenly realm!* (Hebrews 12:26 TPT)

THE LORD'S VOICE THAT once shook Sinai now shakes world systems and demonic structures.

Worship amid darkness is challenging – we often face resistance in the spirit realm. We must come up higher, like eagles that fly into storms to make use of the updrafts to soar above the turbulence. Like John in Revelation 4:1, we are called to ascend. From that higher place, worship carries His Glory and *dunamis* power, spiritual dynamite that pierces the noise of darkness like a sonic boom.

> *I will proclaim the victory of the God of Jacob. My melodies of praise will make him known.* **My praises will break the powers of wickedness,** *while the righteous will be promoted and become powerful!* (Psalm 75:9–10 TPT)

Beyond the Natural: Breaking the Sound Barrier

Many military jets break the sound barrier, but not until after take-off and reaching sufficient speed and altitude. In conflict, this extra impetus is essential.

To break through spiritual sound barriers and resistances, we must abandon our natural limitations and shift momentum into the river of God – His jet streams! I can play worship songs that are nice but ordinary. But once we take off and ascend in the Holy Spirit, the anointing multiplies our worship, and I can go beyond my natural capabilities. The sound and atmosphere change.

However, for good reason, there are rules limiting jets flying at supersonic speeds. When an aircraft penetrates the sound barrier, a cloud forms around it, and people hear a sonic boom. Flying too low supersonically creates damage to buildings and scares people as the sound mimics explosions. Reported incidents occur from time to time.[34]

Years ago, my youngest brother flew the F111 for the Australian Air Force. They often did exercises with other nations across the top end of Australia. On one occasion after he had flown at low level and high speed over a remote community, a report was heard that the locals were convinced the end of the world had come! Even when flying within regulations, it can sound scary to those unaware of what is happening. In war zones, jets sometimes fly supersonically at low altitudes for psychological warfare.

To create a sound that penetrates the noise of darkness, we must ascend and go beyond our usual worship – forsake familiar structures, favourite songs or just louder volume. Prophetic worship is a blend of known songs, tongues and spontaneous creations as we follow the Holy Spirit. For worship to be propelled in the river of God, we must sensitively use the right sound, song or decree at the right time. A song that is powerful one day may be inappropriate the next day and fall flat. A sound can be of a quietly or loudly blown shofar, a bell rung or cymbal clashed, all dependent on being used at an appropriate moment.

When we ascend in worship, our sound changes, like when a car changes gears or a plane takes off. The difference is tangible. The sound becomes like sparkling rarefied air, charged with faith. When our sound goes deep in the Spirit, we go beyond natural sound barriers, piercing dark resistance in the Spirit, which is dangerous to the enemy.

Judgement Shockwaves: His Voice and Our Instruments of Praise

Exceeding the speed of sound causes surges in air pressure, resulting in an explosion or shockwaves. Earthquakes, volcanoes and nuclear weapons all discharge shockwaves, but without warning.

The voice of the Lord is a shockwave to evil! His voice and word exert extreme pressure upon malevolence. His voice flows *through* anointed songs and dance as His sceptre judges nations:

> *Here comes YAHWEH with his mighty power and glory! ...* **hear his awe-inspiring, majestic voice** *... His power will descend in cloudburst, thunderstorm, and hail. And when his rod strikes the Assyrians, they will be terror-stricken by the* **mighty voice of Lord YAHWEH.** *Every stroke of* **YAHWEH's punishing rod** *will be* **to the sound of cymbals and strumming harps.** *God himself fights them in battle* **with dancing!** *(Isaiah 30:27, 29-32 TPT)*

Extraordinary – His punishing rod employs our musical instruments in worship and dance! Before wielding His rod, His voice thunders through storms, hail and fire. Let Isaiah 30 inspire you to accept His invitation to partner with Him. As we align with the sound of heaven, He deals with rebellious nations!

How amazing! The Lord wields His rod through *our* songs of praise with harps and cymbals and dancing. He could act alone, not needing our help. But He has chosen the use of our sounds, our praises, to be the instruments through which He applies His judgement and correction. What an extraordinary privilege.

Psalm 149: Spiritual Nuclear Warhead

Psalm 149 discloses a sound in the Spirit akin to a nuclear warhead for use against the Lord's enemies!

A nuclear weapon combines different components to make it so lethal: fuel, explosives and a delivery system. Psalm 149 has seven components. In isolation, each of these is powerful, but when united, they create a spiritual weapon of mass destruction against the Lord's foes (and ours). For full effect, *all* seven must operate *together*, somewhat like a combination lock.

Seven is the Lord's number for completeness. Complete effectiveness comes as the seventh component merges with the first six. Together, they deliver and execute divine judgements on demonic kings.

Seven Components

1. *Praise and Thanksgiving*

> *Hallelujah! Praise the Lord! (Psalm 149:1 TPT)*

Thanksgiving is a heart posture. Without it, songs are empty and insufficient. We must activate thanksgiving *first*; it is the password or PIN to the Lord's Presence.[35]

When the Lord directed us to do the Grumble Fast, He uncovered hidden pockets of negativity. Grumbling causes us to bring mixed offerings, aligning with the devil's accusations, fostering demands for entertainment. Gratitude and praise from the heart are necessary to activate true worship. Like removing a safety pin on a powerful weapon, thanksgiving and praise unlock the Lord's firepower. Without heart praises from a grateful heart, our weapon is not activated!

2. New Song

> *Sing to the LORD a **new song**, And His praise in the assembly of saints. (Psalm 149:1 NKJV)*

A new song is not necessarily a freshly written song, though it may be. 'New songs' as in Psalms and Revelation are essentially songs of salvation. The Hebrew and Greek words for 'new' is something that is rebuilt or restored rather than brand-new – like a renovated house rather than a brand-new one. These are songs from hearts made new, rebuilt and redeemed by the blood of the Lamb. You can craft new songs ahead of time or you can create them spontaneously. Essentially, such songs are sung with a freshness. In a worship time, these are often released after tongues and fresh tangible anointing increases. Its vibrancy causes even an 'old song' to have the sparkle like a brand-new song.

3. The Nation of Israel

> *Let Israel rejoice in their Maker; Let the children of Zion be joyful in their King. (Psalm 149:2 NKJV)*

Israel plays a major role in Psalm 149's spiritual 'nuclear warhead'. It is Father God's lens, heartbeat and time clock. Israel is central. Jesus will return to Israel, not Palestine. His death and resurrection occurred in Jerusalem and during His Feasts. So, too, will His return.

Israelis joyfully singing and dancing to the Lord in their allotted land is a powerful weapon against the enemy. It is so moving to see young soldiers dancing and singing to the Lord before going into battle. It is the Jewish people in Israel who will physically welcome Jesus to Jerusalem. The church must honour and stand with Israel as Father God does. It strengthens our roots and changes our sound. Replacement theology can cause our weapon to malfunction. Replacement theology must end if our weapon is to be fully effective.[36]

4. Gates of Praise: Dance, Banners and Instruments

> *Break forth with dancing! Make music and sing God's praises with the rhythm of drums [literally, timbrels and harps]! (Psalm 149:3 TPT)*

Gates are sites of judicial decisions and potential invasion points (as in Chapter 28, 'Intercession: Battle at the Gates'), where battles are won through praise.[37]

A spirit-led assembly of musicians, singers and dancers, often with banners, amplifies this spiritual weapon, taking it to another level. Drums and tambourines (played well) supply rhythm for dances and align with the Lord's response, as in Isaiah 30:30–32, where His punishing rod beats in time to music and dance.

5. Intimacy and Enjoying Father's Love

Psalm 149:4 states, 'The LORD takes pleasure in His people.' He enjoys the company and praises of His faithful lovers. God created us for fellowship. You may not consider it a weapon, but amazingly our love refreshes Him, and our worshipping eyes can strengthen Him for battle![38]

> *The Lord stands in full authority to shatter to pieces the kings who stand against you... He will judge ... and will shatter the strongholds of ruling powers. Yet **he himself** will drink from his inheritance ... **refreshed by love** he will stand victorious!* (Psalm 110:5–7 TPT)

6. Humility

Humility releases the Lord's beauty, healing and victory.

> *He adorns the humble with his beauty, and he loves to give them victory.* (Psalm 149:4 TPT)

God gives grace to the humble but resists the proud.[39] Other translations render verse four as 'He will beautify the humble with salvation'. Salvation in Hebrew is *Yeshua*, meaning 'Yah is salvation'. As we humble ourselves to receive salvation through Yeshua, we are healed and adorned with His beauty, releasing His Glory. Unlocking the *shekinah* glory requires humility. Humility is vital fuel for the spiritual warhead.

> *Don't expect to see Shekinah glory until the Lord sees your sincere humility.* (Proverbs 15:33 TPT)

7. Combine High Praise and Wielding Word

Combining high praise with wielding the word is deadly to the enemy, elevating praise to its peak, like ascending from take-off to optimal altitude and speed. High praise is the best spiritual altitude from which to discharge the weapon.

> *Let the **high praises** of God be **in their mouth**,
> And a **two-edged sword in their hand** (Psalm 149:6 NKJV)*

> *God's high and holy praises fill their mouths, for their shouted praises are their weapons of war! (Psalm 149:6 TPT)*

High praise exalts and elevates Yeshua's name, authority and character above every other power – the opposite of self-centred songs. High praise enthrones Jesus above demonic thrones.

Adding the decreed word of God to our songs makes our praise more deadly. Wielding the sword is to use the rod of authority. The Hebrew *yad* (hand) signifies power and strength. When learning to use his rod, Moses' rod turned into a snake. Later, that rod was used to defeat Egypt's magicians, humiliate their gods and deliver Israel.[40]

These two weapons require our mouths for high praises and our 'hands' to wield the two-edged sword, the word of God.[41] Like the elders in Revelation holding a harp and an intercession bowl in their hands, worshippers and intercessors must integrate these two seamlessly, like well coordinated hands on a piano.

The Lord demonstrates this powerful pattern in Isaiah 27:1-2. First, He releases His sword against Leviathan, then sings over His inheritance. Though spoken to Israel, it is also His principle to combine praises and decreeing His word.

> *In that day, the Lord YAHWEH will mercilessly wield his massive, **mighty sword** and punish Leviathan ... He will slay the dragon of the sea ... In that day, they will **sing the song** 'The Vineyard of Delight' ... **a great trumpet will sound**, and – all*

the exiles – will come and bow ...in Jerusalem and worship him! (Isaiah 27:1,2, 13 TPT)

The Lord has been training us in both worship and the word; now we must learn to wield them together as one seamless weapon. Seek His wisdom for strategic timing and places to use them.

You've trained me with the weapons of warfare-worship; now I'll descend into battle with power to chase and conquer my foes. (Psalm 18:34 TPT)

Binding Kings with Chains

*These **warring weapons** will bring vengeance on the nations and every resistant power – to bind kings with chains and rulers with iron shackles. (Psalm 149:7–8 TPT)*

Who is targeted by these weapons? Every institution and nation that commits crimes against God and His people, plus those exerting anti-Christ resistance in governments: elites, intellectuals, media, educators and even terrorists. The kings that are bound are demonic powers with thrones. They are principalities, rulers and powers that govern or make judicial decisions.

For we do not wrestle against flesh and blood, but against principalities, against powers, against the rulers of the darkness of this age ... (Ephesians 6:12)

To 'bind' (in Hebrew, *awsar*) means to yoke, hitch or join in battle, tying up, engaging and capturing demonic forces as prisoners. 'Chains' (Hebrew *ziyqah*) means what leaps forth: a flash of fire, a burning flaming arrow, a firebrand, a *missile!*

Combining the depth of praise songs with decrees from God's word are like arrows or missiles falling on resisting supernatural powers, like the warhead's delivery system.

> *You have an arsenal of lethal weapons ... making your **judgment-arrows shafts of burning fire**. (Psalm 7:12–13 TPT)*

> *Those who plan their evil schemes against the Lord. They will turn and run at the sight of your **judgment-arrow** aimed straight at their hearts. (Psalm 21:11, 12 TPT)*

> *He released his **lightning-arrows**, and routed my foes ... (Psalm 18:14 NKJV)*

Weapons of praise with decrees from the word release the Lord's flaming arrows into the heart of the enemy, inciting fear and causing demonic forces to be taken as prisoners!

Judging Demonic Kings, Enforced by Worshipping Warriors

The World War II pilots who flew the missions to drop the nuclear bombs were enforcing the decrees and instructions of their president. They followed orders. Worshipping warriors are like those pilots enforcing decrees already established by a higher authority.

> *Praise-filled warriors will **enforce** the judgment-doom decreed against their enemies. This is the glorious honor he gives to all his godly lovers ... (Psalm 149:9 TPT)*

> *To execute on them the written judgment – this **honor** have all His saints. (Psalm 149:9 NKJV)*

We are honoured to enforce His previously written decrees – a privilege to partner with Him.

To be a potent weapon, all the components must be operational: heartfelt thanksgiving, a new song, Israel, dance and banners, musical instruments, intimacy with God, humility, praise with decrees from the word. Together, they are the fuel to explode in the enemy's heart. For accuracy and potency, they must all be from the Holy Spirit, thus excluding soulish ideas.

Double-Sided Scroll with Written Judgements

A written judgement is the official transcript of a judge's decision, read out in court. The Hebrew *mishpaòt* includes reading out the law, crime, penalty and sentence. This is the courts of heaven issuing justice against resistant demonic powers. Governments have constitutions and laws; the constitution of heaven has eternal decrees, written judgements against the enemy!

What judgements was the psalmist referring to? The judgements are written on scrolls, and what is known about them gives us insight into what our praises and decrees are enforcing.

Sealed Scroll

Revelation 5 and Ezekiel 2 mention a scroll written on both sides that contain written judgements but is sealed. Daniel speaks of books that are sealed. This heavenly legal document is so important it has seven seals, and not just anybody can open it.

> *I saw a hand holding* **a scroll ... with writing on both sides.** *On it was written 'Lament, Mourning, and Cries of Doom.' (Ezekiel 2:9–10 TPT)*

> *I saw ... the one seated on the throne was holding in his right hand an **unopened scroll** with **writing on the inside and on the outside**, and **it was sealed** with seven seals ...'Who is worthy to open the scroll and able to break its seven seals?' ... I saw the young Lamb ... take the scroll ... (Revelation 5:1–3, 7 TPT)*

Scrolls are not pieces of paper rolled and held together by an elastic band. Ancient scrolls were made from papyrus and sealed with wax or clay. Seals revealed the authenticity of an official court document. Earthly courts maintain scrupulous records – unless there is corruption!

Reliable records for credibility and authority were important in the tabernacle and temple. Appointed scribes recorded events, the history of God and the words of the Lord. Hence, Torah scrolls are revered.

How much more do the courts of heaven maintain scrupulous records – after all, the biblical scrolls belong to the supreme authority overseeing the universe, the highest court of the universe!

Who holds the Scroll?

The Ancient of Days is given books to open (Daniel 7:10). In Revelation 5, the one who sits on the throne holds the scroll. The scroll is in the Father's right hand, signifying His power, strength and authority; hence, no one can snatch it from His hand.

Scroll written both sides; what is written on it?

Usually written on the inside only, the scroll of heaven is written inside and outside and tightly sealed. Why is so much written on it? Scholars suggest the scroll contains the title deed of the universe, with God's ownership, timing, plans and His destiny for nations. Heaven's court judges nations. Are they sheep nations or goat nations? Did they obey the word of God and fulfil their destiny and how did they treat Israel?

God's word is eternal, established in heaven – and Yeshua is *the* Word! When on earth, Yeshua said He judges no one, but it is the established word that judges. His judgements are righteous, not arbitrary.

Perhaps one side of the parchment is His eternal word, the plan of salvation and nations' destiny. The other side could be the consequences – the woes or rewards – for adhering to or violating His word. Ezekiel notes judgements bring mourning.

> *I saw a hand holding a scroll … He unrolled it in front of me with writing on both sides. On it was written* **'Lament, Mourning, and Cries of Doom.'**
> (Ezekiel 2:9–10 TPT)

Who can open the Seals?

Why is it so hard to find someone who can open the seals? The scroll is sealed with seven seals, representing full completeness: full salvation and complete justice over all of eternity. Not just anybody can open it. Jesus, the pure Lamb who prevailed over all rebellion, death and hell, is the only one who has the jurisdiction and authority to unseal the documents.

Heaven and earth witness and accompany the heavenly scene by worshipping Jesus. Our Psalm 149 high praises, worship and decrees must align with Revelation 5's worship scene where Yeshua is found worthy to open the scroll. His judgements are against demonic kings and all who oppose Messiah.

Worship warriors have the privilege to enforce these decrees. Our weapons of praise and prayer are truly like a nuclear bomb, a sonic boom or a flaming arrow into the enemy's heart.

'One Sound' Amplifies God's Original Sound

Linking Psalm 149 with Revelation 5 (and Ezekiel and Daniel), we discover worship plays an enormous role in heaven and on earth. By intentionally embracing all aspects of worship in Psalm 149, we enforce the contents of the scrolls that only Jesus can open – a profound privilege.

Heaven is filled with His Glory, and a 'one sound' that is linked to the Ark. As the original Ark is in heaven, we should pay attention to the sounds accompanying the Ark even on earth. Corporate worship attuned to the Holy Spirit creates this unified sound. What is it?

After hosting a major worship conference, many of us had a bad winter flu. The event had been physically and emotionally taxing with some tricky relationship issues thrown into the mix. I was tired, sick, confused and felt betrayed. Our next meeting was a challenge; only eight attended and most of us had raspy voices. I cried out to God for supernatural help. We worshipped for a while and then sang Irene Swan's 'Hallelujah', which was inspired by angelic singing. The simple song echoes between male and female voices.

As we continued singing this song, the anointing thickened and all our voices were strengthened. Our crackling voices became stronger and clearer. Eight voices sounded like a choir of three hundred! Visions were seen of angels everywhere in the room, plus we had been allocated three angels each. Each of us and the angels were united in one sound! Our volume was amplified – I am sure the angels were singing too. The unity in sound and in the Spirit realm was tangible. We were literally as one! No one was out of sync musically or spiritually. It was a miracle that resulted in a powerful, multiplied sound. Angelic presence, frequencies of the glory and 'one sound' intertwined.

A symphony orchestra ensures that each instrument is tuned to the same frequency before a performance to avoid even a slight dissonance. They rehearse to ensure they are as one rhythmically and harmonically. The symphony orchestra is a great analogy of oneness in the Body of Messiah.

The 'one sound' is not only beautiful but more powerful than a single instrument. With God, one can put a thousand to flight, two put ten thousand to flight – a multiplication of ten![42] The 'one sound' manifests the multiplication effect.

Ark in Temple: 'One Sound'

King David received the plans for the temple from the Holy Spirit and passed them to his son Solomon.[43] At the dedication during the Feast of Tabernacles, Solomon used David's worship model. The priests processed the Ark into the temple as appointed psalmists, led by Asaph, Heman and Jeduthun, released 'one sound' to the Lord.[44]

> *... having cymbals, stringed instruments and harps, and with them one hundred and twenty priests sounding with trumpets ...* **when the trumpeters and singers were as one,** *to make* **one sound** *...* **praising and thanking the Lord** *... that the house of the Lord, was filled with a cloud, so that the priests could not continue ministering because of the cloud; for the glory of the Lord filled the house of God. (2 Chronicles 5:13–14)*

The exact size of these worship teams is unknown, but there were one hundred and twenty shofar players! They praised the Lord as one and made 'one sound'! The glory cloud fell; no one could remain standing. The Lord's *shekinah* invaded the temple.

PSALM 149: NUCLEAR WARHEAD

The unified sound of glory terrifies the enemy. God's Glory will cover the earth like the waters cover the sea.[45] Glory waves and its sound will roll across the earth. Let us take our place as priests and kings and press into producing 'one sound'. May His light and voice release a sonic boom against darkness.

The glorious angelic 'one sound' through our eight worshippers on that bleak winter's day restored my soul and helped me remain faithful during a bleak time. Demonic rage is escalating, as shown by the rising persecution of Christians globally. As darkness increases on the earth, we need angels joining us in the 'one sound'.

If God's voice is shaking nations and demonic realms, then the Church must arise, and echo His voice, with our shouts and songs of praise.

> *God arises **with** the earsplitting shout of his people! God goes up with a trumpet blast ... Sing your highest song of praise to our King! For God is the **triumphant King;** all the powers of the earth are his. So sing your celebration songs of highest praise to the glorious Enlightened One! (Psalm 47:5-7 TPT)*

> *Before the gods I will sing praises to You. (Psalm 138:1 NKJV)*

> *I bow ... and bring you my deepest worship ... For your Word and the fame of your name have been magnified above all else! You strengthened me deep within my soul and breathed fresh courage into me. (Psalm 138:2-3 TPT)*

May the worshippers on earth echo and resonate the sounds of heaven.

CHAPTER THIRTY-THREE

The Harp: End-Time Instrument

Harp Resurgence

IT IS NO COINCIDENCE that the harp is having a renaissance during a period of turbulent contention in the spirit realm. As the enemy rages against God's people, seeking to destroy civilisation built on Judeo-Christian morality, the harp is being heard again in Israel and the Church. It may seem crazy to think that within this season of war and confusion, God would release the gentle sound of the harp. But come with me through scriptures and events and discover why the resurgence of the harp is prophetic and powerful confirmation for this season – even to have victory over the spirit of anti-Christ!

The strings of the harp reverberate with heaven, with earth, human souls and bodies. The sound of the harp:

- comforts those who mourn
- brings joy to celebrate victory in the spiritual war
- breaks the sound barrier of demonic oppression
- woos prodigals and wounded souls to the Father's loving arms

- heralds a new sound in worship, connected to heaven
- is a sign the tabernacle of David is being restored

Gentle Strength

The harp is a gentle instrument. But gentle does not mean weak.

King David said, 'Your gentleness has made me great' (Psalm 18:3) and Isaiah said, 'in quietness and confidence is your strength' (Isaiah 30:15). Greatness and strength come through the Lord's gentleness and *shalom*. In Israel's history and into the prophetic future, the harp is an instrument to console His people and destroy the enemy.

The harp, associated with King David and the nation of Israel, symbolises joy, blessings, comfort and deliverance. The harp is so aligned with heavenly worship that most caricatures of heaven include angels and harps!

Silent harps signified bondage, as when Israel hung them up in Babylonian captivity (Psalm 137:2), lamenting, 'How can we sing the Lord's song in a foreign land?' After seventy years, they returned, rebuilt the temple and resumed worship, and harps were heard again.

Harps fell silent in Israel after the destruction of the temple in AD 70.

> *Silenced for 2,000 years, the restoration of the ancient harp of David began when the first Harrari harp was built in 1984.*[46]

The harp's resurgence in modern Israel signals Israel's prophetic return to the land of promise and growing in her maturity and freedom. Despite nations attempting to annihilate her, she has established a strong economy and leads in technology, innovation, security and military.

Adding the harp to worship in Israel, and in many nations, is a prophetic call for worship in the throne room and for ending captivity in spiritual Babylon. The Lord urges His people to flee from Babylon and its seductive harlotry (Revelation 18:4) before final judgement falls on it and its sounds.

Though David famously played the harp to soothe King Saul, do we also realise the Lord will employ the harp in the end-times? Chapter Fifteen of both Exodus and Revelation. Coincidence? The number fifteen means 'act of divine grace'.[47]

Pharaoh: Exodus 15

Pharaoh typifies a cruel ruler, enslaving people using tyrannical control and witchcraft, foreshadowing the anti-Christ. After deliverance from Egypt and reaching the other side of the Red Sea, Israel sang the Song of Moses, a celebratory anthem of deliverance. Exodus 15 contains the celebratory song, which was an 'act of divine grace'. Miriam and the women danced with tambourines as all Israel sang, proclaiming freedom from Pharaoh's tyranny.

Anti-Christ: Revelation 15

Revelation 15 repeats the Song of Moses, now with harps celebrating victory over the dragon and the beast (anti-Christ) – another 'act of divine grace'! A stronger enemy is defeated, yet a gentler instrument accompanies the same Song of Moses.

According to Revelation 12:9, the dragon is the 'serpent of old, called the Devil and Satan'. Commentators consider 'the beast' as a metaphor of the anti-Christ (singular person or spirit) or our beastly old nature. Those opposing Messiah as anti-Christ seeks to replace Jesus as the false Messiah.

The dragon and the beast blaspheme God, the tabernacle and the saints (Revelation 13). They are loud, obnoxious, violent, loud, seductive, aggressive and dissonant – demonic manifestations are rarely quiet!

Those who triumph over the anti-Christ sing the song of Moses, accompanied by harps! These worshippers do not go through the Red Sea but stand on the Sea of Glass. Sea is a metaphor of humanity, and glass is transparent. Overcomers are fully devoted to the Lord, at peace amid anti-Christ's rants, with unwavering trust in God. They are transparent worshippers whose lives are full of integrity and sing victory songs with harps.

Tracking the Harp Resurgence

This chapter sprouted from a 2012 Praise Alert newsletter article. Upon reflection, I have realised harp stories weave like golden threads through my life.

- Around 2008, the Lord nudged me about the harp during a Sydney throne room worship event where a friend played hers. Soon after, my sister gave me our mother's old, dilapidated zither – I had played it as a child – but repairs proved impossible.

- In 2010, Andrew Ironside (formerly at Hillsong Sydney) connected with a harp maker wanting to make harps for worship. Andrew started using the harp for worship and helping other worship leaders and musicians – which is how I got my harp.

- A harp school has operated in Jerusalem since 2010, recording worship songs at the Temple's Southern steps since 2023.[48] It is part of Tom Hess's Jerusalem House of Prayer for All Nations (since 1987 on the Mount of Olives). Global worshippers and harpists – learners and experts – increase the sound of harps being used in worship.

- In 2014, I met Michael David within a short distance of the Begin Heritage Centre in East Jerusalem, to discuss harps. Hours later, an assassination attempt targeted Yehuda Glick there for his Temple Mount prayer advocacy. As we returned home amid police helicopters hunting the gunman, the day's links between end-time harps and third temple animosity etched into my memory.

This surge in Spirit-led harp worship over recent years, in Israel and the Church, is no coincidence. The Lord is preparing the way for Messiah through the sound of harps – in itself, a thrilling reason to embrace and encourage the release of harps.

Four Reasons for End-Time Harps

Affiliated with the return of Messiah are four specific reasons for the harp in the end-times:

1. *Comfort and Deliverance*

Music therapy traces its roots to King David's harp – though ironically, it is now often linked to New Age practices.

At the hospital where our first granddaughter was born, the harp is used in palliative care but also to joyfully announce new births – so precious for this new grandma to hear.

Those who summoned a harpist to soothe King Saul must have understood the instrument's healing effect. As a shepherd, David had spent hours worshipping YHWH on his harp, likely sharing those same songs with the troubled king.

While Greeks used the harp to express sorrow, the Jews used it to celebrate joy, blessing, deliverance, praise and worship. That is why in Babylonian captivity, their harps and songs were silent.

> '*Comfort my people! Comfort them!*' *says your Elohim.* '*Speak tenderly to Jerusalem …*' *(Isaiah 40:1–2 NOG)*

Many ministries to Israel have embraced this word in various ways, through aid, reconciliation and music. Many friends play music especially for Holocaust survivors in Israel. There is a sound from the Lord that brings comfort and deliverance.

In our worship gatherings, many testify to emotional healing and the lifting of depression. The resurgence of the harp is prophetic, coinciding with rising PTSD and trauma caused by the pandemic, war, rising anti-Semitism, and global instability. In an increasingly chaotic world, many long for the comforting arms of the Lord. Through the harp, the Holy Spirit is releasing His comfort to individuals and nations.

We are in a time of great global distress – earthquakes, riots, terrorism, injustice, financial and political instability. Jesus warned that in the end-times, people would 'faint at the prospect of what is overtaking the world; for the powers in heaven will be shaken' (Luke 21:26 CJB).

Just as parents sing over frightened children, the Lord sings over us. The resurgence of the harp aligns with the fresh revelation of the Father's love, bringing comfort and healing. The harp's gentle, calming resonance stands in stark contrast to the cacophony of daily life – traffic, machinery, screens and devices.

It's worth asking: does the loudness of popular culture mirror the noise in people's heads, their daily stresses and traumatic memories? Could it reflect the Babylonian system itself? Unhealed trauma, abuse, offences and choosing not to forgive are all restrictive weights.

Yet God offers peace amid the chaos. As nations rage like roaring oceans, He declares, 'Be still and know that I am God'

(Psalm 46:10). Stillness is possible because He remains on His throne, He ends wars and destroys the enemies weapons. The Lord is calling His people into His sanctuary, a refuge from a truth-starved, morally broken world. The harp reflects His quietness, assurance, comfort and rest. It restores the soul and draws our hearts upward to hide in His heart.

2. Worship and Restored Temple

Without delving into debate about the third temple, nevertheless, serious preparation is underway in Jerusalem. Since the 1967 war and the brief reclamation of the Temple Mount, the Temple Institute has been preparing articles for a future temple with musical instruments (including harps and trumpets), furniture and the training of priests and Levites.

> *Since 1987, the House of Harrari has worked in partnership with the Temple Institute… to prepare the harps that will be needed for the future temple.*[49]

This significant preparation is not political – it's a faith statement that the Messiah is coming. If Israel is preparing to release the sound of the harp, it should be no surprise that the Holy Spirit would also simultaneously release the harp across the Church globally.

Historically, God often moves at the same time in Israel naturally and in the Church spiritually. Multiple ministries in Israel are making harps to release a unique sound across the land. But this revival is not limited to Israel alone.

There is an overlap in the harp's return for both the rebuilt temple and the restored tabernacle of David. Since the late 1980s, the Holy Spirit has been restoring the tabernacle of David throughout the earth.[50] Even my personal journey reflects what God is doing in Israel and the global Church: the resurgence of the harp as a sign of the restoration of worship, pointing to the end-times.

3. Worship and Restored Tabernacle of David

King David, the 'sweet psalmist of Israel' (2 Samuel 23:1), worshipped at the altar of the Lord with his harp (Psalm 43:4). He then spoke of a 'harp in my heart' (Psalm 71:22 TPT), connecting his worship to something deeper and more internal.

> *My loving God, the* **harp in my heart will praise you.** *Your faithful heart toward us will be the theme of my song. Melodies and music will rise to you, the Holy One of Israel. (Psalm 71:22 TPT)*

The psalmist suggests we have a harp in our heart! Is there a correlation between the harp and heart? Could our physical and spiritual hearts be tuned like a harp?

Modern neuroscience supports this idea. An ABC documentary once explained that every neuron in the brain corresponds to a specific string on a piano. When I began learning harp, I immediately noticed the similarity to a grand piano, except that the harp's strings are vertically aligned.

A 2018 SBS program highlighted that:

> *The harp could be particularly effective ... the playing of multiple strings produces 'a wide range of vibrations and overtones (harmonics) that can resonate ... with the complex and vast range of cellular vibrations in the human body and mind'. These vibrations enter the body through the central nervous system, bones, muscles and even skin.*[51]

This reveals something powerful: our physical and spiritual hearts *resonate with the harp strings*. The thoughts, memories and emotions in our hearts can be comforted, even massaged, as the Lord Himself sings over us. In return, the 'harp in our heart' aligns with the actual instrument to complete the cycle of praise, as we give praise to our King from our heart. 'The harp in my heart will praise you.'

The harp is the instrument of choice in heaven. The twenty-four elders hold harps and prayer bowls in each hand. While opinions differ on who the elders are, they clearly represent mature leadership, entrusted with governmental worship and intercession.

Some prayer houses use 'harp and bowl' (worship and intercession) more like a ritual than a worship archetype. Personally, I avoid formulas in worship. However, when these two giftings flow in the Holy Spirit together in tandem, they lift one another, powerfully enhancing both. This enables more effective warfare, and the level of authority increases.

Before King David brought the Ark into Jerusalem, it first took 'divine grace' for Israel to defeat the mocking Jebusites.

David established his tabernacle, installed the Ark in the heart of Israel's government, and surrounded it with 24/7 throne room worship. David replicated heaven's worship pattern, and his instrument of choice was the harp.

Acts 15 confirms that this tabernacle is being restored, as Jews and Gentiles could have fellowship together. Number 15 representing acts of divine grace,. It takes divine grace, the blood of Yeshua removing enmity between Jews and Gentiles, to produce 'one new man' (Ephesians 2:11–22).

In this new era, God is releasing a fresh sound on the earth. As David's tabernacle is being restored, harps return to our praise and worship. Harps release the sound of heaven, and His Glory. Many anticipate glory waves, massive revival and reformation. It should not be a surprise for throne room worship with harps and tambourines to herald the wave!

On a podcast, Andrew Ironside shared that while he leads worship with guitar and piano, the harp opens the Spirit realm faster.

I also believe that alongside the harp, God wants to restore the sound of the believer's voice. Revelation 19:6 describes multitudes singing in victorious praises that sound like rushing waters and mighty thunder.

Imagine for a moment: the sound of multitudes singing in the Spirit accompanied by harps. Other sounds may be fine, but this is the sound the Spirit is releasing in His Church for these end days. This releases both heavenly worship and is a powerful weapon against an increasingly hostile enemy.

4. The Lord Judges His Enemies with Tambourines and Harps

Surprisingly, the Lord declares He judges His enemies with both tambourine and the harp.

In Isaiah 30:15, the Lord speaks of 'quietness and confidence' being our strength and then suddenly shifts to judging Assyria, at the sound of the harp!

> *Here comes YAHWEH with his mighty power and glory! ... his words are a devouring fire! His breath is as overwhelming... He sifts the nations ... But you will have a joyous song ... as one celebrating a holy, consecrated feast... celebrating to the sound of a flute and dancing up the mountain of YAHWEH ... power will descend in cloudburst, thunderstorm, and hail. And when his rod strikes the Assyrians, they will be terror-stricken by the mighty voice of Lord YAHWEH. Every stroke of YAHWEH's* **punishing rod will be to the sound of cymbals and strumming harps.** *God himself fights them in battle with dancing! (Isaiah 30:27–32 TPT)*

CHAPTER THIRTY-THREE

Reminiscent of Israel coming out of Egypt, the scene begins with a Passover celebration with songs of joy and deliverance on the Lord's mountain. Then comes divine warfare; God's voice thunders, releasing wind, fire and hail. The Biblical imagery is quite breathtaking. His breath sifts nations while His people ascend His mountain with songs of joy. (They must be fit going up the mountain while dancing, singing and playing flutes and harps!)

To defeat the Egyptians, Moses used his rod, but against the Assyrians, the Lord used His own rod, His royal sceptre. The sound of glorious praises, cymbals, harps and pounding, dancing feet accompanies the Lord's punishing rod falling on and shattering the Assyrians (Isaiah 30:27–33). The Lord's voice thunders and His fists pound, terrorising the Assyrians, while the gentle harp plays!

The Assyrians today include the countries of Iraq, Iran and parts of Syria. Is the Lord now restoring the harp to comfort war-torn lands and simultaneously to war against demonic principalities, powers and spiritual world rulers behind the conflict?

Despite hostile regimes, Iran has the world's fastest growing Church, and these believers love Israel! Their government admits there are too many Christians to jail![52] Many are former Muslims – evidence of spiritual breakthrough.

Could the sound of the harp and the Lord's voice (shofar) be critical weapons of intercession today, even for the Middle East?

Historically, tambourines and harps were used to celebrate great victories, as recorded in the 15th chapters of Exodus and Revelation, reminding us of the importance of these instruments in end-time worship. The surge in those playing the harp in the nations is prophetic of Messiah's victory, and His divine grace to His people. The sound of the harp in Israel and the Church is a reminder to the enemy: Messiah cannot be mocked nor defeated. The Lamb wins every battle – and His return is near.

This is the time for heaven's sound to be heard on earth again.

CHAPTER THIRTY-FOUR

Glory Sounds From Church Confront World Powers

IN THE END-TIMES, THERE is a ramped-up battle over whom mankind will worship: Almighty God or the dragon. This confrontation escalates as the gods from Bible times return, as written by Jonathan Cahn[53], and referred to earlier in Chapter 8, 'Music, Marx and Recycling the Gods'.

Oh, To Be Like the Early Church

People often lament, 'Oh, that we were like the early Church'. The desire is understandable. We long for their miracles and transformational growth, but it is too easy to romanticise the results while forgetting the environment of persecution in which they preached and sang.

Five characteristics of the early church are often overlooked or misunderstood, yet we are hurtling towards a similar environment at a frightening pace. Hence, we must engage and multiply the glory sounds with the help of the Holy Spirit.

A few features of the early church to remember:

- The leadership was predominantly Jewish. Pentecost first touched Jewish disciples of Jesus before grace opened the gospel to Gentiles.
- House churches resembled synagogues (ten men for a minyan)[54] more than Western structures, especially mega churches.
- Persecution was brutal. Christians faced lions for Roman entertainment at the Colosseum!
- Paul ministered in cities steeped in paganism.
- There was a sound of glory linked to miracles. Music, worship and prayer were common features of the early Church.

In this chapter, we focus on the last two points as they relate to the cities of Philippi and Ephesus.

Paul and Silas Sing

Philippi was steeped in syncretism. Some worshipped the Roman Emperor, others Isis and others Yahweh. On the Sabbath, Paul and Silas joined a riverside prayer and worship gathering and soon faced trouble.

They encountered a slave girl with a spirit of Python, a powerful demonic power tied to the gods, divination and false prophecy. Anne Hamilton notes that Python[55] and its allies belong to the 'powers above' of Ephesians 6:12.[56]

This confrontation came at a key moment: Paul was crossing a threshold – bringing the gospel from Israel into the world of Gentile paganism. They were also on their way to a house of prayer and worship. These two dynamics – threshold and intercessory worship – always threaten the enemy. In such major clashes of kingdoms, demons often manifest!

After delivering the girl, Paul and Silas were accused, beaten and jailed. Yet despite their distress, wounds and shackles, they finished their day with a worship watch. Their chains did not silence their voices – they sang! Their praises set off a shockwave in the Spirit, an earthquake in the natural and revival in the prison.

> *At midnight Paul and Silas were praying and singing hymns to God... Suddenly there was a great earthquake, so that the foundations of the prison were shaken; and immediately all the doors were opened and everyone's chains were loosed. (Acts 16:25–26)*

For them to sing in prison, worship had to already be their lifestyle. You do not sing for the first time in those circumstances. The New Testament gives few direct references to singing (apart from in Revelation); however, it is an incorrect assumption that singing in the early church was not a priority – it was a well-established practice.

Whether in prison or at home under trial, singing praise in dark hours is key to a victorious sound. It defies the flesh, breaks demonic intimidation and releases joy, glory and divine intervention. Paul and Silas' praise in the darkness shifted the atmosphere and changed their situation.

Ephesus: Witchcraft and Idol Worship

Many consider the book of Ephesians to be the 'constitution' of the church. It continues to speak through the timeline of history to us today. Ephesus was a godless environment but had the greatest revival. Some forty to fifty entities ruled the city. The book of Ephesians contains the wisdom for contending for and worshipping God in a society filled with idol worship, immorality and witchcraft.

Ephesus was an important seaport, a major trading and political centre of the ancient world. It was also a focal point for pagan worship and witchcraft. Ephesus was home to the temple of Artemis. This temple was so significant it became one of the seven wonders of the ancient world and Acts 19:27 identified the Ephesus temple as the worldwide centre of Diana worship. These were not just local gods, but world powers.

The Greeks knew the goddess as Artemis, the daughter of Zeus and sister of the god Apollo. To the Romans she was Diana, the Phrygians called her Cybele, the Phoenicians knew her as Astarte, and among the Assyrians she was Ishtar. Regardless of her name, she was known as the goddess of fertility or the mother goddess of the earth. Ephesus was morally depraved, as it was under the control of the prostitutes affiliated with the Artemis/Diana temple.

Paul's ministry in Ephesus was explosive. The truth of Jesus confronted and collided with the strong witchcraft and idolatry. Extraordinary miracles took place. Many people forsook the false gods and depravity, burning occult books and paraphernalia worth millions of dollars.

> *Great fear fell over the entire city, and the authority of the name of Jesus was exalted...Large numbers of those who had been practicing magic took all of their books and scrolls of spells and incantations and publicly burned them. When the value of all the books and scrolls was calculated, it all came to several million dollars. (Acts 19:17, 19 TPT)*

The makers of the idols became very upset. Their businesses were in danger. Revival undermined the tourist trade from the big temple.

> *So not only is this trade of ours in danger of falling into disrepute, but also the temple of the great goddess Diana may be despised and her*

*magnificence destroyed, whom **all Asia and the world worship**. (Acts 19:27)*

As we witness exponential resurgences in our own day of New Age and occult festivals and temples to other gods, the book of Ephesians becomes extremely helpful to us right now. What sounds, songs and theology enabled the Ephesian church to have many victories in a society filled with immorality, strong witchcraft and idol worship? They:

- nullified the prince of the power of the air
- exalted Jesus above the gods
- sang to the Lord

Nullifying the Prince of the Airwaves

Paul described the atmosphere over Ephesus, where many believers had once obeyed the dark spiritual ruler of the airwaves. Ephesus was the world centre of goddess worship.

*… you once walked … **according to the prince of the power of the air** … (Ephesians 2:2 NKJV)*

*… you lived in the religion, customs, and values of this world, obeying the **dark ruler of the earthly realm** who fills the atmosphere with his authority, and works diligently in the hearts of those who are disobedient to the truth of God. (Ephesians 2:2 TPT)*

These believers had been under the influence of the 'prince of the power of the air'. No wonder Paul's teaching on the armour of God was addressed to the Ephesian church – warfare was their daily reality!

Jesus, the Son of God, is light. In contrast, darkness is not just an absence of light but a ruling entity that covers the atmosphere of cities like Ephesus like a suffocating blanket. This same darkness governs many modern cities and nations, seducing citizens to rebel against the Lord. Whenever we proclaim Jesus the light, a collision occurs in the spirit realm – the Prince of Peace is confronting the prince of the power of the air.

Anointed sound plays a vital role in this unseen conflict. Just as unseen radio and Wi-Fi frequencies to our various devices shape our modern lives, so spiritual frequencies affect the atmosphere. We take these for granted, despite their power and invisibility to the natural eyes – the unseen realm is real. Having worked in radio, I've become increasingly aware of how sound and spirit intertwine in warfare. Before every broadcast we intentionally pray for truth and the name of Jesus to fill the airwaves. The enemy seeks to dominate the airwaves so as to corrupt and control minds, promote rebellion and mock God. Therefore, we must release the frequencies of glory into the airwaves to shatter demonic influence and reclaim the atmosphere for Christ.

The enemy wants to dominate these. He uses the airways to control the minds of humanity to deny, rebel and mock God, His holiness and His Messiah. Hence, it is into this realm of the airways that we must release the frequencies of glory to shatter demonic sorcery and reclaim the atmosphere for Yeshua.

Paul's reminder was apt for the Ephesians, who would have clearly understood the dynamics of the supernatural unseen realms. Pagan worshippers believed strongly in unseen beings influencing daily life. Only later, during the 18th century's Age of Enlightenment,[57] did Western thought strip away the supernatural worldview of spirits and supernatural beings. Some people still struggle to believe in the supernatural. However, as demonic activity increases and society unravels, even non-believers recognise that an invisible spiritual war is raging.

In 2008, I had a dream about fierce contention over a worship meeting which the enemy wanted closed. After praying into the dream, the Lord said: 'If you do not prioritise to take control of the airwaves, then the enemy will, and he will release anarchy, murder and spiritual blindness.'

As darkness increases, we need to tap into the sound in the Spirit that can overwhelm and shatter the dominion of the prince of the power of the air.

Conflict remains until the Prince of Peace reigns. Penetrating this realm requires the anointing of the Prince of *shalom*. Only His peace can silence the turbulence of the enemy's domain.

Battle of Britain: Spiritual Air Supremacy

During World War II, Britain realised that to defeat Hitler, they needed air supremacy. The Lord also raised up a spiritual air force in intercessors like Rees Howells and his students at the Swansea Bible College. The Lord gave them words to pray, and they put many of them into songs as they worshipped and prayed until they broke through. Prophetic worship and intercession changed history by restraining evil agendas aimed at global domination.

Churchill said the Battle of Britain was about the survival of Christian civilization, yet the enemy initially outnumbered RAF pilots four to one. The Swansea Bible College was in danger because it was near a vital port, but Rees Howells believed God would protect them – and He did. They worshipped and prayed during air raids, singing, 'Holy Spirit in Thy Majesty'.[58]

On 4 September 1940, Rees Howells said, 'The situation because of air raids is very serious. The important thing to find out is where God is in this. We have bound the devil over and over again ...' On 7 September, he wrote:

> *If you can believe you have been delivered from hell, why can't you believe you have been delivered from air raids? Unless we are really trusting Him, where does the praise come in? ... You cannot hear things in the Spirit while you have any turmoil or fear in you. You cannot take a shade of fear into the presence of God.*

On 12 September, 'we prayed last night that London would be defended and that the enemy would fail to break through, and God answered prayer'.[59] The Nazis turned away right when all hope seemed lost. The RAF won the battle.

British Intelligence questioned three German air crews that were captured.

> *Globally we are being reminded that God is again calling for air supremacy – in the Spirit.*

Q: Why did you retreat when there were only two planes attacking you?

A: Two? There were hundreds! Where did you get all the planes you threw into the battle over Britain?

Air Chief Marshall Lord Dowding, chief of Fighter Command during the Battle of Britain said, 'At the end of the battle, I had the sense there had been some sort of divine intervention to alter some sequence of events which would otherwise have occurred.'

Globally we are being reminded that God is again calling for air supremacy – in the Spirit. The 'spiritual air force' comprises worshippers and intercessors who release the unique sounds of heaven: songs, decrees and prophetic sounds from the throne of God which strike the enemy like divine warheads. The anointing that rested on Rees Howells is being released anew. Heaven's air force must arise.

Exalt Jesus, Not Demons

Paul's message to Ephesus was simple and powerful: preach Jesus. The authority of the resurrected and ascended Jesus far surpasses Artemis/Diana and every world ruler.

> *This is the mighty power that was released when God raised Christ from the dead ... **he is exalted as first above every ruler, authority, government, and realm of power in existence!** He is gloriously enthroned over every name that is ever praised, not only in this age, but in the age that is coming! (Ephesians 1:19–22 TPT)*

Whatever god or goddess rules your city or nation, Jesus reigns with a higher authority. The prophetic Psalm of Jesus on the cross declares:

> *But You are holy, Enthroned in the praises of Israel. (Psalm 22:3 NKJV)*

After decades of leading worship in a city filled with idols and immorality, I have found the quickest breakthrough in the spirit realm is to exalt Jesus above every other name and power. In our praises, we enthrone Him.

Though proclaiming Jesus caused a riot, Paul and the Ephesian church did not blaspheme the demons or mock the local gods.

> *For you have brought these men here who are neither robbers of temples **nor blasphemers of your goddess.** (Acts 19:37)*

We must learn from their restraint. It is neither wise nor scriptural to mock or 'shout' at the enemy. We may have the keys to the kingdom, but we do not have the authority to blaspheme the gods whom Jesus defeated. When Israel faced overwhelming armies in 2 Chronicles 20, their singers were instructed to praise the Lord, not to address their foes, nor to slander, mock or ridicule the enemy to their faces. Their victory came through worship, not confrontation. We should do likewise.

Jude warns that even Michael the archangel did not revile the devil when contending over Moses' body (Jude 1:9-10). It is dangerous to lambaste the devil. Our authority is not in attacking demons but in affirming the victory of Jesus. Salvation is in His name.

However, we are not to be ignorant of the enemy, nor be in denial of his existence and devices. Rather, we seek the Lord's wisdom and strategies to outwit a cunning and vicious enemy. As darkness grows, we must rise above the second heaven – where conflict rages – and come before the throne of God and tap into the sound of heaven. Our praises enthrone Jesus on the highest throne; His Glory frequencies scatter darkness. Demons flee from the sound made from consecrated hearts who bow and exalt the Lamb.

Ephesian's New Lifestyle: Sing to the Lord

Paul's pastoral counsel to the Ephesian converts who had renounced Artemis/Diana was threefold:

1. surrender to the extravagant love of God
2. be filled with the Holy Spirit
3. sing to the Lord

> *... be filled continually with the holy Spirit. And your hearts will overflow with a joyful song to the Lord. Keep speaking to each other with words of Scripture,* **singing the Psalms with praises** *and* **spontaneous songs** *given by the Spirit! (Ephesians 5:19 TPT)*

The old life of idolatry and immorality was to be replaced with a new life in Jesus, overflowing with His love, Spirit and song. Paul encouraged them in the Davidic practice of singing the Psalms, and spontaneous songs as previously discussed as singing in the Spirit.

For those emerging from a culture full of idols and witchcraft, this provided essential stability and maturity in God. They need to declare scripture, sing to the Lord, sing His songs and to give thanks.

For those raised in church, giving thanks and singing to the Lord might seem basic, but daily gratitude and praise outside a weekly church service are not always easy but necessary disciplines. We discovered this during our first ever Grumble Fast which was tough but transformative, providing lasting breakthroughs.[60]

If it is transformational for mature believers to engage in thanksgiving and singing praise, imagine what it does for those who have been in a society full of idols? If consistent gratitude can shift mature believers, imagine the power it releases for those emerging from an environment full of idols and spiritual darkness.

Music in the Early Church

The New Testament frequently quotes the Psalms because music and singing were already central in Jewish worship[61] and culture. There was no need to reiterate the revelation of worship to the Jewish audience of the early church. Paul was a rabbi trained by Gamaliel (Acts 22:3) who would have sung Psalms daily. The book of Psalms commands singing over four hundred times. Today, singing is being revived. In 2022, six hundred Levites prepared by the Temple Institute sang on the Temple Mounts steps.[62]

Rabbi Paul would have sung the Psalms long before encountering Jesus the Messiah. The few times Paul mentions singing in his writings, he reaffirms what the Jewish believers already practised, which was in sharp contrast to the practices of the Gentile's pagan customs.

Whether in prison or being tested in our homes, singing praise in dark hours of trial is powerful. It defies the reaction of our flesh, breaking demonic intimidation and discouragement. It honours the Lord's name, releasing His joy, glory and intervention. Paul and Silas' singing in the darkness of the prison confines shifted the atmosphere and changed their situation.

Supernatural Understanding in the Early Church

Jesus took His disciples to Caesarea Philippi to teach them about the keys of the kingdom prevailing over the gates of hell. That site is now in ruins, but when Jesus took His disciples there, temples to Zeus and Pan were active, including child sacrifices to Moloch at the head of the River Jordan. This was an intentional backdrop for His lesson on spiritual authority, a powerful and pertinent sermon.

Paul's missionary journeys continued this theme. He preached in cities dominated by similar pagan temples which were world centres of idolatry. In such cities, he exhorted believers to sing the song of the Lord amid demonic strongholds. The sound of glory shifted the atmosphere; his circumstances changed, and demonic kings were terrified!

Persecution came to the church because the world was filled with ancient gods, the same spirits now at work in our culture to silence and eradicate Jews, Christians and biblical truth.

Have we prepared our hearts and character to release the glory sounds needed in this clash of kingdoms? We can be like the early church, but it requires a renewed mindset and practice. The Western church must awaken from ease, recognise the real conflict and respond, like Paul, with songs of praise amid a hostile atmosphere. There is an urgency for us to upgrade.

The Glory Terrifies Demonic Kings

The glory of the Lord strikes terror into the heart of demonic kings.

> *When You arise to intervene, all the nations and kings will be stunned and will fear your awesome name, trembling before Your glory! (Psalm 102:15 TPT)*

> *According to their deeds, accordingly He will repay, Fury to His adversaries, Recompense to His enemies ... So shall they fear The name of the LORD from the west, And His Glory from the rising of the sun ... (Isaiah 59:18–19 NKJV)*

The sound connected to the glory strikes terror into the heart of those who oppose the Lord and His people. We must look beyond the seen realm for end-time confrontation with the gods, their adherents and their music. As we pursue restoring true worship, these principles of His Glory are vital to grasp and implement.

CHAPTER THIRTY-FIVE

Ark Defeats Dagon: But Yahweh's Glory is *No* Lucky Charm!

IN THE AFTERMATH OF 7 October, Israeli PM Benjamin Netanyahu declared:

> We are in a battle of civilisation against barbarism. I've been through wars. I've seen horrible things. I've never seen things this horrible. This is a battle of our common civilization.[63]
>
> It is a time for everyone to decide where they stand. Israel's fight is your fight. Should Hamas and Iran's axis of evil win, you will be their next target.[64]

Ark Vs. Dagon: Showdown in Worship War

Is it possible Israel's war with Hamas is connected to the ancient confrontation between the Ark and Dagon? Is this conflict an earthly manifestation of the spiritual war to be fought in the end-times between God and Satan? Of all the pagan gods worshipped in the ancient world, why was Dagon the *only* one that came face to face with the Glory of God, as represented by the Ark? Why did the Ark never contend with Baal? Does the Dagon episode point to the end-time war over worship?

When Yahweh confronts Satan and false gods, get out the camera – there will be fireworks. Lightning. Thunder. Storms. Idols crashing. The sea being split. The sun standing still.

The Ark being stolen and placed in the temple of Dagon is one of those. It was the *only* recorded incident when the Ark had a direct confrontation with a false god. Why did God allow His Glory to be face to face with Dagon, the chief god of the Philistines? It must be even more significant than we realise. It was strategic, tactical and brilliant.

Is this ancient showdown important for us today?

On two separate occasions while working on this chapter, I have had several intercessors phone or message me (unsolicited and without prior knowledge) with dreams and visions about Dagon! In two separate dreams in late 2025, Dagon was rising up out of the sea, as a great monster threatening the earth, demanding to be obeyed or be killed. In both cases, these believers had difficulty discerning if the ferocious creature was good or evil. I spoke to them of the importance of knowing the word well – vital for discernment.

In another vision, the person was given keys for prayer and worship – which are shared at the end of this chapter.

I am convinced the Lord is wanting us to pay attention to this often overlooked or underrated principality. There is much to learn from this incident for end-time cosmic battles; hostage taking, captivity, culture wars, struggles for land and inheritance, and victory![65] Join me as we uncover the mystery of Dagon when it meets the awesome Glory of God.

Dagon's Real Identity: Sea Dragon

Often called a fish god, Dagon was far more than a god in charge of the local fish' n' chip shop. He was the supreme deity of the Philistines⁶⁶ and is the father of Baal.⁶⁷ Let that sink in – *father* of Baal!

Baal worship in scripture was the nemesis of Israel. But Dagon is the *father*, the one who gave 'life' to Baal. In Greek mythology, Dagon would correspond to Zeus. Biblically, he parallels the dragon in the sea. Some link him to Neptune or Poseidon, gods of the sea and storms. But Dagon is the *father*, making these two his offspring.⁶⁸ Ancient images depict him as a merman – half man, half fish. It is more apt to think of Dagon as a monster of the sea.

According to Dr Tom Knotts,⁶⁹ one arm bore a serpent like a python, the other arm a sundial, while his hand held fruit – symbols of fertility, provision, and mastery over time and harvest. He claimed lordship over the food chain and human fertility.

Is this the same spirit behind globalists demanding allegiance to the climate change ideology, threatening food chains, economies and human fertility? Is this the thief of the physical and spiritual harvests? Dagon's temple was in Gaza. Though the physical structure is destroyed, is this principality still causing trouble in Gaza?

Clash of Cloud Riders: Yahweh Supreme King

> *Let them sing their celebration-songs for the* **coming of the cloud rider whose name is Yah!** *(Psalm 68:4 TPT)*

Yah is the shortened name of Yahweh, the always existent one, His sacred name. Hallelujah means to 'praise Yah'. He rides the clouds.

CHAPTER THIRTY-FIVE

> *You ... ride as King in a chariot you made from clouds. You fly upon the wings of the wind. (Psalm 104:3 TPT)*

At His trial, the priests asked Jesus if He was the Messiah. He replied:

> *I am. And you will see the Son of Man sitting at the right hand of the Power, and **coming with the clouds of heaven**. (Mark 14:62)*

The high priest was so outraged he tore his garment. Not only did Jesus say yes, I am Messiah – He inferred He was Yah – coming on the clouds. Jesus ascended in a cloud and will return in a cloud.

> *For the LORD is the **great King above all gods**. Oh come, let us worship ... kneel before the LORD our Maker. (Psalm 95:3, 6)*

Not only is Yahweh King above all gods, but a time is coming when Yah, the cloud rider, will deal with Dagon worshippers as well as the principality they bow to.

> *At that time, I will **punish all who worship Dagon**[70] and fill the palace of their rulers with violence and deception. (Zephaniah 1:9 TPT)*

Like Dagon, every false god ultimately collapses in the Lord's holy Presence. Hostility to the Glory of God is futile. However, the resistance is vicious, exemplifying the battle for true worship. The demonic realm fights His Glory. Hence the glory angels (as per Jenny Hagger's vision in the Prophetic Snapshot) need to be escorted by warrior angels.

The false cloud rider crashed to earth. Sometimes the devil's only weapon is to intimidate and seduce our flesh because it resists the Spirit. At the Fall, Satan was cursed to eat dirt. Our flesh is his food. If we succumb, we help him out. We cannot resist this principality in our flesh. But when we align with the Presence and Glory of God, we will overcome. The scriptures above are powerful to war with.

Return of the Gods: Dagon, Merman, Mermaid and Mitre Hat

Though Samson and the Maccabees destroyed Dagon's temples at Gaza and Ashdod, is this principality resurfacing in the spirit realm today? Jonathan Cahn in *Return of the Gods* suggests so. Events in Gaza since World War II and especially since 7 October suggest yes.

Dagon and his consort, as merman and mermaid, also intrude into our popular culture to influence our children: Disney mermaids, video games, films like Conan the Destroyer, where Dagoth the evil god is named Dagon.[71] His influence seeps into art and entertainment, shaping our culture towards false worship. Some believe Dagon symbolism is in religious rituals through Catholicism.[72] Hislop suggests the Pope's hat, called the mitre, represents Dagon, the fish god.[73]

Dagon, Dragon: Mystery Babylon and End-Time Victories

Rev. Alexander Hislop in *The Two Babylons* suggests Nimrod introduced the worship of Dagon, who 'civilised the Babylonians, teaching them the arts, science, politics, and religion'.[74] Dagon a teacher of Babylon! The plot thickens.

The father of lies morphs and shape-shifts across cultures and eras to deceive and steal, trying to take credit for creation and civilisation. Mesopotamia and Sumer (which predates but is in the same area as Babylon) have their creation stories – and it's not Yahweh!

Netanyahu's warning of a 'battle of civilisation' may be deeper than many realise.

The only difference between Dagon and dragon is the letter 'r', and both of them share imagery of reptilian tails and consorts of the sea. Dagon's link with Babylon is twofold: as the one who enlightened Babylon, and as the king of Babylon, married to the queen of Babylon – Mystery Babylon, the queen of heaven!

As the male merman, Dagon's consort was a mermaid, corresponding to Aphrodite or Ashtoreth, the 'queen of heaven', goddess of war and lust.[75] The dragon's consort is Mystery Babylon, described in Revelation as the harlot enthroned on many waters.

> *The **waters** that you saw, upon which the **great prostitute is seated**, represent peoples, multitudes, nations, and languages. (Revelation 17:15 TPT)*

This queen sits on and rules people and nations through sorcery.[76] Water spirits are very dangerous. Mystery Babylon is enthroned and draws power from worship – it is her spiritual oxygen! Yet Jeremiah declared her waters would dry up:

> *A drought is against her waters, and **they will be dried up**. For it is the land of carved images, And they are insane with their idols. (Jeremiah 50:38)*

Fish die out of water, because they get their oxygen from the water. This end-time judgement is a powerful prayer. The numbers of those who will worship the Babylonian gods will eventually dry up! Babylon's worship will cease. One day, every knee will bow before the Name above all names:

> *... the **name** of **Jesus** causes **every knee to bow** in reverence ... in the heavenly realm, in the*

earthly realm, **and** *in the* **demonic realm**. *(Philippians 2:10 TPT)*

Find strength, knowing the language of Revelation 12 is victorious. The dragon has already been defeated and cast out of heaven. On earth, he is overcome by the blood of the Lamb,[77] our testimony and total commitment to Yeshua.

Dagon Bowed Once, Twice! Rat Plague and Haemorrhoids!

Dagon fell prostrate before the Ark at the threshold.[78] Thresholds are markers of covenants – but the Philistines had none with Yahweh, and Israel had broken theirs.[79]

Yahweh declared Himself the supreme Elohim. What humiliation for the 'father of Baal' who thought *he* was the cloud rider! Dagon is no match for the Holy God of Israel. Dagon fell prostrate, was propped up, fell again and then shattered. Dagon fell once, twice, and then was humiliated before Yahweh.

> *The* **head of** *Dagon and* **both the palms** *of its hands were broken off on the threshold; only Dagon's torso was left … (1 Samuel 5:4)*

Decapitated, Dagon lost his ability to rule and lead and was stripped of honour, power and authority. The Ark stood; Dagon lost its headship.

> *An avalanche of evil will come upon you that* **no magic spell will be able to avert**. *Great disaster is about to fall upon you that* **you will not be able to ward off**! *(Isaiah 47:11 TPT)*

Dagon encountered the strong right arm of Yahweh and lost his right hand of sorcery, divination and witchcraft.

Enchantments cannot succeed against the glory. These are powerful scriptures to pray, decree and sing.

Dagon's left hand, symbolising dominion over time and the food chain, was also cut off. Then plague struck. Rats ruined the crops while the Philistines suffered tumours and haemorrhoids in their genitalia. The Lord rendered Dagon impotent to protect their crops and their health – and Dagon was powerless as a fertility god.[80] Yahweh alone is the giver and sustainer of life.

> *I am the Alpha and the Omega, the Beginning and the End ... (Revelation 1:8)*

> *While the earth remains ... seedtime and harvest ... shall not cease. (Genesis 8:22)*

Proclaim this word of the Lord: Yahweh alone rules.

Dagon Must Bow Before Yahweh

Yahweh's strong right arm cut off Dagon's authority, power, witchcraft and sorcery.

Is this the same spirit now working to block spiritual harvests, destroy food supplies, lower fertility rates, interrupt trade and supply and hinder Israel's inheritance of Gaza? Is this the same spirit working through the footprint of the dragon in Pacific nations? Declare the word of the Lord:

> *O YAHWEH, Lord God of Angel Armies! ... **You rule over oceans** ... You crushed the strongholds of Egypt, and all your enemies were scattered at the mighty display of your glory-power. (Psalm 89:8-11 TPT)*

> *Strong is Your hand, and high is Your right hand. (Psalm 89:13 NKJV)*

Once, twice, Dagon must bow! But so must we – before the Lamb, who gave everything for us.

Why the Ark Was Captured

How could the Philistines defeat Israel and capture the Ark? For the same reason the Church has struggled against ancient gods re-entering our culture through media, entertainment and corporations.

Israel had been given clear instructions both before the Ark was stolen and after it was returned. The first time they disobeyed and lost; the second time, Israel obeyed God and won a glorious victory. God's grace restored Israel then – and it is the same grace to restore us too.

Joshua warned Israel of covenant infidelity.

> *If after YAHWEH has been gracious to you, you turn and forsake him to **worship other gods**, then he will **turn** and deal harshly with you and **totally consume you!** (Joshua 24:20–22 TPT)*

Broken Covenant in a Time of War

Prior to the Ark being captured, Israel's spiritual leadership were setting a disastrous example. The covenant was openly violated. Eli's sons, Hophni and Phinehas, were priests but corrupt, 'sons of Belial' who did not even know the Lord![81] They profaned the holy things, exacted sexual favours within the tabernacle, served other gods and broke covenant.

When the Philistines attacked, Israel panicked and said:

> *Let us bring the Ark of the Covenant … that when it comes among us it may save us from … our enemies. (1 Samuel 4:3)*

Though they had neglected God's Presence, with war on their doorstep, it was like the Ark was a weapon of last resort. Did Israel take God's Presence for granted? When all else fails, try God? Despite all that was wrong, the Philistines trembled when they heard the Ark had entered the camp.

Sound of the Ark Shook the Ground

Despite having defiled the covenant, as Israel carried the Ark into battle, the sound released struck terror into the Philistines. Israel and the Philistines both encountered the fear of God that day.

> ... all Israel shouted so loudly that **the earth shook** ... the **Philistines heard the noise** ... So the Philistines were afraid, for they said, **'God has come into the camp!'** (1 Samuel 4:6–7)

The glory has a distinct sound! When God Himself shows up, it sets off shock waves, causing the ground of nations to shake.

> The earth shook ... Sinai itself was moved **at the presence of God**, the God of Israel. (Psalm 68:8)

Sinai shook, Isaiah saw doorposts tremble when angels sang 'Holy' and now the Philistines quaked. Though Israel had become corrupt, even their *sound* changed as they carried the Ark, like King Saul, who twice prophesied[82] near the anointing of the prophets, but soon returned to violence. Israel's transformation was temporary – a sober warning for us too.

We too can change momentarily in a meeting, but like Saul, can soon go back to murderously chucking spears at each other with our words – even as we leave His Presence! A worship team may sound 'anointed' and can sing nice songs, but how many can safely accompany the Ark? Carriers of the glory must heed the lessons of 1 Samuel 4–5.

The Ark is *Not* a Lucky Charm

When the covenant was violated, the Ark did not save Israel – it brought judgement. Eli and his sons died, Ichabod was born ('the glory is gone'), the Ark was captured, Israel was defeated and the inheritance was gone.

The middle of a war is not the time to pretend God is your friend and protector. To invoke His Glory while harbouring idols is dangerous (like the sons of Sceva in Acts 19). The Lord is holy; His Glory is not a lottery ticket but the weight of His Presence. If there are idols in our hearts and we try to invoke His Glory, our songs may entertain people, but it can be dangerous. Demonic entities have hovered over worship teams.[83]

> *The Lord is holy; His Glory is not a lottery ticket but the weight of His Presence.*

The glory is about Him, not us! When we desperately want His Glory in our midst, it is not just singing songs about the glory. The glory sound is formed *inside* of us as Jesus lives in us and transforms us.

In a time of war, victory depends on obedience to His voice. Saul aligned with rebellion and witchcraft, was killed in battle and his head nailed to the temple of Dagon.[84] Remember, Saul's head was not nailed to the temple of Baal, but Dagon. Ultimately flesh bows to a principality and ends in defeat. Pampered flesh resists the glory and can cause us to end up nailed to a false god! Only crucified flesh can carry the glory.

> *Don't expect to see Shekinah glory until the Lord sees your sincere humility. (Proverbs 15:33 TPT)*

> *... turn back to Yahweh before the appointed time arrives. Repent before ... the day of YAHWEH's burning fury. (Zephaniah 2:1–2 TPT)*

The Lord's glory wave is coming. As His Glory confronts principalities, we must choose – with Him or against Him. Zephaniah 1:9 speaks of the Lord dealing with Dagon worshippers! Then in chapter two, he warns the people to repent before YAHWEH judges the gods. Judgement begins at the house of God. It is important to be correctly positioned to ride the glory wave rather than be judged by it!

> *I, YAHWEH, will be terrifying to them, for I will make **all the gods** of the earth **vanish**. And the people of every nation **will bow down and worship me** wherever they live. (Zephaniah 2:11 TPT*

Yet again, it is about the gods being judged and nations worshipping the Lord. Our praises must enthrone Him.

Return of the Ark and Stolen Land

After seven months of suffering, the Philistines returned the Ark on a cart. They were not repentant or willing to worship Yahweh, only desperate to get rid of Him! They sent a bonus guilt offering: five gold rats and tumours, a grotesque acknowledgment of their affliction.

When life goes pear-shaped, people either run from God to false comforts or run to Him in repentance and worship, asking for His comfort and help. Israel's response was mixed. At Beth Shemesh, joy erupted when the Ark arrived, but curiosity led many to unwisely take a peek inside. Judgement fell, and they cried, 'Who is able to stand before this holy LORD God (1 Samuel 6:20)?'

For twenty years, the Ark rested at Kirjath Jearim until David brought it to Jerusalem. Yet even in Israel's failures, a yearning for God's Presence was rekindled. The key to victory was a hunger for His Presence, readiness to obey and a healthy dose of the fear of the Lord.

Samuel repeated the same call Joshua once gave: repent, remove idols and return to the Lord. This time the people obeyed, putting away Baal, Ashtoreth and every foreign god. They fasted and confessed.

Right on cue, in the middle of consecration and worship, the Philistines attacked again! This time, Israel's heart was right with Yahweh, and as Samuel interceded,

> ... **the LORD thundered** with a loud thunder upon the Philistines ... so confused ... they were **overcome before Israel**. *(1 Samuel 7:10)*

The enemy was routed, hostilities ceased and Israel recovered every piece of land they had lost. They recovered all!

The lesson for us is clear: obedience, prayer and pure worship release God's power. But mixture of other gods intermingled into our worship is a serious hindrance to the Church and even brings defeat! It is not Him plus something else.

Gaza: Giants, Judah, ANZACs and Hamas

After long flights from Australia to Israel, a day at Tel Aviv beach to recover from jet lag is welcome. This Mediterranean coastline, including Gaza, has magnificent beachfronts. But historically and biblically, Gaza has been a graveyard, a stronghold of giants that few have subdued. Does Dagon still lurk over Gaza?

This same battleground stretches into history. Gaza's Hebrew root, *azzah,* means strong, fierce, harsh, greedy, to prevail. It was the last refuge of the Anakim giants (Joshua 11:22, Deuteronomy 2:10–11), the stronghold of Philistine lords (Judges 3:2–3), and the site of Samson's final act, to destroy the temple of Dagon in Gaza.

Gaza was allocated to the tribe of Judah as their inheritance, yet they always struggled to possess it. Yes, David defeated Goliath and they had possession during Solomon's reign, but Gaza has remained a spiritual and physical flashpoint. Israel's withdrawal from Gaza in 2005 and subsequent wars with Hamas are rooted in this severe spiritual war. The ancient battle between the Ark and Dagon is the key, even for Gaza battles today!

The international peacekeepers for the Gaza peace deal are set to be established in Goliath's hometown of Kiryat Gat! Is another David vs. Goliath and Ark vs. Dagon showdown being set-up?

ANZACs at Gaza

Gaza was a defensive stronghold of the Ottoman Turks and became a graveyard of troops during World War I. The British and Allies fought bitterly for Gaza. It was strategic because of the water wells needed for the horses. ANZAC forces (Australian and New Zealand) suffered catastrophic defeats in March and April 1917 and many soldiers thought it was another Gallipoli disaster. A changed leadership and tactic brought the breakthrough at Beersheba with the famous Lighthorse charge on 31 October 1917. The story became personal after visiting there, making friends in the area and discovering my dad's brother had served in the 4th Australian Lighthorse, though repatriated in 1916 after sustaining injuries in the Sinai. Finally, in November 1917, Gaza fell to the Allies, opening the way to Jerusalem.[85]

The pattern repeats: Gaza as a hostile stronghold, Gaza as the gate to inheritance.

Gaza and Hamas

The same spiritual forces seem visible today. Are these ancient gods the real thorn in Israel's side today? In Hebrew, *chamas* means violence, injustice, oppression – the very name of Hamas! Scripture first uses it before the flood: *'The earth was filled with violence (chamas)'* (Genesis 6:11).

The horrific atrocities of 7 October – massacres, kidnappings, destruction – fit this pattern of ancient violence. Israel's withdrawal in 2005 left behind three thousand greenhouses that could have made Gaza self-sufficient in food.[86] Hamas destroyed them, then poured resources into tunnels – and rats live in tunnels! The nickname of Sinwar, the former Hamas leader in Gaza, was 'the rat'. Is Dagon once again exposed? The god of food and fertility replaced by rats, tunnels and bloodshed?

As in Samuel's day, the confrontation is not only military but spiritual.

Worship and the Inheritance of Judah

As we witness the rising tide of evil, I believe we are in a time of the return of the Nephilim giants. We are also in a time of the Davidic worshipping warriors arising. David's worship carried the sound of confident authority.

Judah's inheritance is Gaza, and Judah leads with praise. David faced Goliath with confidence because the Lord had trained and delivered him from bears and lions. His heart was also trained in worship, so in the moment of confrontation, David was confident the Lord of angel armies was fighting for him. Likewise, today's battle is not only for land but for worship. What bears and lions has the Lord trained you on? The Lion of Judah has triumphed all the works of the devil at the cross[87] and our sound must echo His victory as we embrace His cross.

The ancient god of Gaza needs to hear Davidic worshippers releasing frequencies of the glory. The fierce physical battles over Gaza are a picture of the fierce battle over worship and for the inheritance of the Lord. Davidic worshippers, arise!

In several of our worship watches, the Lord has given visions of Him carrying our praises (along with the prayers of millions of others) into Gaza, even into the tunnels! These glimpses remind us that glory sounds and the prayers of many can pierce darkness even where soldiers cannot. Many freed hostages speak of the presence of the Lord with them in the tunnels – even His light!

The Lord Himself promises, *'I will send a fire on Gaza, and the kings of Gaza shall be cut off'* (Amos 1:6-7, Zechariah 9:5-6). The ancient god of Gaza needs to hear Davidic worshippers releasing the fire of God and the frequencies of His Glory!

Obadiah declares the end game:

> *On Mount Zion there shall be deliverance, And there shall be holiness; The house of Jacob* **shall possess their possessions***. (Obadiah 1:17)*[88]

Our worship, prayers and decrees can be that nuclear warhead in the Spirit as we align heaven and earth until His kingdom triumphs.

Word From the Lord

A series of visions and words from the Lord received by an intercessor in 2022 about the Ark in the temple of Dagon provide insight of how to pray in this battle (excerpts reprinted here with permission).[89]

> *Governments cannot stop a holy revival. Fires within My people will go out from their bellies, their hearts, along the veins of the earth.*

She saw Dagon falling and heard the words: 'Every knee will bow!' Then the Spirit of God said, 'Robbing My people. Grain and Harvest'.

In the vision, she saw Dagon falling again, accompanied by the words, 'Every knee will bow!' Dagon fell again, broken, while people sang, 'Surely the presence of the Lord is in this place …' The Holy Spirit continued:

> *If they think they can capture Me and rob My people, let them remember Dagon! My people strayed, but they are returning – weeping and turning back to Me in consecration at the altar of mercy. They are seeking My presence and bringing Me into their midst; I dwell in their worship, in their consecration, and their sacrifices of service and praise.*

The Lord's final instructions:

> *Let My people worship Me; I will have My harvest. No one robs the Lord!* **Demolish the stronghold of Dagon with Me.** *The weapons I have given you are mighty spiritual weapons, petitions and declarations. Use them to bring down strongholds and refute proud, arrogant reasoning, and empty philosophies. Declare that doctrines of demons will fall down, their heads broken, and the hands that do Dagon's bidding will be cut off.*

CHAPTER THIRTY-FIVE

The Glory and His Sword

As in the temple of Dagon, only the Lamb of God, the King of kings, can confront and finish this principality. He does so with His sword and His Glory, which terrifies demonic kings.

> *In that day, the Lord YAHWEH will **mercilessly** wield his **massive, mighty sword** and punish Leviathan, the swift, slithering serpent. **He will slay the dragon of the sea – Leviathan**, the twisting serpent. In that day, **they** will **sing** the song 'The Vineyard of Delight'. (Isaiah 27:1–2 TPT)*

After the Lord's sword – His word – cuts off the head of the sea dragon, a song rises over His inheritance! Warfare is joined to worship for harvest and legacy. The enemy comes to rob, kill and destroy, but the Lord preserves His inheritance with a sound and a song.

We are called to join Him, lifting weapons of worship, prayers and declarations to demolish strongholds. Our worship should not be scattergun but precise. We war for destiny with His praises and word. Songs tuned to His Glory and aligned with His throne are like guided missiles against dark powers. For though the war is against the Lamb, the Lamb always wins. So, too, the faithful ones who stand with Him.

CHAPTER THIRTY-SIX

Silencing Babylon: Praise Eruption

THE CULMINATION OF THE cosmic war is accompanied by sound – or lack of! Babylon's music is silenced. Heaven erupts into a Hallelujah chorus and bridal joy. The galloping hooves of the great white horse carry Jesus wielding His sceptre as it swooshes through the nations, arresting and throwing the dragon and beast into sizzling flames.

Relief From Babylon

The prophecy of Revelation 18:21–22 offers great relief: the *sounds of Babylon* will be *silenced* forever:

> *Then a mighty angel took up a stone like a great millstone and threw it into the sea, saying, 'Thus with violence the great city Babylon shall be thrown down, and shall not be found anymore. The sound of harpists, musicians, flutists, and trumpeters shall* **not** *be heard in you anymore ...'* (Revelation 18:21–22)

The seductive music of Babylon will cease. Every sound that once enticed and enslaved nations will be silenced.

As a musician, I am deeply sensitive to how sound influences atmospheres. Dissonance, imbalance and hypnotic repetition unsettle the soul. The disordered sound of Babylon brings confusion and unrest to humanity. But when the Lord's judgement falls, those chaotic frequencies will stop, replaced by the harmony and joyful melodies of heaven.

Final Battle Over Worship

At the heart of the end-time conflict is worship. The ultimate confrontation between God and Satan will not be over politics or power – but over *who people worship*.

> *At the heart of the end-time conflict is worship.*

Those not redeemed by the blood of the Lamb will succumb to the dragon's sadistic deception. They will bow and worship. A day is coming when the lawless one will sit on God's throne in the rebuilt temple. He will exult himself and ensure that,

> *Everyone on earth **will worship** the wild beast – those whose names have not been written ... in the Book of the Life of the Lamb who was slain. (Revelation 13:8 TPT)*

> *So they **worshiped the dragon** who gave authority to the beast; and **they worshiped the beast** ... (Revelation 13:4 NKJV)*

Only two choices remain – worship the dragon or the Lamb.

True believers, regardless of what they have to face, are called to endure and remain faithful:

> *This is a call for the **endurance and faithfulness** of the holy believers. (Revelation 13:10 TPT)*

Faithful overcomers follow the Lamb wherever He goes – and they sing songs no one else can learn.

> *I heard a tremendous sound coming out of heaven, like the roar of a waterfall … The sound of music that I heard was like the sound of many harpists playing their harps … (Revelation 14:2 TPT)*

> *They sang as it were a new song before the throne … and no one could learn that song … **except** the … **redeemed from the earth**. (Revelation 14:3 NKJV)*

Don't be too distracted by the hundred and forty-four thousand and who they might be. The important focus should be this: they did *not* defile themselves with a woman. That would suggest immorality, either physically or spiritually, with the harlot of Mystery Babylon, or both. The only ones who could sing this particular song are those not defiled by immorality or seduced by the Babylonian spirit. Their sound was pure.

Anti-Christ Demands Worship – Destroyed by the Breath of God

Good news – Jesus thwarts the plans of the lawless one in *one* breath!

> *… for the Day (of Jesus returning) will not come unless the rebellion comes first and the man of lawlessness … exalts himself above every so-called god or object of worship … he sits in the Temple of God, proclaiming himself that he is God … The Lord Yeshua will slay him with the breath of His mouth … (2 Thessalonians 2:1, 3–4)*

Jesus will slay the lawless one with the *breath from His mouth*. The people who will not bow and worship the beast are the only true lovers of God who, with their own breath, will worship the Lamb who was slain. Everyone else will bow and worship the beast, the dragon.

Regardless of the different theological persuasions of when and how this occurs, the point is a time is coming when the demarcation line is over worship. The choice is you either bow to the Lamb of God, or you will bow and worship the dragon and the beast.

Last Mercy Call to the Earth

Despite rebellion and wickedness, there appears to be a last mercy call *to* the *whole earth* to worship the Lord. After the hundred and forty-four thousand harpists worship the Lord, an angel shouts a message calling all the earth to worship God. Though the timeframe is uncertain, this call seems to happen after everyone has bowed to the dragon, so it appears to be the last and final plea to worship the Lord.

> *... another angel ... carrying a message of eternal good news to **announce to the earth** – to every tribe, language, people, and nation ... '**You must reverence God and glorify him**, for the **time** has come for **him to judge**. Worship at the feet of the Creator of heaven, earth, and sea ...' (Revelation 14:6–7 TPT)*

Such mercy of God to extend a last call to repent! If the breath of God destroys the lawless one, the call reminds us of our choice. How will we use our breath – giving praise to Jesus or the beast?

Judgement on Ancient and Mystery Babylon

Once the last call to earth to worship God is complete, then comes the judgement on Babylon. There is a striking resemblance between Isaiah 13-14, 47, Jeremiah 50-51 and Revelation 17-19. God judged ancient Babylon because they destroyed the Lord's temple, His house of prayer in Jerusalem.

> ... *YAHWEH's plan is to destroy Babylon. This is YAHWEH's **revenge for destroying his temple**. (Jeremiah 51:11 TPT)*

The enemies target to destroy the Lord's house (and houses) of prayer is something Yahweh deals with. This is important while praying for Jerusalem, rebuilding the temple and houses of prayer.[90]

The title above the text of Jeremiah 51 in my Bible is 'Yahweh's War against Babylon', compared with Revelation 18's title, 'The Fall of Babylon'. Where the Lord judged ancient Babylon, similarly in the end-times, He *will* judge Mystery Babylon – it will fall! Proclaim, pray, and sing these powerful passages prophesying judgement on Babylon.[91]

Sounds of Nebuchadnezzar and the Beast Imposing Worship

Nebuchadnezzar, king of Babylon, foreshadowed the end-time worship demands of Mystery Babylon. He built a golden statue of himself and commanded all nations to bow in worship, a prophetic picture of what is to come.

> ... *cause as many as would not worship the image of the beast to be killed. (Revelation 13:15 NKJV)*

When Nebuchadnezzar's orchestra played – the shofar, flute, lyre, harp and drums – *every nation and language bowed* in worship.

CHAPTER THIRTY-SIX

> *As soon as they heard **the musical instruments** ... those present **from all nations** and languages **bowed down and worshiped** the golden image ...* (Daniel 3:7 TPT)

It is likely the beast will utilise technology, setting up a hologram of the beast (looking handsome) and with techno music enticing and commanding all to bow.

Babylon's roots trace back to the tower of Babel, where men built a tower to make a name for themselves. From its inception, Babylon's spirit has exalted self and manipulates through sorcery, seduction and witchcraft to control. Its modern sounds through media, entertainment, music and culture still seek to captivate hearts and minds through a mix of pleasure, power and a cacophony of sorcery. Dean Briggs summarises the Revelation description of Babylon being a dwelling place for every kind of demon: 'a petri dish of moral and spiritual bacteria'.[92]

Sorcery is a form of witchcraft that operates through specific objects like music and drugs. Music industries, from rock music through to the electronic music of Tomorrowland and Supernova, combine drugs, music and witchcraft paraphernalia to destroy lives.[93]

Babylon does not just bark orders to bow and worship; it subtly crafts seductive *atmospheres*. Nebuchadnezzar used music to create emotional compliance. The spirit of Babylon still whispers today, but rewards worship by offering fame, pleasure and power. Refusal brings death.

Living in the Western world does not protect us from Satan's manipulations, seductions or revenge. Mystery Babylon has one objective – to get all of mankind to turn away from God and worship the dragon.[94]

We must guard our hearts against its lure; even believers can become enticed. When Israel defeated Jericho, Achan coveted a Babylonian garment and silver and gold. These are symbols of covering, greed and false worship. His disobedience brought disaster when Israel went against Ai. So, too, the church must ensure that Babylon's garments do not clothe or cover us nor its glittering wealth corrupt our worship. Any spirit of control or compromise in the church opens the door to Babylon's influence, even takeover. Nor can we war against Babylon or Ai (AI) if we are wearing Babylon's garments or harbouring its beliefs and attitudes.

Both Jeremiah and Revelation sound the same blunt warning – escape from any Babylonian activity before God judges it. This includes pornography, immorality, prostitution, idols, witchcraft and corrupt trading.

> *Leave Babylon behind, my people. Each of you, save your lives from YAHWEH's furious anger. (Jeremiah 51:45 TPT)*

> *My people, come out from her (Mystery Babylon) so that you don't participate in her sins and have no share with her in her plagues … (Revelation 18:4 TPT)*

The choice remains clear: *bow* or *burn*. Shadrach, Meshach and Abednego refused to compromise. When thrown into the fire, they found the Son of God walking with them. Their courageous loyalty to God preserved them – they emerged without even a whiff of smoke on them!

Let us rise with the same courage, refusing Babylon's song and standing firm in worship to the Lamb alone.

Lucifer and the Sound of Babylon

Isaiah 14 records a taunt against the king of Babylon, revealing the principality ruling behind him – Lucifer, heaven's first worship leader.

His pride and arrogance mirror the tower of Babel where men sought to 'make a name' for themselves. The music gift which once allowed Lucifer to lead worship before God's throne was corrupted into a sound that now drives nations to bow and dance to his perverse tunes and rhythms so he can rule as a king.

Babylon Will Be Judged

The Lord judged ancient Babylon and will judge Mystery Babylon.

The first judgement scattered humanity at Babel, confusing languages and separating people groups by borders and different gods. Later, Nebuchadnezzar, Babylon's proud king, lost his mind like an animal until he repented and worshipped the Most High.

Spiritually, Babylon represents a seductive and blasphemous system – a fusion of religion, power, perversion and grotesque abuse. Lucifer, the fallen 'king of Babylon', is no longer perfect beauty but a 'horror' (Isaiah 14:4–12), working through the Babylonian system like a rampaging bull to demand global worship and spread spiritual corruption.

Revelation 17–19 unveils Babylon's final collapse. Mystery Babylon, the harlot, the consort of the dragon, intoxicates nations through harlotry and sorcery. She sits on the waters of humanity, representing nations and tongues. She blasphemes God and is drunk with the blood of the saints. Yet her downfall is certain: *'Babylon is fallen, is fallen!'*

The very judgements she planned for apostles, prophets and holy believers boomerangs back upon her. Her music ceases, her trade stops and her lights go out forever. Hallelujah!

As the *Ekklesia*, we hold the keys of the kingdom. We are called to forbid every work and sound of Babylon, and to release the song of the Lamb that overcomes her.

Characteristics of Babylon

- seduces nations by sorcery, drugs and witchcraft (pharmakia) (Revelation 18:23, Isaiah 47:9)
- pride (Isaiah 47:10)
- nations deranged by her wine (Jeremiah 51:7)
- merchant trading (Revelation 18:11–13)
- human trafficking (Revelation 18:13)
- living luxuriously (Revelation 18:7)
- boasts no grief losing husband or children (Revelation 18:7, Isaiah 47:8)
- murders prophets and saints (Revelation 17:6; 18:24)
- makes war with the Lamb and the faithful (Revelation 17:14)
- mental illness from idols (Jeremiah 50:38)
- no mercy (Isaiah 47:6)
- yoke on the elderly (Isaiah 47:6)

Babylon's Judgements

Decree and sing these in intercession.[95]

- Babylon will fall (Revelation 18:2, Isaiah 21:9)
- Babylon is burned with fire (Revelation 18:9)
- Babylon is made desolate (Revelation 18:19, Jeremiah 50:3, 14, 23, 51:1, 29)
- Babylon's idols are broken and humiliated (Jeremaih 50:2, Isaiah 21:9)
- Babylon is exposed (Isaiah 47:3)

- no music, arts or factories (Revelation 18:22, Isaiah 47:5)
- darkness – lights out (Revelation 18:23, Isaiah 47:5)
- Babylon's waters are dried up (Jeremiah 50:38)
- Babylon loses her husband and children (Isaiah 47:9, Revelation 17:21–23)

When Babylon is Silenced

When the spiritual tower of Babel crumbles and Babylon is silenced, all these things end:

- man building his own name – stops
- separation and confusion of many languages and nations – gone
- war against and mockery of God – gone
- Babylon cacophony in society – gone
- sound of enticements, corrupt trading – gone
- sound of perversion and human trafficking – gone
- sound of music and false worship – gone
- sound of grief over martyrdom – gone.

Babylon's Final Judgement – Silence!

> ... *Babylon shall be thrown down ... The sound of harpists, musicians, flutists, and trumpeters shall not be heard in you anymore ... (Revelation 18:21–22)*

Babylon's final judgement is silence – an eerie, unsettling stillness. No music. No artists. No factories. No bread making. No weddings. No lights. The sound and light show is over.

Death. Destruction. Desolation. Silence.

Extended silence can be deafening.

When the seventh seal is opened, there is silence in heaven for half an hour – a terrifying pause. The hush before a storm, the stillness of a full eclipse in the middle of the day, or the empty streets during lockdowns – all carry that same eerie haunting pregnant pause. Where sound and motion once reigned, the absence of them becomes its own judgement.

The seductive sounds of Babylon will be silenced, but the sounds of heaven will swell in greater glory and even more beauty. Heavenly choirs will rise, their harmonies filling creation with praise.

It is time for the Church to resist the seductive strains of Babylon's music and wealth, and instead, arise with a new song, declaring and affirming the Lord's righteous judgements.

> *The seductive sounds of Babylon will be silenced, but the sounds of heaven will swell in greater glory and even more beauty.*

> *Fallen, fallen is Babylon the great! You who were once the great and powerful city Babylon, now **in one hour** your **complete devastation** has come!* (Revelation 18:2, 10 TPT)

Tale of Two Women, Two Cities and Two Rivers

Scripture paints a vivid metaphor contrasting two women and the cities they represent: a bride and a harlot:

1. Israel and her offspring, who birthed Messiah and those holding His testimony
2. Babylon, the mother of harlots.

The Lord of Hosts is warring to purify His people, to unite Israel and Gentile believers as one spotless bride through the redeeming and cleansing blood of Jesus.[96]

By contrast, Mystery Babylon, the end-time spirit, embodies corruption, sorcery and witchcraft to defile, disqualify, deceive and destroy.

Two rivers also flow through this story: the River of Life and the rivers of Babylon. The rivers of Babylon are where the songs of Zion were once silenced.[97] Though Babylon muted the songs of Zion for a season, God's judgements will silence Babylon's songs forever!

The River of Life, like Eden, inspires melodies of joy. The songs of the Lord's lovers will increase eternally, carried by the river of life flowing from His throne, nourishing fruit trees whose leaves bring healing to the nations.

At the end of time, two great celebrations will take place:

1. the marriage supper of the Lamb
2. the fall of Babylon

Surrounding both is the pure and triumphant worship filling heaven and earth.

Hallelujah Chorus: All Creation Sings!

As Babylon falls silent, a roar of praise erupts across heaven, earth and all creation. The celebration resounds with joy as heaven and earth sing together:

> *Then the heavens and the earth and all that is in them shall sing joyously over Babylon. (Jeremiah 51:48 NKJV)*

Joy reverberates through creation as the battle of the ages concludes and Babylon is no more. The Hebrew wording even hints that stars and planets join the song! The Bible often links deliverance from Babylon with a new sound of singing.[98]

Israel celebrated upon return from ancient Babylon, and there was a celebration when the Holocaust camps were freed. While writing this chapter, all the living hostages were finally freed from Gazan captivity. All Israel, and much of the world, rejoiced with tears. October 7th occurred on Simchat Torah, the eighth day of the Feast of Tabernacles. Two years later, the remaining living hostages were returned on the eve of Simchat Torah, the eighth day of the Feast of Tabernacles.[99] When captives go free, singing and dancing breaks out.

When Babylon is judged, multitudes will sing Hallelujah.

> ... ***a great multitude of voices***, *saying: 'Hallelujah! Salvation and glory and power to our God! All his judgments are right and true, For he has **judged the great prostitute who corrupted the earth** with her sexual immorality. He has avenged on her the blood of his loving servants'... Then I heard what seemed to be the thunderous voice of a great multitude, like the sound of a massive waterfall and mighty peals of thunder, crying out: 'Hallelujah! For the Lord our God, the Almighty, reigns!'(Revelation 19:1–2, 6 TPT)*

The most famous echo of this heavenly celebration may well be Handel's 'Hallelujah Chorus' from *Messiah*. History records that Handel wrote the entire oratorio – fifty-three songs spanning two hundred and sixty pages in just twenty-four days – without a computer or music-writing software! Overcome by divine inspiration, he reportedly fell to his knees, exclaiming, 'I did think I saw all heaven before me!' At the end of his manuscript, he inscribed SDG – *Soli Deo Gloria*, 'To God alone the glory'.[100]

Hallelujahs, The Wedding and the White Horse

After the first wave of hallelujahs, heaven bursts into another:

> *'Alleluia! For the Lord God Omnipotent reigns! Let us be glad and rejoice and give Him glory, for the marriage of the Lamb has come, and His wife has made herself ready.' (Revelation 19:6–7)*

Finally, the Bride is ready!

Revelation 19 follows a powerful sequence – the fall of Babylon, the marriage supper of the Lamb and then the appearance of Yeshua the Messiah on a white horse:

> *Now out of His mouth goes a sharp sword, that with it He should strike the nations. And He Himself will rule them with a rod of iron … (Revelation 19:15)*

The King of kings rides forth, conquering every ruler on earth, and capturing the beast and false prophet. That is worth another Hallelujah!

Intergenerational 'One Sound' and the Glory

Throughout history, the enemy has sought to steal or corrupt worship meant for God alone. If theft fails, he tries to defile or sabotage it. Yet, though the cosmic war is fierce, the Lamb *wins every* battle! Joined by His faithful heavenly worshipping army (human and angelic), He conquers the old serpent, the dragon, the beast and all their followers. Heaven's sound triumphs and Babylon's music is forever silenced.

In these end-time wars, the church must come higher in its understanding of God's purposes for music and worship. In this era, a spiritual air force is arising – those who release heaven's decrees through songs and sounds birthed from the throne. Anything less is powerless against cosmic forces.

The enemy knows the difference between fleshly worship and worship filled with the glory. Compromised worship gives him permission to exploit it; glory-filled worship terrifies him. The flesh is his domain – the snake feeds on dirt (Genesis 3:14). Give him an inch, and he will take a mile. But he knows what pure worship sounds like – it was his original home. When our songs carry the weight of being tuned to the glory, Babylon's sounds are silenced.

It is time for the *Ekklesia* to release a new sound – glorious, prophetic and aligned with heaven – to activate angelic hosts and bring down the final curtain on Babylon's reign of tyranny.

> *The breath of God is releasing a new sound through a 'new breed' of prophet-psalmists. These are intergenerational voices in the spirit of Elijah*

The breath of God is releasing a new sound through a 'new breed' of prophet-psalmists. These are intergenerational voices in the spirit of Elijah – as fathers and mothers join with sons and daughters to release one sound in His Presence.

It is time to uproot the generational divide caused by the sexual revolution of the 1960s and 1970s. In 1 Chronicles 25, King David organised musicians for the temple worship. Those appointed to prophesy on instruments and sing were trained and under the direction of their fathers. The 'one sound' that released the glory as the Ark was dedicated into the temple, was undergirded by fathers and sons worshipping together to produce one sound. It was this oneness of sound and heart in the presence of Almighty God, that released His Glory to fill the temple. The priests could no longer stand.

CHAPTER THIRTY-SIX

The worshipping church must arise in the spirit of Elijah –intergenerational voices of fathers and mothers joined with sons and daughters in one sound, tuned to His Glory.

> *I, YAHWEH, Commander of Angel Armies, will shake every nation, and the treasures of the nations will flow in, and I will fill this temple with glory. (Haggai 2:7 TPT)*

Let us arise with a new governing sound in our instruments and the voice of every believer.

> *Long live this King! May there be ceaseless praise and prayer to him ... May the cities be full of praising people, fruitful and filled ... May all the earth overflow with his glory! Faithful is our King! Amen! (Psalm 72:15–16, 19 TPT)*

ENDNOTES - PART 4

1. https://succathallel.com/spiritual-vision-tsunami/.
2. https://www.reuters.com/world/asia-pacific/scientists-struggle-monitor-tonga-volcano-after-massive-eruption-2022-01-17/; https://www.nytimes.com/2022/01/19/climate/scientists-tonga-volcano-eruption-effects.html; https://www.gizmodo.com.au/2022/01/tonga-eruption-was-so-powerful-scientists-propose-new-ultra-classification/. More prophetic insights shared at our Passover after the Tonga volcano and linked with the Covid vaccine: https://rumble.com/v122vqo-prophetic-pointers-passover-2022.html?e9s=src_v1_s%2Csrc_v1_s_o&sci=4004533b-0477-4330-8e9b-c52c3582154d.
3. Richard Wurmbrand: Marx & Satan, p. 84.
4. https://www.rebelnews.com/police_confirm_use_of_controversial_lrad_device_at_canberra_protest/.
5. *The New Citizen*, 'The Satanic Roots of Rock', Vol. 2 March/April/May.
6. The act went viral, igniting debates on cultural decay, devilish themes in pop, and secular vs. religious interpretations: https://wm.wts.edu/read/the-deathwork-of-devilish-dance-what-a-grammy-performance-reveals-about-secular-thought; https://www.skynews.com.au/insights-and-analysis/piers-morgan-sam-smiths-satanic-unholy-performance-at-the-grammys-made-a-deliberate-mockery-of-most-of-america/news-story/296127b56ae5e1fdf27d823ad501ff54.
7. https://medium.com/@indropajaro/inside-the-fairy-tale-festival-how-does-tomorrowland-work-a26629afce65.
8. https://cds.cern.ch/record/745737.
9. ibid.
10. https://www.nbcnews.com/slideshow/bizarre-stage-show-opens-35-mile-rail-tunnel-under-swiss-n583986.
11. The Lord revealed Greek mythology and Dionysius as a root of music of sexual revolution. More detail in Vol. 2.
12. Isaiah 14:11.
13. CNN, 16 Feb 2023, https://edition.cnn.com/style/article/uae-abrahamic-family-house-david-adjaye-intl/index.html.
14. Galatians 6:8.
15. https://www.opendoorsuk.org/persecution/.
16. Brim, Billye. *The Blood and the Glory*, Harrison House, Tulsa, 1995, p. 45.
17. EUN is an acronym of the Unified Team in French. It comprised twelve of fifteen former USSR countries. They finished first overall, though second in swimming. https://www.olympedia.org/countries/EUN.
18. Huch, Larry. *The 7 Places Jesus Shed His Blood*, Whitaker House, New Kensigton, 2012.
19. My radio program on this topic: https://youtu.be/2pID3AQFXLg?si=CH70mAsv2B9-T3DP.

20. Webb, Ruth, *Grumble Fast: 40-Day Gratitude Feast*, Day 27, Heart of the Psalmist Inc, Bendigo, 2020; my song 'By His Stripes' (recorded on Holy One) is my testimony of physical healing from whooping cough and of betrayal. https://www.tabernacleofdavid.org.au/shop/digital/holy-one-digital.html
21. James 3:5-9
22. Briggs, Dean. *The Great Communion Revival*, 2023, pp. 154–164.
23. ibid. pp. 87–89.
24. Thompson, Adam F, Beale, Adrian, and King, Patricia. *The Divinity Code to Understanding Dreams and Visions*, Destiny Image Publishers, Shippensburg, 2011, p. 392.
25. To understand this thread of thought, read ESV version of Deuteronomy 32:8–9. Imperative reading is Michael Heiser's *The Unseen Realm*.
26. Ephesians 2.
27. Oasis Church, 6 October 2025, 'Governing Authority', https://www.youtube.com/watch?v=vodU0SfitSY.
28. Seven spirits of the Lord in Isaiah 11:1–2; seven flames of fire in Revelation 4:5, 5:6.
29. 1 Corinthians 14:15 TPT.
30. Webb, Ruth, *Grumble Fast*, p. 182.
31. ibid. Day 33.
32. Strong's Concordance, G2570.
33. Psalm 55:9.
34. *Daily Mail*, 13 March 2025, http://www.dailymail.co.uk/news/article-2579977/Dai-way-danger-zone-US-fighter-jet-pilot-hot-water-supersonic-flight-Welsh-town-800mph-smashed-windows-left-locals-terrified.html.
35. Psalm 100. Webb, Ruth: *Grumble Fast*.
36. Replacement theology claims God has finished with Israel, replacing her with the church. Romans 9–11 reveals the opposite. My teaching on YouTube has important information: https://www.youtube.com/playlist?list=PL_KPX_YdtY4-Rc941rm5r0OJyGB-mgGQm; 'For if their temporary rejection released the reconciling power of grace into the world, what will happen when Israel is reinstated and reconciled to God? It will unleash resurrection power throughout the whole earth!' (Romans 11:15 TPT).
37. Isaiah 60:18.
38. Song of Solomon 4:7–9 TPT.
39. 1 Peter 5:6.
40. Exodus 4:1–4.
41. Hebrews 4:12.
42. Deuteronomy 32:30, Joshua 23:10.
43. 1 Chronicles 28: 9–13, 22:5-8.
44. 2 Chronicles 5.
45. Habakkuk 2:14, Numbers 14:21.

46. https://www.harrariharps.com/temple-harp-project.
47. Thompson, Adam F, and Beale, Adrian. *God's Prophetic Symbolism in Everyday Life: the Divinity Code to Hearing God's Voice Through Natural Events and Divine Occurrences*, Destiny Image Publishers, Shippensburg, 2017
48. Youtube, 'The King's Harpists'.
49. https://www.harrariharps.com/single-post/2017/02/09/Temple-Harp-Project
50. Volume 3 will be devoted to the restored tabernacle of David.
51. https://www.sbs.com.au/whats-on/article/the-healing-power-of-the-harp/yjywmlxvo.
52. Bradley, Mark. 'Too Many to Jail: The Story of Iran's New Christians', 2018; Webb Ruth, www.TabernacleofDavid.org.au.
53. Jonathan Cahn, *Return of the Gods*, Frontline, NY, 2022.
54. *Minyan* is the Hebrew word that describes the quorum of ten Jewish adults required for certain religious obligations. The word itself comes from the Hebrew root *maneh*, meaning to count or to number; https://www.myjewishlearning.com/article/minyan-the-congregational-quorum/#:~:text=Minyan%20is%20the%20Hebrew%20word,to%20count%20or%20to%20number (accessed 5 Sept 2024).
55. Hamilton, Anne. *Dealing with Python: Spirit of Constriction: Strategies for the Threshold #1,* Armour Books, Australia, 2017.
56. 'For we do not wrestle against flesh and blood, but against principalities, against powers, against the rulers of the darkness of this age, against spiritual hosts of wickedness in the heavenly places.' (Ephesians 6:12 NKJV).
57. Michael D Heisler gives details about this shift in thinking in *Supernatural* and *The Unseen Realm*.
58. Backholer, Matthew. *Rees Howells, Vision Hymns of Spiritual Warfare Intercessory Declarations: World War II Songs of Victory, Intercession, Praise and Worship, Israel and the Every Creature Commission*, ByFaith Media, UK, 2021, pp. 93–94.
59. ibid. p. 90.
60. Webb, Ruth. *Grumble Fast*. (Amazon books or www.tabernacleofdavid.org.au)
61. https://www.biblicalarchaeology.org/daily/ancient-cultures/daily-life-and-practice/ancient-music-biblical-psalms/.
62. https://www.hughsnews.com/newsletter-posts/600-levites-rehearse-worship-songs-for-the-third-temple-on-temple-mount-steps, https://templeinstitute.org/.
63. 23 October 2023, https://economictimes.indiatimes.com/news/defence/were-in-battle-of-civilisation-against-barbarism-netanyahu-to-dutch-pm/articleshow/104659855.cms?utm_source=contentofinterest&utm_medium=text&utm_campaign=cppst (accessed 4 Sept 2024).
64. 23 October 2023, https://www.timesofisrael.com/liveblog_entry/netanyahu-to-dutch-leader-this-war-is-civilization-vs-barbarism/(accessed 4 Sept 2024).
65. See also Webb, Ruth. 'The Ark, Dagon And Gaza', https://youtu.be/PpfKqUNwEzc?si=nkSH0W008vBDBfAA.

66. Jeremiah 47:4. The Philistines settled the coastal areas of Israel, especially Gaza and Ashdod, during the 12th century BC. Greek mythology influenced them, and they were often at war with Israela https://mythology.net/others/gods/dagon/ (accessed 25 Aug 2024).
67. 'In the Ugaritic epics, one of Baal's epithets is "Son of Dagon," … sometimes held by the Canaanites to be identical with Il [El], "the father of the gods." Philo of Byblos (first century CE), who described the Phoenician religion according to ancient sources, identifies Dagon with Chronos, the father of Greek gods.' https://www.jewishvirtuallibrary.org/dagon (accessed 25 Aug 2024).
68. Knotts, Tom. 'Dagon – Chief god of the Philistines', 20 Aug, https://www.youtube.com/watch?v=8tPn9FUYp0c&list=PL_KPX_YdtY48jW0Lso15IEbL9iW_A-bzB&index=47 (accessed 25 Aug 2024).
69. ibid.
70. Several translations render it as those who 'leap over the threshold'. After Dagon fell at the threshold, the Philistines leapt over the threshold. Thresholds are a significant boundary and of covenant. Explore this important subject in Anne Hamilton's work, https://gracedropswithanne.com/?s=thresholds.
71. https://mythology.net/others/gods/dagon/ (accessed 25 Aug 2024).
72. ibid.
73. Hislop, Alexander. *The Two Babylons: or, the Papal Worship Proved to be the Worship of Nimrod and his Wife*, Loiseaux Brothers, New Jersey, 1959, pp. 215, 241–3, 252–5.
74. ibid. p .243.
75. Jeremiah 17:2–4; 1 Kings 11:5, 33.
76. Revelation 17:1, 14, 18:23.
77. Revelation 12:7–12.
78. 1 Samuel 5:3–4.
79. Our honour of God is tested at the threshold. We recommend Anne Hamilton 'Strategies for the Threshold' series: #1 Dealing with Python, #2 Dealing with Ziz, #3 Name Covenant, #4 Hidden in the Cleft, #5 Dealing with Leviathan, #6 Dealing with Resheph, #7 Dealing with Azazel, #8 Dealing with Belial, and #9 Dealing with Kronos.
80. 1 Samuel 6:5.
81. 'Now the sons of Eli were corrupt (worthless, sons of Belial); they did not know the LORD' (1 Samuel 2:12); 'Corrupt men have gone out from among you and enticed the inhabitants of their city, saying, "Let us go and serve other gods" which you have not known' (Deuteronomy 13:13). Belial is a big subject (see Anne Hamilton, *#8 Dealing with Belial*). Simply, it is a demonic entity also known as lord of the flies. Belial is considered a demon of lawlessness and death and is behind abuse. Such men ministering before the holy things of God was an open door to disaster.
82. 1 Samuel 10:10–13; 1 Samuel 19:19–24.
83. More details in Volume 2 of *Restoring True Worship*.
84. 1 Samuel 31:10; 1 Chronicles 10:10.

85. https://www.dva.gov.au/newsroom/latest-news-veterans/remembering-battles-gaza-first-world-war.
86. Kennedy, John F Jr. 'Don't Blame Israel for Gaza Crisis'., https://www.youtube.com/watch?v=INcHXmuNIN8 (accessed 5 Sept 2024). International agencies have given Gaza more than ten times per capita what the USA gave to rebuild all of Europe after World War II: $621 pr capita rebuilt all of Europe; (in equivalent value) $8,300 per capita in Gaza. What have they done with money? Stolen by top five billionaires used to build tunnels and rockets.
87. Revelation 5:11–13; 1 John 3:8.
88. 'For violence against your brother Jacob, Shame shall cover you, And you shall be cut off forever … For the day of the LORD upon all the nations is near; As you have done, it shall be done to you … But on Mount Zion there shall be deliverance, And there shall be holiness; The house of Jacob shall possess their possessions. Then saviors shall come to Mount Zion To judge the mountains of Esau, And the kingdom shall be the LORD's. (Obadiah 1:10, 15, 17, 21)
89. Private email received 29 Aug 2024.
90. Read my article re the Hamas attack targeting the temple rebuild, https://www.tabernacleofdavid.org.au/israel/406-what-connection-hamas-gaza-war-al-aqsa-red-heifers-turmoil-prayer-movement.html.
91. Isaiah 13–14, 47; Jeremiah 50–51; Revelation 17–19.
92. Briggs, Dean, *The Great Communion Revival*, p. 138.
93. Revelation 18:11–13, 23–24.
94. Revelation 13:4, 7–8.
95. Isaiah 13–14, 21, 47; Jeremiah 50–51; Revelation 17– 19.
96. Ephesians 2:11–22, 5:25–27, 32.
97. Psalm 137
98. Isaiah 30:29–33, 48:20, 49:13; Revelation 18:20; Revelation 19:1–6.
99. The Feasts do not run according to our calendar; hence, captivity and freedom did not both occur on 7 October, but both occurred at the end of the Feast.
100. 'Handel's Messiah – Stories to Inspire!', Ruth Webb https://youtu.be/W3LCTXrtdkY?si=BI2eGHSGe2SlpD3s.

OTHER RESOURCES BY RUTH WEBB

Grumble Fast – Gratitude Feast
A 40-day devotional journey that invites readers into a shift from grumbling to gratitude, and into a deeper awareness of God's goodness in everyday life.

Be Still
Instrumental piano and orchestral worship designed for prayer, reflection and rest in God's presence.

Gardens of Love
A collection of instrumental pieces exploring four aspects of God's love through gentle, contemplative music.

Holy One
Live worship recordings capturing spontaneous praise and prophetic worship moments.

Welcome King of Glory (3-disc set)
Extended live worship sessions recorded with the Tabernacle of David Worship Team, creating space for deep corporate worship and ministry.

All Your Works Shall Praise
An instrumental worship DVD featuring Ruth at piano playing her composition superimposed by beautiful footage of the stars and the heavens, creating a visual and musical meditation on the glory of God.

ABOUT THE AUTHOR

Ruth Webb (B.Mus. Ed.), and husband Laurence, co-founded Heart of the Psalmist Inc and Tabernacle of David (Bendigo).

Tabernacle of David is an apostolic hub for intercessory throne-room worship. As an anointed psalmist, prophetic worship leader, watchman and author, Ruth hosts weekly worship watches, and a monthly regional meeting to teach, equip and facilitate a space for worshipping-warriors. She also hosts a weekly radio broadcast "Sundays at the Tabernacle", where she provides Biblical perspective on prophecy and global events especially related to Israel and worship.

Ruth serves as worship leader for The Global Watch Oceania War Room, and on the leadership of Global Watch Oceania Council.

She has a passion to see every believer engaged in intimate worship, reflecting the pure and powerful sounds of heaven. Ruth's expertise and gifting are well recognised as evidenced by numerous invitations to serve congregations, prayer houses and ministries both across Australia and Internationally.

You can connect with Ruth here:

Sundays at The Tabernacle (Life FM):
www.life1051.org.au/shows/prophecy-teaching

YouTube:
www.youtube.com/@TabernacleofDavidBendigo

Website and shop:
www.tabernacleofdavid.org.au/shop

www.ingramcontent.com/pod-product-compliance
Lightning Source LLC
Chambersburg PA
CBHW062055290426
4411OCB000022B/2597